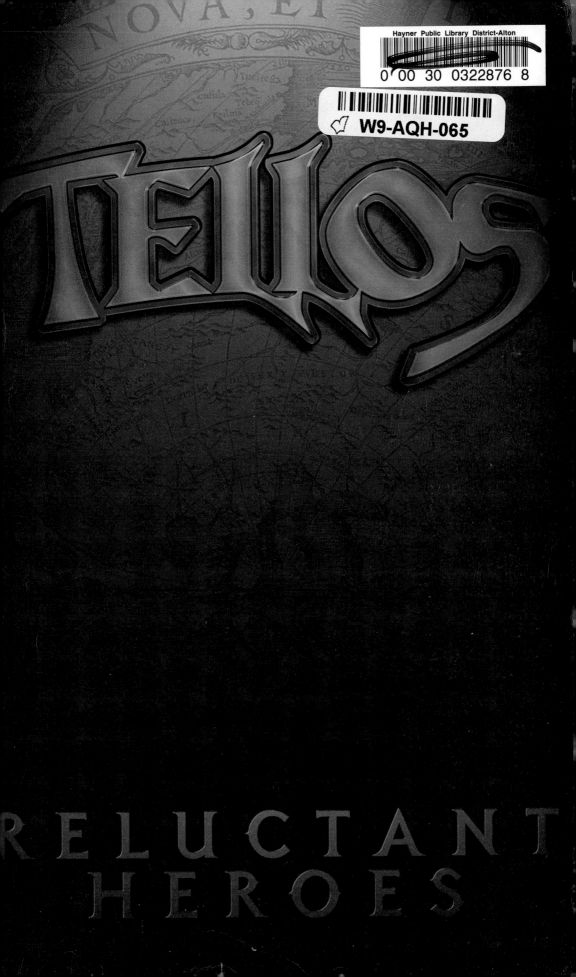

NOVA, ET

TELLOS

RELUCTANT
HEROES

For Image Comics:
Jim Valentino–Publisher
Traci Hale–Controller
Anthony Bozzi–Director of Marketing
Brent Braun–Director of Production
Doug Griffith–Art Director
Kenny Felix–Graphic Designer

Special Thanks to
Jim, Brent, Bozzi and
Everyone at Image for all
of their help and support!

TELLOS: Reluctant Heroes, Vol.1. February 2001. First Printing. Published by Image Comics, 1071 N. Batavia St. Ste. A, Orange CA 92867. Direct Market: $17.95 US/ $24.50 Can. Tellos is a registered trademark and copyright c Todd Dezago and Mike Wieringo.

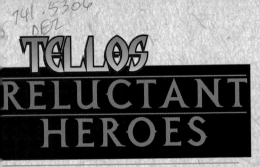

TELLOS
RELUCTANT HEROES

STORY
Todd Dezago and Mike Wieringo

ARTIST
Mike Wieringo

WRITER
Todd Dezago

INKS
Tellos 1-3
Nathan Massengill with Rich Case,
Rick Ketchum, and Rob Stull
Tellos 4-5
Rob Stull with Howard Shum
Tellos:Prelude
Rich Case
Tellos:Prologue
Rob Stull

COLORS
Bongotone's
Paul Mounts and Ken Wolak

LETTERING
Tellos 1-3 and Prelude
Richard Starkings and
ComicCraft's Wes Abbott
Tellos 4-5 and Prologue
Bongotone's Paul Mounts

FILM OUTPUT
Kell-O-Graphics

TELLOS created by
Todd Dezago and Mike Wieringo

BROTHERS-IN-ARMS

or
HE BROUGHT HIM STRINGS AND SEALING WAX AND OTHER FANCY STUFF

As a child, the only thing I wanted more than my own Komodo Dragon was a Siberian Tiger. What do you mean, why? That's a silly question, didn't you? Besides, it was Christmas and I'd been good (relatively speaking). Oddly enough, my parents didn't come through on that one, some grownup nonsense about getting eaten for lunch. I decided I was never going to be a grownup; those people had no imagination at all.

Despite my best efforts, growing up turned out to be inevitable. It wasn't all bad. There were girls, motorcycles, the Blues. But I never lost my fascination for the joys of my youth: animation, baseball, Dr. Seuss. All things done professionally by people older than me. The secret, it would seem, was in growing up without growing old. To take the training and experience that comes with age and meld it with the innocence and wonder of childhood.

Given the above, is it any surprise I fell for this book? Tellos is a portal to our youth. At first glance you cock your head a bit, then your eyes widen in happy recognition as you straighten up. Like deja vu all over again, you're there. The land of Anything Can Happen. Some of this comes from references to Kipling or Peter, Paul & Mary, but these would fall flat were the work not done from the heart. This isn't some bridge they're trying to pawn off, they actually believe this stuff. Cobblestones are cooler than pavement. Tigers should talk. And, most importantly, pirate ships should always be captained by beautiful women while sailing through dragon-filled skies. When I become King, that last one becomes law.

Here we find out that this is more than just a trip down memory lane. Tellos is familiar enough that it feels like home. The buildings are real, not facades. When we open the door, we find a room, not a back lot. We believe our feet to be firmly planted, then discover we're standing on a flying carpet that no longer touches the ground. And someone else has the controls. All we can do, like the riders on a roller coaster, is trust the engineers to know what they're doing, hang on and enjoy the ride.

Speaking of our engineers, who are these guys and why should we trust them? For all we know, they could slam us right into the wall.

Todd's work is new to me. I'm sure there's a bio here somewhere, full of wonderful accomplishments, but I can only speak of what I've seen. What I've seen is a bit of a magician, using enough stage magic and misdirection to keep us on our toes while quietly weaving a larger spell in the background. Larger spells, as we all know, take time. With a pinch of this and a dash of that, Todd reveals what he wants, when he wants, all in the right order. He gives us a world that we think we know, and then little by little starts peeling away the outer layers until, much like real life, we realize all is not what it seems.

'Ringo's work is not new to me and there had better be a bio here somewhere recounting his wonderful accomplishments. Not that you need it when this work speaks as eloquently as it does. While always possessing an individual sense of charm, his early work, like most artists, survived more on energy than craftsmanship. Unlike most artists, who seem to trade one for the other over time, his abilities keep improving with no corresponding loss of fire. Trust me, that's harder than it sounds. He gives us all he's got, yet never stoops to visual bragging. He knows what he can do and, when he deems the time is right, you will too.

Together they've given us a world stable enough for us to believe and just shaky enough to keep us on edge. They know that while good and evil can come in unexpected forms, it takes more than a pair of horns to make a villain, and more than an icon on a well muscled chest to make a hero. It's what's on the inside that counts.

So let's go inside. But, before we do, a toast. To Todd and 'Ringo, my brothers-in-arms, and to childhood.

Happy trails,

Paul Smith
Groundhog's Day 2001

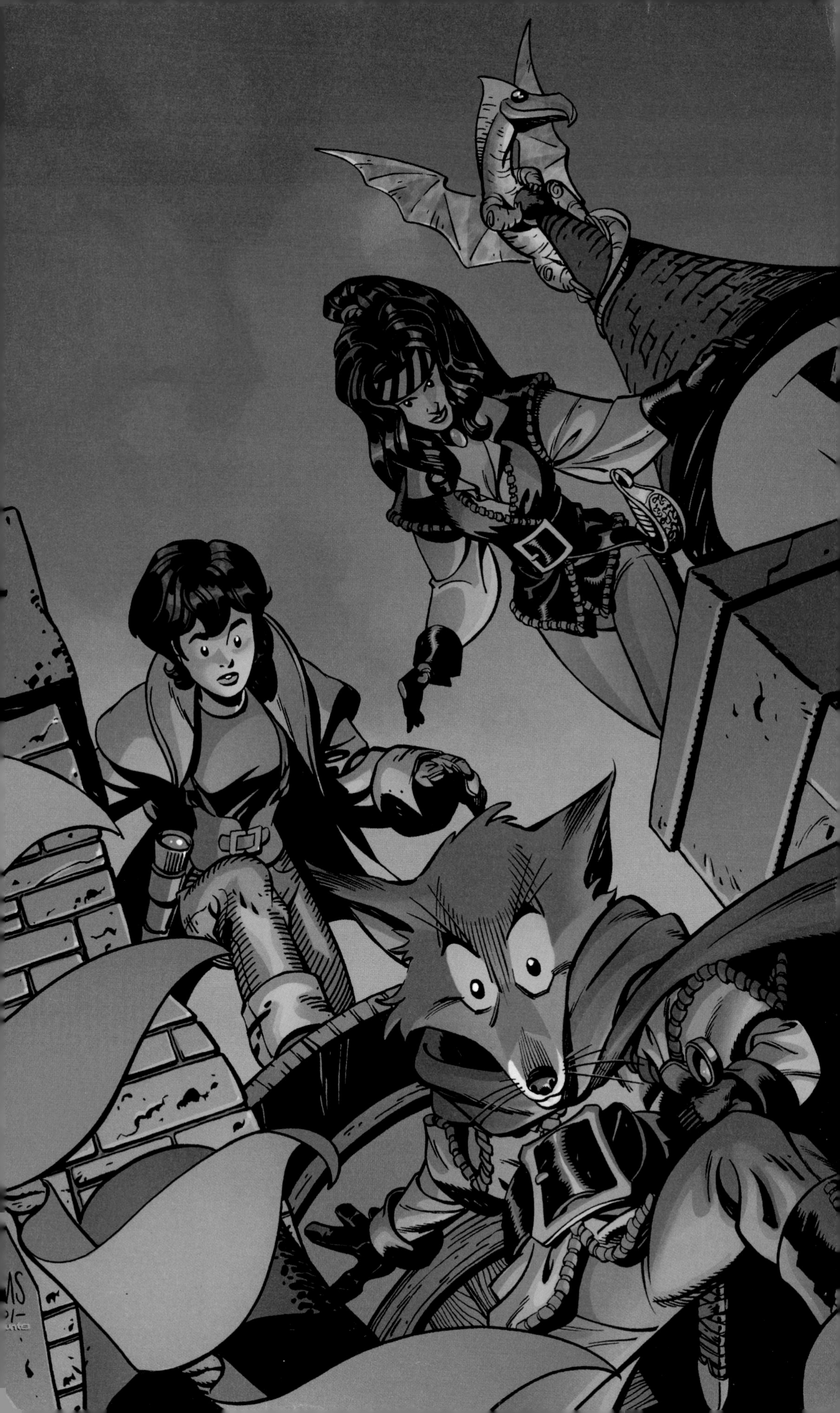

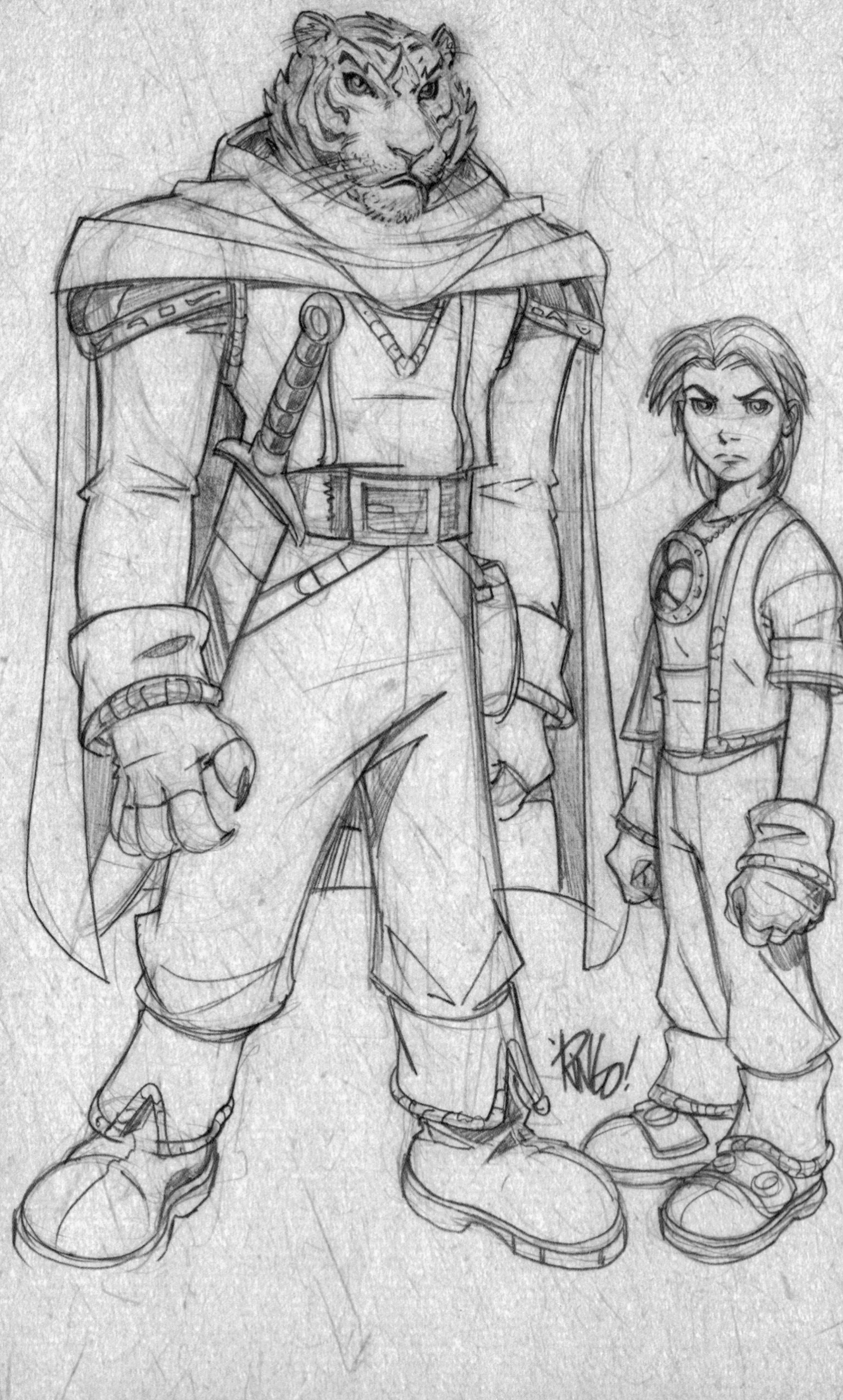

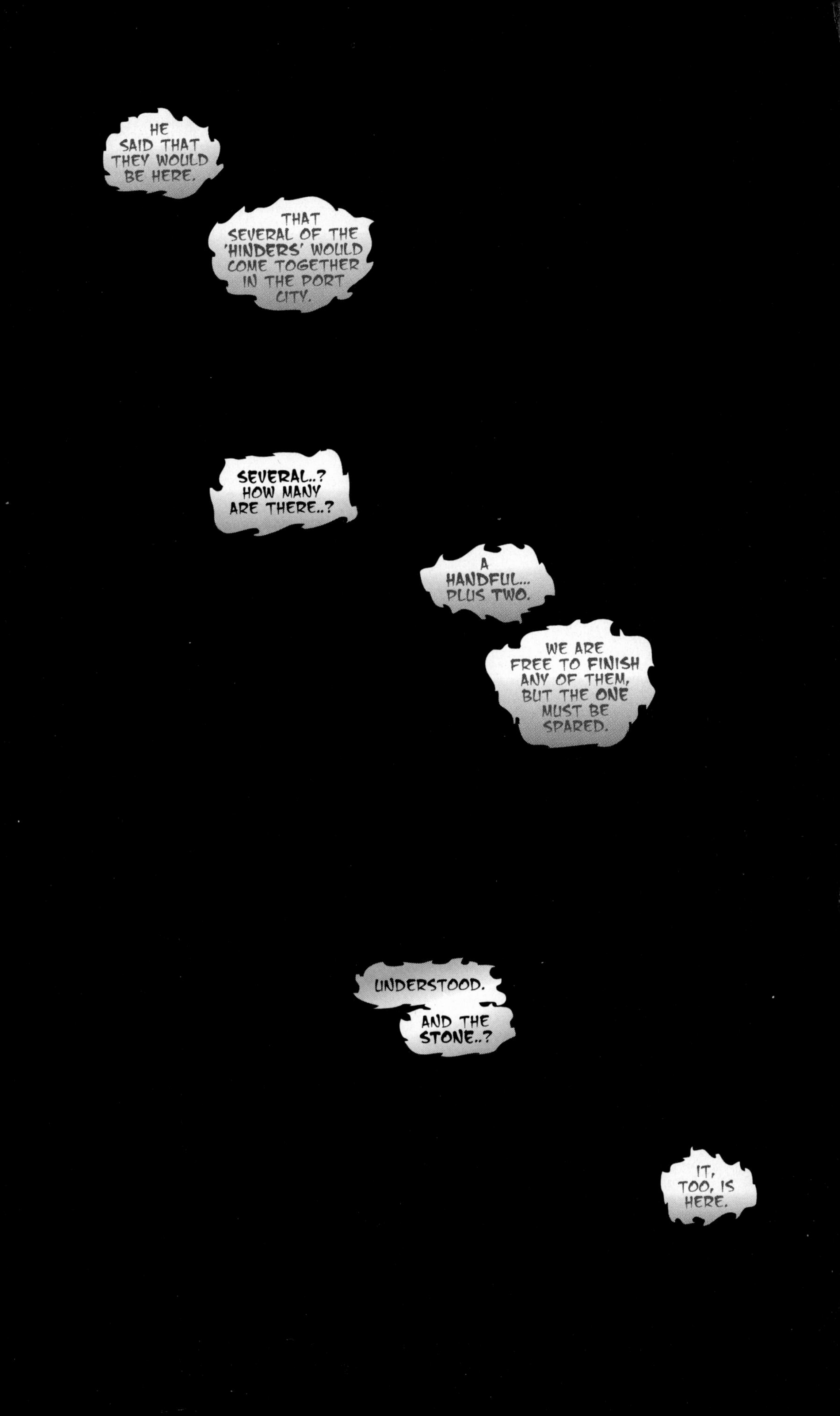
HE SAID THAT THEY WOULD BE HERE.
THAT SEVERAL OF THE 'HINDERS' WOULD COME TOGETHER IN THE PORT CITY.
SEVERAL..? HOW MANY ARE THERE..?
A HANDFUL... PLUS TWO.
WE ARE FREE TO FINISH ANY OF THEM, BUT THE ONE MUST BE SPARED.
UNDERSTOOD.
AND THE STONE..?
IT, TOO, IS HERE.

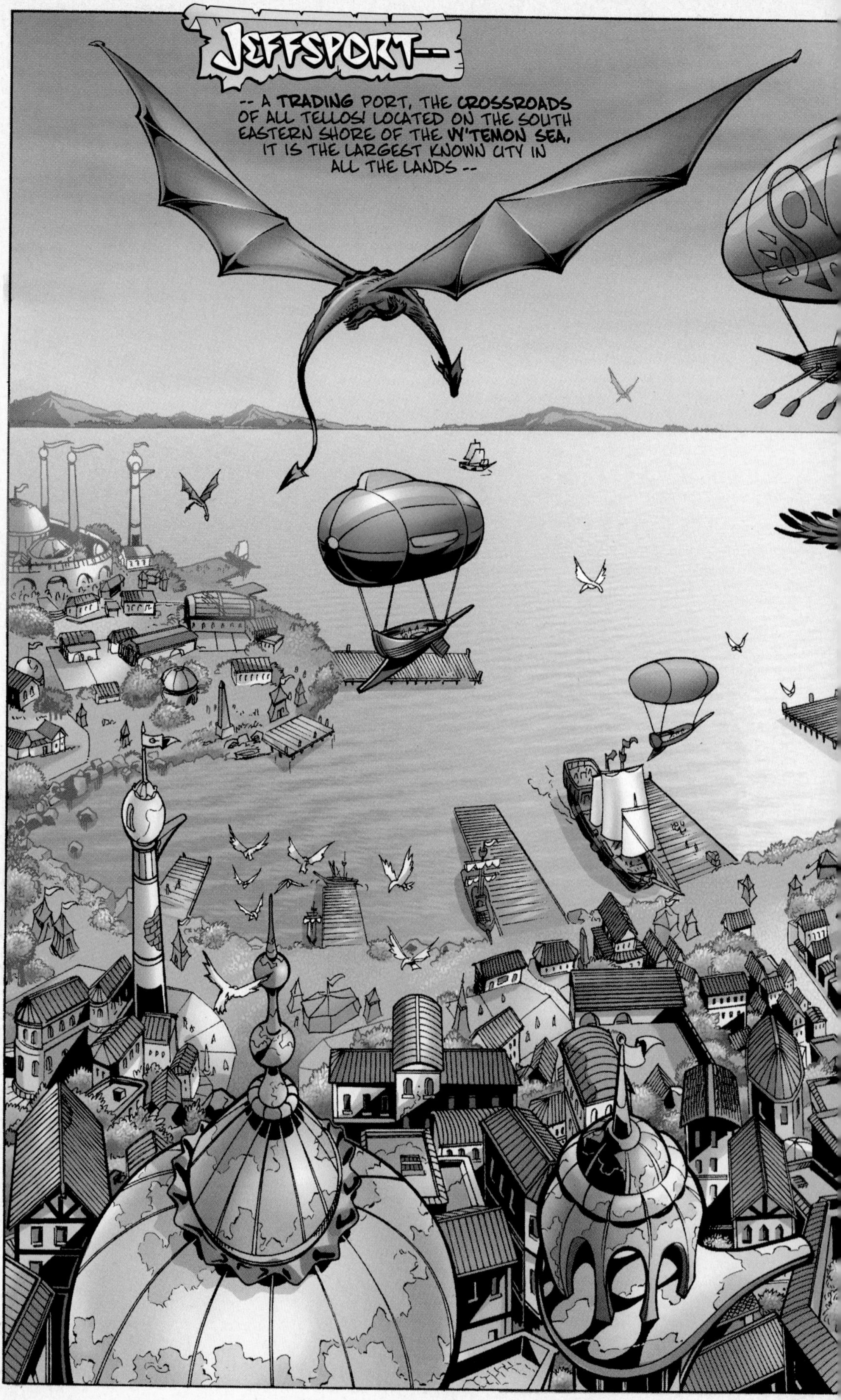
JEFFSPORT--
-- A TRADING PORT, THE CROSSROADS OF ALL TELLOS! LOCATED ON THE SOUTH EASTERN SHORE OF THE VY'TEMON SEA, IT IS THE LARGEST KNOWN CITY IN ALL THE LANDS --

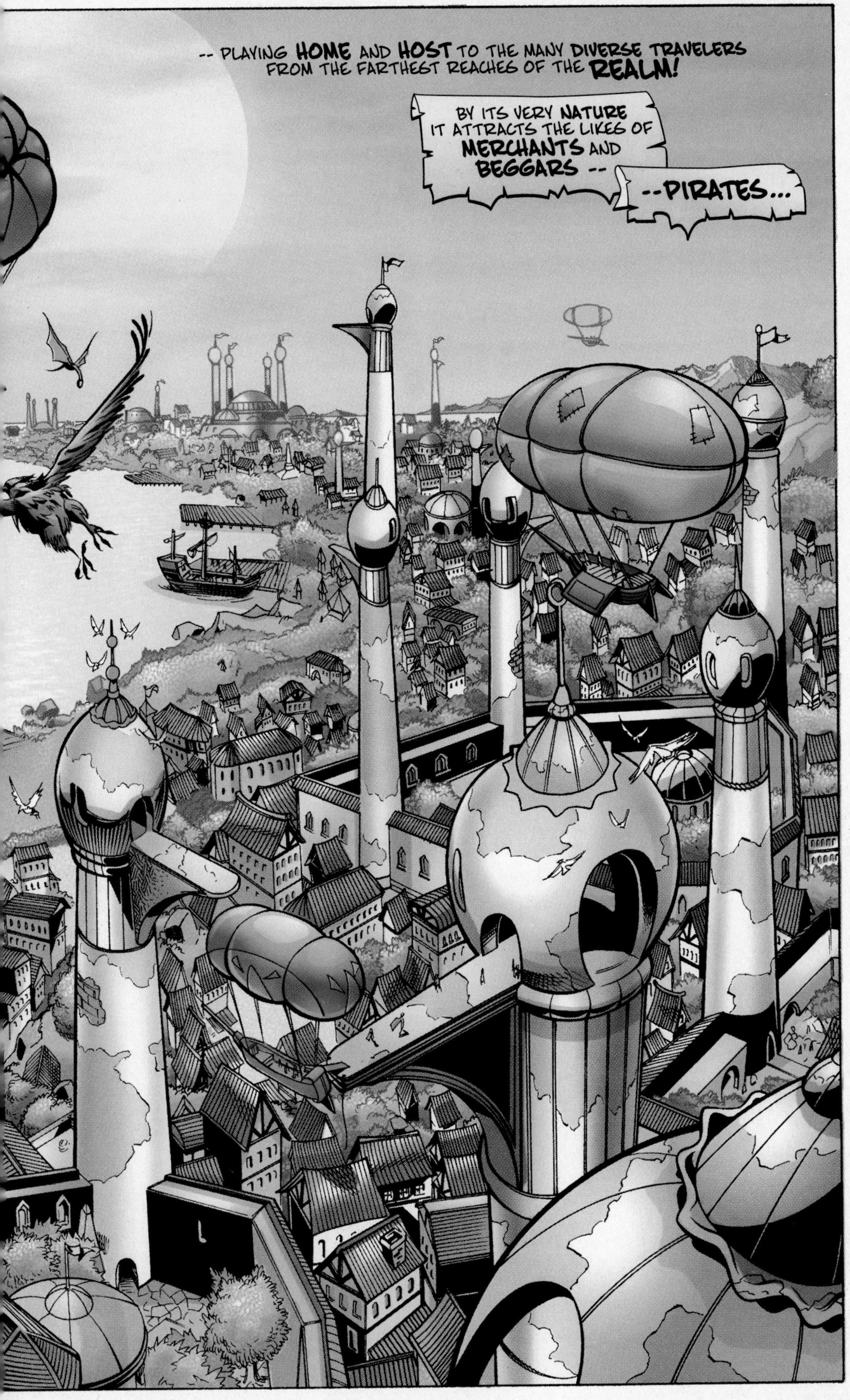
-- PLAYING **HOME** AND **HOST** TO THE MANY **DIVERSE TRAVELERS** FROM THE FARTHEST REACHES OF THE **REALM!**
BY ITS VERY **NATURE** IT ATTRACTS THE LIKES OF **MERCHANTS** AND **BEGGARS** --
--**PIRATES...**

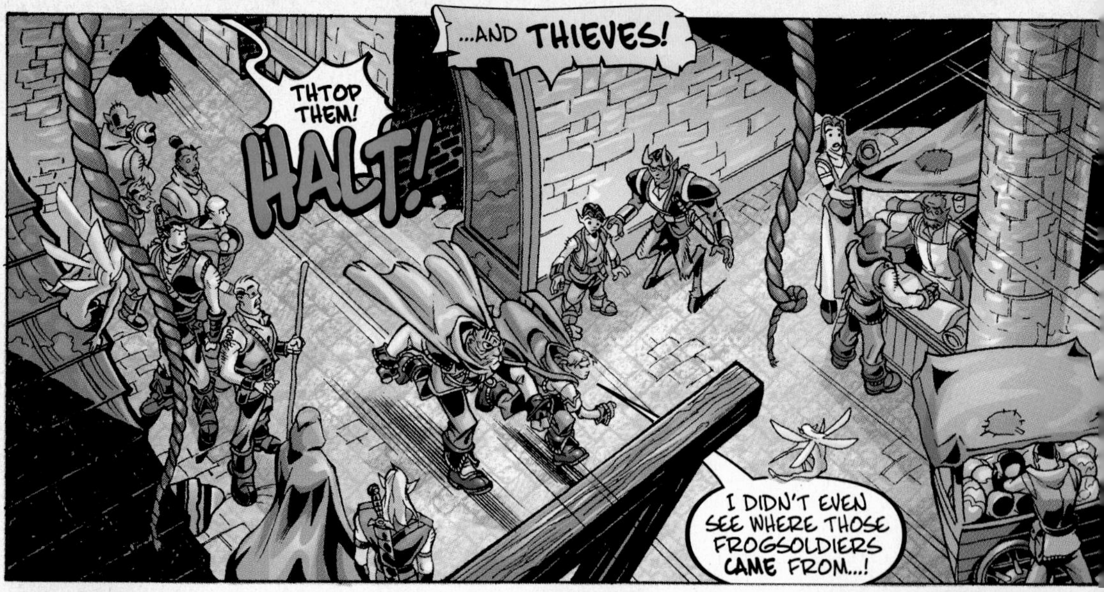
...AND THIEVES!
THTOP THEM!
HALT!
I DIDN'T EVEN SEE WHERE THOSE FROGSOLDIERS CAME FROM...!
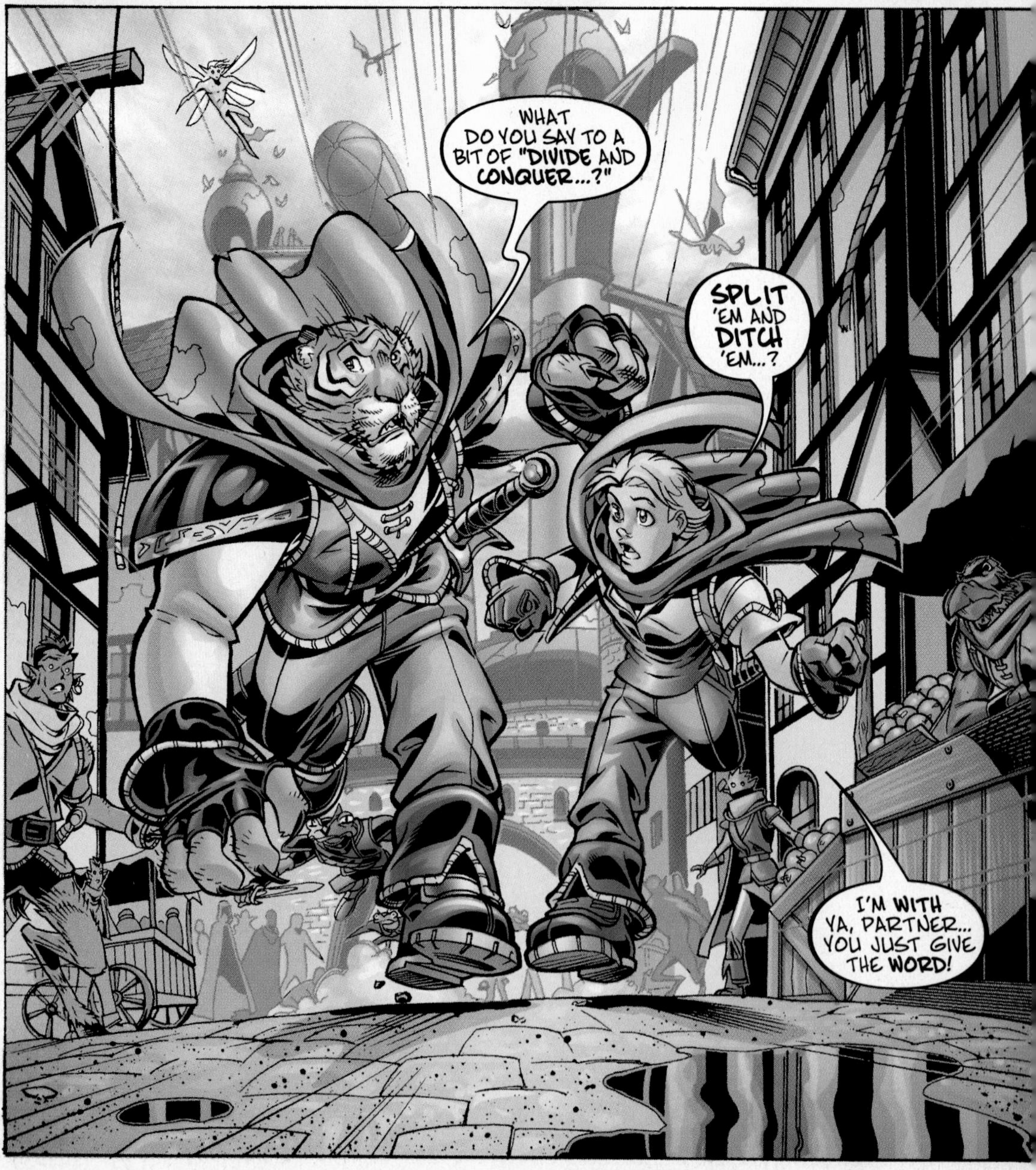
WHAT DO YOU SAY TO A BIT OF "DIVIDE AND CONQUER...?"
SPLIT 'EM AND DITCH 'EM...?
I'M WITH YA, PARTNER... YOU JUST GIVE THE WORD!

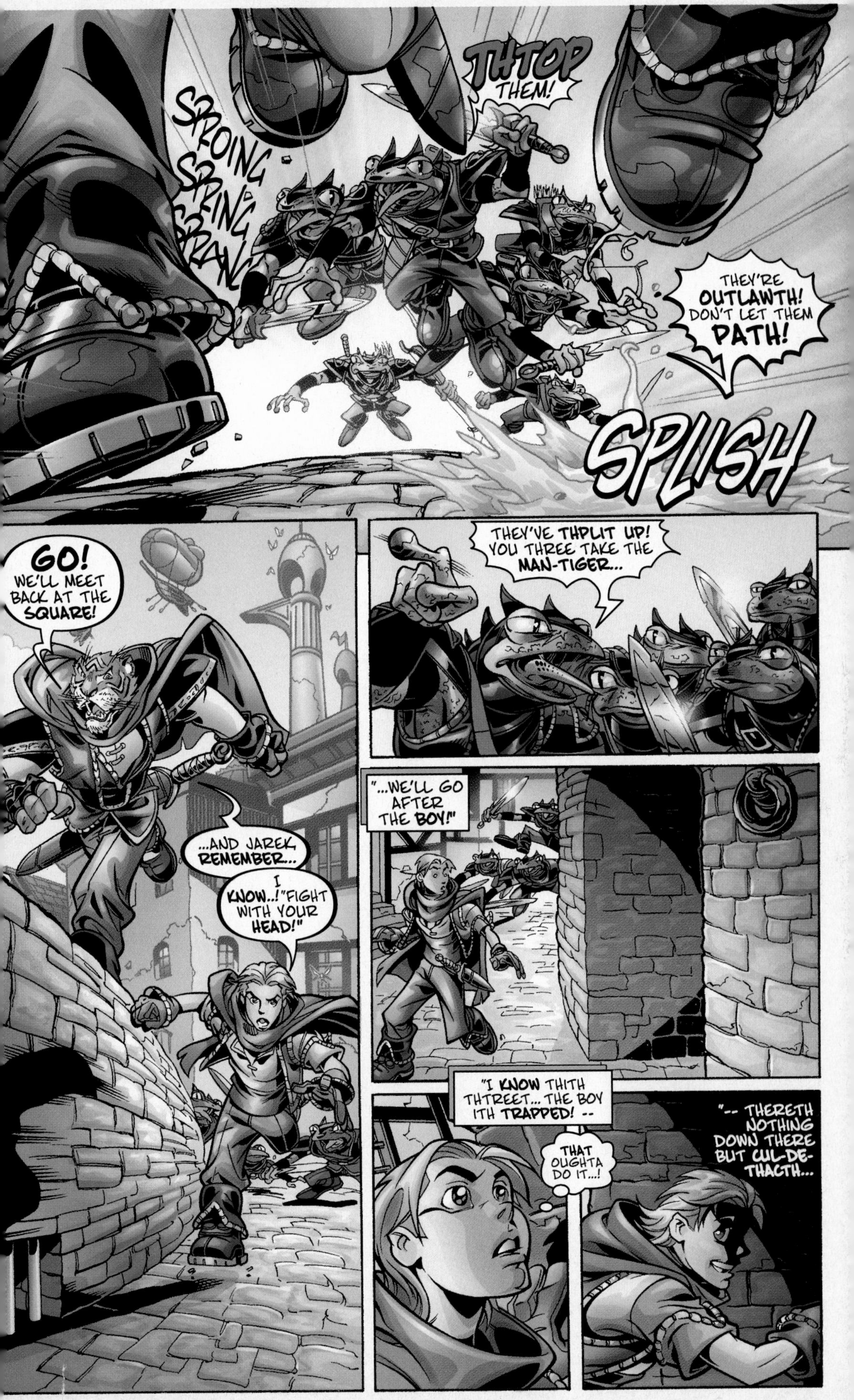

SPROING SPRING SPRANG
THTOP THEM!
THEY'RE OUTLAWTH! DON'T LET THEM PATH!
SPLISH
GO! WE'LL MEET BACK AT THE SQUARE!
...AND JAREK REMEMBER...
I KNOW..! "FIGHT WITH YOUR HEAD!"
THEY'VE THPLIT UP! YOU THREE TAKE THE MAN-TIGER...
"...WE'LL GO AFTER THE BOY!"
"I KNOW THITH THTREET... THE BOY ITH TRAPPED! --
"-- THERETH NOTHING DOWN THERE BUT CUL-DE-THACTH...
THAT OUGHTA DO IT...!

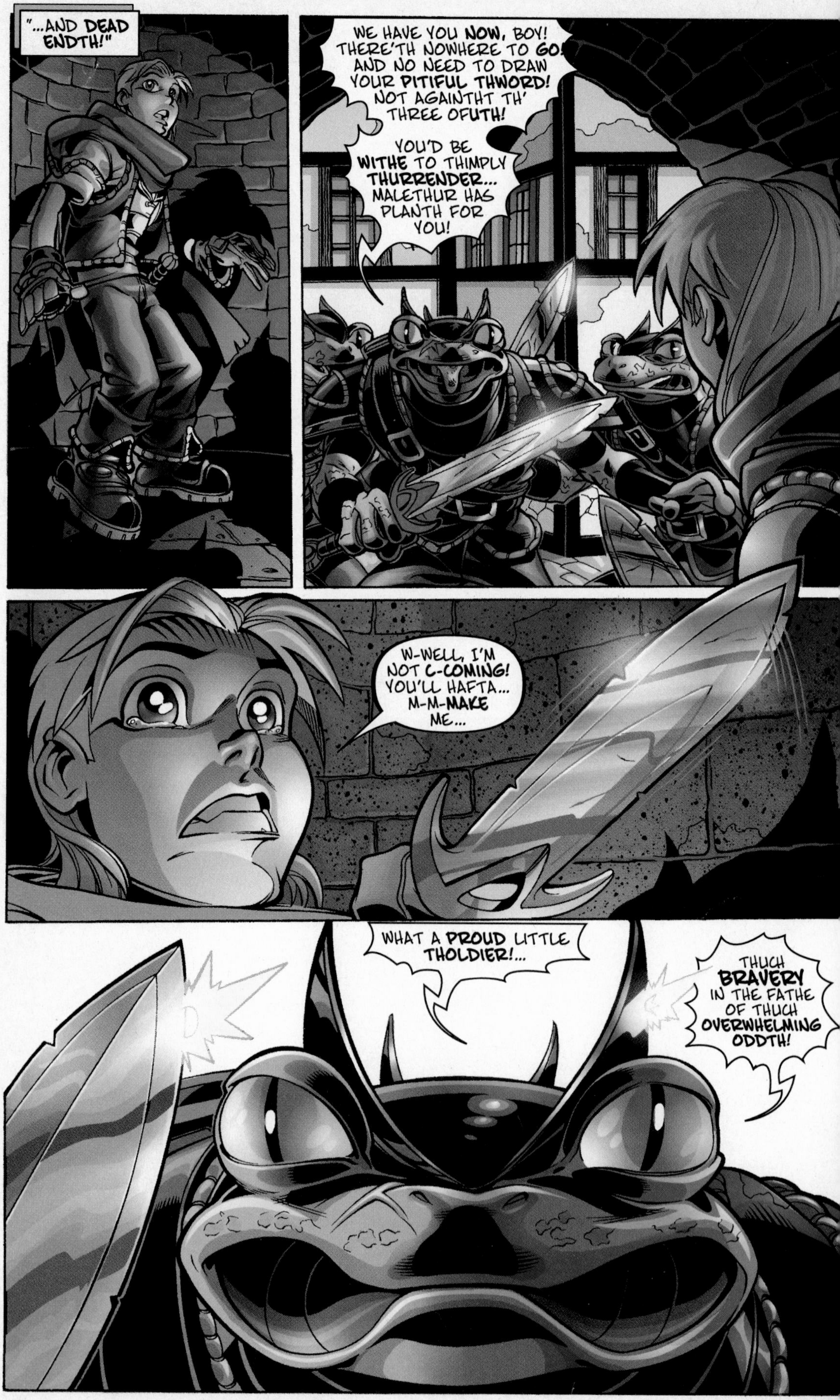
"...AND DEAD ENDTH!"
WE HAVE YOU NOW, BOY! THERE'TH NOWHERE TO GO! AND NO NEED TO DRAW YOUR PITIFUL THWORD! NOT AGAINTHT TH' THREE OFUTH!
YOU'D BE WITHE TO THIMPLY THURRENDER... MALETHUR HAS PLANTH FOR YOU!
W-WELL, I'M NOT C-COMING! YOU'LL HAFTA... M-M-MAKE ME...
WHAT A PROUD LITTLE THOLDIER!...
THUCH BRAVERY IN THE FATHE OF THUCH OVERWHELMING ODDTH!

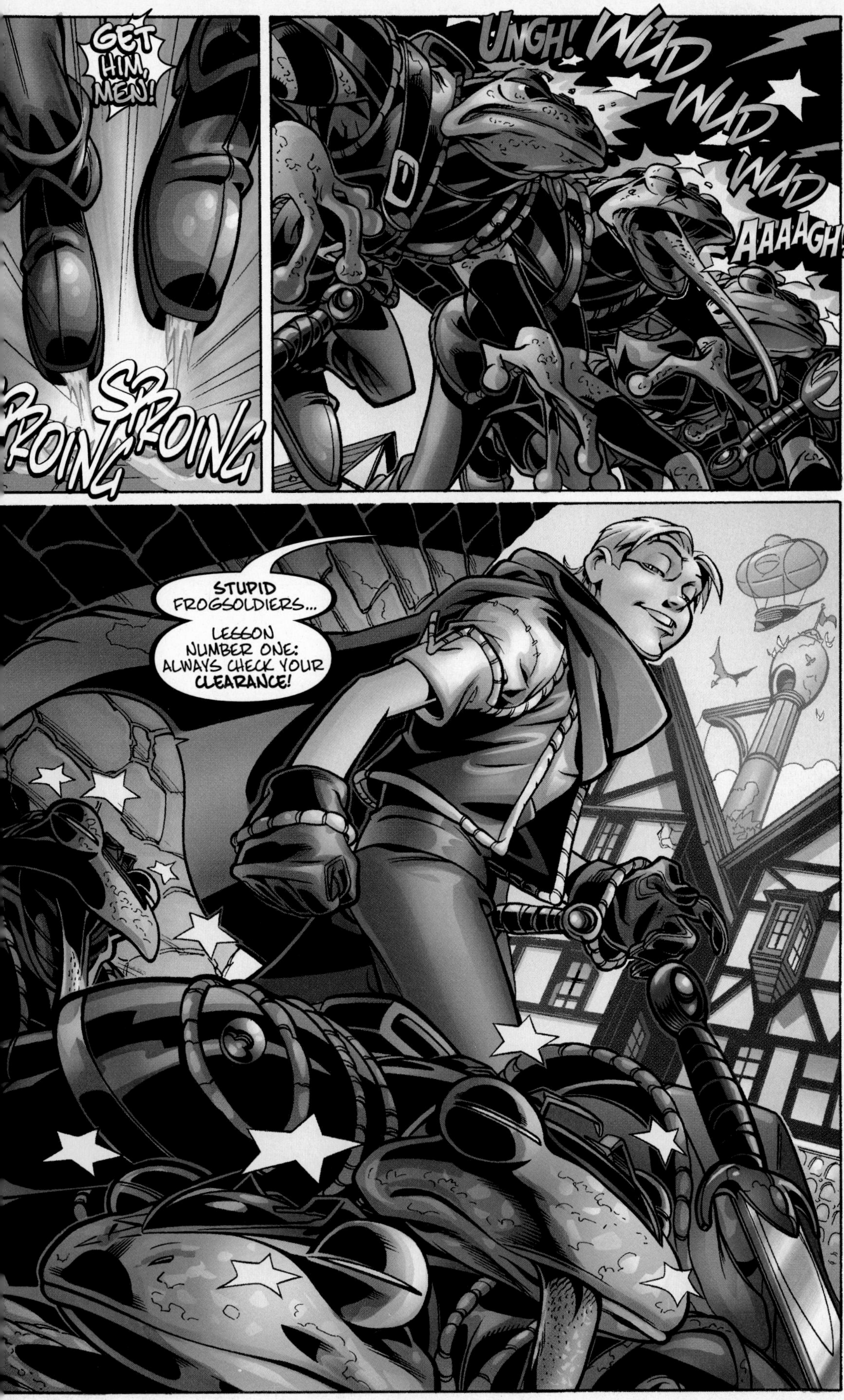
GET HIM, MEN!
SPROING
SPROING
UNGH!
WUD
WUD
WUD
AAAAGH!
STUPID FROGSOLDIERS...
LESSON NUMBER ONE: ALWAYS CHECK YOUR CLEARANCE!

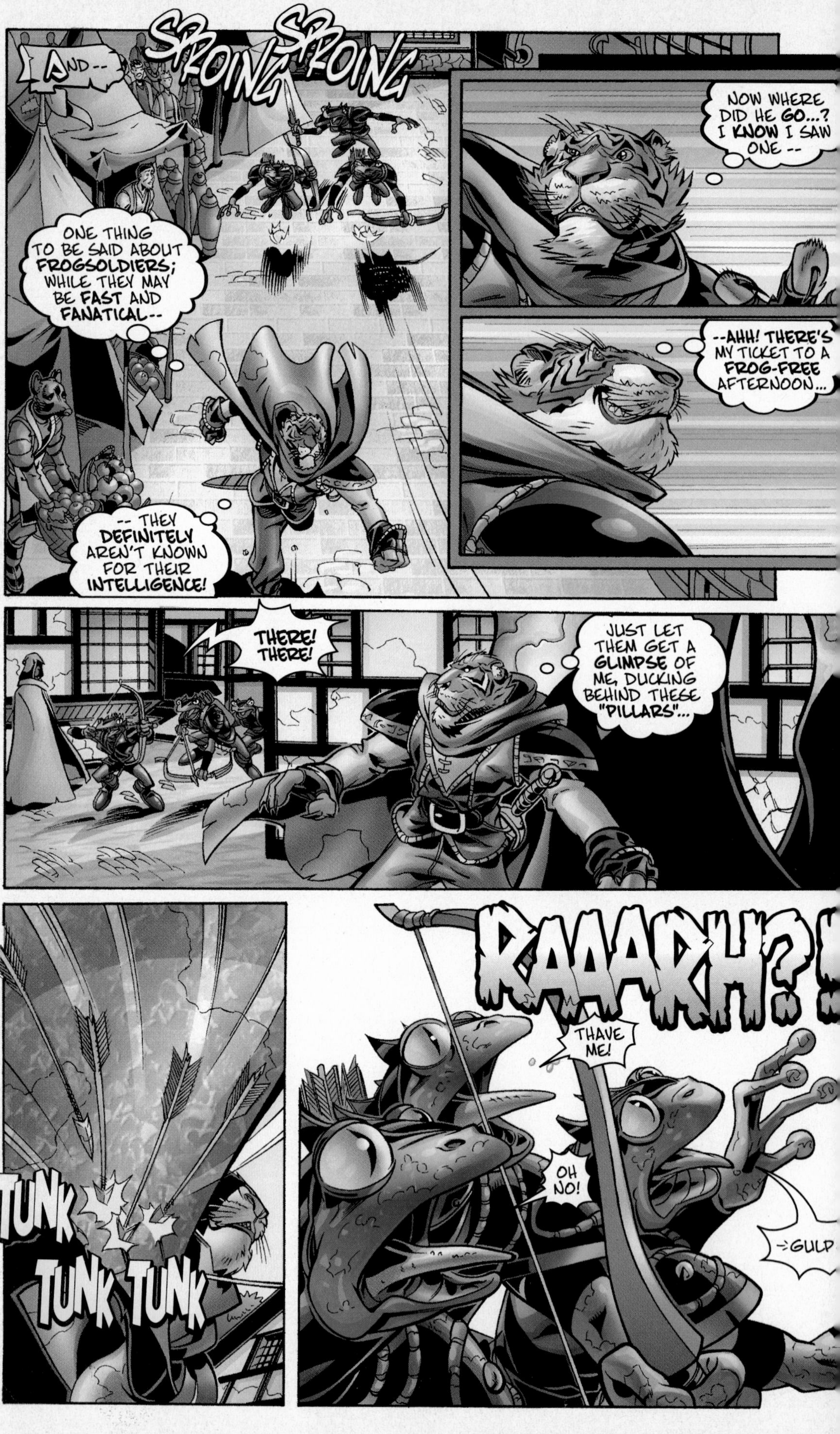
AND --
SPROING SPROING
ONE THING TO BE SAID ABOUT FROGSOLDIERS; WHILE THEY MAY BE FAST AND FANATICAL--
-- THEY DEFINITELY AREN'T KNOWN FOR THEIR INTELLIGENCE!
NOW WHERE DID HE GO...? I KNOW I SAW ONE --
--AHH! THERE'S MY TICKET TO A FROG-FREE AFTERNOON...
THERE! THERE!
JUST LET THEM GET A GLIMPSE OF ME, DUCKING BEHIND THESE "PILLARS"...
TUNK TUNK TUNK
RAAARH?!
THAVE ME!
OH NO!
GULP

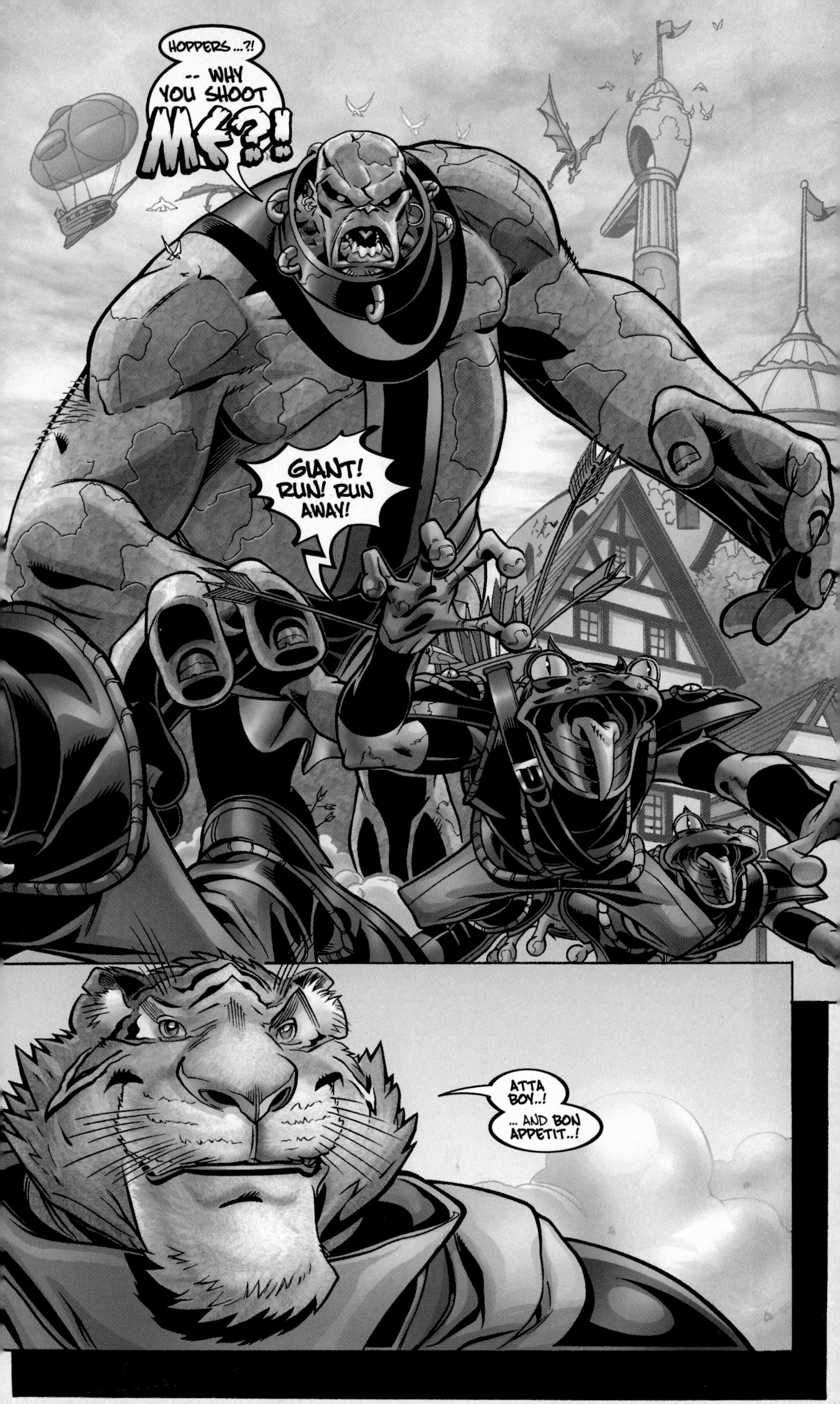
HOPPERS...?!
-- WHY YOU SHOOT ME?!
GIANT! RUN! RUN AWAY!
ATTA BOY..!
... AND BON APPETIT..!

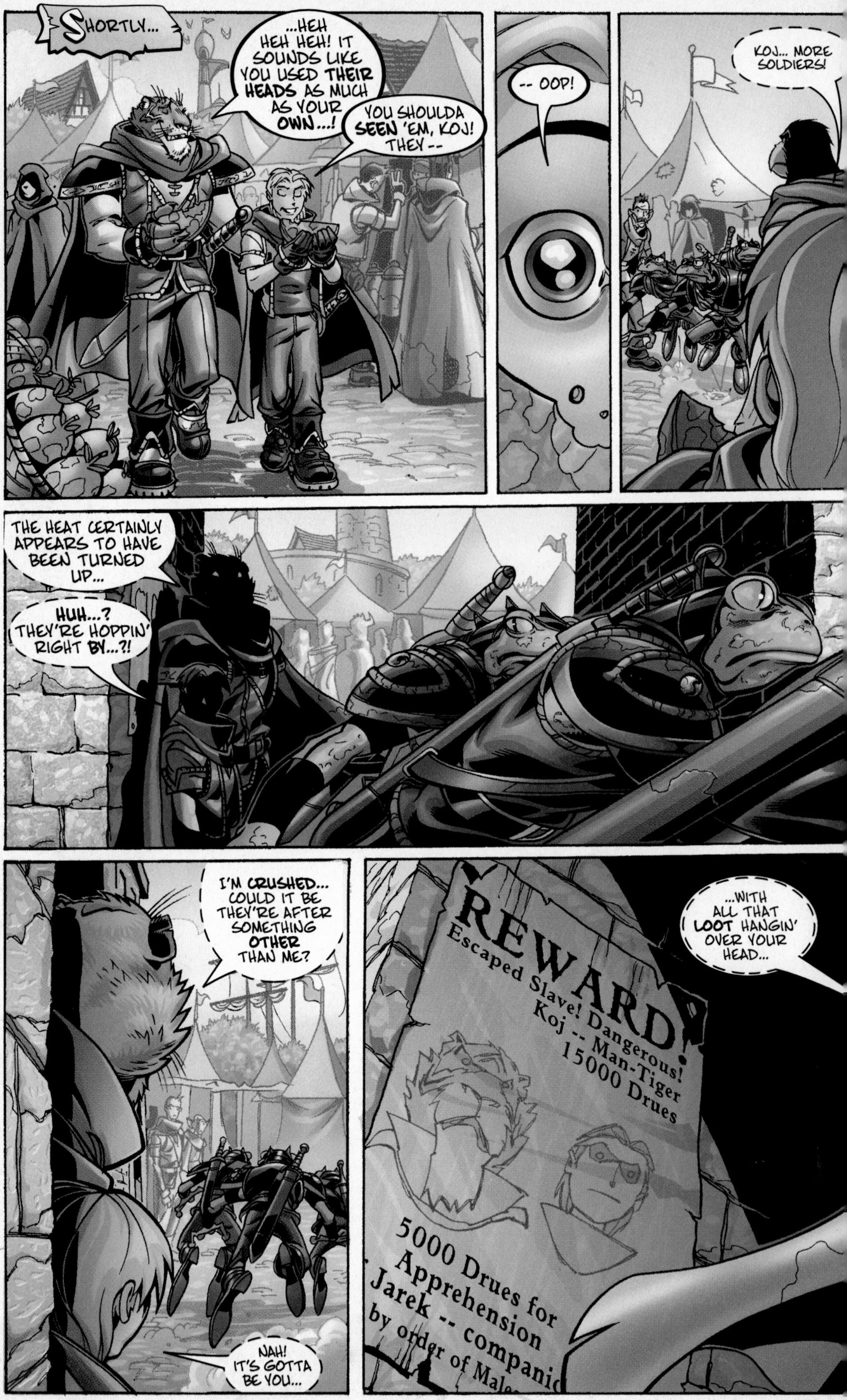
SHORTLY...
...HEH HEH HEH! IT SOUNDS LIKE YOU USED THEIR HEADS AS MUCH AS YOUR OWN...!
YOU SHOULDA SEEN 'EM, KOJ! THEY --
-- OOP!
KOJ... MORE SOLDIERS!
THE HEAT CERTAINLY APPEARS TO HAVE BEEN TURNED UP...
HUH...? THEY'RE HOPPIN' RIGHT BY...?!
I'M CRUSHED... COULD IT BE THEY'RE AFTER SOMETHING OTHER THAN ME?
NAH! IT'S GOTTA BE YOU...
...WITH ALL THAT LOOT HANGIN' OVER YOUR HEAD...
REWARD!
Escaped Slave! Dangerous!
Koj -- Man-Tiger
15000 Drues
5000 Drues for
Apprehension
Jarek -- companio
by order of Male

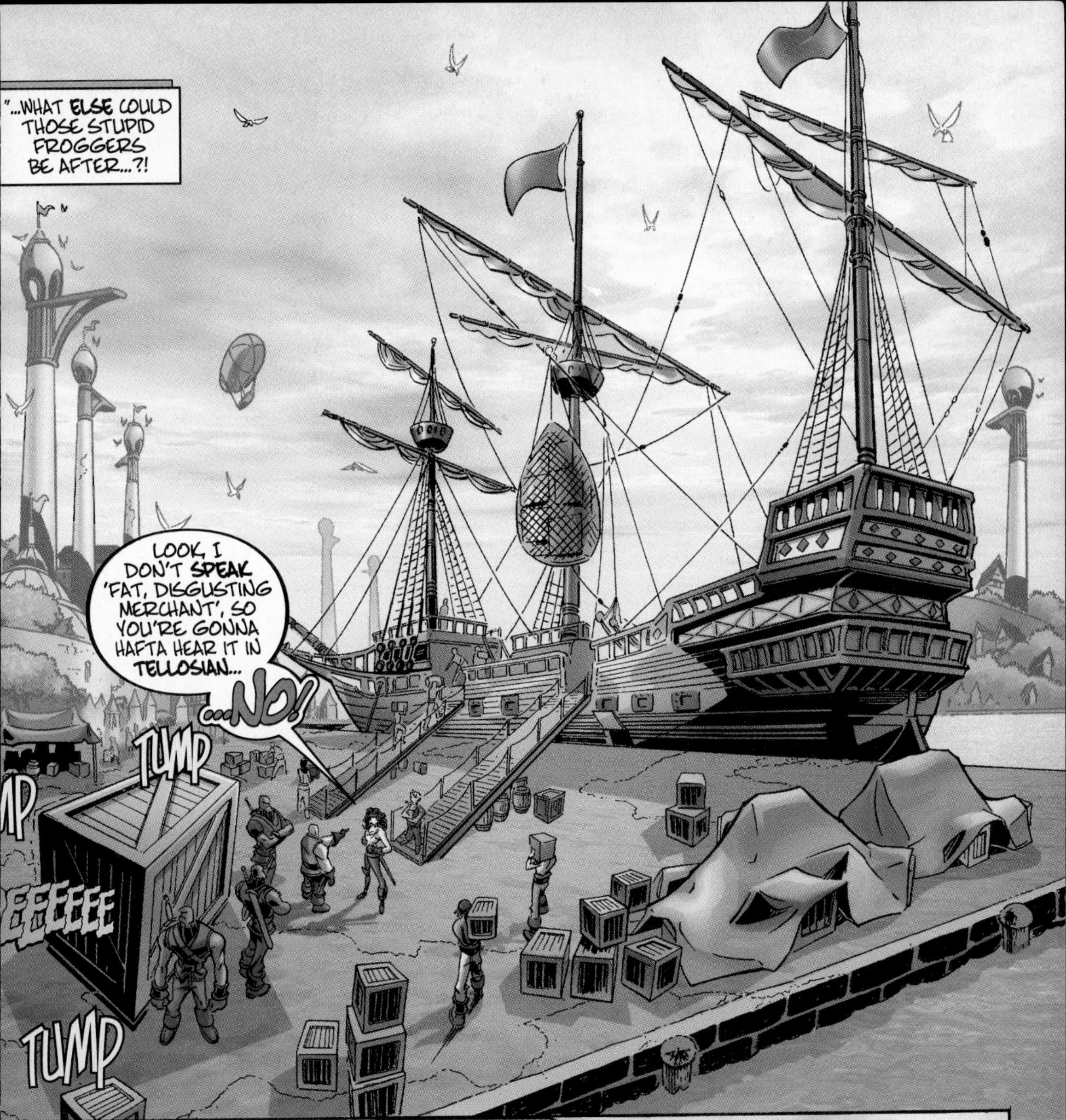
"...WHAT ELSE COULD THOSE STUPID FROGGERS BE AFTER...?!
LOOK, I DON'T SPEAK 'FAT, DISGUSTING MERCHANT', SO YOU'RE GONNA HAFTA HEAR IT IN TELLOSIAN...
...NO!
TUMP
TUMP
EEEEEEE
TUMP

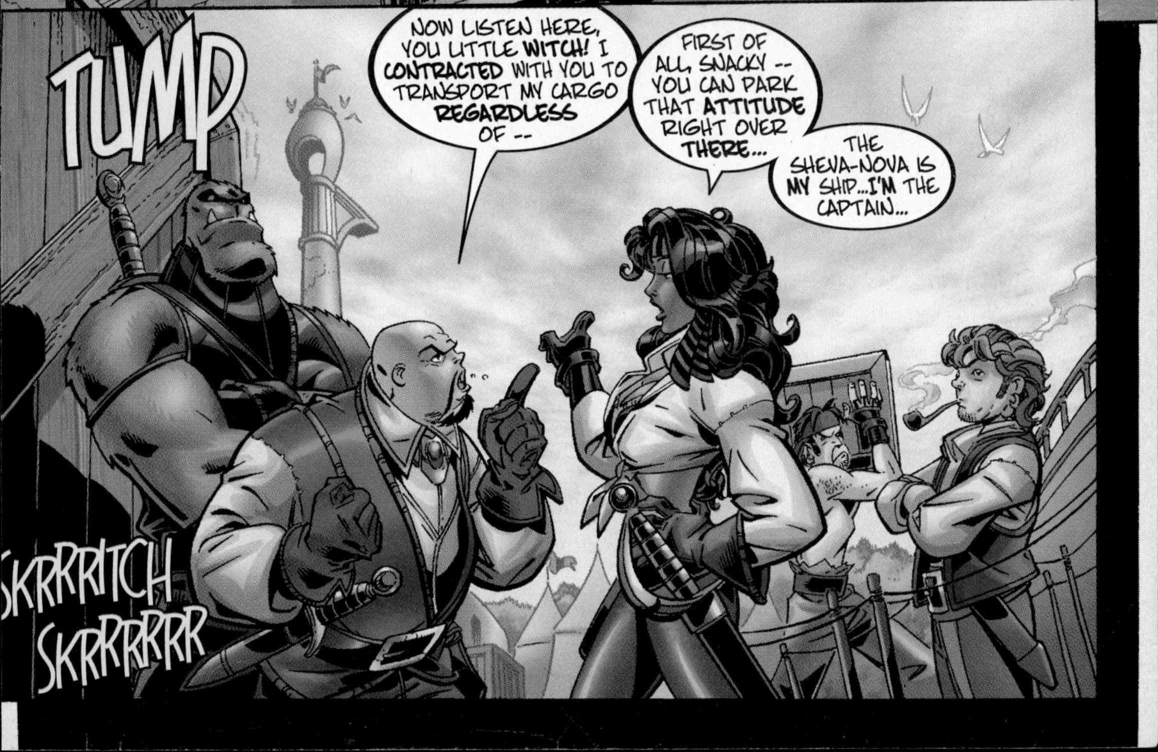
TUMP
NOW LISTEN HERE, YOU LITTLE WITCH! I CONTRACTED WITH YOU TO TRANSPORT MY CARGO REGARDLESS OF --
FIRST OF ALL, SNACKY -- YOU CAN PARK THAT ATTITUDE RIGHT OVER THERE...
THE SHEVA-NOVA IS MY SHIP...I'M THE CAPTAIN...
SKRRRITCH
SKRRRRRR

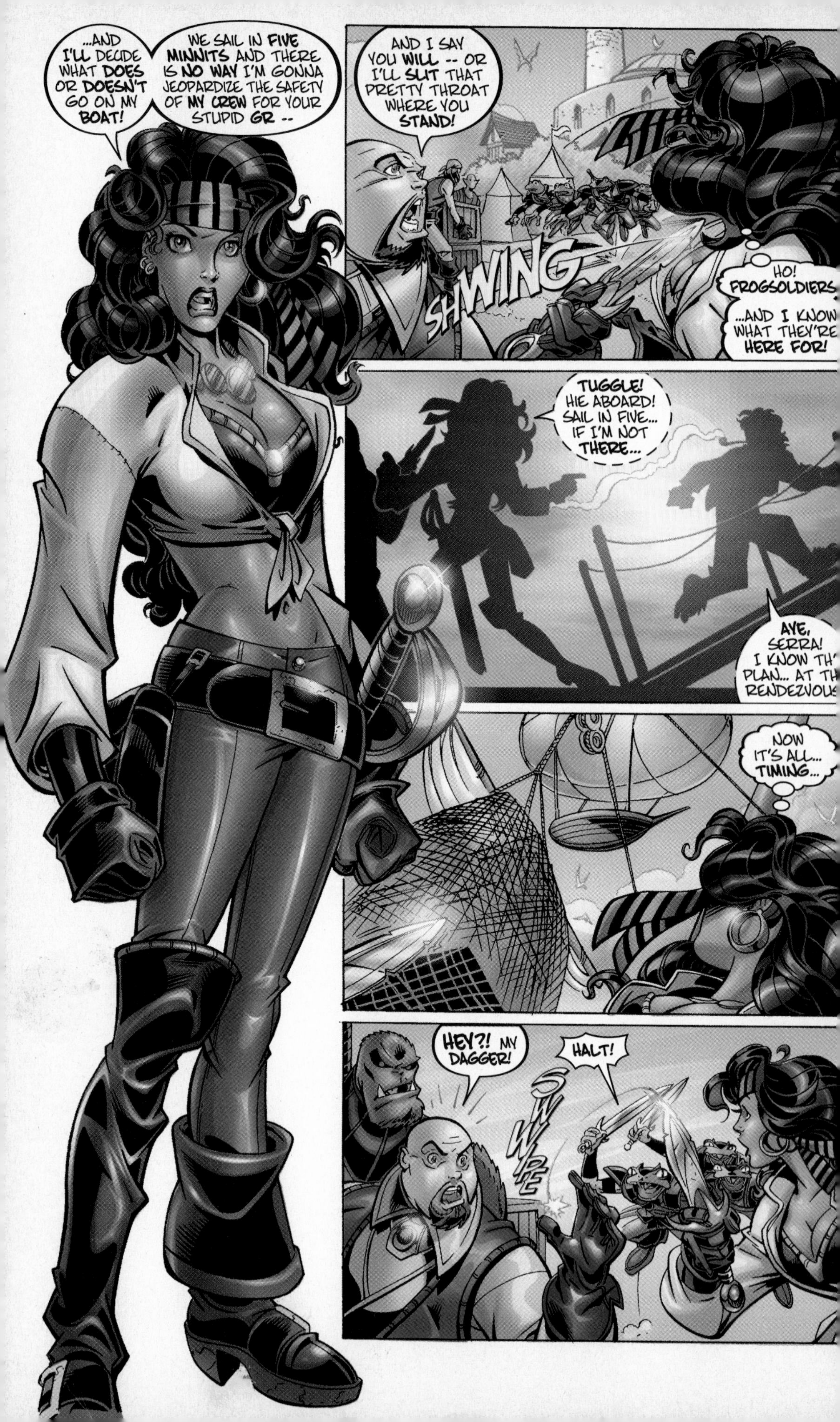
...AND I'LL DECIDE WHAT DOES OR DOESN'T GO ON MY BOAT!
WE SAIL IN FIVE MINNITS AND THERE IS NO WAY I'M GONNA JEOPARDIZE THE SAFETY OF MY CREW FOR YOUR STUPID GR --
AND I SAY YOU WILL -- OR I'LL SLIT THAT PRETTY THROAT WHERE YOU STAND!
SHWING
HO! FROGSOLDIERS
...AND I KNOW WHAT THEY'RE HERE FOR!
TUGGLE! HIE ABOARD! SAIL IN FIVE... IF I'M NOT THERE...
AYE, SERRA! I KNOW TH' PLAN... AT TH RENDEZVOUS
NOW IT'S ALL... TIMING...
HEY?! MY DAGGER!
HALT!
SWWIPE

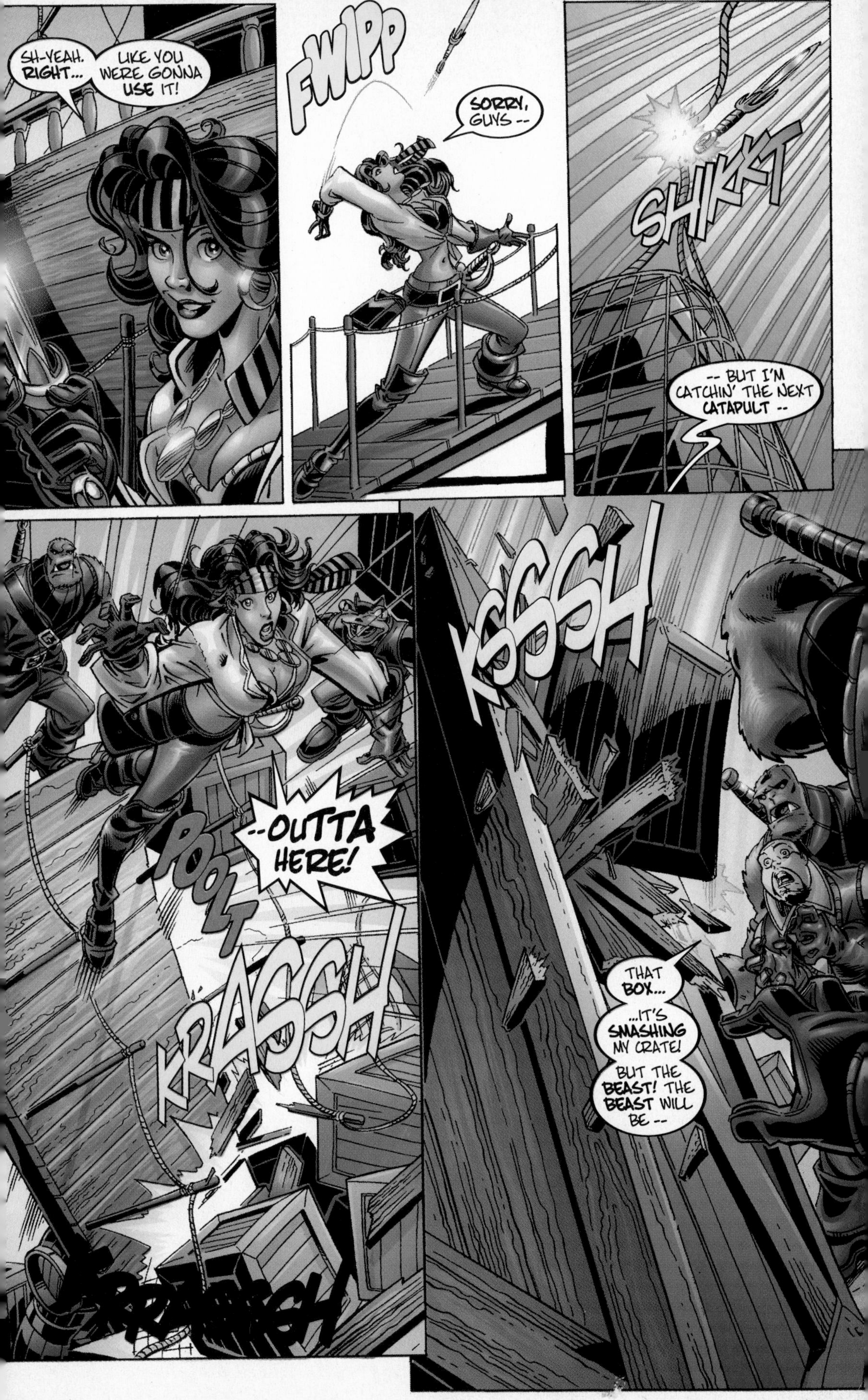
SH-YEAH. RIGHT...
LIKE YOU WERE GONNA USE IT!
FWIPP
SORRY, GUYS --
SHIKKT
-- BUT I'M CATCHIN' THE NEXT CATAPULT --
--OUTTA HERE!
KRASSH
KSSSH
THAT BOX...
...IT'S SMASHING MY CRATE!
BUT THE BEAST! THE BEAST WILL BE --

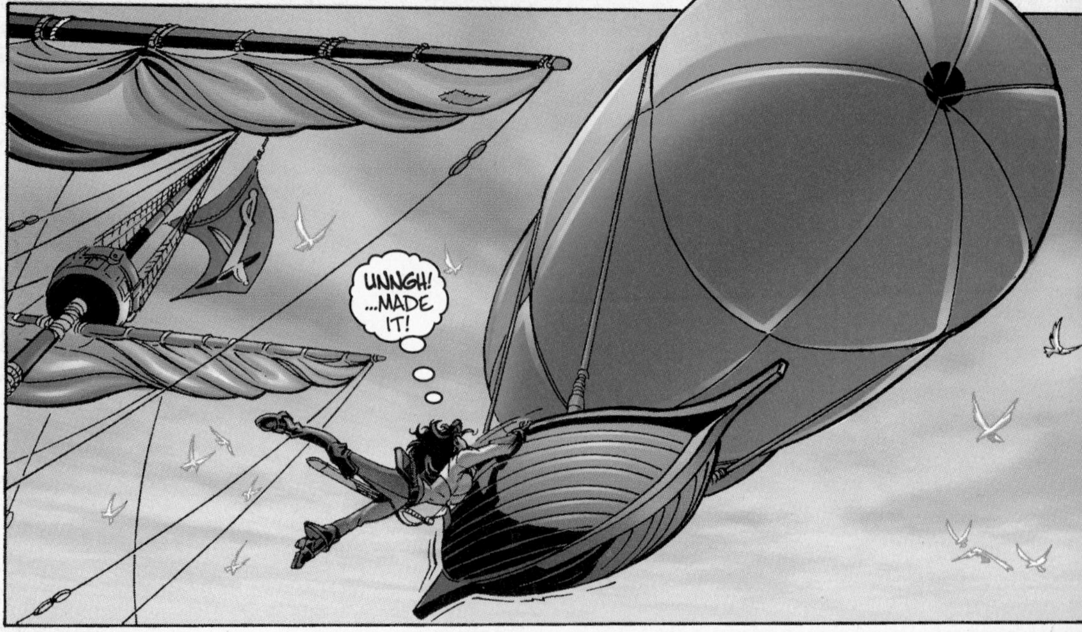
UNNGH! ...MADE IT!

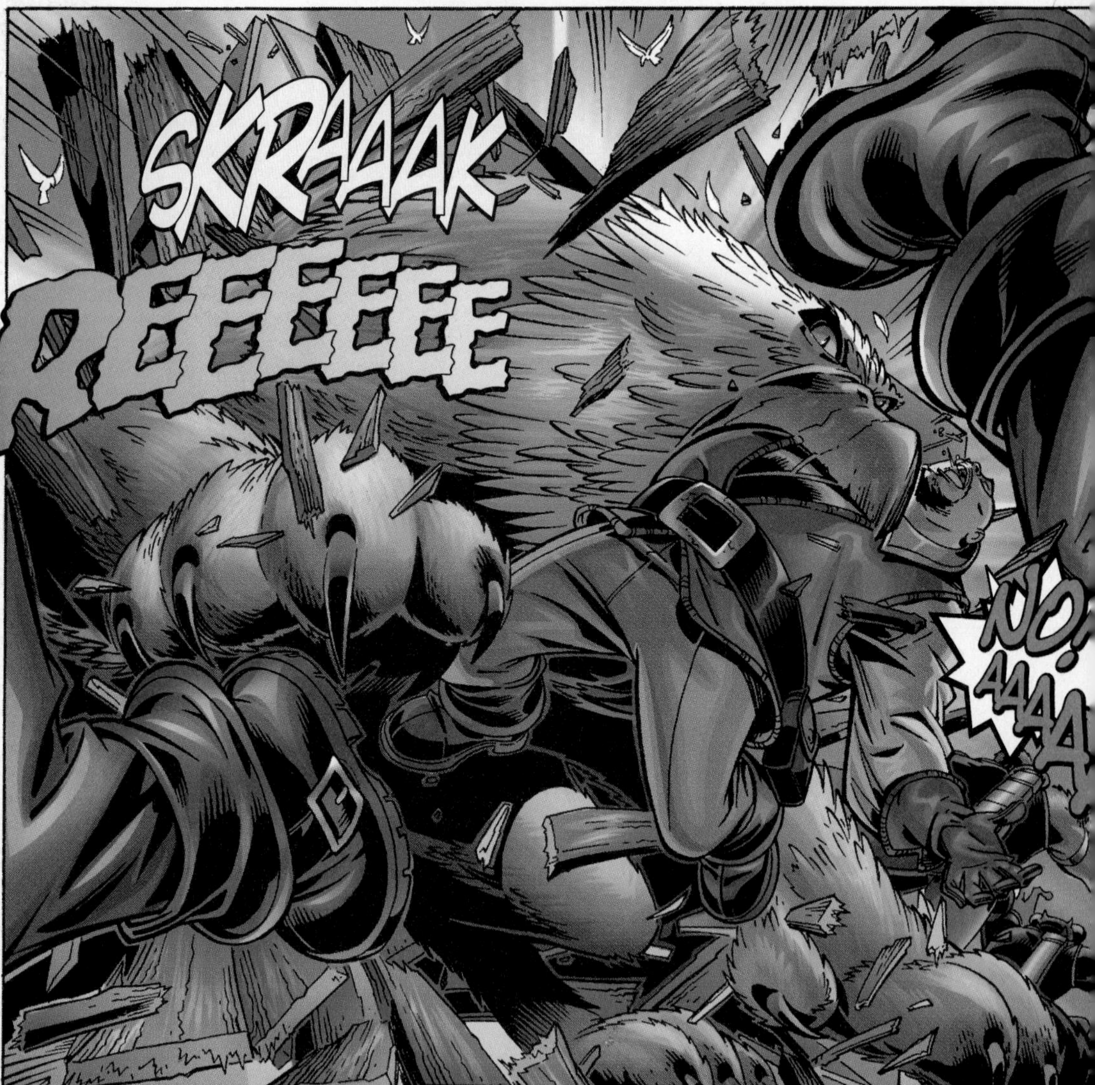
SKRAAAK
REEEEEE
NO! AAAA

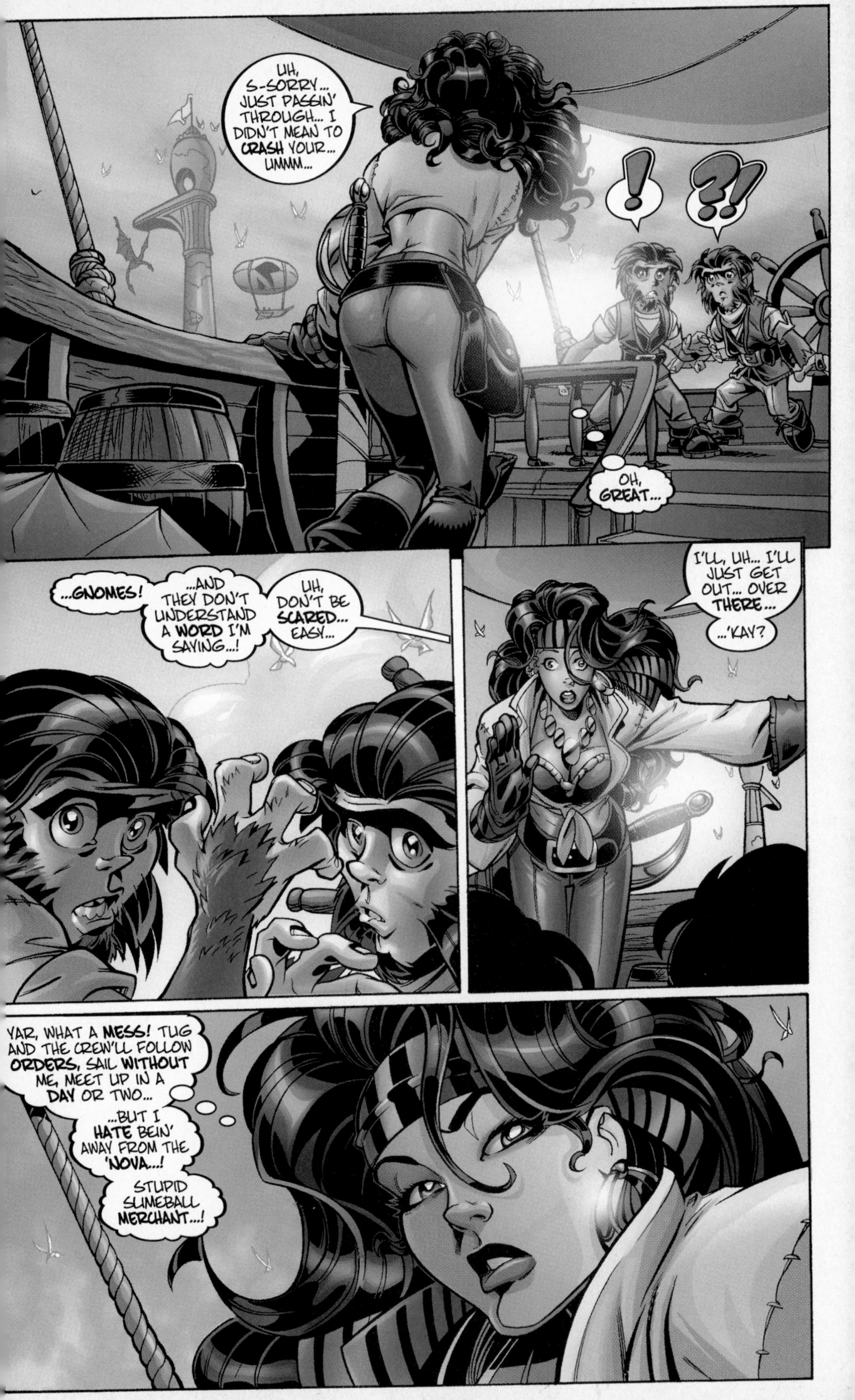
UH, S-SORRY... JUST PASSIN' THROUGH... I DIDN'T MEAN TO CRASH YOUR... UMMM...
!
?!
OH, GREAT...
...GNOMES!
...AND THEY DON'T UNDERSTAND A WORD I'M SAYING...!
UH, DON'T BE SCARED... EASY...
I'LL, UH... I'LL JUST GET OUT... OVER THERE...
...'KAY?
YAR, WHAT A MESS! TUG AND THE CREW'LL FOLLOW ORDERS, SAIL WITHOUT ME, MEET UP IN A DAY OR TWO...
...BUT I HATE BEIN' AWAY FROM THE 'NOVA...!
STUPID SLIMEBALL MERCHANT...!

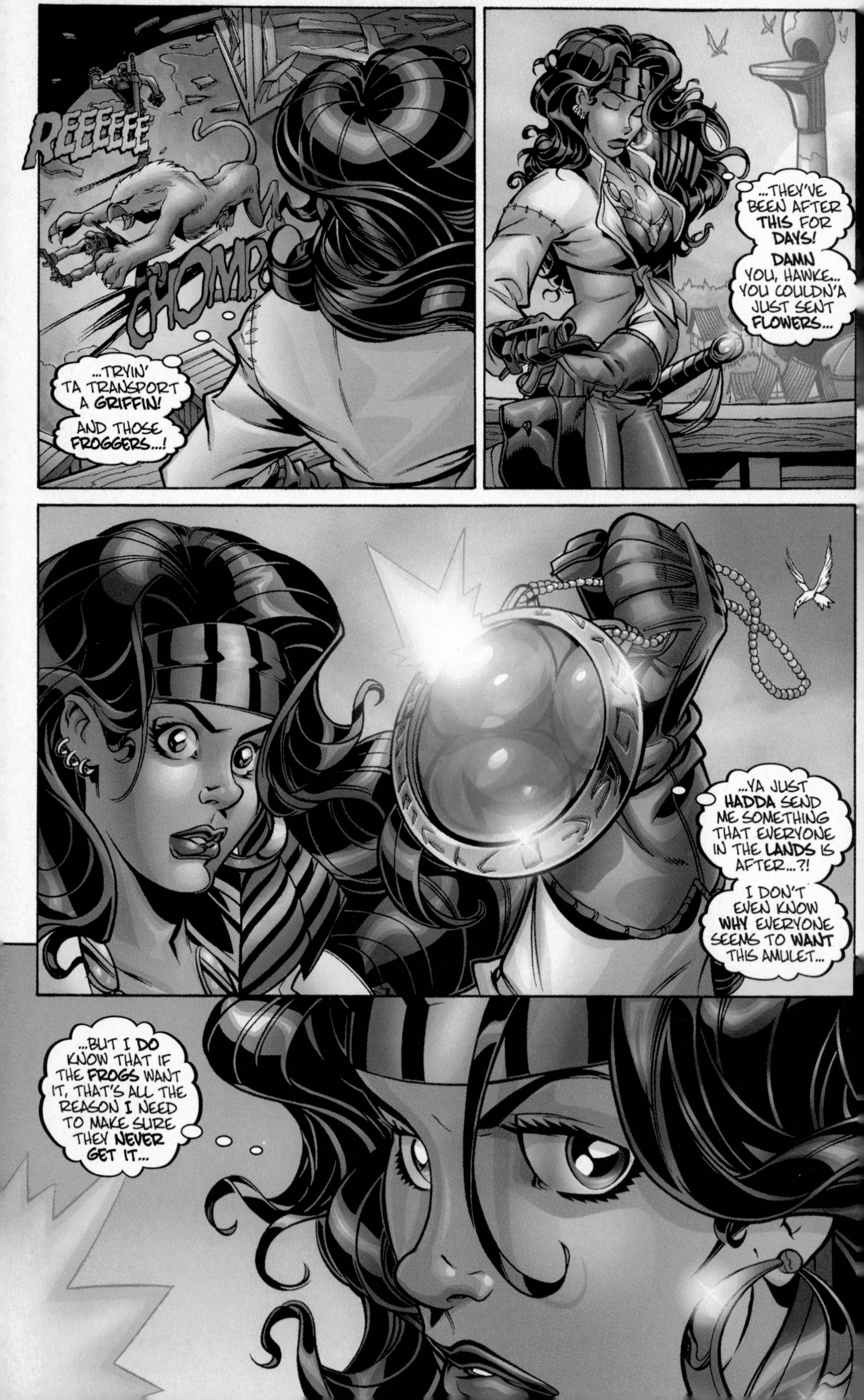
REEEEEE
CHOMP
...TRYIN' TA TRANSPORT A GRIFFIN!
AND THOSE FROGGERS...!
...THEY'VE BEEN AFTER THIS FOR DAYS! DAMN YOU, HAWKE... YOU COULDN'A JUST SENT FLOWERS...
...YA JUST HADDA SEND ME SOMETHING THAT EVERYONE IN THE LANDS IS AFTER...?!
I DON'T EVEN KNOW WHY EVERYONE SEEMS TO WANT THIS AMULET...
...BUT I DO KNOW THAT IF THE FROGS WANT IT, THAT'S ALL THE REASON I NEED TO MAKE SURE THEY NEVER GET IT...

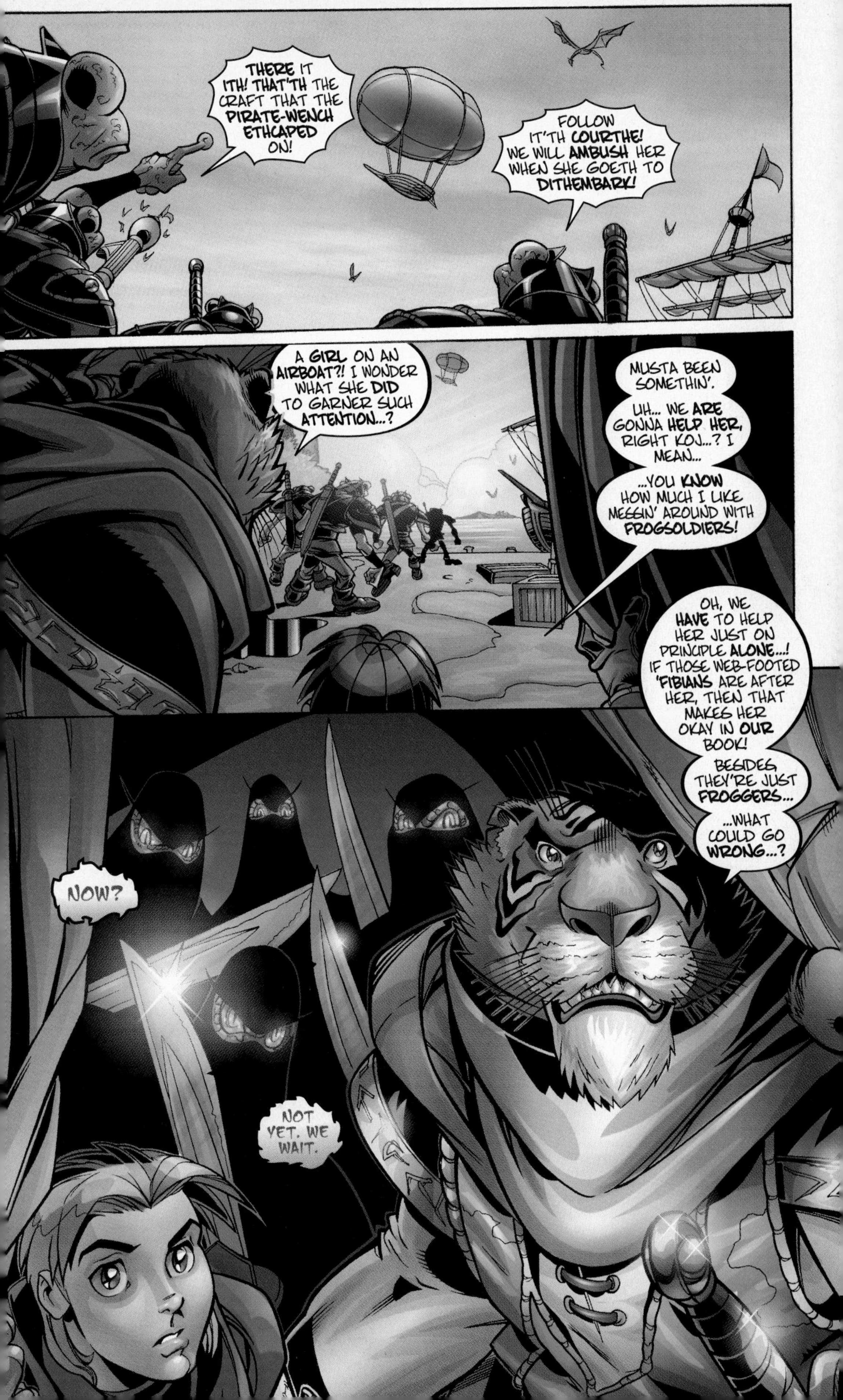

THERE IT ITH! THAT'TH THE CRAFT THAT THE PIRATE-WENCH ETHCAPED ON!
FOLLOW IT'TH COURTHE! WE WILL AMBUSH HER WHEN SHE GOETH TO DITHEMBARK!
A GIRL ON AN AIRBOAT?! I WONDER WHAT SHE DID TO GARNER SUCH ATTENTION...?
MUSTA BEEN SOMETHIN'.
UH... WE ARE GONNA HELP HER, RIGHT KOJ...? I MEAN...
...YOU KNOW HOW MUCH I LIKE MESSIN' AROUND WITH FROGSOLDIERS!
OH, WE HAVE TO HELP HER JUST ON PRINCIPLE ALONE...! IF THOSE WEB-FOOTED 'FIBIANS ARE AFTER HER, THEN THAT MAKES HER OKAY IN OUR BOOK!
BESIDES THEY'RE JUST FROGGERS...
...WHAT COULD GO WRONG...?
NOW?
NOT YET. WE WAIT.

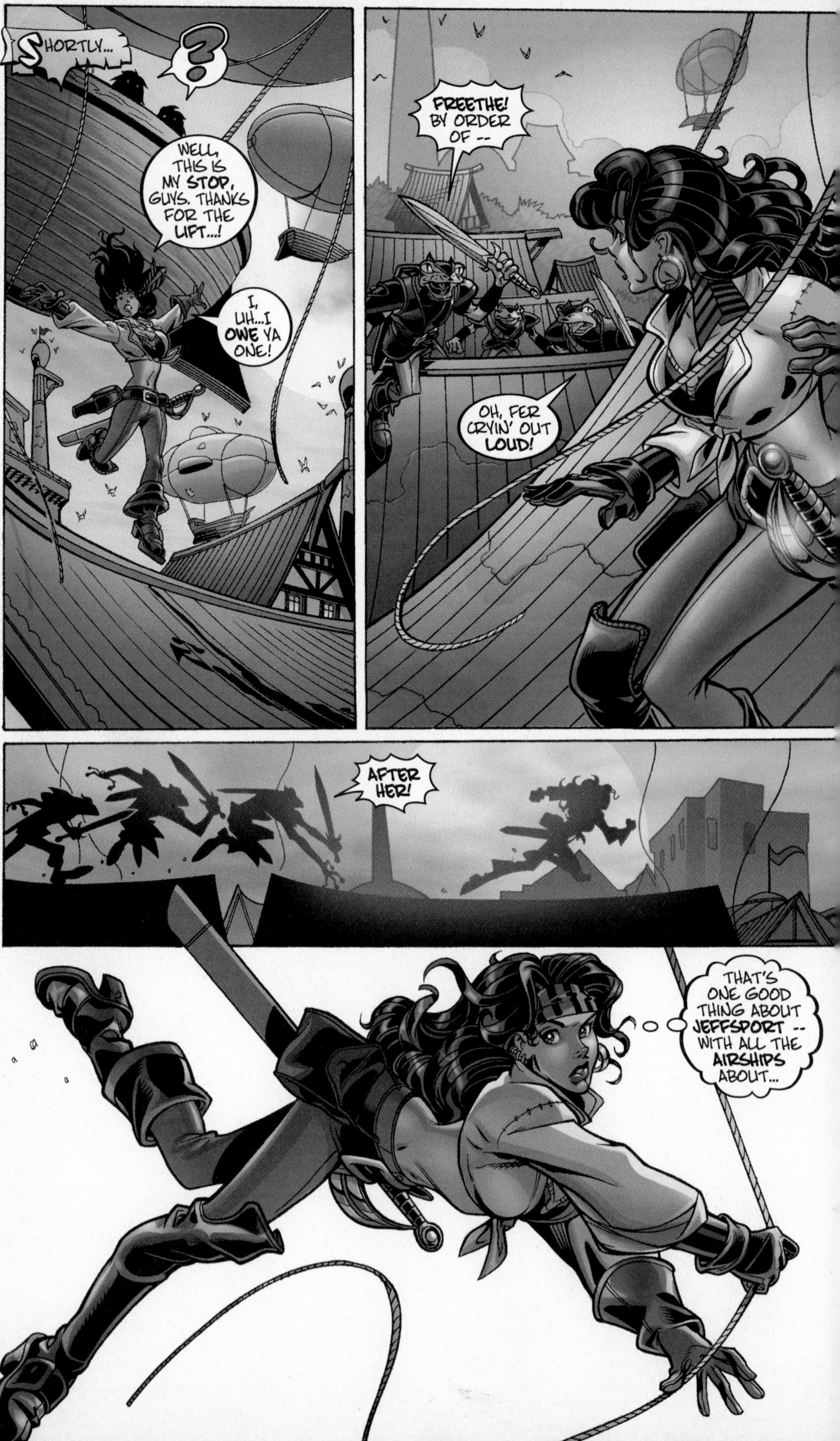
SHORTLY...
?
WELL, THIS IS MY STOP, GUYS. THANKS FOR THE LIFT...!
I, UH...I OWE YA ONE!
FREETHE! BY ORDER OF --
OH, FER CRYIN' OUT LOUD!
AFTER HER!
THAT'S ONE GOOD THING ABOUT JEFFSPORT -- WITH ALL THE AIRSHIPS ABOUT...

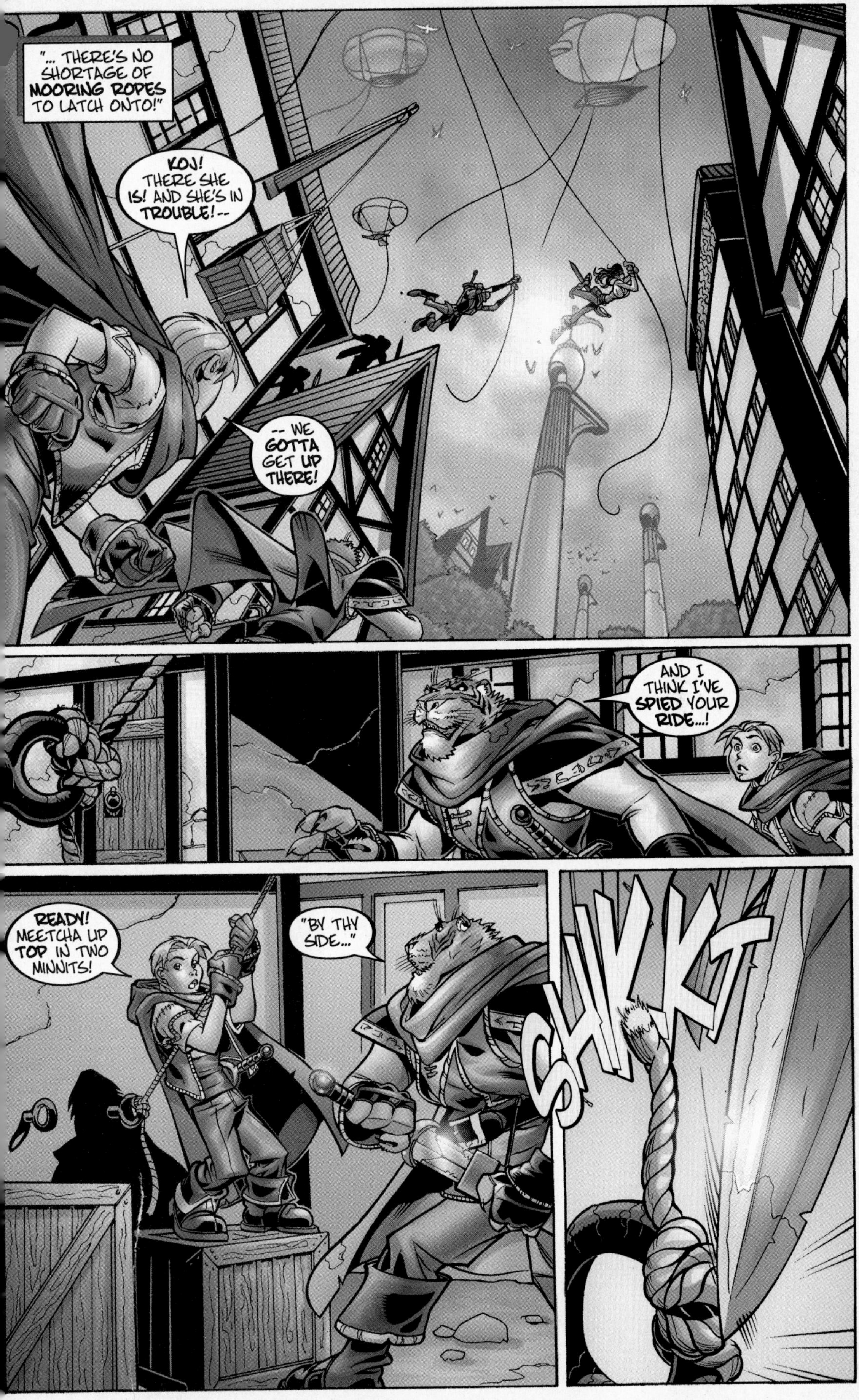
"... THERE'S NO SHORTAGE OF MOORING ROPES TO LATCH ONTO!"
KOJ! THERE SHE IS! AND SHE'S IN TROUBLE! --
-- WE GOTTA GET UP THERE!
AND I THINK I'VE SPIED YOUR RIDE...!
READY! MEETCHA UP TOP IN TWO MINNITS!
"BY THY SIDE..."
SHKKT

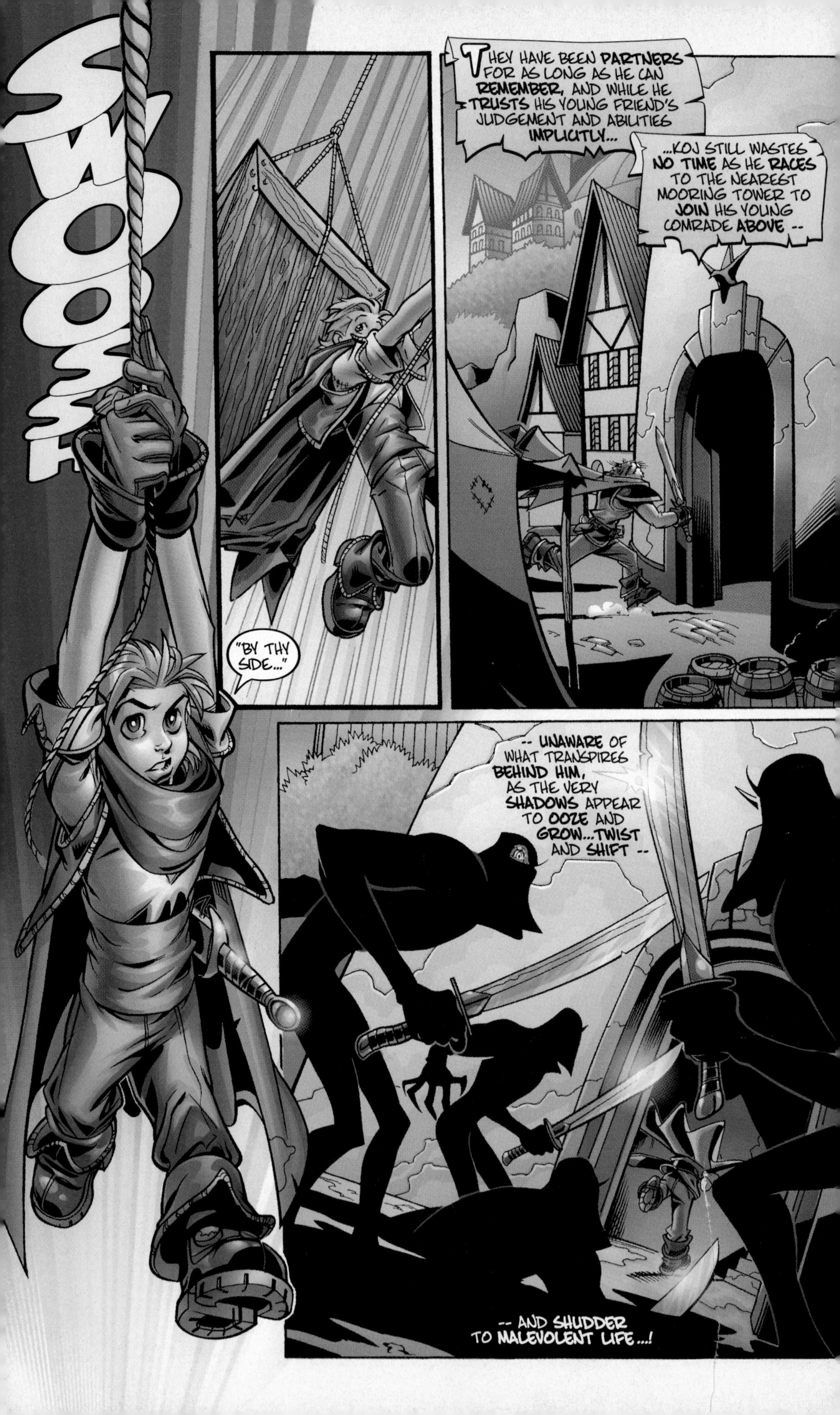
SWOOSH!
"BY THY SIDE..."
THEY HAVE BEEN PARTNERS FOR AS LONG AS HE CAN REMEMBER, AND WHILE HE TRUSTS HIS YOUNG FRIEND'S JUDGEMENT AND ABILITIES IMPLICITLY...
...KOJ STILL WASTES NO TIME AS HE RACES TO THE NEAREST MOORING TOWER TO JOIN HIS YOUNG COMRADE ABOVE --
-- UNAWARE OF WHAT TRANSPIRES BEHIND HIM, AS THE VERY SHADOWS APPEAR TO OOZE AND GROW...TWIST AND SHIFT --
-- AND SHUDDER TO MALEVOLENT LIFE...!

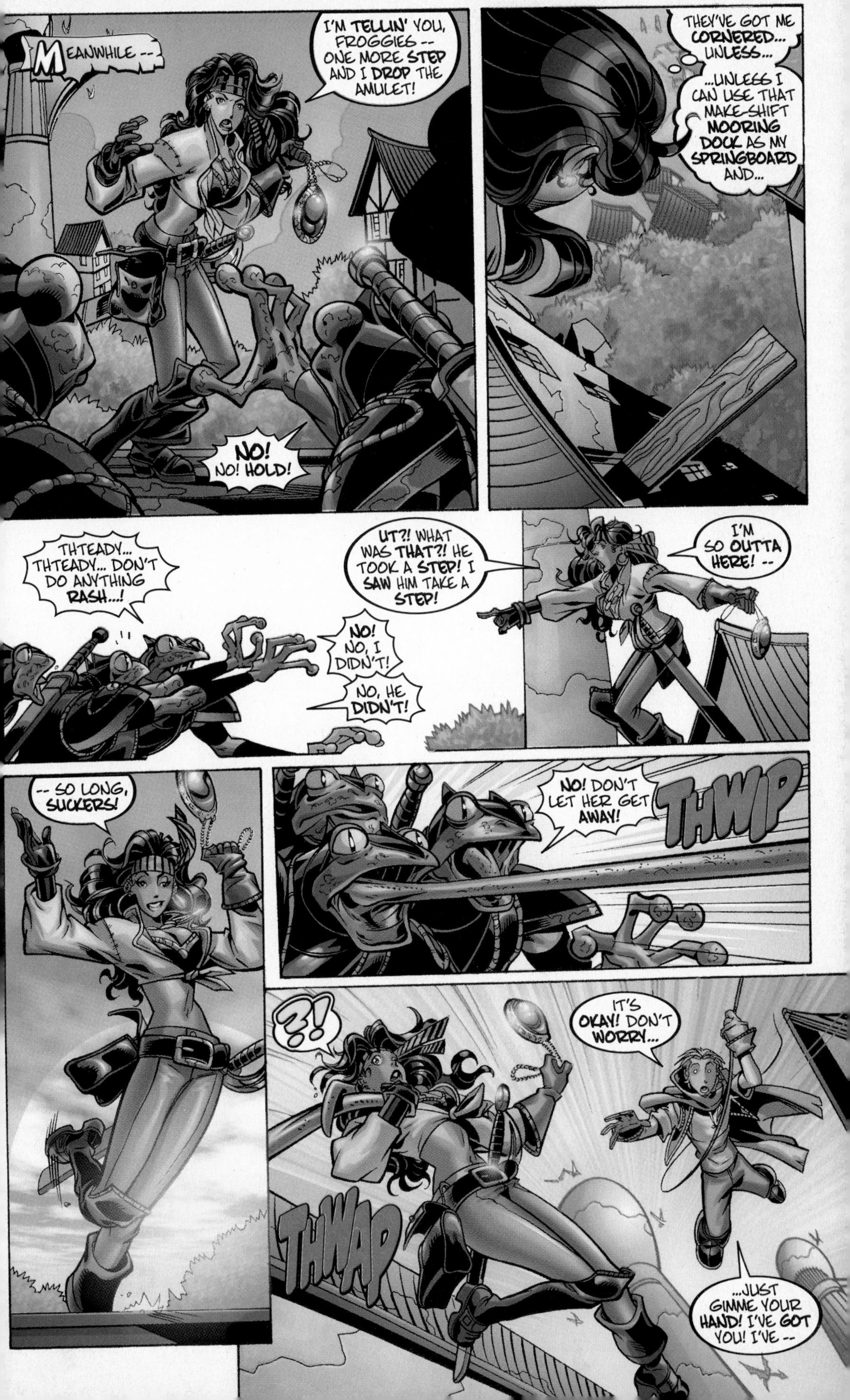
MEANWHILE --
I'M TELLIN' YOU, FROGGIES -- ONE MORE STEP AND I DROP THE AMULET!
NO! NO! HOLD!
THEY'VE GOT ME CORNERED... UNLESS...
...UNLESS I CAN USE THAT MAKE-SHIFT MOORING DOCK AS MY SPRINGBOARD AND...
THTEADY... THTEADY... DON'T DO ANYTHING RASH...!
UT?! WHAT WAS THAT?! HE TOOK A STEP! I SAW HIM TAKE A STEP!
NO! NO, I DIDN'T!
NO, HE DIDN'T!
I'M SO OUTTA HERE! --
-- SO LONG, SUCKERS!
NO! DON'T LET HER GET AWAY!
THWIP
?!
IT'S OKAY! DON'T WORRY...
THWAP
...JUST GIMME YOUR HAND! I'VE GOT YOU! I'VE --

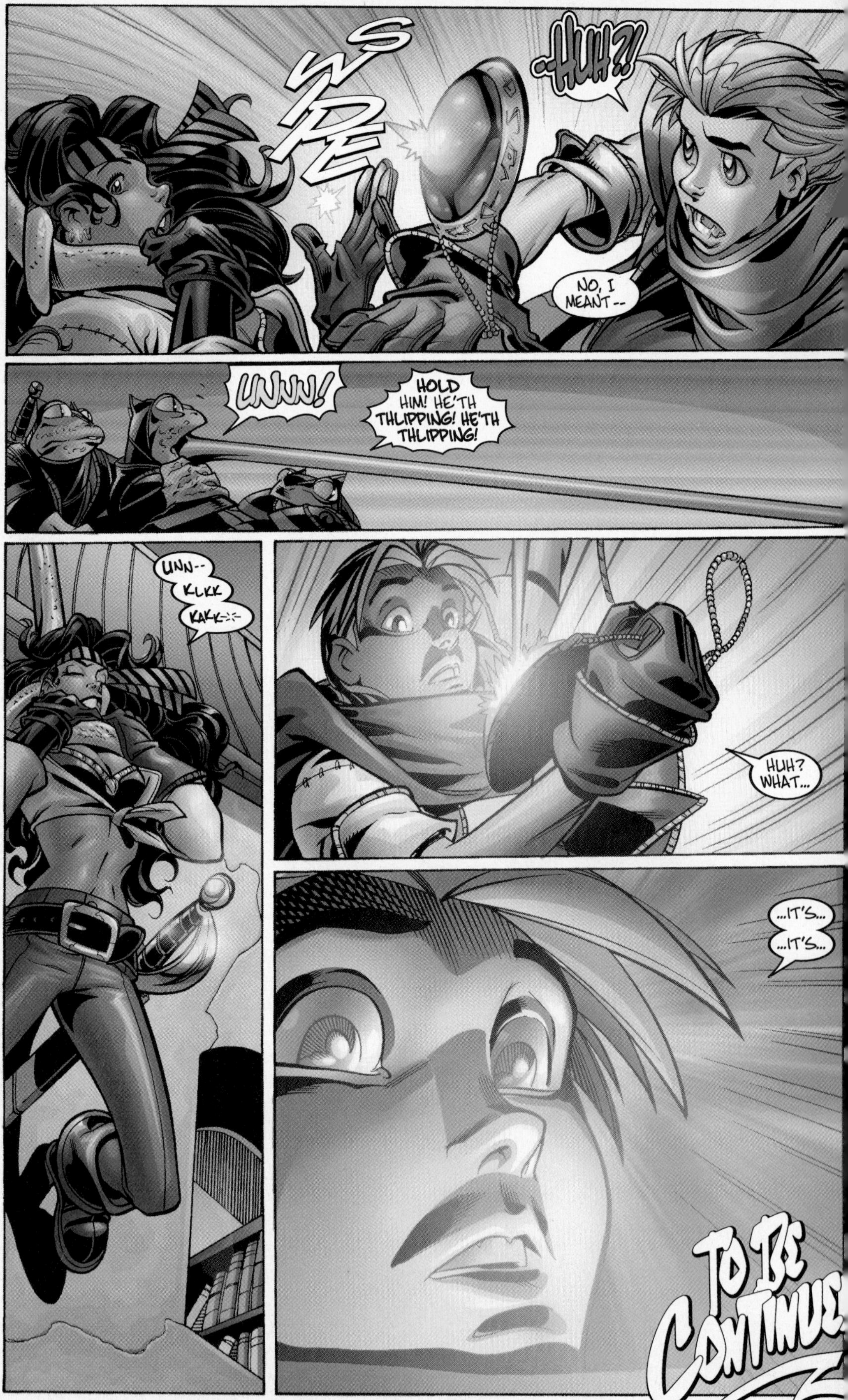
SWIPE
-HUH?!
NO, I MEANT--
UNNN!
HOLD HIM! HE'TH THLIPPING! HE'TH THLIPPING!
UNN-- KLKK KAKK-
HUH? WHAT...
...IT'S... ...IT'S...
TO BE CONTINUED

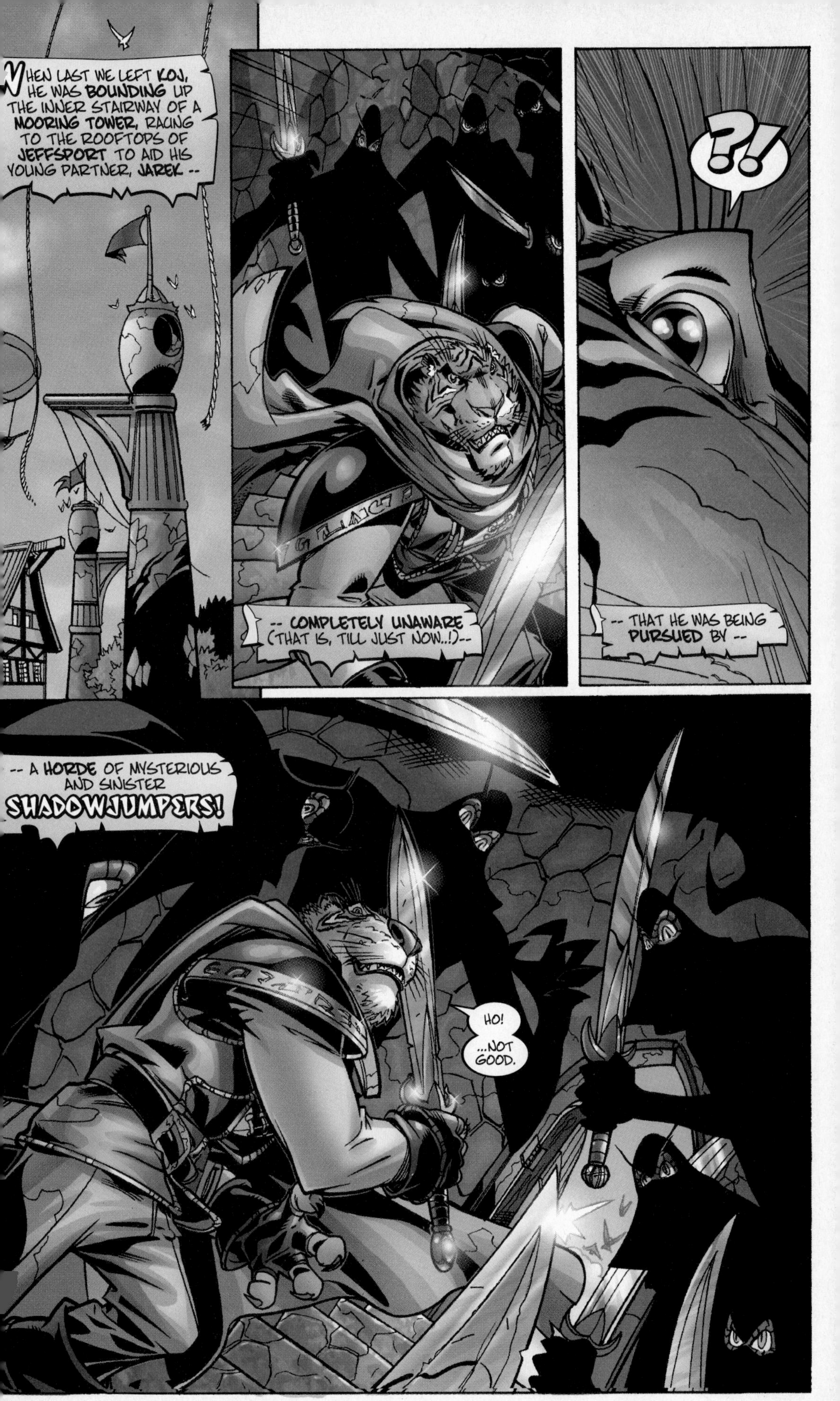
WHEN LAST WE LEFT KOJ, HE WAS BOUNDING UP THE INNER STAIRWAY OF A MOORING TOWER, RACING TO THE ROOFTOPS OF JEFFSPORT TO AID HIS YOUNG PARTNER, JAREK --
-- COMPLETELY UNAWARE (THAT IS, TILL JUST NOW..!)--
?!
-- THAT HE WAS BEING PURSUED BY --
-- A HORDE OF MYSTERIOUS AND SINISTER SHADOWJUMPERS!
HO! ...NOT GOOD.

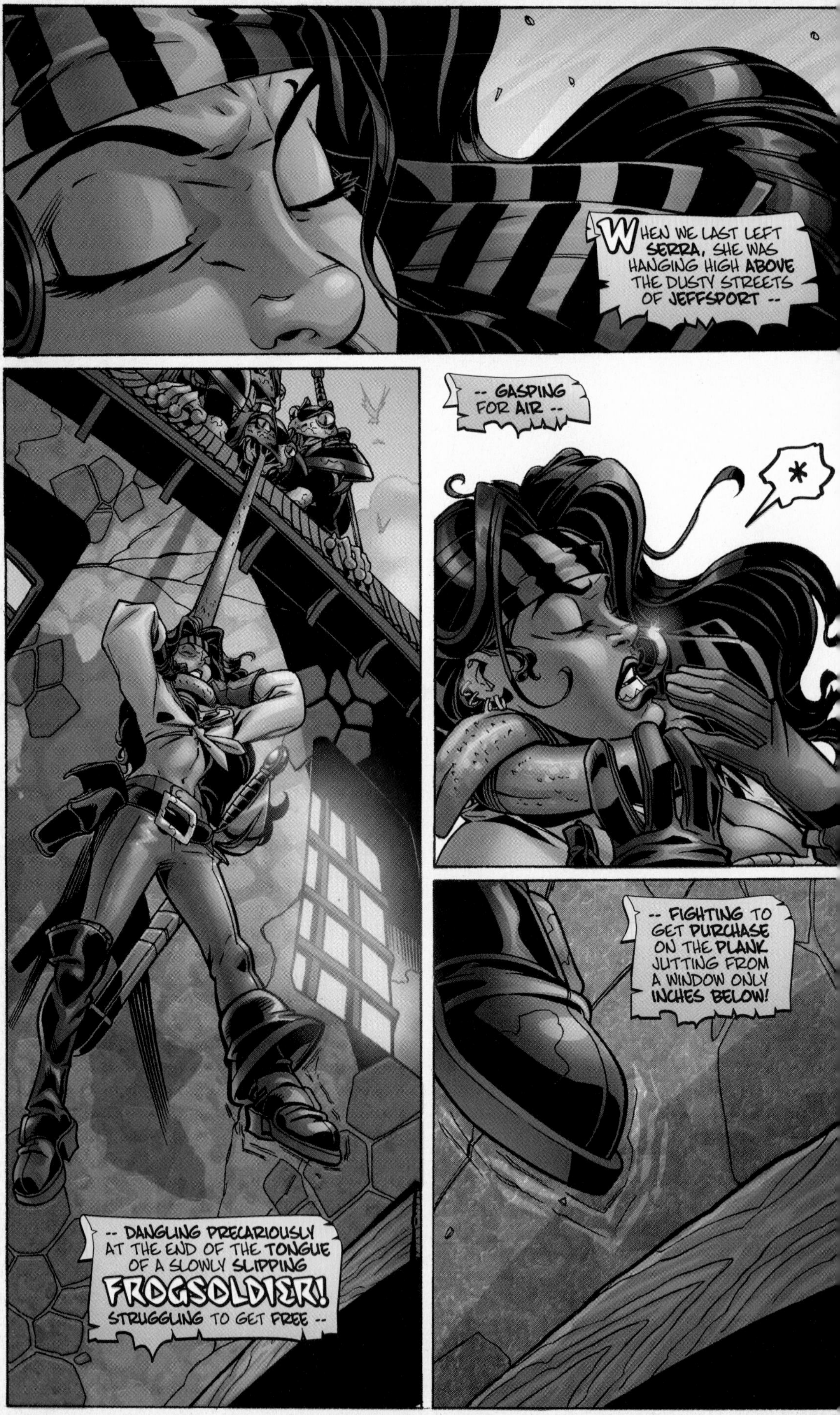
WHEN WE LAST LEFT SERRA, SHE WAS HANGING HIGH ABOVE THE DUSTY STREETS OF JEFFSPORT --
-- GASPING FOR AIR --
*
-- DANGLING PRECARIOUSLY AT THE END OF THE TONGUE OF A SLOWLY SLIPPING FROGSOLDIER! STRUGGLING TO GET FREE --
-- FIGHTING TO GET PURCHASE ON THE PLANK JUTTING FROM A WINDOW ONLY INCHES BELOW!

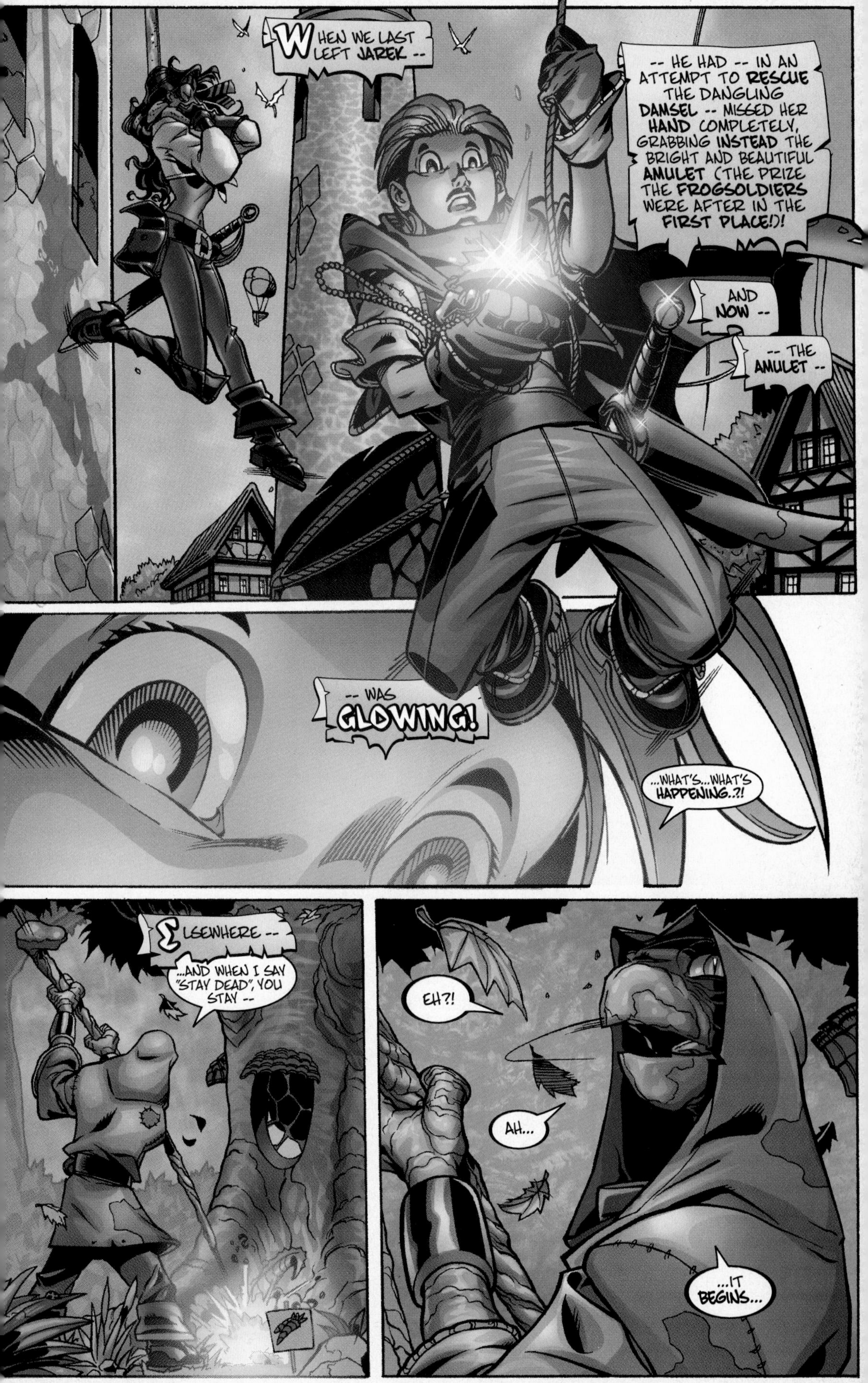
WHEN WE LAST LEFT JAREK --
-- HE HAD -- IN AN ATTEMPT TO RESCUE THE DANGLING DAMSEL -- MISSED HER HAND COMPLETELY, GRABBING INSTEAD THE BRIGHT AND BEAUTIFUL AMULET (THE PRIZE THE FROGSOLDIERS WERE AFTER IN THE FIRST PLACE!)!
AND NOW --
-- THE AMULET --
-- WAS GLOWING!
...WHAT'S...WHAT'S HAPPENING..?!
ELSEWHERE --
...AND WHEN I SAY "STAY DEAD", YOU STAY --
EH?!
AH...
...IT BEGINS...

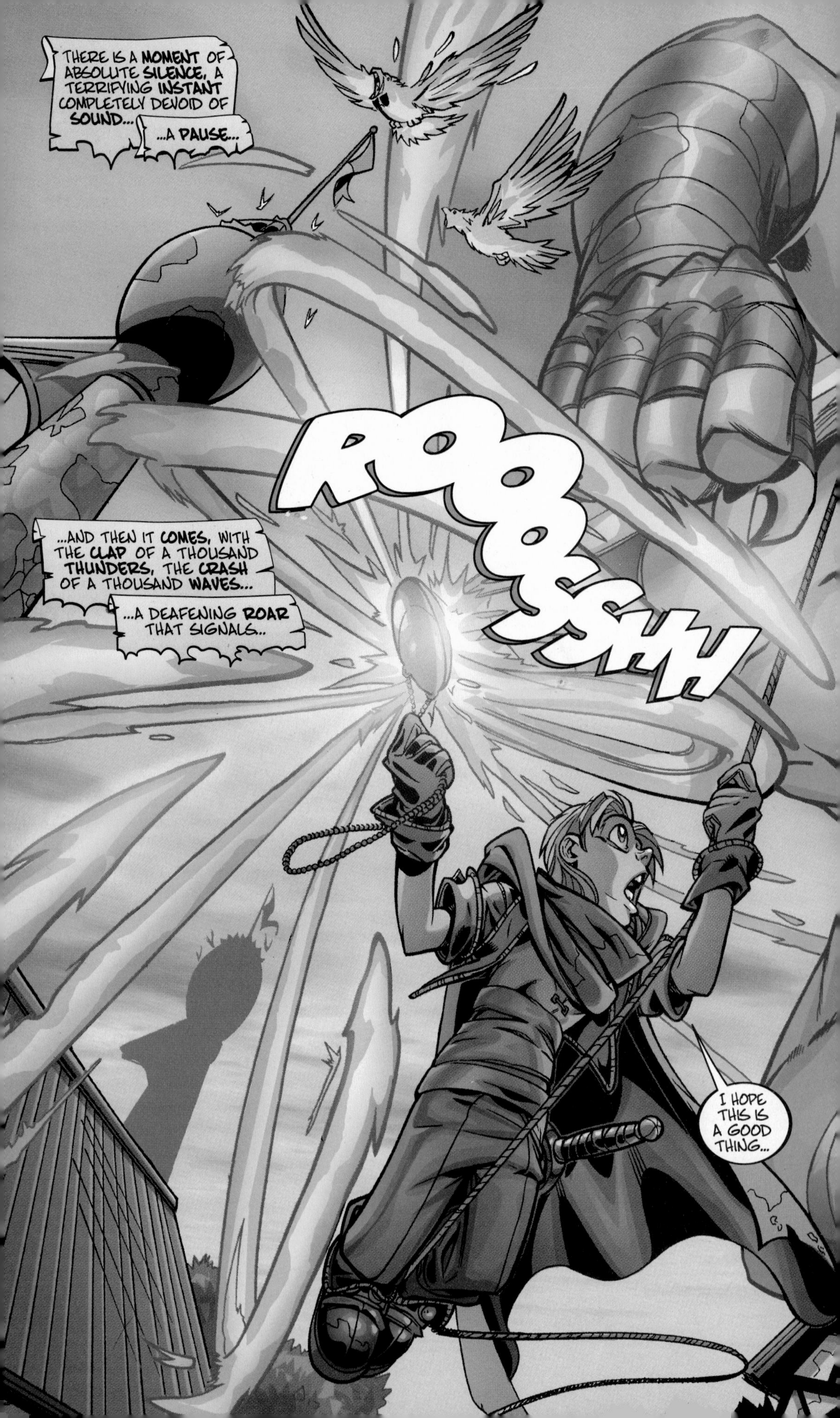
THERE IS A MOMENT OF ABSOLUTE SILENCE, A TERRIFYING INSTANT COMPLETELY DEVOID OF SOUND...
...A PAUSE...
ROOOOSHH
...AND THEN IT COMES, WITH THE CLAP OF A THOUSAND THUNDERS, THE CRASH OF A THOUSAND WAVES...
...A DEAFENING ROAR THAT SIGNALS...
I HOPE THIS IS A GOOD THING...

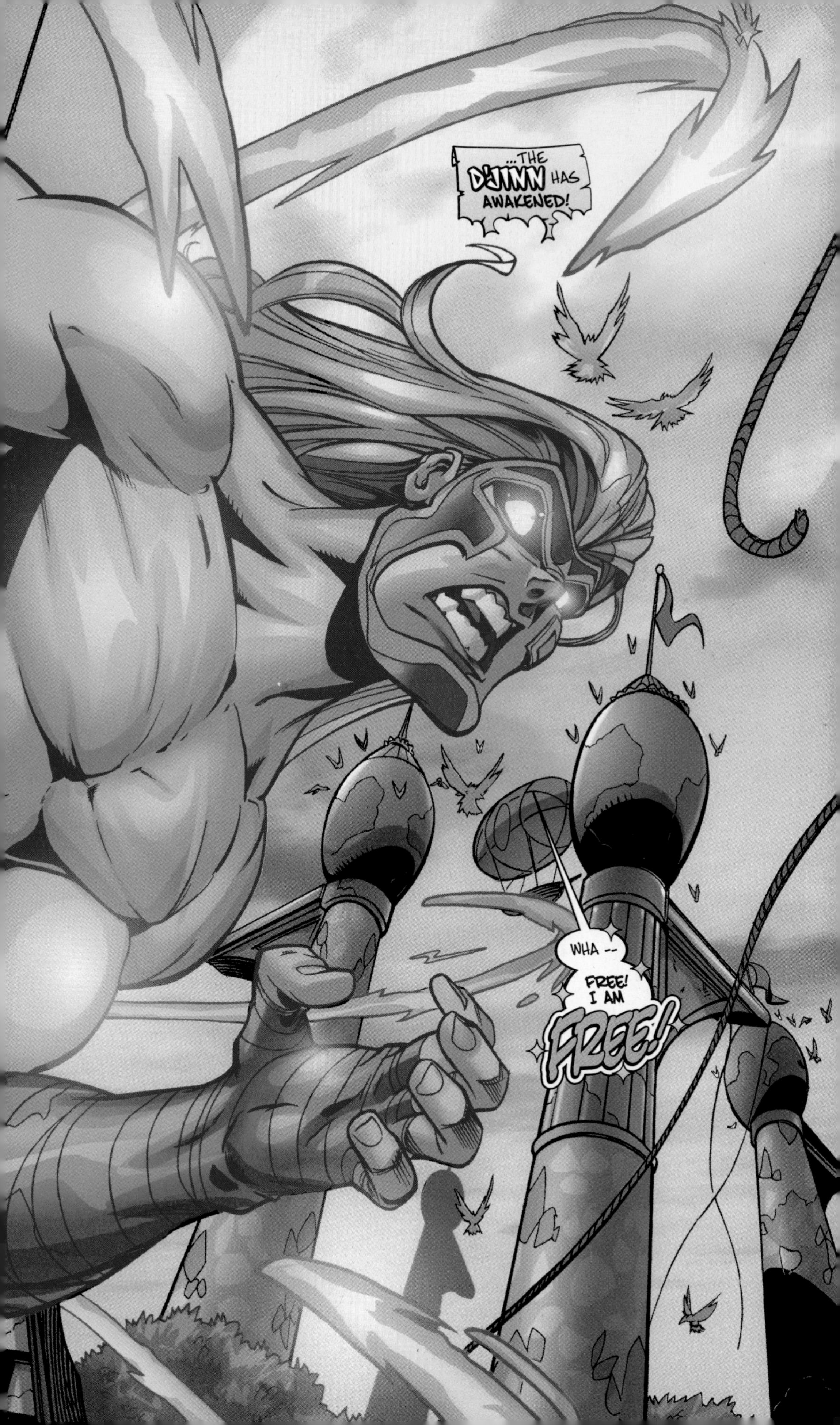

...THE D'JINN HAS AWAKENED!
WHA --
FREE! I AM FREE!

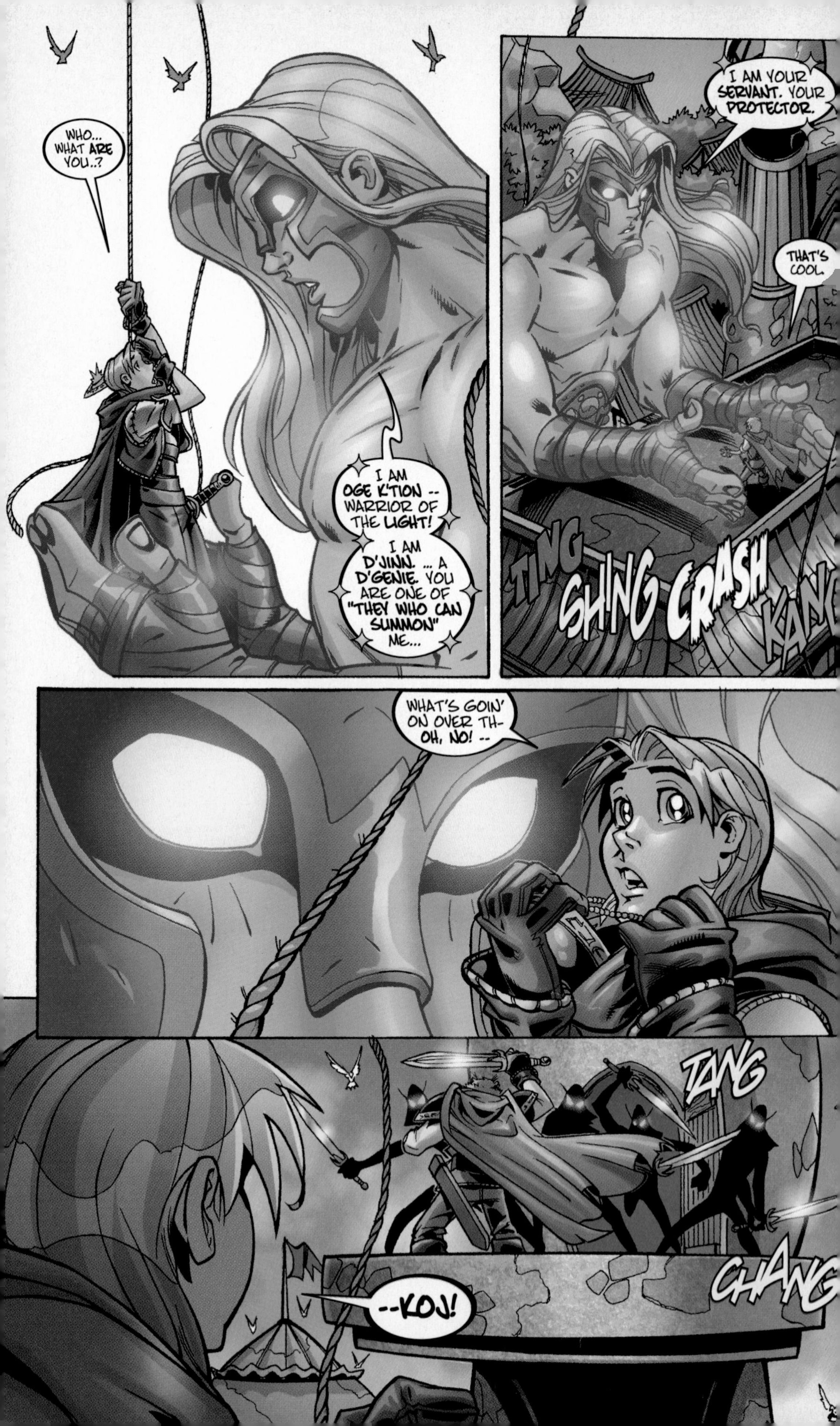
WHO... WHAT ARE YOU..?
I AM OGE K'TION -- WARRIOR OF THE LIGHT!
I AM D'JINN. ... A D'GENIE. YOU ARE ONE OF "THEY WHO CAN SUMMON" ME...
I AM YOUR SERVANT. YOUR PROTECTOR.
THAT'S COOL.
TING
SHING
CRASH
WHAT'S GOIN' ON OVER TH- OH, NO! --
TANG
CHANG
--KOJ!

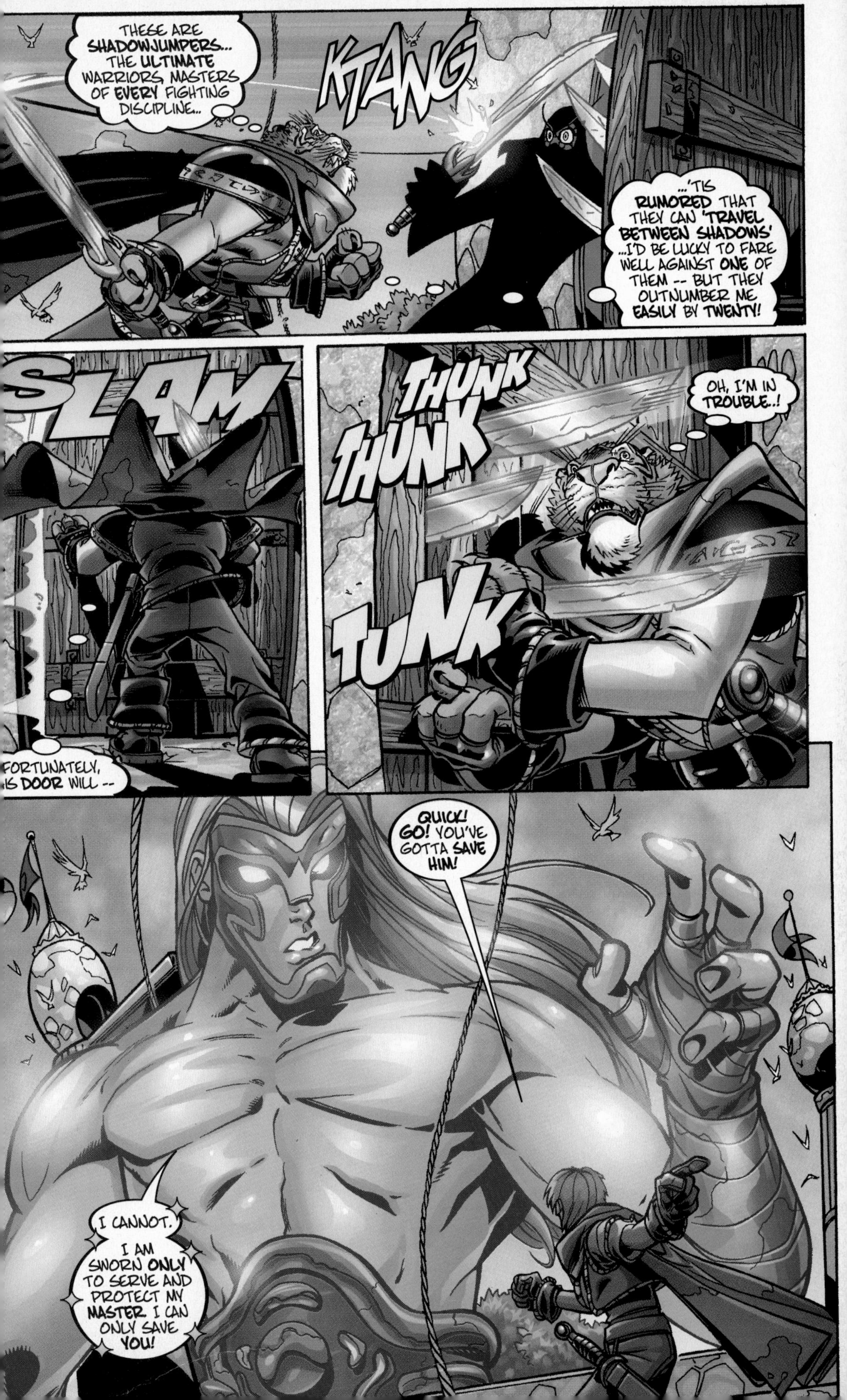
THESE ARE SHADOWJUMPERS... THE ULTIMATE WARRIORS, MASTERS OF EVERY FIGHTING DISCIPLINE...
KTANG
...'TIS RUMORED THAT THEY CAN 'TRAVEL BETWEEN SHADOWS' ...I'D BE LUCKY TO FARE WELL AGAINST ONE OF THEM -- BUT THEY OUTNUMBER ME EASILY BY TWENTY!
SLAM
FORTUNATELY, IS DOOR WILL --
THUNK
THUNK
OH, I'M IN TROUBLE..!
TUNK
QUICK! GO! YOU'VE GOTTA SAVE HIM!
I CANNOT.
I AM SWORN ONLY TO SERVE AND PROTECT MY MASTER. I CAN ONLY SAVE YOU!

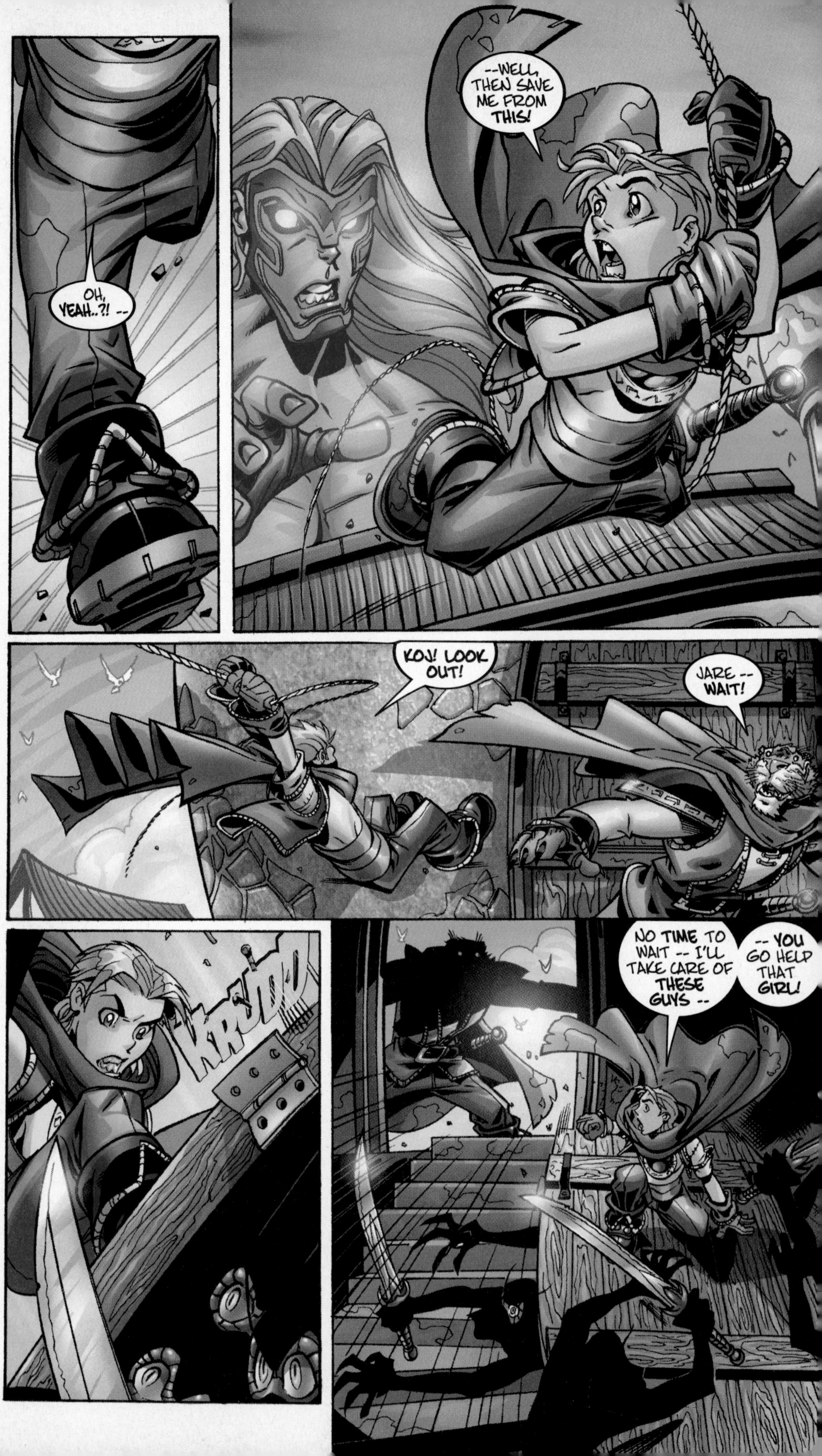
OH, YEAH..?! --
--WELL, THEN SAVE ME FROM THIS!
KOJ! LOOK OUT!
JARE -- WAIT!
KRUDD
NO TIME TO WAIT -- I'LL TAKE CARE OF THESE GUYS --
-- YOU GO HELP THAT GIRL!

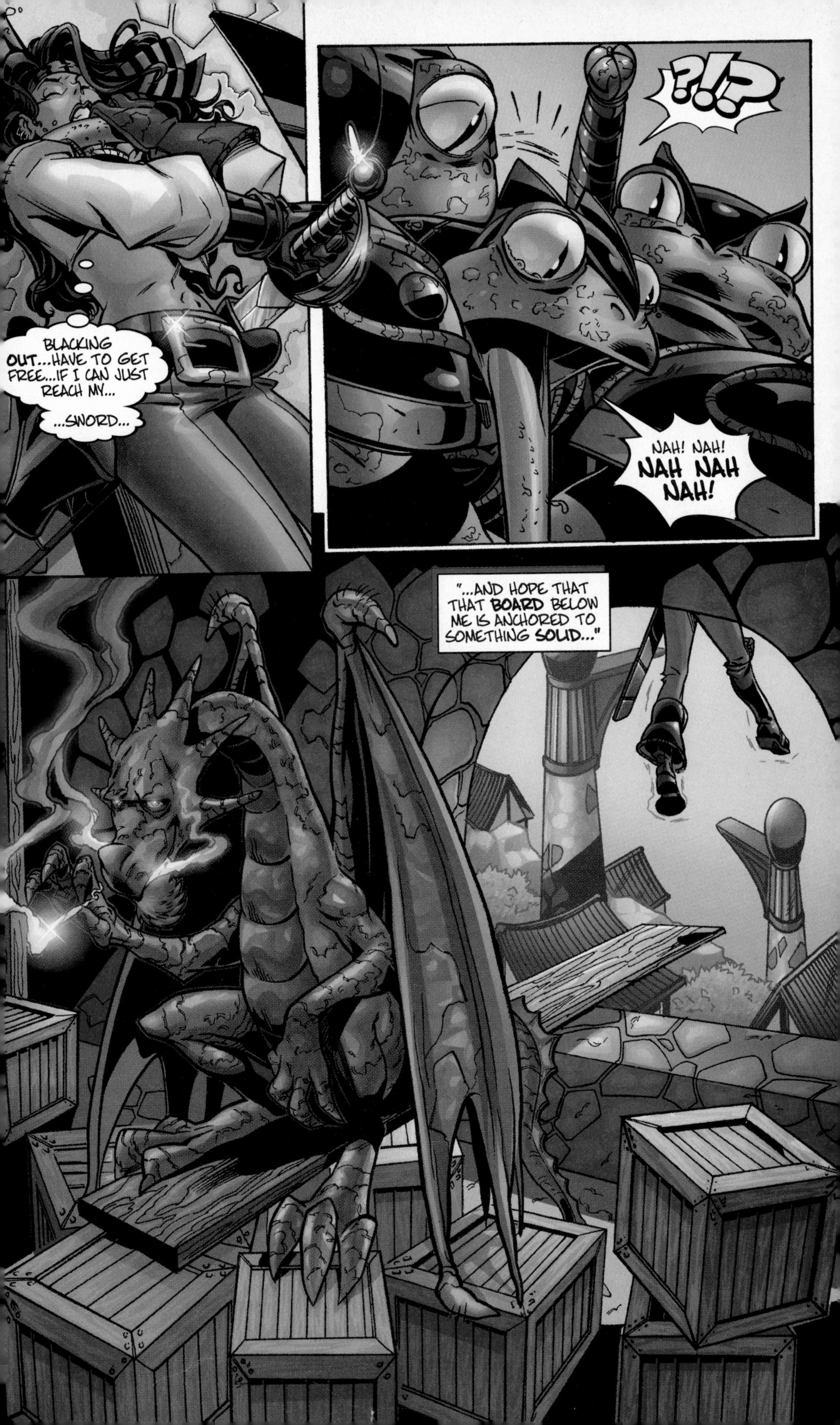
BLACKING **OUT**...HAVE TO GET FREE...IF I CAN JUST REACH MY...
...SWORD...
?!?
NAH! NAH! **NAH NAH NAH!**
"...AND HOPE THAT THAT **BOARD** BELOW ME IS ANCHORED TO SOMETHING **SOLID**..."

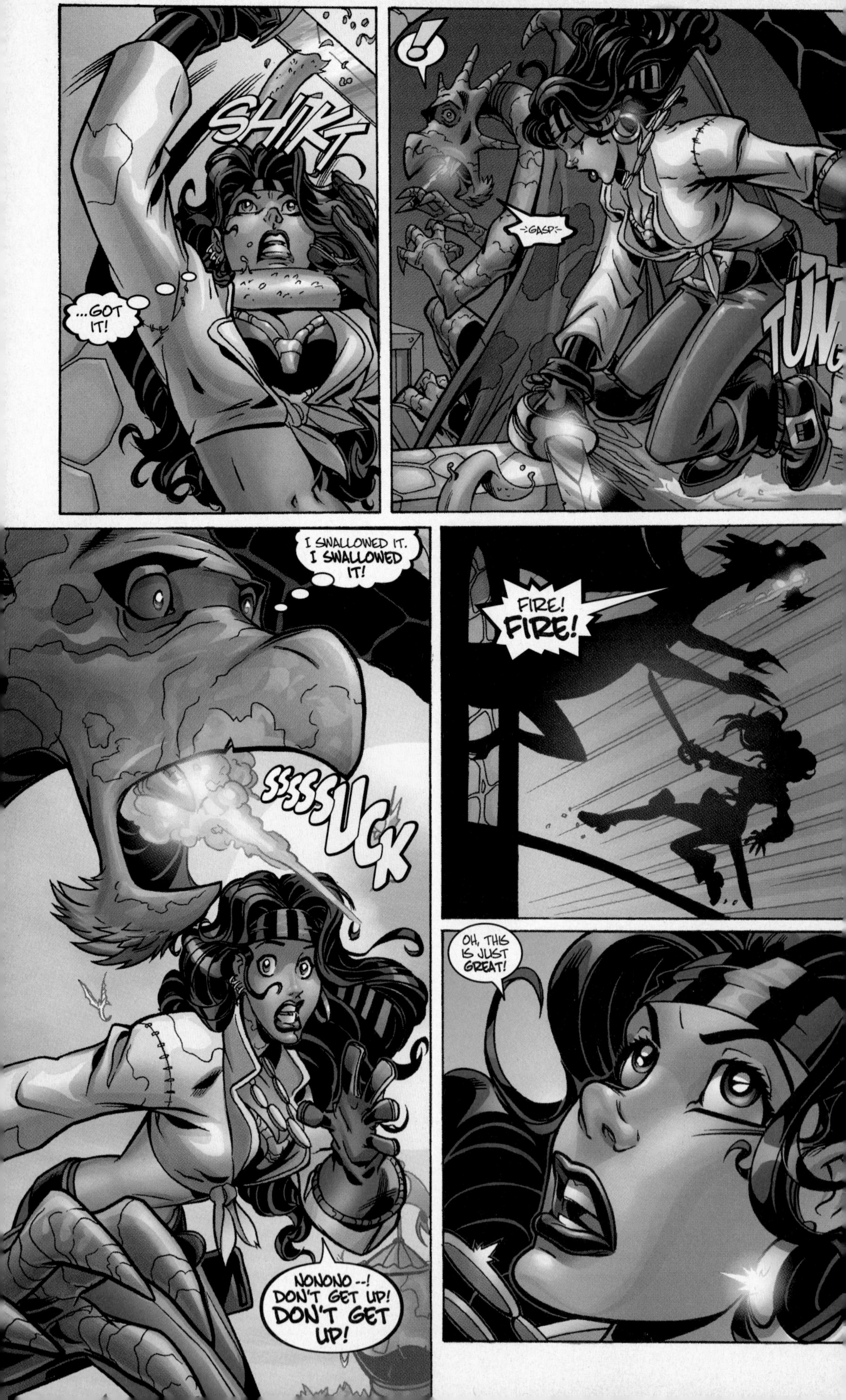
SHIKT
...GOT IT!
!
-GASP-
TUNG
I SWALLOWED IT. I SWALLOWED IT!
SSSSSUCK
NONONO --! DON'T GET UP! DON'T GET UP!
FIRE! FIRE!
OH, THIS IS JUST GREAT!

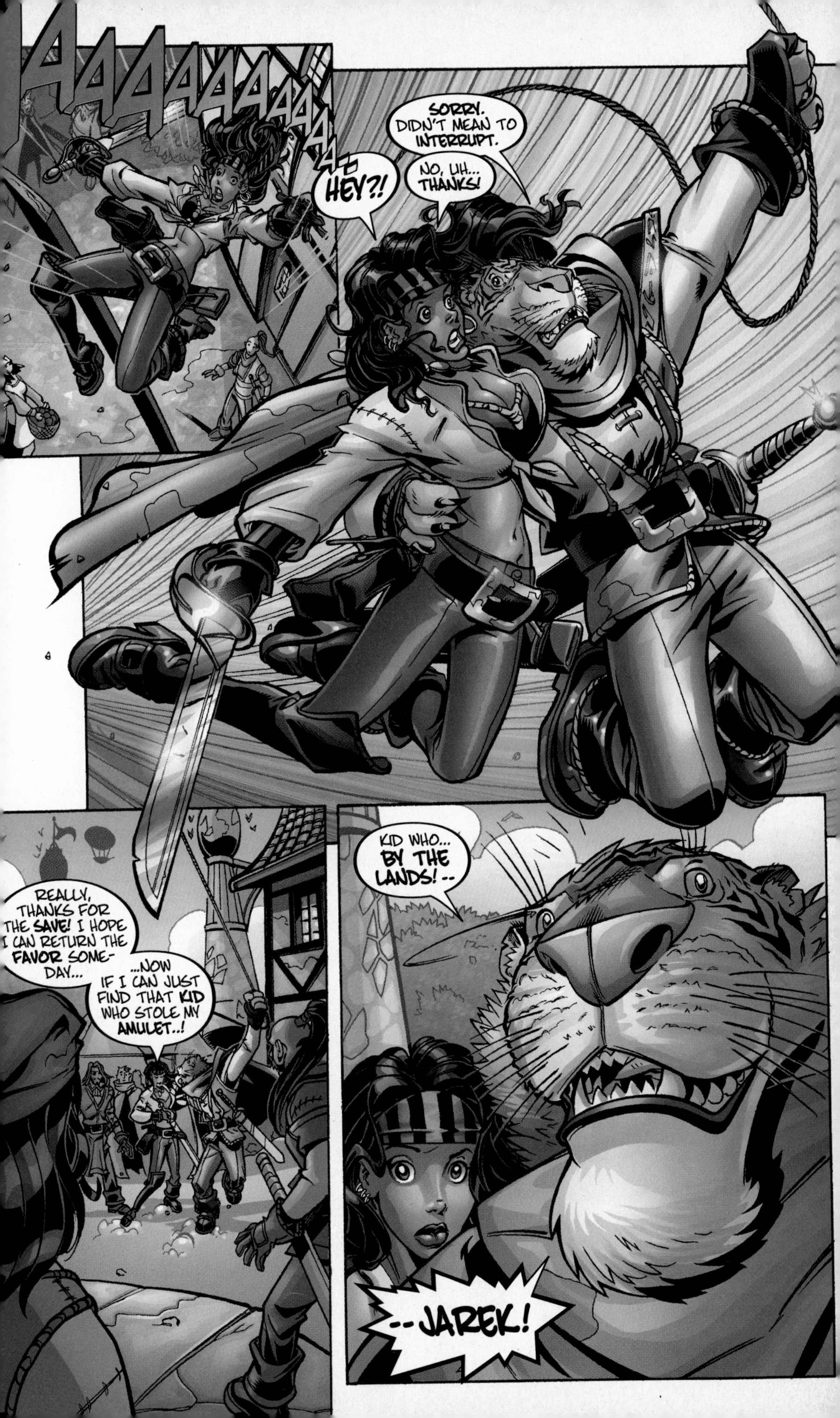
AAAAAAAAAAA
HEY?!
SORRY. DIDN'T MEAN TO INTERRUPT.
NO, UH... THANKS!
REALLY, THANKS FOR THE SAVE! I HOPE I CAN RETURN THE FAVOR SOME-DAY...
...NOW IF I CAN JUST FIND THAT KID WHO STOLE MY AMULET..!
KID WHO... BY THE LANDS! --
--JAREK!

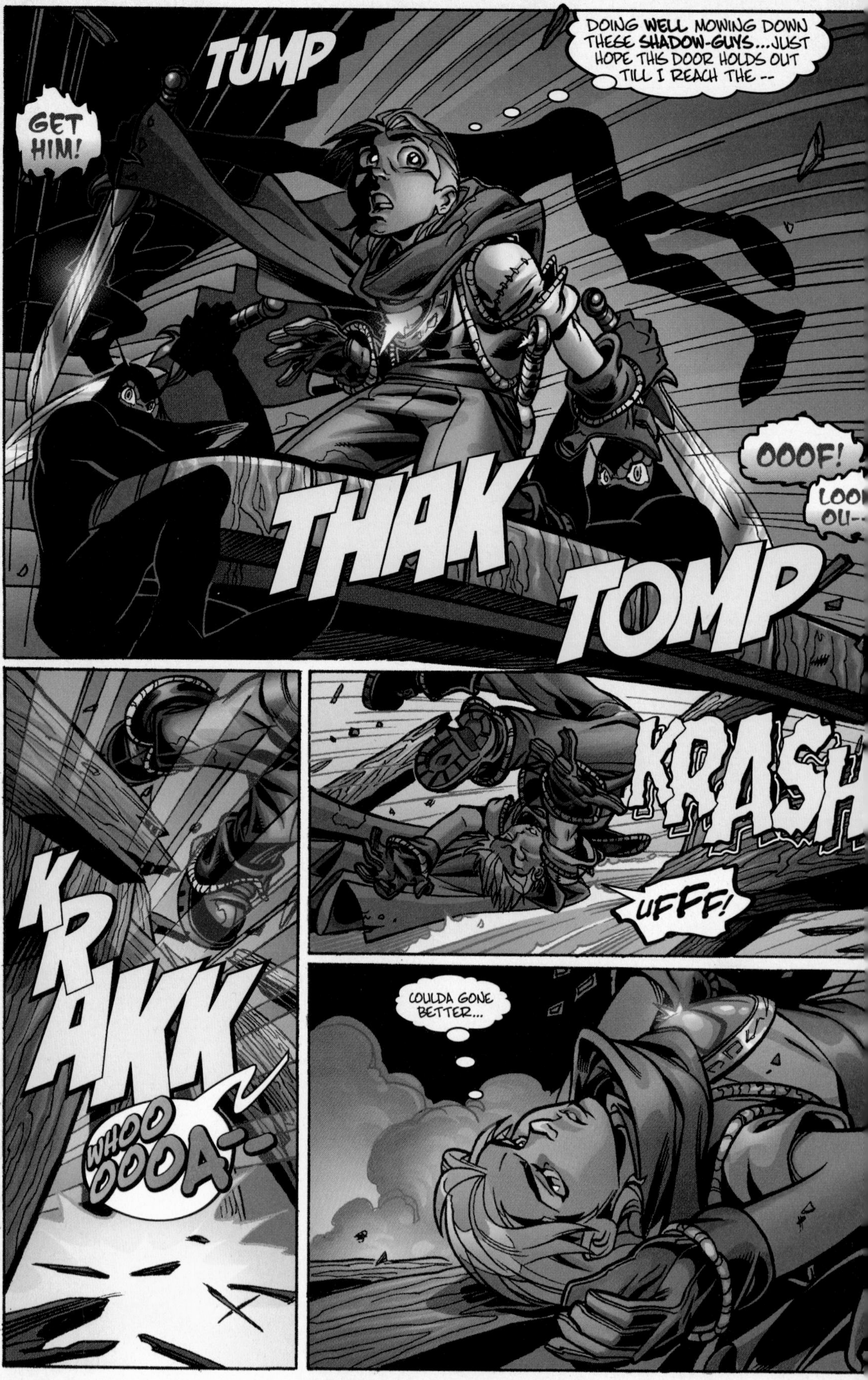
TUMP
DOING WELL MOWING DOWN THESE SHADOW-GUYS...JUST HOPE THIS DOOR HOLDS OUT TILL I REACH THE --
GET HIM!
OOOF!
THAK
TOMP
KRASH
UFFF!
KRAKK
WHOO OOOA--
COULDA GONE BETTER...

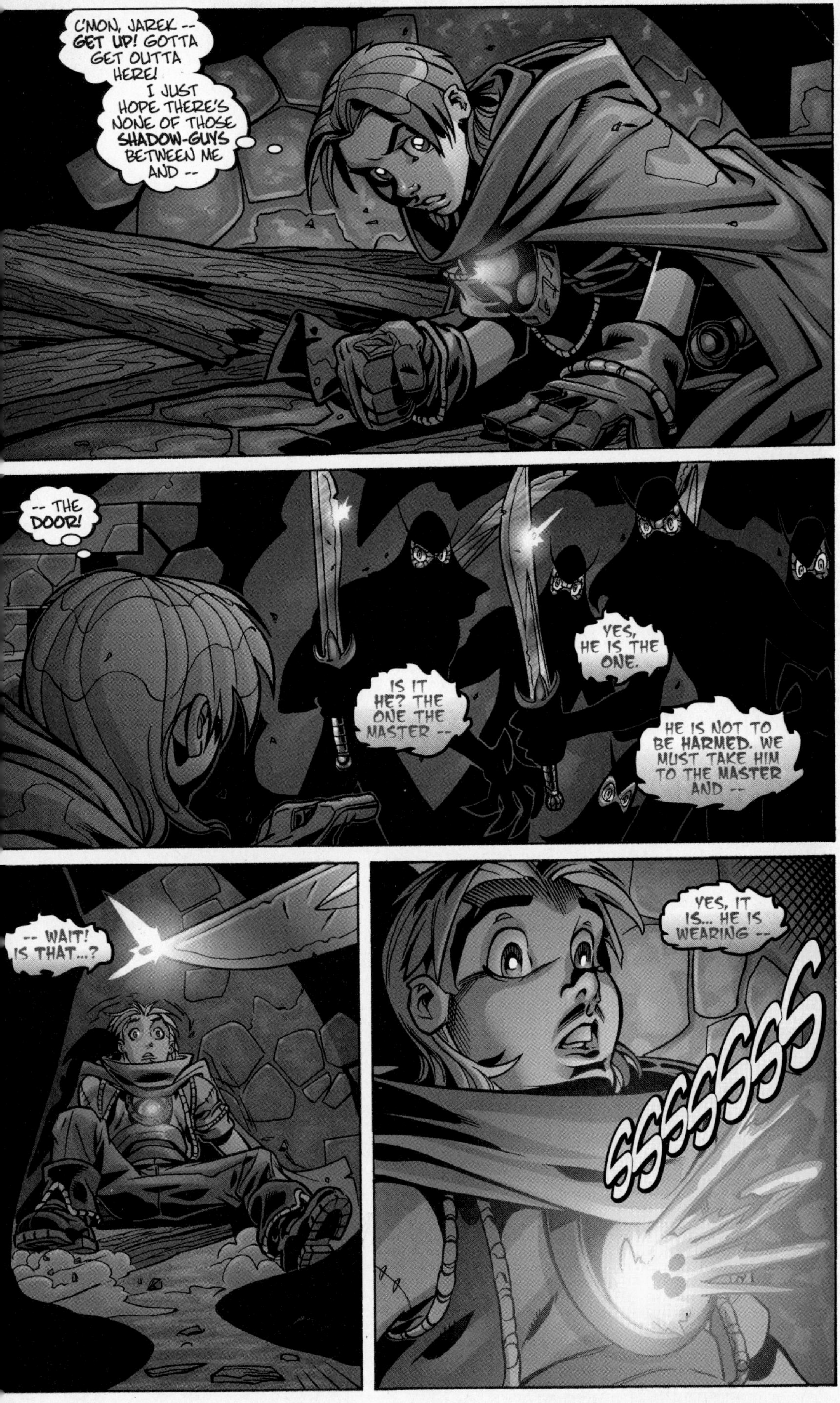

C'MON, JAREK -- GET UP! GOTTA GET OUTTA HERE!
I JUST HOPE THERE'S NONE OF THOSE SHADOW-GUYS BETWEEN ME AND --
-- THE DOOR!
IS IT HE? THE ONE THE MASTER --
YES, HE IS THE ONE.
HE IS NOT TO BE HARMED. WE MUST TAKE HIM TO THE MASTER AND --
-- WAIT! IS THAT...?
YES, IT IS... HE IS WEARING --
SSSSSSS

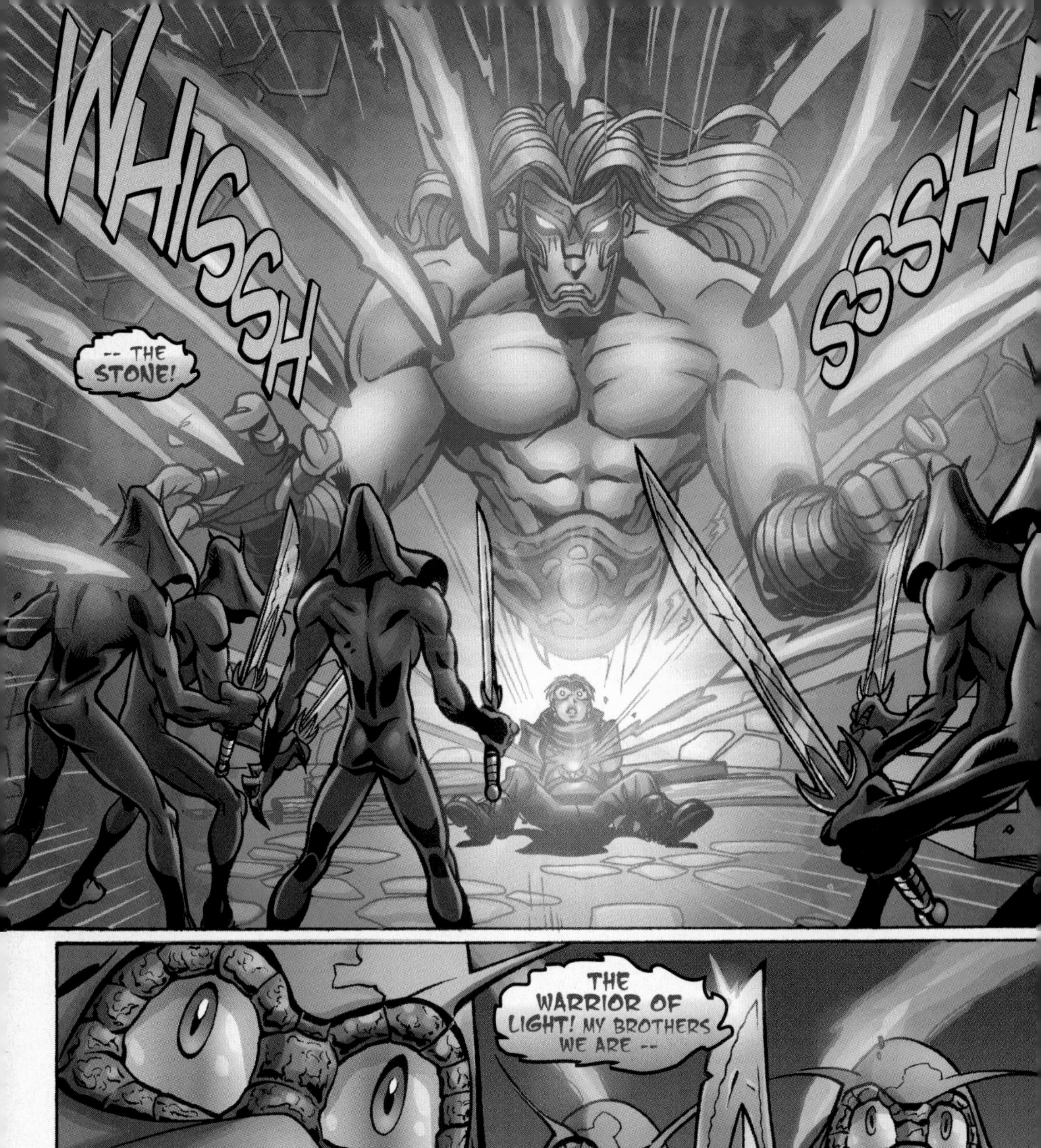
WHISSSH
SSSHH
-- THE STONE!

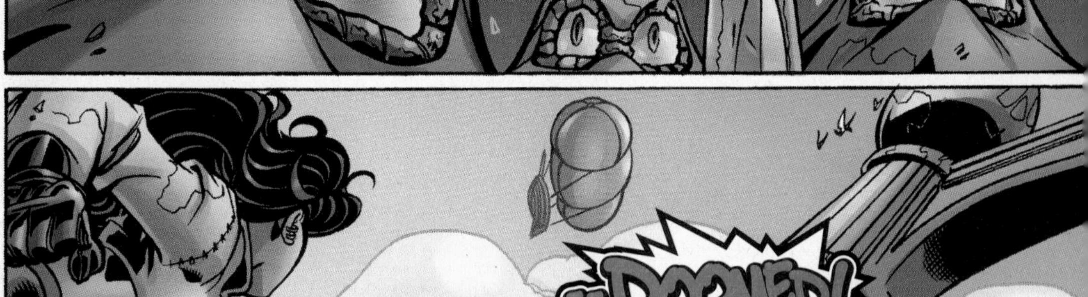
THE WARRIOR OF LIGHT! MY BROTHERS WE ARE --

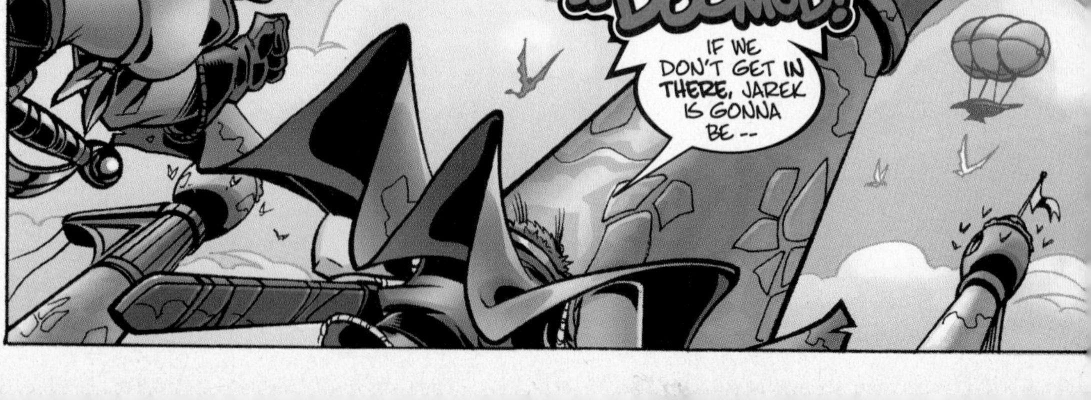
--DOOMED!
IF WE DON'T GET IN THERE, JAREK IS GONNA BE --

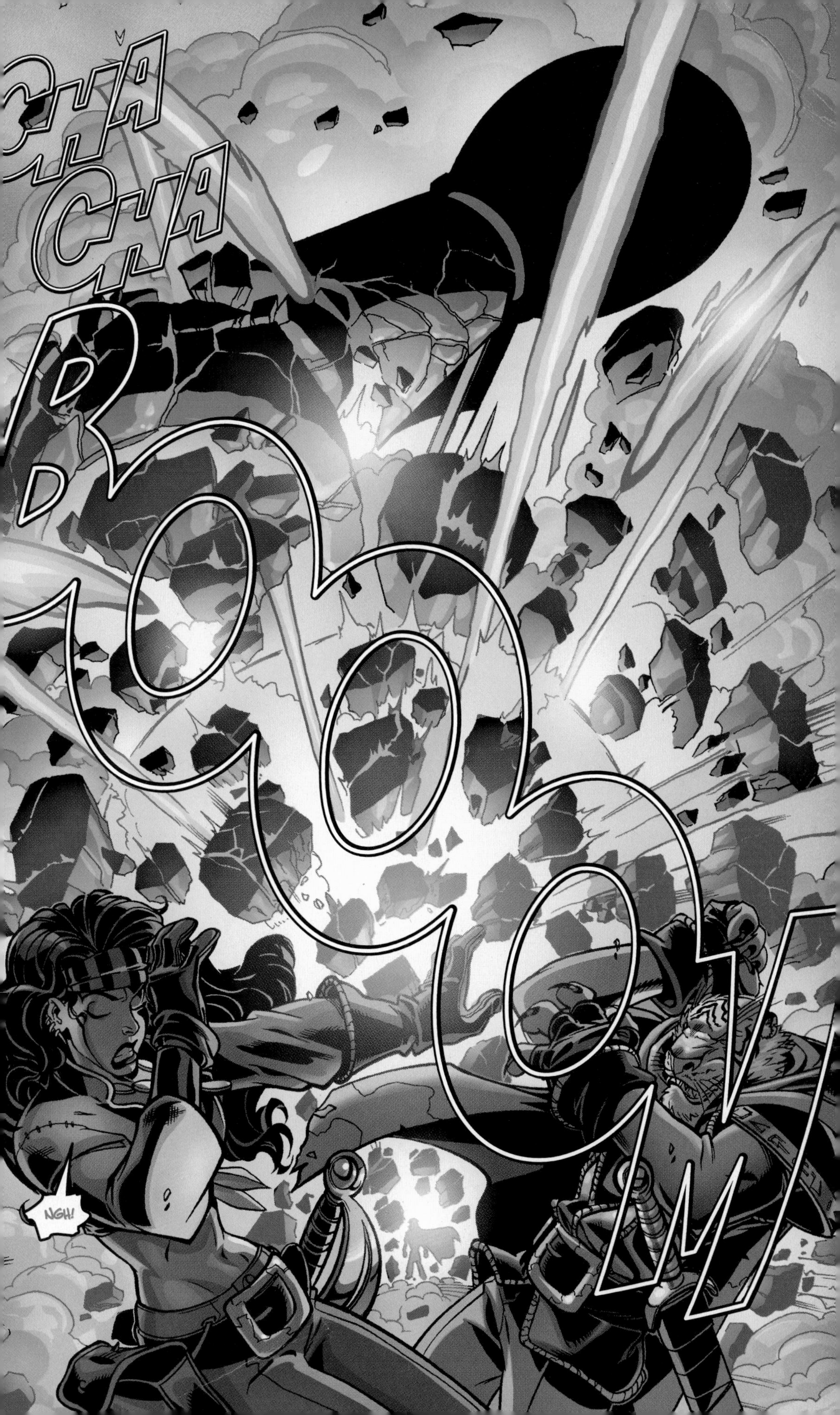
CHA
CHA
BROOOOOOM!
NGH!

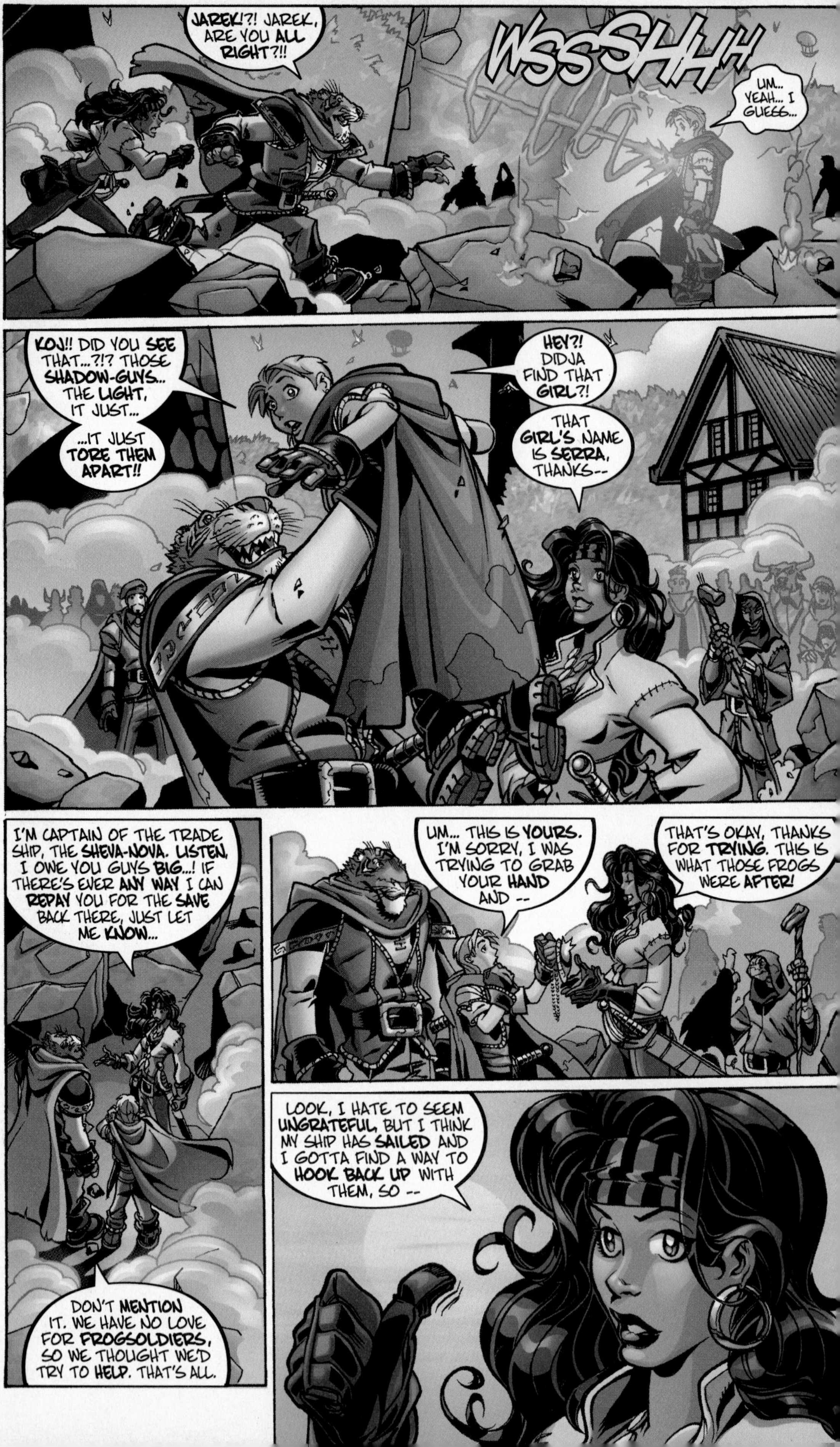
JAREK!?! JAREK, ARE YOU ALL RIGHT?!!
WSSSHHH
UM... YEAH... I GUESS...
KOJ!! DID YOU SEE THAT...?!? THOSE SHADOW-GUYS... THE LIGHT, IT JUST...
...IT JUST TORE THEM APART!!
HEY?! DIDJA FIND THAT GIRL?!
THAT GIRL'S NAME IS SERRA, THANKS--
I'M CAPTAIN OF THE TRADE SHIP, THE SHEVA-NOVA. LISTEN, I OWE YOU GUYS BIG...! IF THERE'S EVER ANY WAY I CAN REPAY YOU FOR THE SAVE BACK THERE, JUST LET ME KNOW...
DON'T MENTION IT. WE HAVE NO LOVE FOR FROGSOLDIERS, SO WE THOUGHT WE'D TRY TO HELP. THAT'S ALL.
UM... THIS IS YOURS. I'M SORRY, I WAS TRYING TO GRAB YOUR HAND AND --
THAT'S OKAY, THANKS FOR TRYING. THIS IS WHAT THOSE FROGS WERE AFTER!
LOOK, I HATE TO SEEM UNGRATEFUL, BUT I THINK MY SHIP HAS SAILED AND I GOTTA FIND A WAY TO HOOK BACK UP WITH THEM, SO --

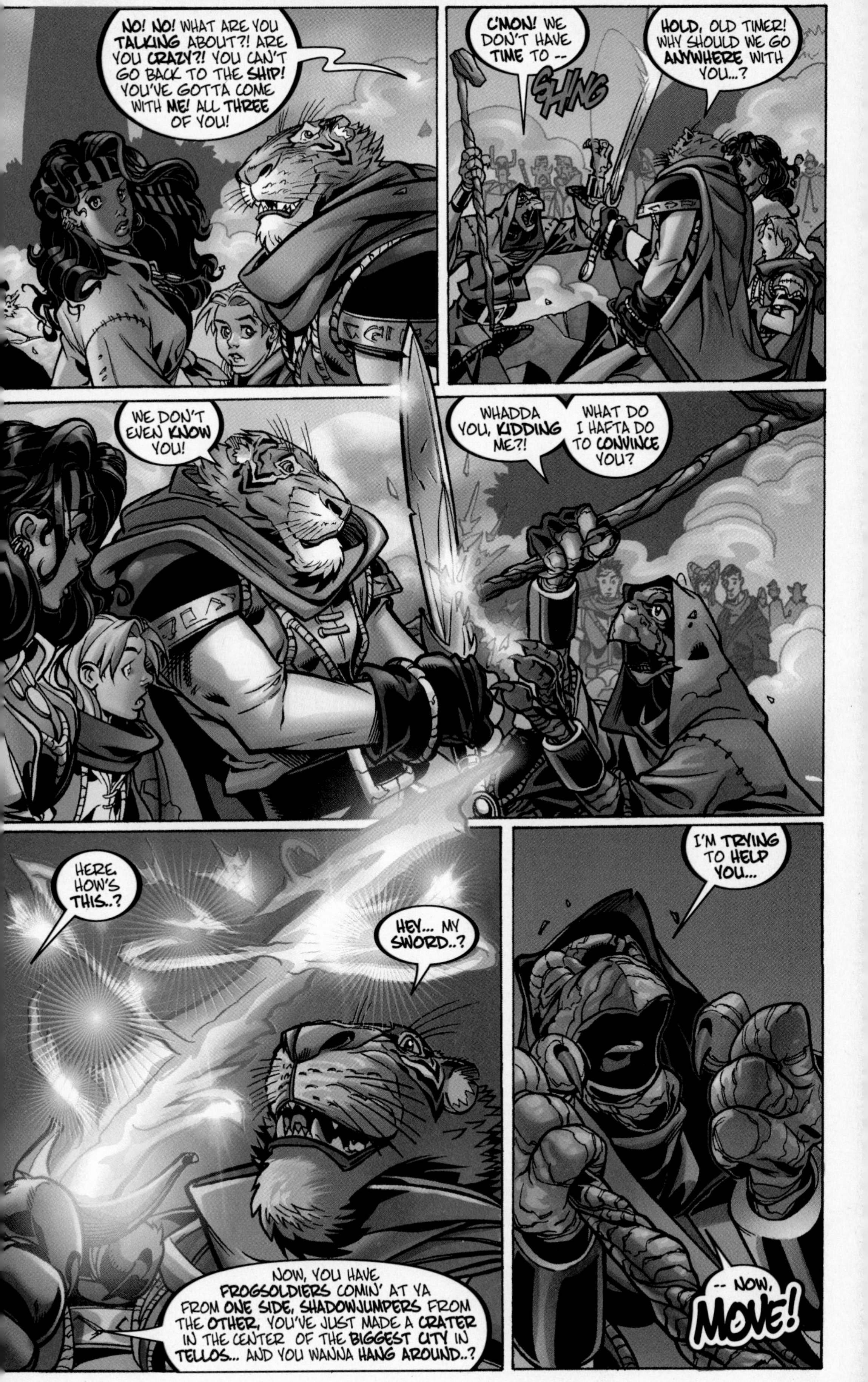
NO! NO! WHAT ARE YOU TALKING ABOUT?! ARE YOU CRAZY?! YOU CAN'T GO BACK TO THE SHIP! YOU'VE GOTTA COME WITH ME! ALL THREE OF YOU!
C'MON! WE DON'T HAVE TIME TO --
SHING
HOLD, OLD TIMER! WHY SHOULD WE GO ANYWHERE WITH YOU...?
WE DON'T EVEN KNOW YOU!
WHADDA YOU, KIDDING ME?!
WHAT DO I HAFTA DO TO CONVINCE YOU?
HERE. HOW'S THIS..?
HEY... MY SWORD..?
NOW, YOU HAVE FROGSOLDIERS COMIN' AT YA FROM ONE SIDE, SHADOWJUMPERS FROM THE OTHER, YOU'VE JUST MADE A CRATER IN THE CENTER OF THE BIGGEST CITY IN TELLOS... AND YOU WANNA HANG AROUND..?
I'M TRYING TO HELP YOU...
-- NOW, MOVE!

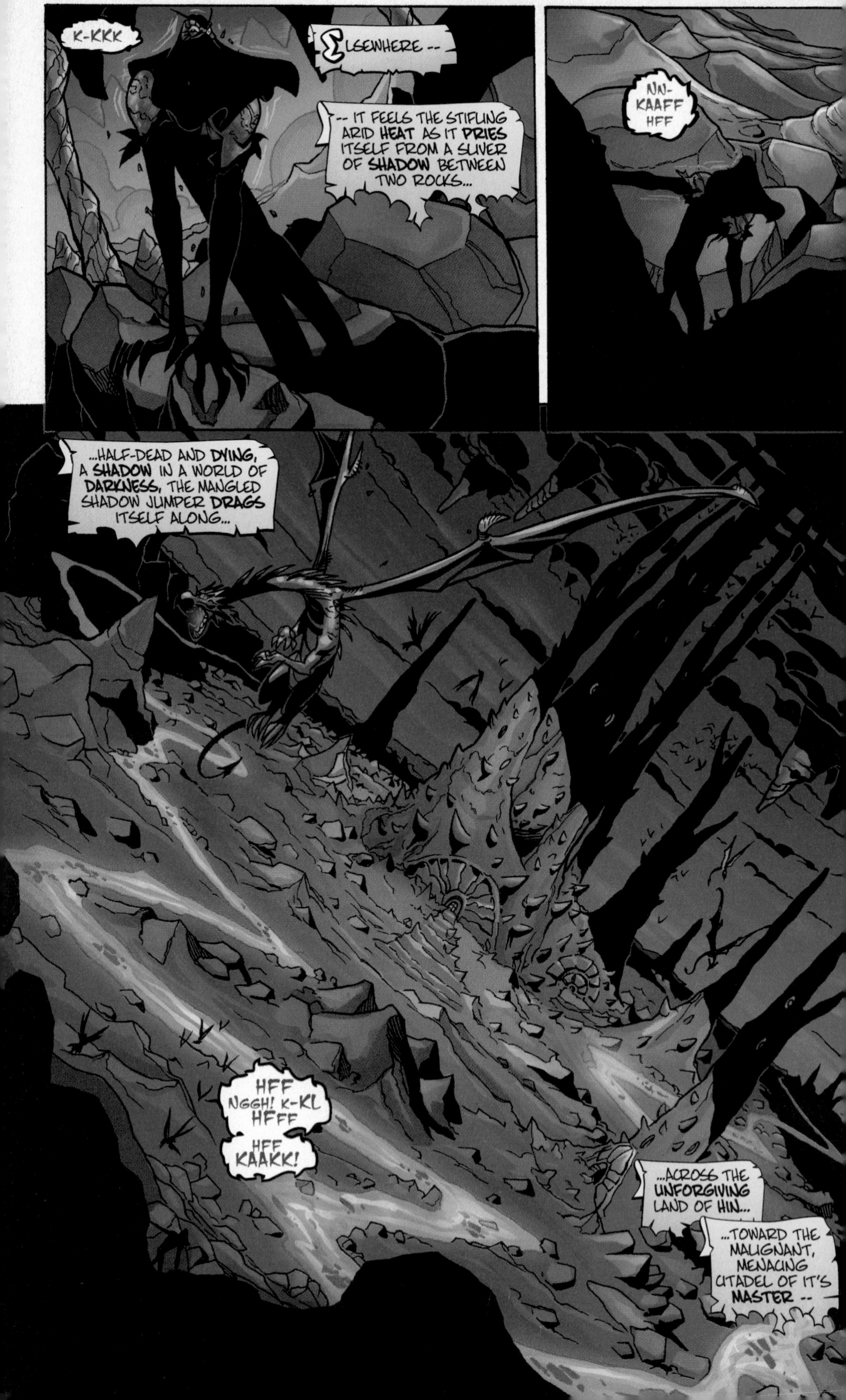
K-KKK
ELSEWHERE --
-- IT FEELS THE STIFLING ARID HEAT AS IT PRIES ITSELF FROM A SLIVER OF SHADOW BETWEEN TWO ROCKS...
NN-KAAFF HFF
...HALF-DEAD AND DYING, A SHADOW IN A WORLD OF DARKNESS, THE MANGLED SHADOW JUMPER DRAGS ITSELF ALONG...
HFF NGGH! K-KL HFFF HFF KAAKK!
...ACROSS THE UNFORGIVING LAND OF HIN...
...TOWARD THE MALIGNANT, MENACING CITADEL OF IT'S MASTER --

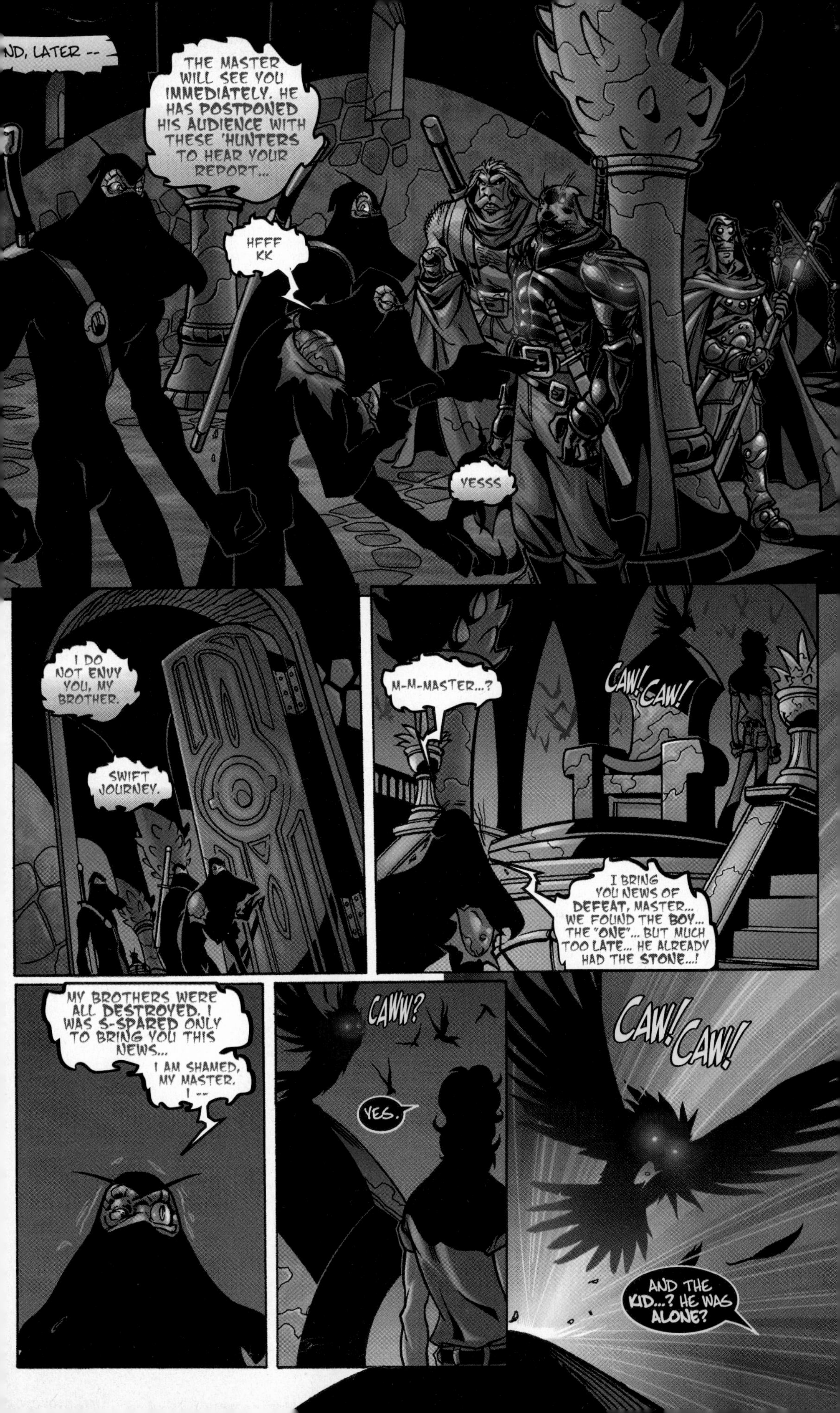
ND, LATER --
THE MASTER WILL SEE YOU IMMEDIATELY. HE HAS POSTPONED HIS AUDIENCE WITH THESE 'HUNTERS TO HEAR YOUR REPORT...
HFFF KK
YESSS
I DO NOT ENVY YOU, MY BROTHER.
SWIFT JOURNEY.
M-M-MASTER...?
CAW! CAW!
I BRING YOU NEWS OF DEFEAT, MASTER... WE FOUND THE BOY... THE "ONE"... BUT MUCH TOO LATE... HE ALREADY HAD THE STONE...!
MY BROTHERS WERE ALL DESTROYED. I WAS S-SPARED ONLY TO BRING YOU THIS NEWS...
I AM SHAMED, MY MASTER. ! --
CAWW?
YES.
CAW! CAW!
AND THE KID...? HE WAS ALONE?

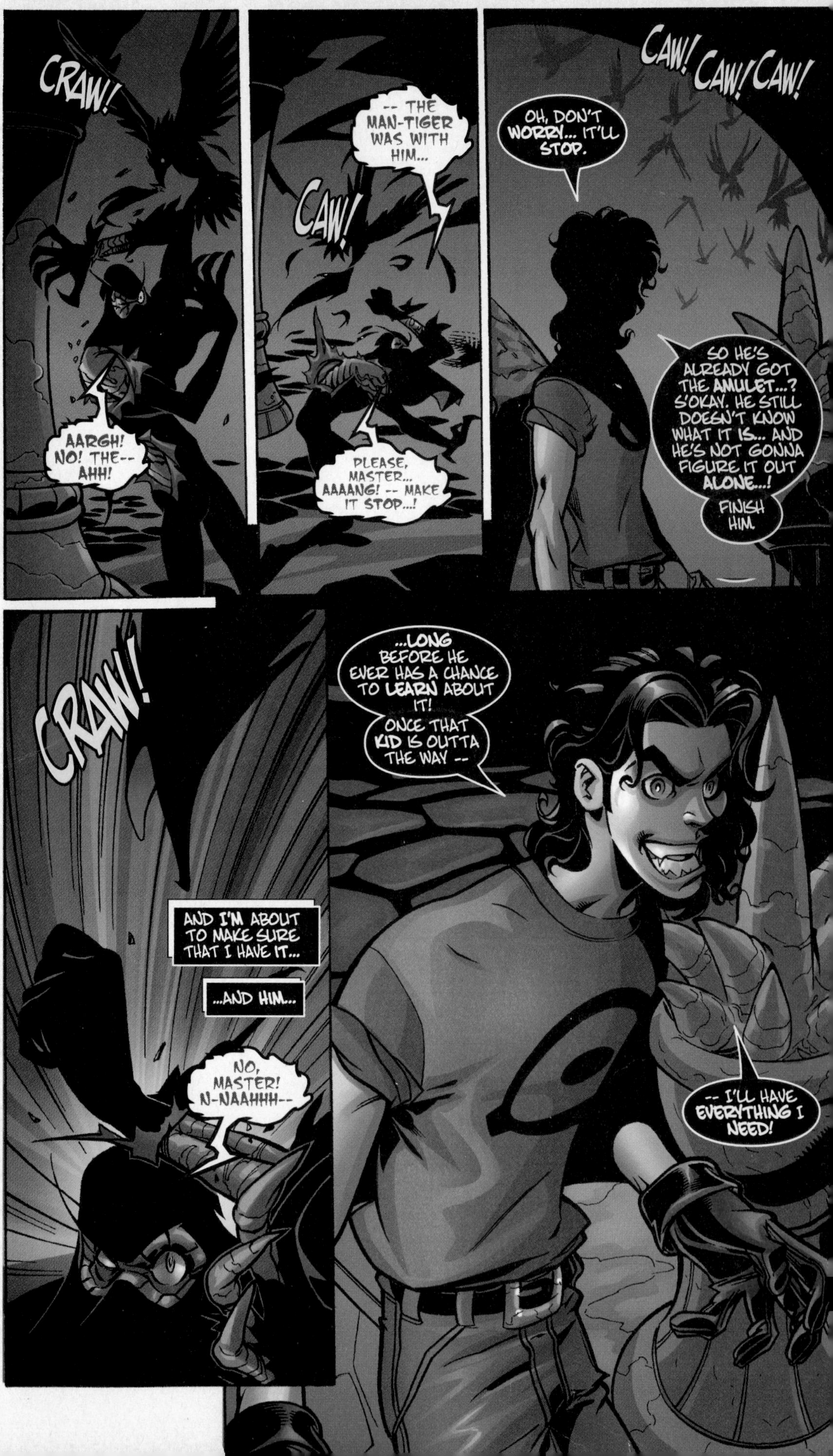
CRAW!
AARGH! NO! THE-- AHH!
-- THE MAN-TIGER WAS WITH HIM...
CAW!
PLEASE, MASTER... AAAANG! -- MAKE IT STOP...!
CAW! CAW! CAW!
OH, DON'T WORRY... IT'LL STOP.
SO HE'S ALREADY GOT THE AMULET...? S'OKAY. HE STILL DOESN'T KNOW WHAT IT IS... AND HE'S NOT GONNA FIGURE IT OUT ALONE...!
FINISH HIM.
CRAW!
AND I'M ABOUT TO MAKE SURE THAT I HAVE IT...
...AND HIM...
NO, MASTER! N-NAAHHH--
...LONG BEFORE HE EVER HAS A CHANCE TO LEARN ABOUT IT!
ONCE THAT KID IS OUTTA THE WAY --
-- I'LL HAVE EVERYTHING I NEED!

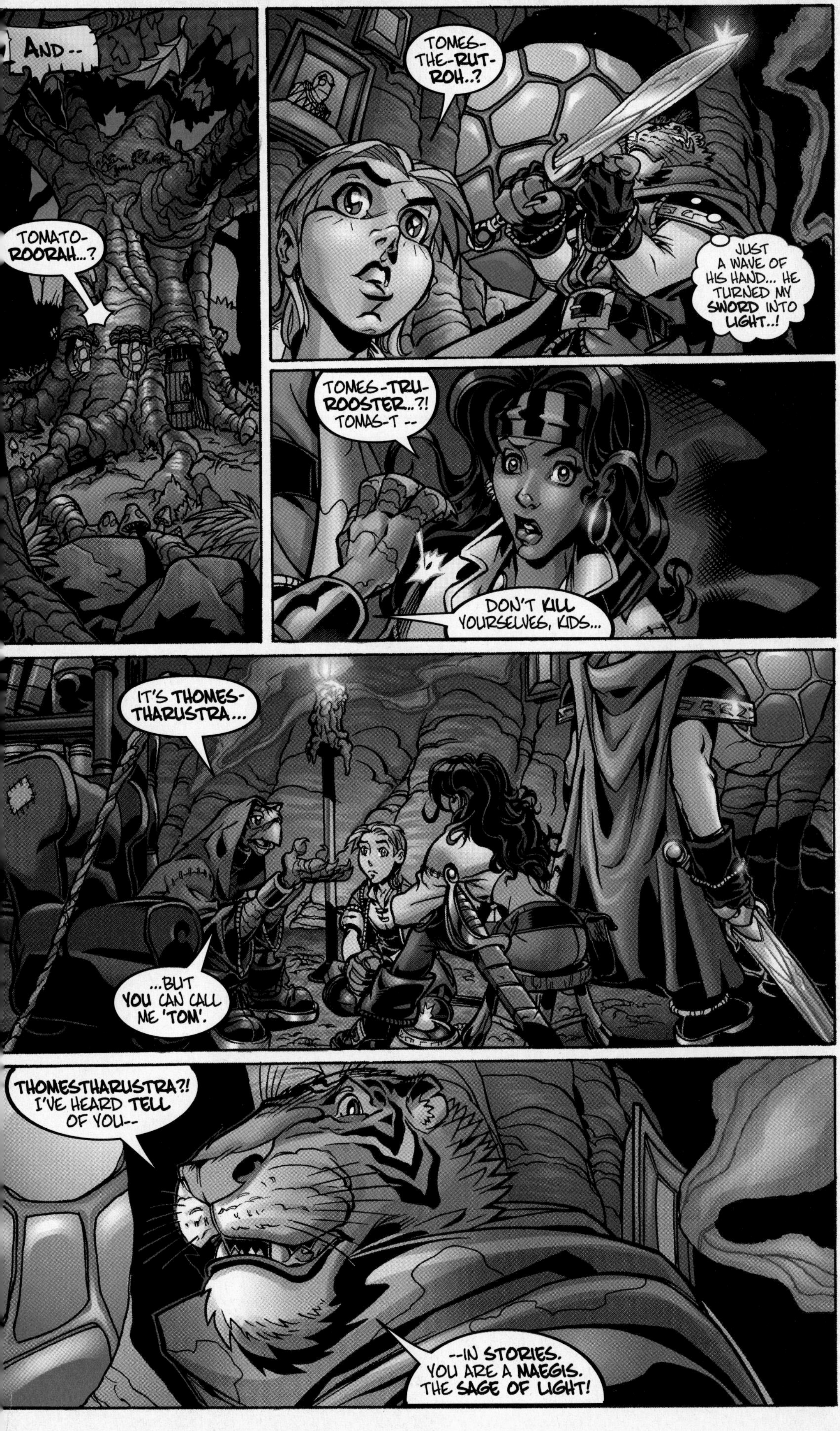
AND--
TOMATO-ROORAH...?
TOMES-THE-RUT-ROH..?
JUST A WAVE OF HIS HAND... HE TURNED MY SWORD INTO LIGHT..!
TOMES-TRU-ROOSTER...?! TOMAS-T --
DON'T KILL YOURSELVES, KIDS...
IT'S THOMES-THARUSTRA....
...BUT YOU CAN CALL ME 'TOM'.
THOMESTHARUSTRA?! I'VE HEARD TELL OF YOU--
--IN STORIES. YOU ARE A MAEGIS. THE SAGE OF LIGHT!

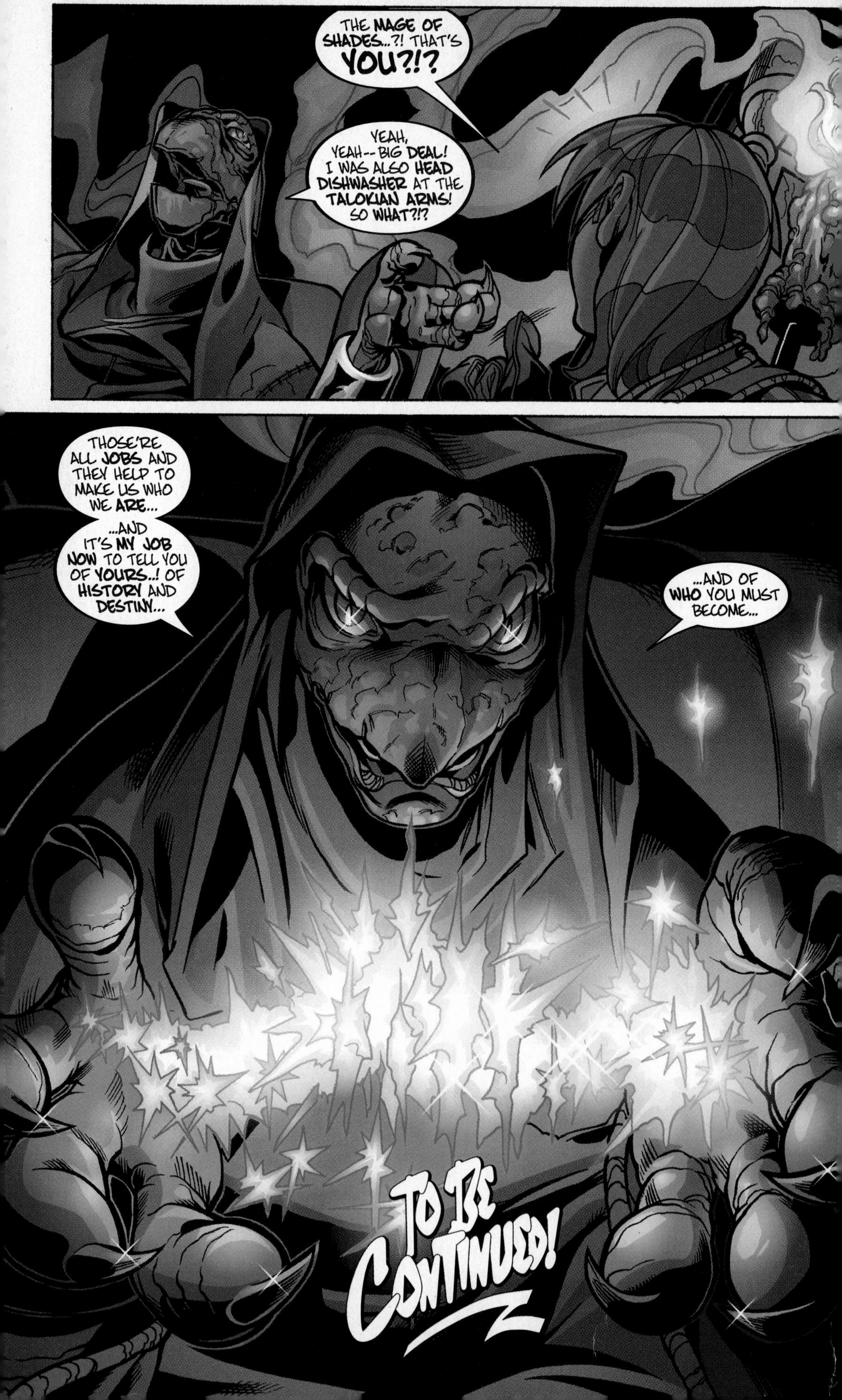
THE MAGE OF SHADES...?! THAT'S YOU?!?
YEAH, YEAH--BIG DEAL! I WAS ALSO HEAD DISHWASHER AT THE TALOKIAN ARMS! SO WHAT?!?
THOSE'RE ALL JOBS AND THEY HELP TO MAKE US WHO WE ARE...
...AND IT'S MY JOB NOW TO TELL YOU OF YOURS..! OF HISTORY AND DESTINY...
...AND OF WHO YOU MUST BECOME...
TO BE CONTINUED!

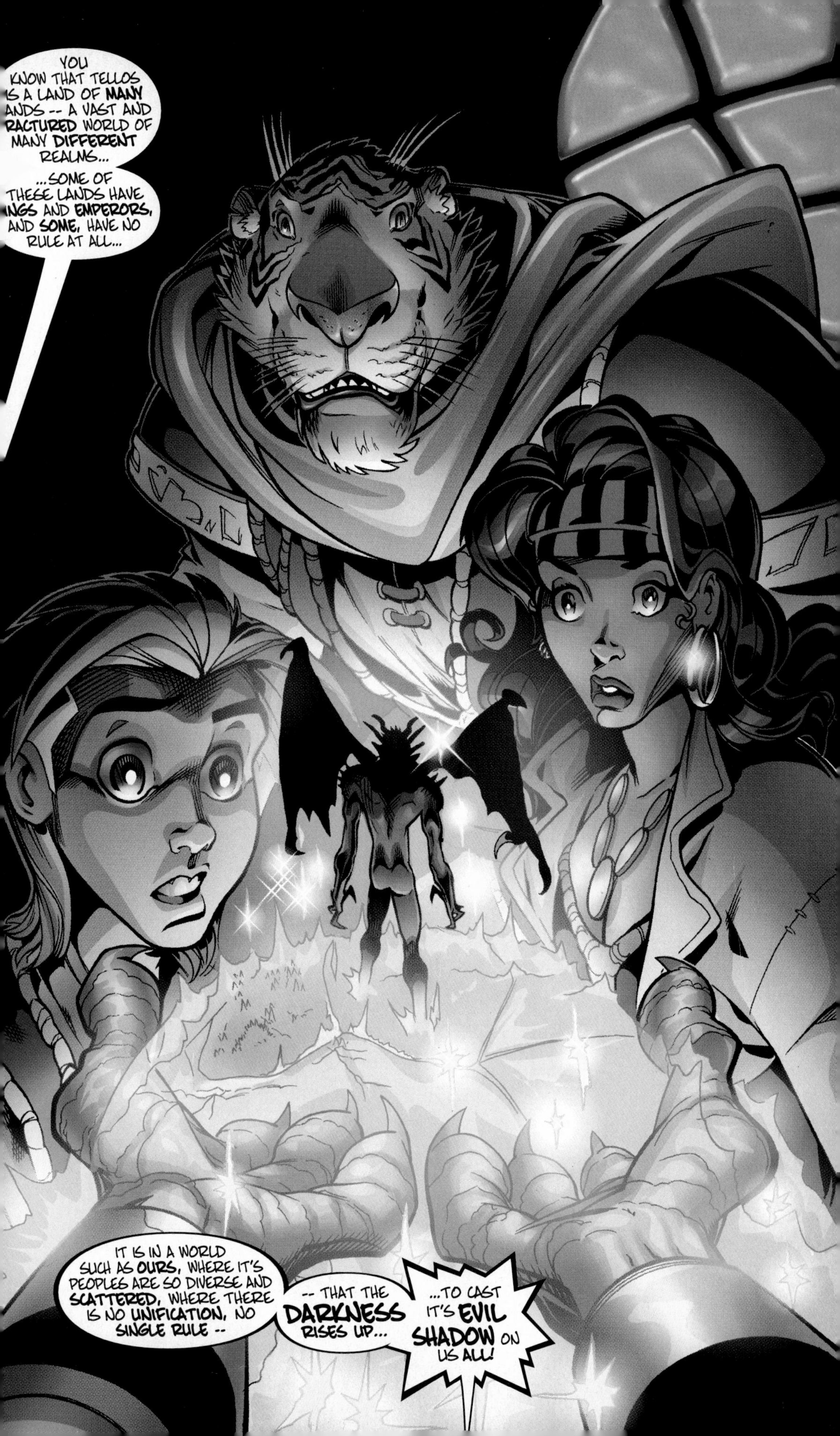
YOU KNOW THAT TELLOS IS A LAND OF MANY LANDS -- A VAST AND FRACTURED WORLD OF MANY DIFFERENT REALMS...
...SOME OF THESE LANDS HAVE KINGS AND EMPERORS, AND SOME, HAVE NO RULE AT ALL...
IT IS IN A WORLD SUCH AS OURS, WHERE IT'S PEOPLES ARE SO DIVERSE AND SCATTERED, WHERE THERE IS NO UNIFICATION, NO SINGLE RULE --
-- THAT THE DARKNESS RISES UP...
...TO CAST IT'S EVIL SHADOW ON US ALL!

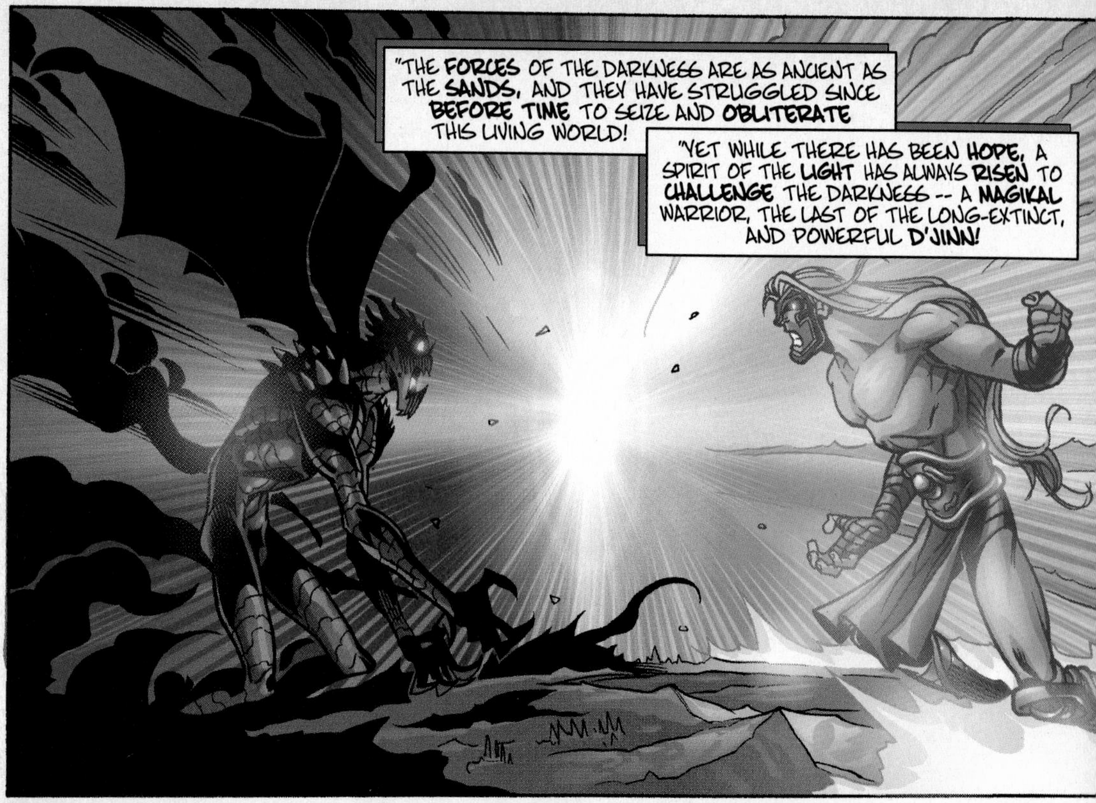
"THE FORCES OF THE DARKNESS ARE AS ANCIENT AS THE SANDS, AND THEY HAVE STRUGGLED SINCE BEFORE TIME TO SEIZE AND OBLITERATE THIS LIVING WORLD!
"YET WHILE THERE HAS BEEN HOPE, A SPIRIT OF THE LIGHT HAS ALWAYS RISEN TO CHALLENGE THE DARKNESS -- A MAGIKAL WARRIOR, THE LAST OF THE LONG-EXTINCT, AND POWERFUL D'JINN!

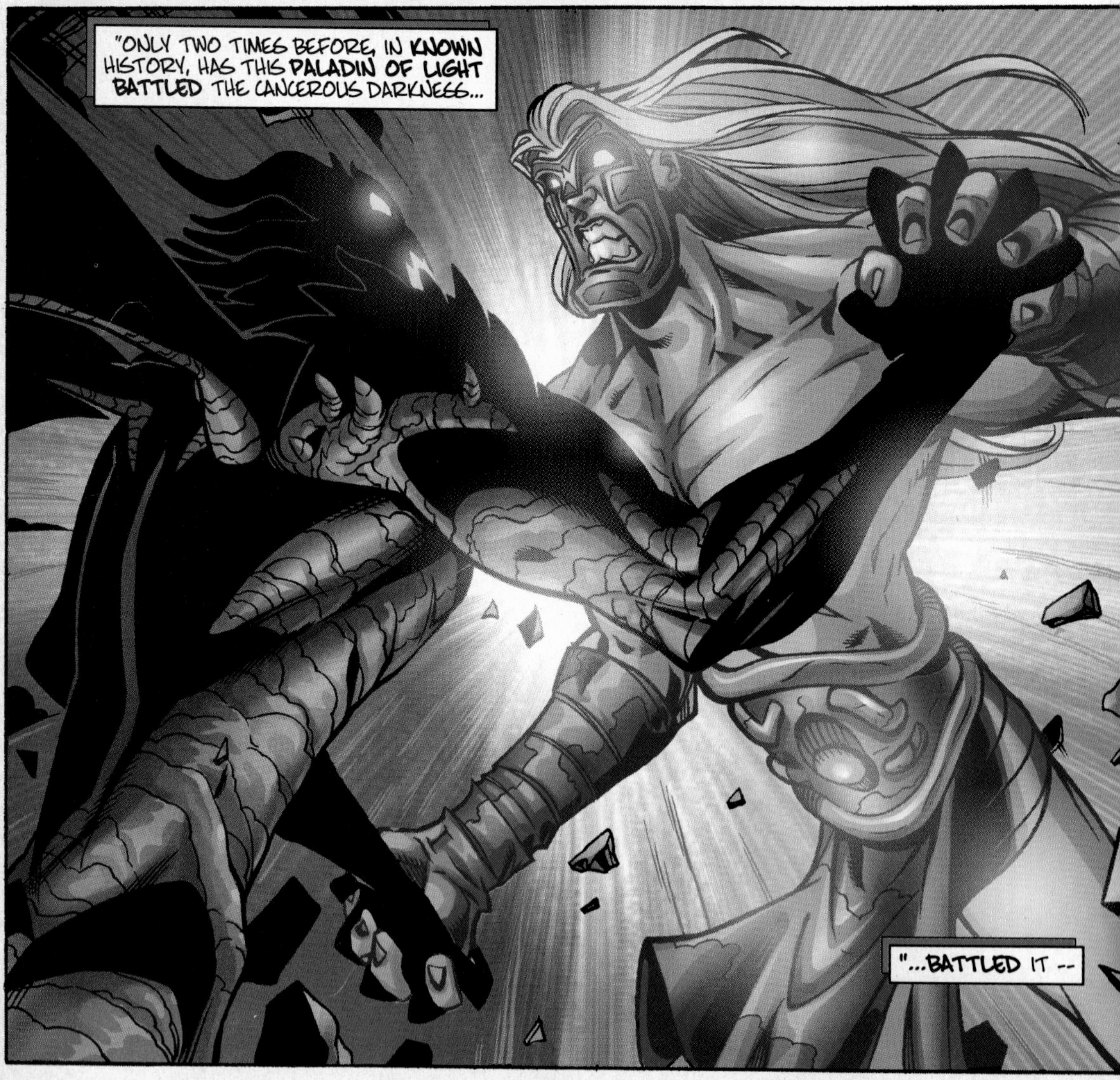
"ONLY TWO TIMES BEFORE, IN KNOWN HISTORY, HAS THIS PALADIN OF LIGHT BATTLED THE CANCEROUS DARKNESS...
"...BATTLED IT --

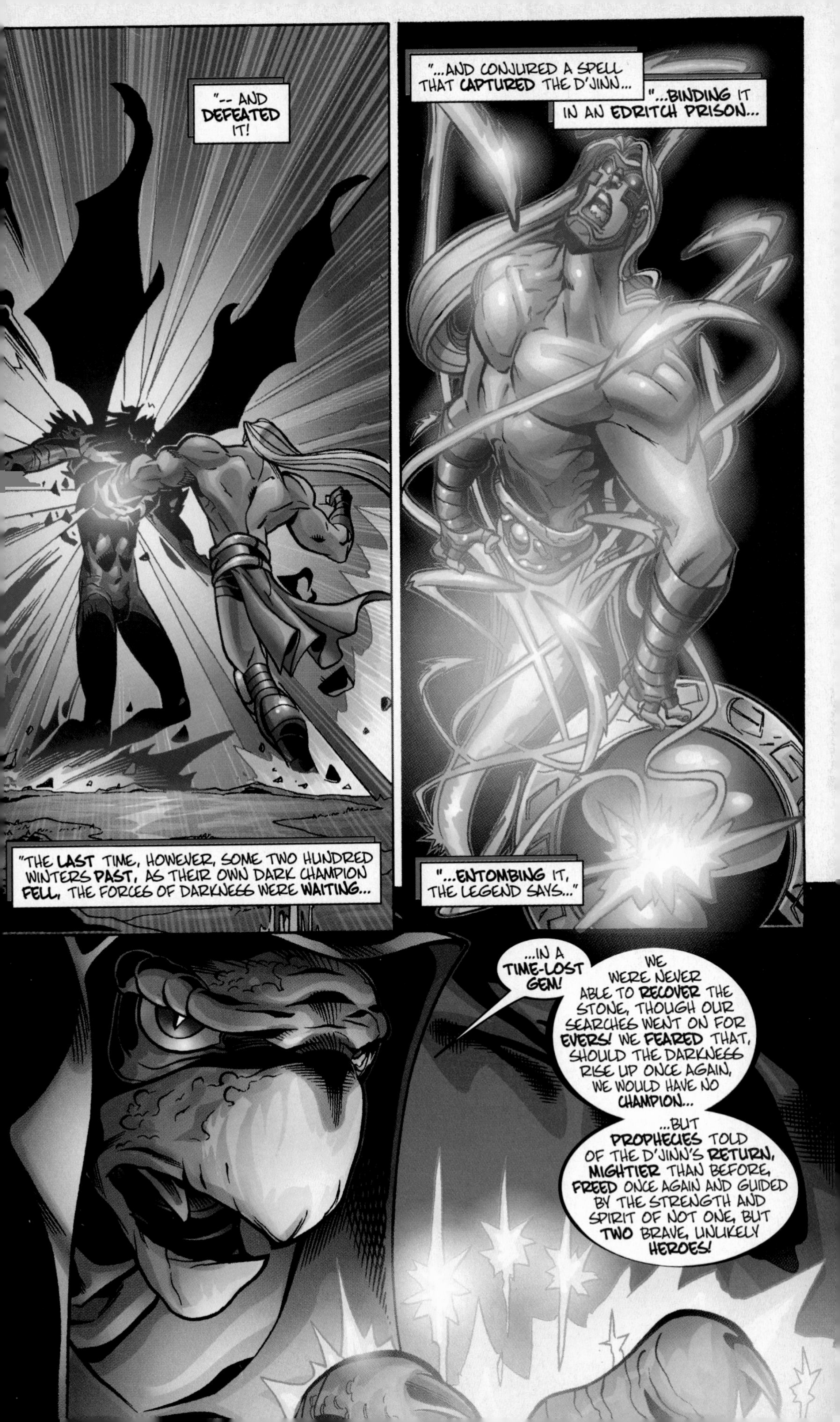
"-- AND DEFEATED IT!
"THE LAST TIME, HOWEVER, SOME TWO HUNDRED WINTERS PAST, AS THEIR OWN DARK CHAMPION FELL, THE FORCES OF DARKNESS WERE WAITING...
"...AND CONJURED A SPELL THAT CAPTURED THE D'JINN...
"...BINDING IT IN AN EDRITCH PRISON...
"...ENTOMBING IT, THE LEGEND SAYS..."
...IN A TIME-LOST GEM!
WE WERE NEVER ABLE TO RECOVER THE STONE, THOUGH OUR SEARCHES WENT ON FOR EVERS! WE FEARED THAT, SHOULD THE DARKNESS RISE UP ONCE AGAIN, WE WOULD HAVE NO CHAMPION...
...BUT PROPHECIES TOLD OF THE D'JINN'S RETURN, MIGHTIER THAN BEFORE, FREED ONCE AGAIN AND GUIDED BY THE STRENGTH AND SPIRIT OF NOT ONE, BUT TWO BRAVE, UNLIKELY HEROES!

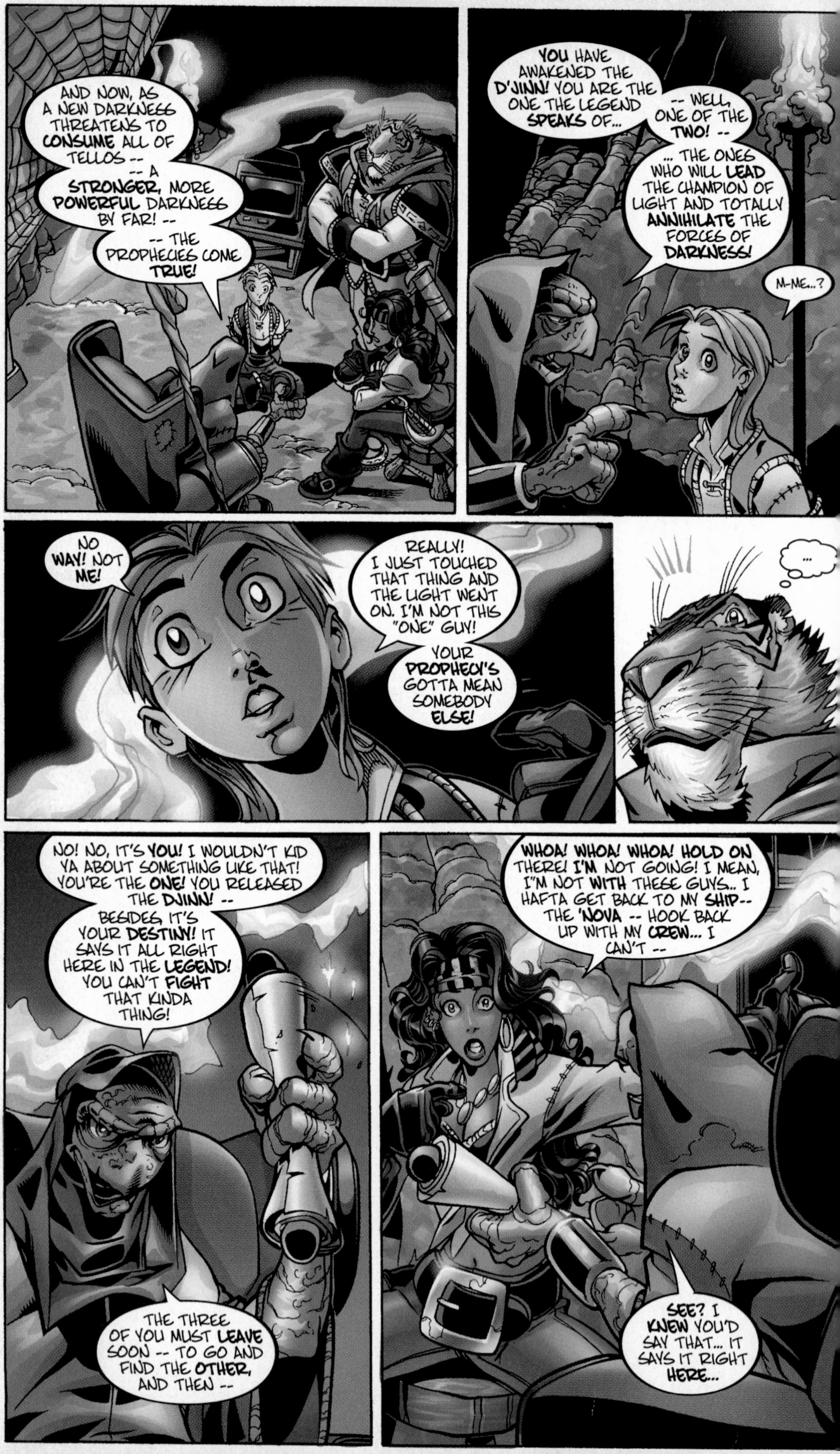
AND NOW, AS A NEW DARKNESS THREATENS TO CONSUME ALL OF TELLOS --
-- A STRONGER, MORE POWERFUL DARKNESS BY FAR! --
-- THE PROPHECIES COME TRUE!
YOU HAVE AWAKENED THE D'JINN! YOU ARE THE ONE THE LEGEND SPEAKS OF...
-- WELL, ONE OF THE TWO! --
... THE ONES WHO WILL LEAD THE CHAMPION OF LIGHT AND TOTALLY ANNIHILATE THE FORCES OF DARKNESS!
M-ME...?
NO WAY! NOT ME!
REALLY! I JUST TOUCHED THAT THING AND THE LIGHT WENT ON. I'M NOT THIS "ONE" GUY!
YOUR PROPHECY'S GOTTA MEAN SOMEBODY ELSE!
...
NO! NO, IT'S YOU! I WOULDN'T KID YA ABOUT SOMETHING LIKE THAT! YOU'RE THE ONE! YOU RELEASED THE DJINN! --
BESIDES, IT'S YOUR DESTINY! IT SAYS IT ALL RIGHT HERE IN THE LEGEND! YOU CAN'T FIGHT THAT KINDA THING!
THE THREE OF YOU MUST LEAVE SOON -- TO GO AND FIND THE OTHER, AND THEN --
WHOA! WHOA! WHOA! HOLD ON THERE! I'M NOT GOING! I MEAN, I'M NOT WITH THESE GUYS... I HAFTA GET BACK TO MY SHIP-- THE 'NOVA -- HOOK BACK UP WITH MY CREW... I CAN'T --
SEE? I KNEW YOU'D SAY THAT... IT SAYS IT RIGHT HERE...

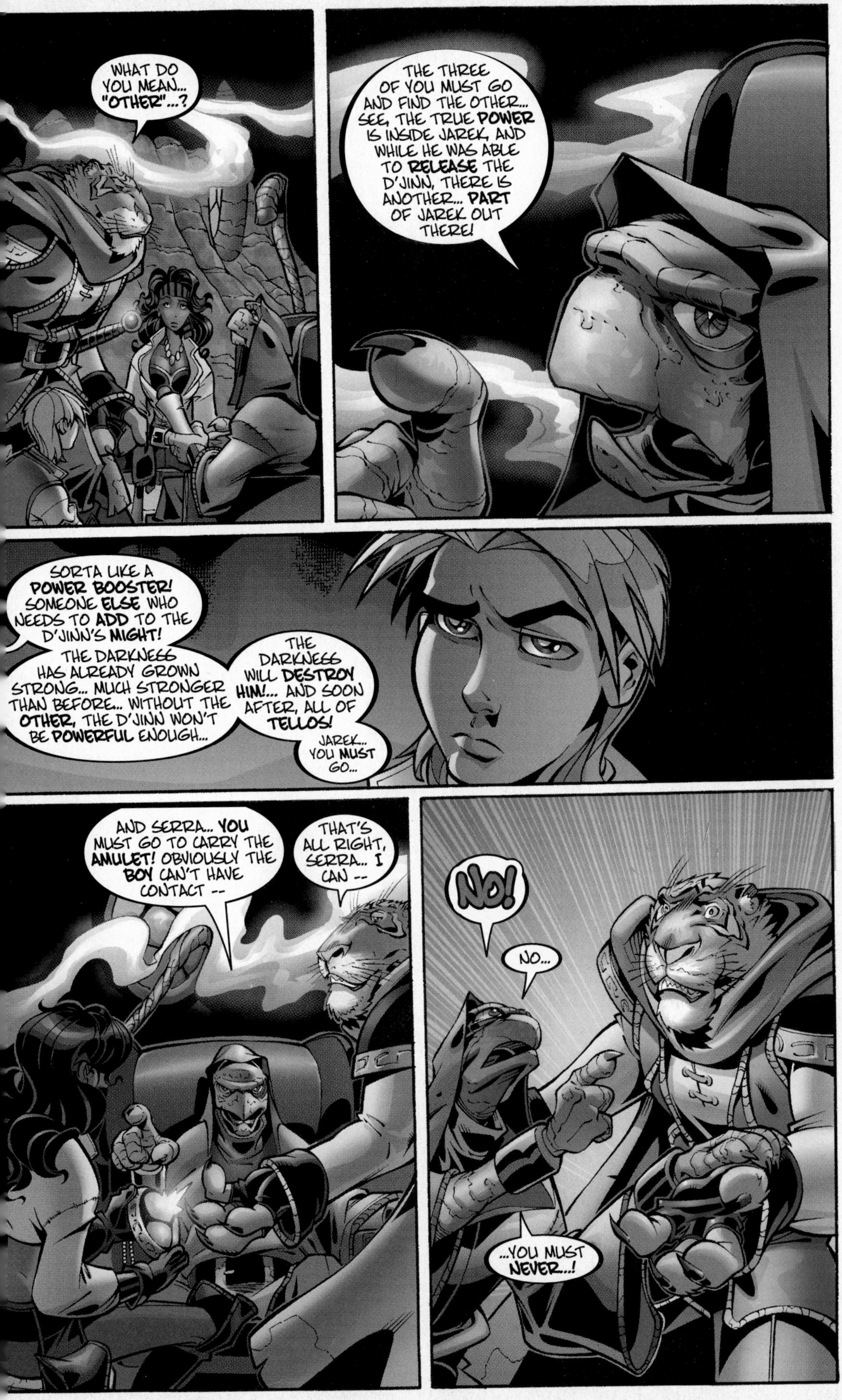
WHAT DO YOU MEAN... "OTHER"...?
THE THREE OF YOU MUST GO AND FIND THE OTHER... SEE, THE TRUE POWER IS INSIDE JAREK, AND WHILE HE WAS ABLE TO RELEASE THE D'JINN, THERE IS ANOTHER... PART OF JAREK OUT THERE!
SORTA LIKE A POWER BOOSTER! SOMEONE ELSE WHO NEEDS TO ADD TO THE D'JINN'S MIGHT!
THE DARKNESS HAS ALREADY GROWN STRONG... MUCH STRONGER THAN BEFORE... WITHOUT THE OTHER, THE D'JINN WON'T BE POWERFUL ENOUGH...
THE DARKNESS WILL DESTROY HIM!... AND SOON AFTER, ALL OF TELLOS!
JAREK... YOU MUST GO...
AND SERRA... YOU MUST GO TO CARRY THE AMULET! OBVIOUSLY THE BOY CAN'T HAVE CONTACT --
THAT'S ALL RIGHT, SERRA... I CAN --
NO!
NO...
...YOU MUST NEVER...!

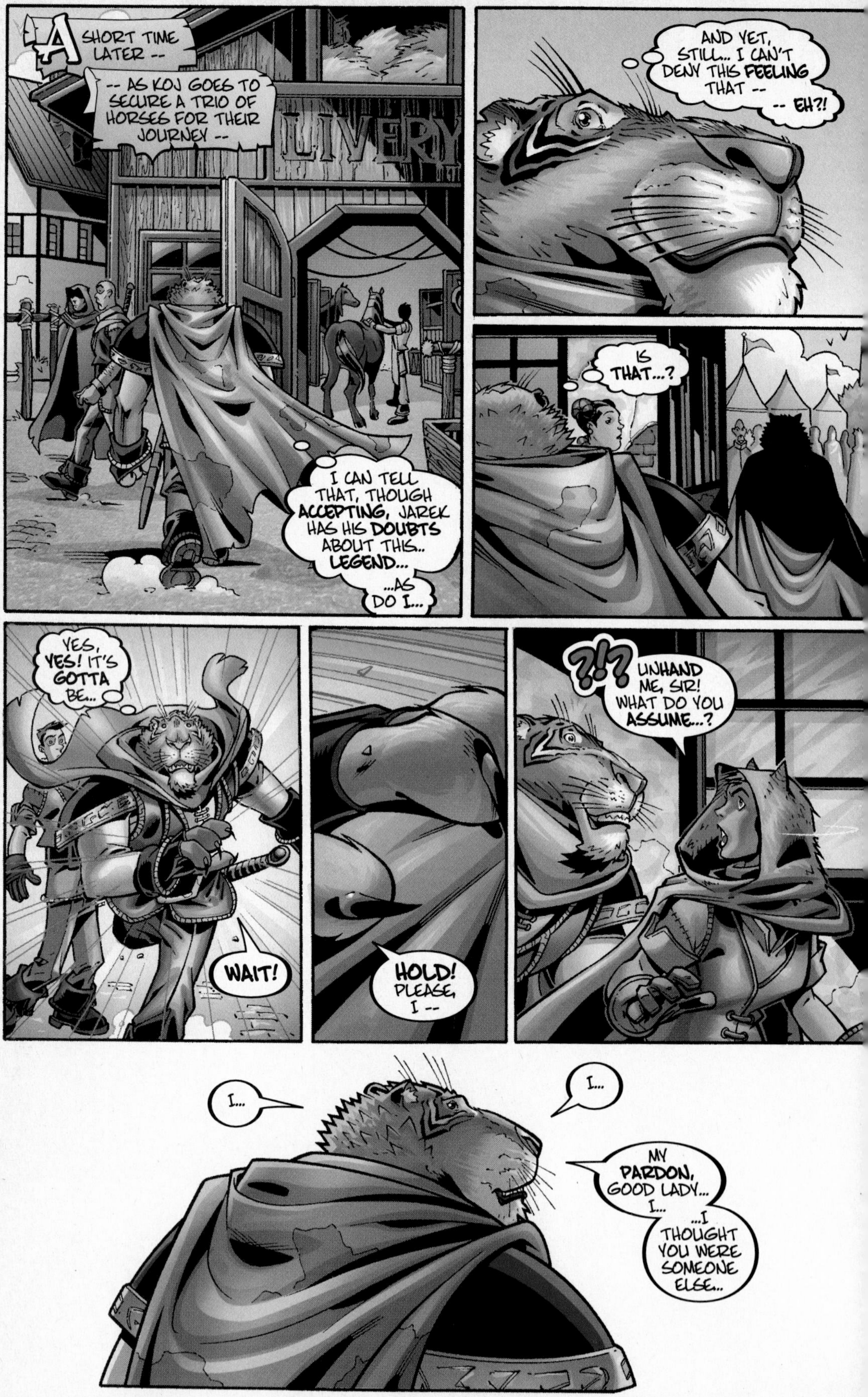
A SHORT TIME LATER --
-- AS KOJ GOES TO SECURE A TRIO OF HORSES FOR THEIR JOURNEY --
LIVERY
I CAN TELL THAT, THOUGH ACCEPTING, JAREK HAS HIS DOUBTS ABOUT THIS.. LEGEND...
...AS DO I...
AND YET, STILL... I CAN'T DENY THIS FEELING THAT --
-- EH?!
IS THAT...?
YES, YES! IT'S GOTTA BE...
WAIT!
HOLD! PLEASE, I --
?!?
UNHAND ME, SIR! WHAT DO YOU ASSUME...?
I...
I...
MY PARDON, GOOD LADY... I...
...I THOUGHT YOU WERE SOMEONE ELSE...

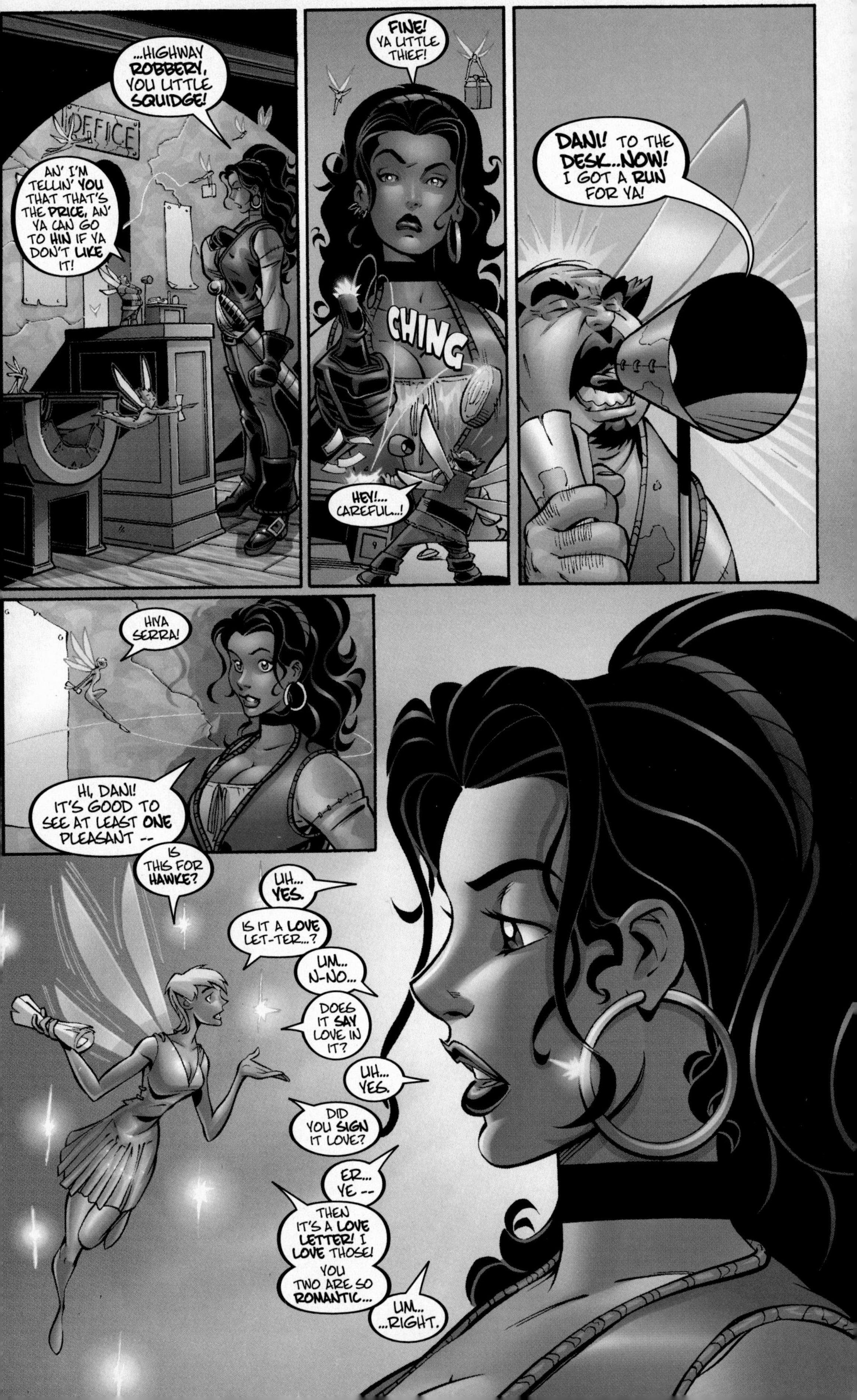
...HIGHWAY ROBBERY, YOU LITTLE SQUIDGE!
OFFICE
AN' I'M TELLIN' YOU THAT THAT'S THE PRICE, AN' YA CAN GO TO HIN IF YA DON'T LIKE IT!
FINE! YA LITTLE THIEF!
CHING
HEY!... CAREFUL...!
DANI! TO THE DESK...NOW! I GOT A RUN FOR YA!
HIYA SERRA!
HI, DANI! IT'S GOOD TO SEE AT LEAST ONE PLEASANT --
IS THIS FOR HAWKE?
UH... YES.
IS IT A LOVE LET-TER...?
UM... N-NO...
DOES IT SAY LOVE IN IT?
UH... YES.
DID YOU SIGN IT LOVE?
ER... YE --
THEN IT'S A LOVE LETTER! I LOVE THOSE!
YOU TWO ARE SO ROMANTIC...
UM... ...RIGHT.

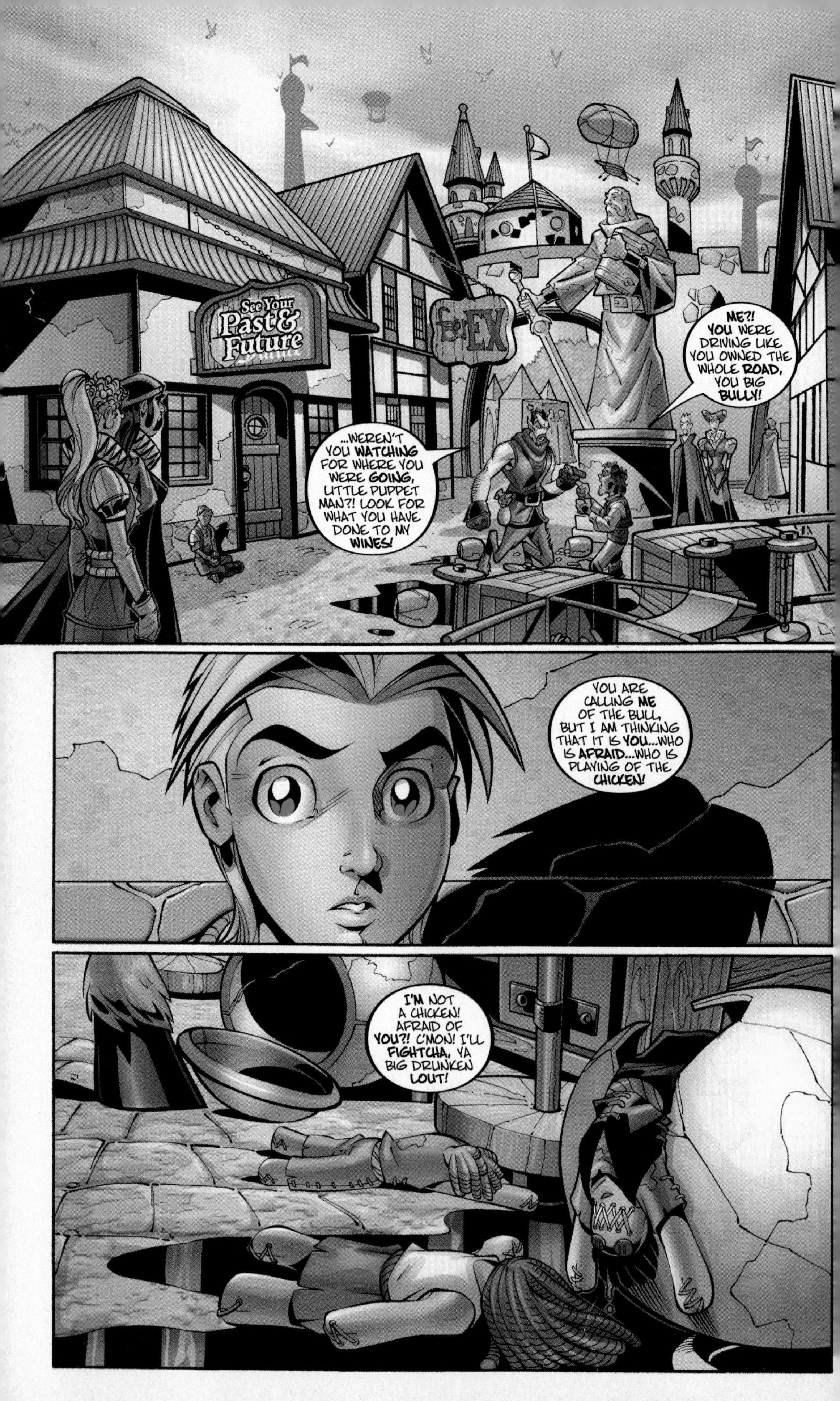
See Your Past & Future
...WEREN'T YOU WATCHING FOR WHERE YOU WERE GOING, LITTLE PUPPET MAN?! LOOK FOR WHAT YOU HAVE DONE TO MY WINES!
ME?! YOU WERE DRIVING LIKE YOU OWNED THE WHOLE ROAD, YOU BIG BULLY!
YOU ARE CALLING ME OF THE BULL, BUT I AM THINKING THAT IT IS YOU...WHO IS AFRAID...WHO IS PLAYING OF THE CHICKEN!
I'M NOT A CHICKEN! AFRAID OF YOU?! C'MON! I'LL FIGHTCHA, YA BIG DRUNKEN LOUT!

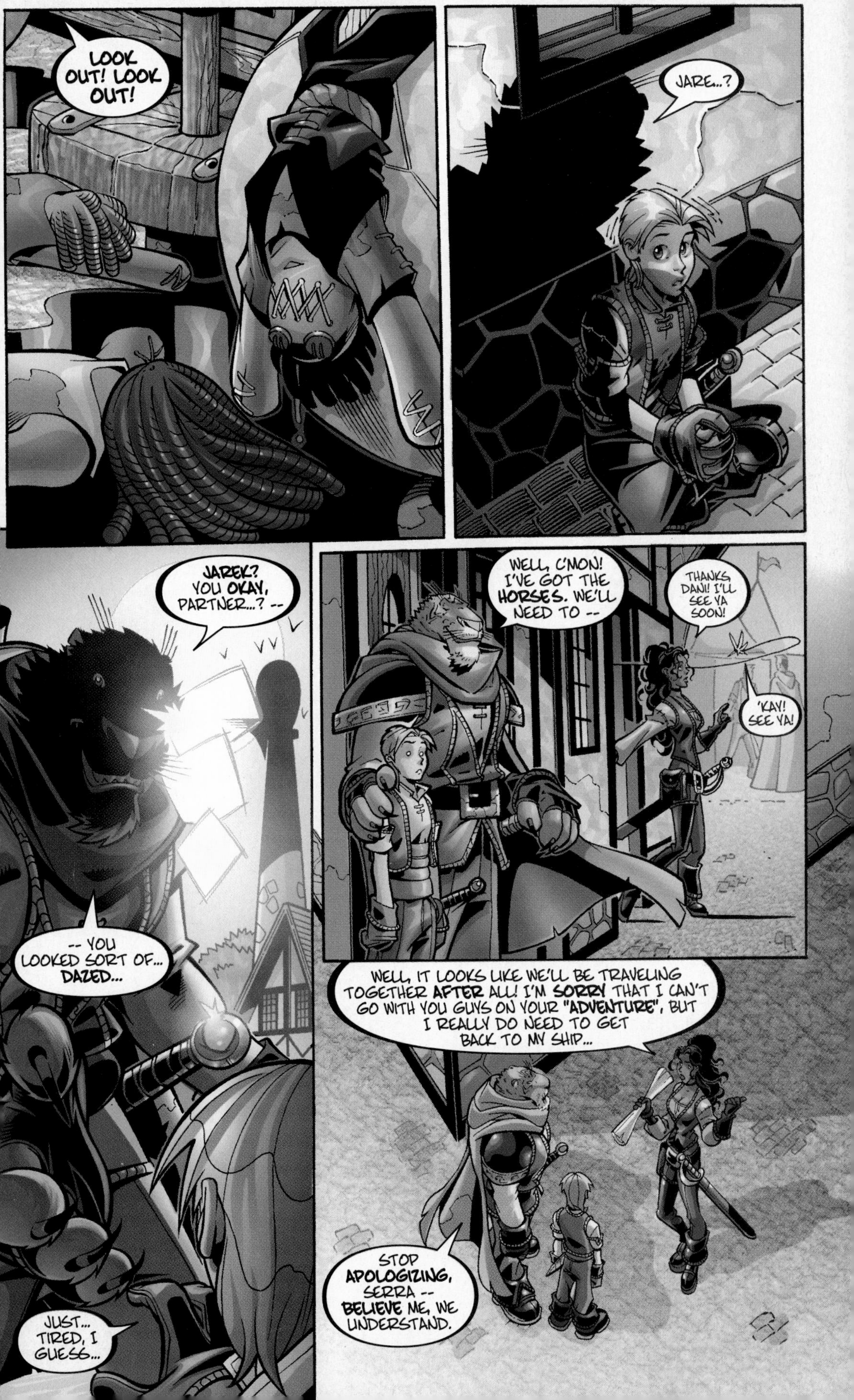
LOOK OUT! LOOK OUT!
JARE...?
JAREK? YOU **OKAY**, PARTNER...? --
-- YOU LOOKED SORT OF... **DAZED**...
JUST... TIRED, I GUESS...
WELL, C'MON! I'VE GOT THE **HORSES**. WE'LL NEED TO --
THANKS DANI! I'LL SEE YA SOON!
'KAY! SEE YA!
WELL, IT LOOKS LIKE WE'LL BE TRAVELING TOGETHER **AFTER** ALL! I'M **SORRY** THAT I CAN'T GO WITH YOU GUYS ON YOUR **"ADVENTURE"**, BUT I REALLY DO NEED TO GET BACK TO MY SHIP...
STOP **APOLOGIZING**, SERRA -- **BELIEVE** ME, WE UNDERSTAND.

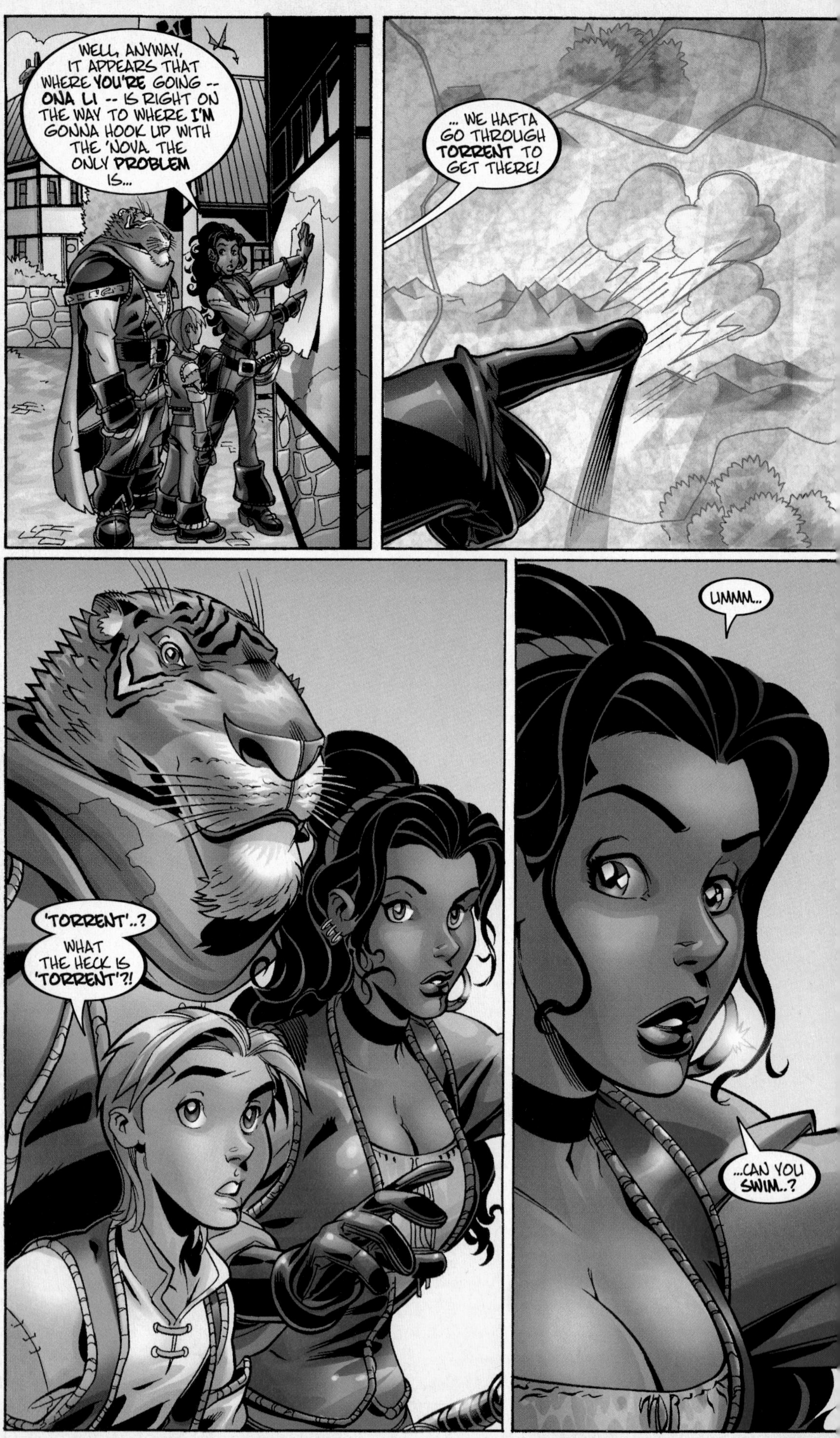
WELL, ANYWAY, IT APPEARS THAT WHERE YOU'RE GOING -- ONA LI -- IS RIGHT ON THE WAY TO WHERE I'M GONNA HOOK UP WITH THE 'NOVA. THE ONLY PROBLEM IS...
... WE HAFTA GO THROUGH TORRENT TO GET THERE!
'TORRENT'..? WHAT THE HECK IS 'TORRENT'?!
UMMM...
...CAN YOU SWIM..?

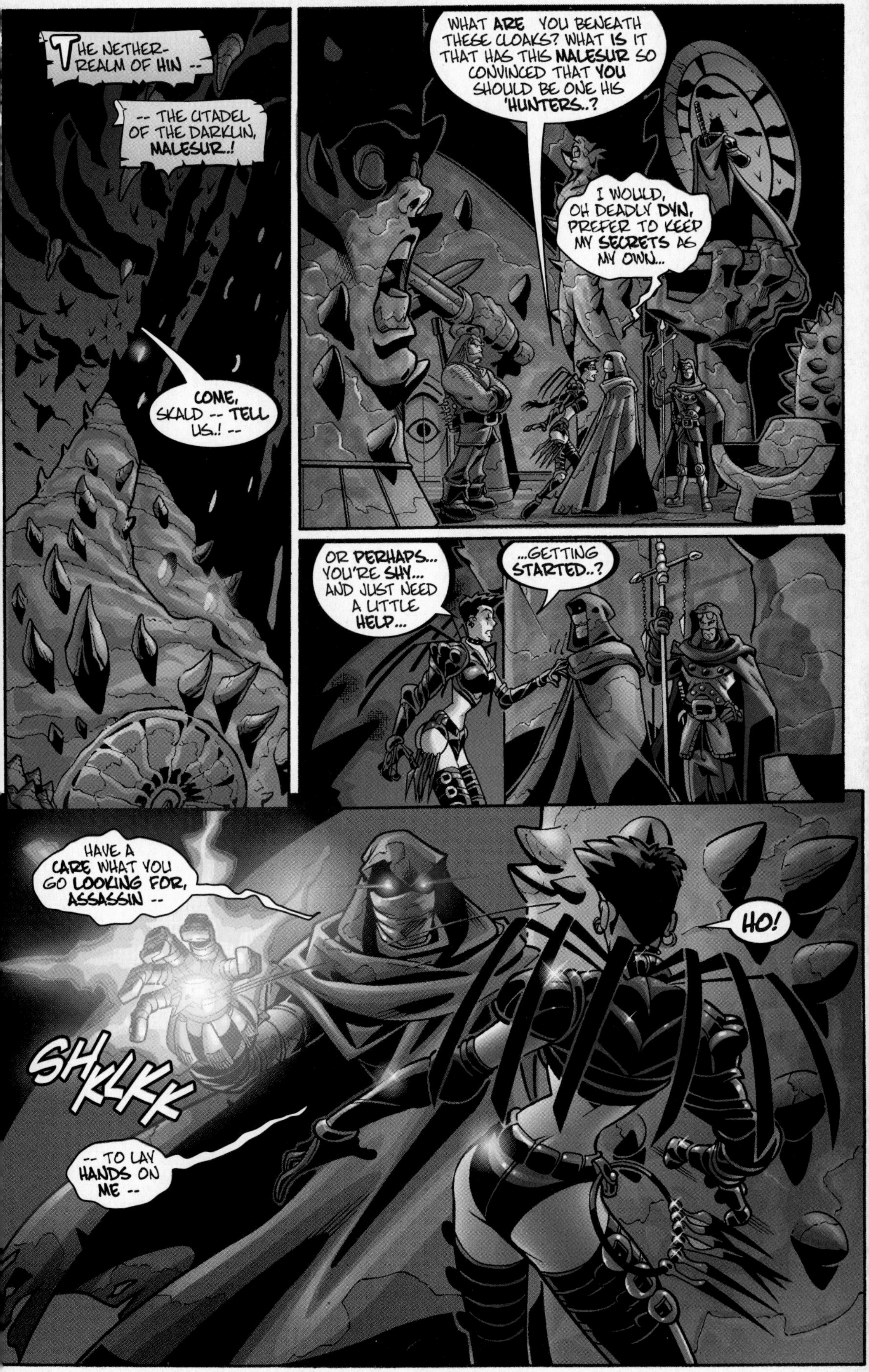
THE NETHER-REALM OF HIN --
-- THE CITADEL OF THE DARKLIN, MALESUR..!
COME, SKALD -- TELL US..! --
WHAT ARE YOU BENEATH THESE CLOAKS? WHAT IS IT THAT HAS THIS MALESUR SO CONVINCED THAT YOU SHOULD BE ONE HIS 'HUNTERS..?
I WOULD, OH DEADLY DYN, PREFER TO KEEP MY SECRETS AS MY OWN...
OR PERHAPS... YOU'RE SHY... AND JUST NEED A LITTLE HELP...
...GETTING STARTED..?
HAVE A CARE WHAT YOU GO LOOKING FOR, ASSASSIN --
HO!
SHKLKK
-- TO LAY HANDS ON ME --

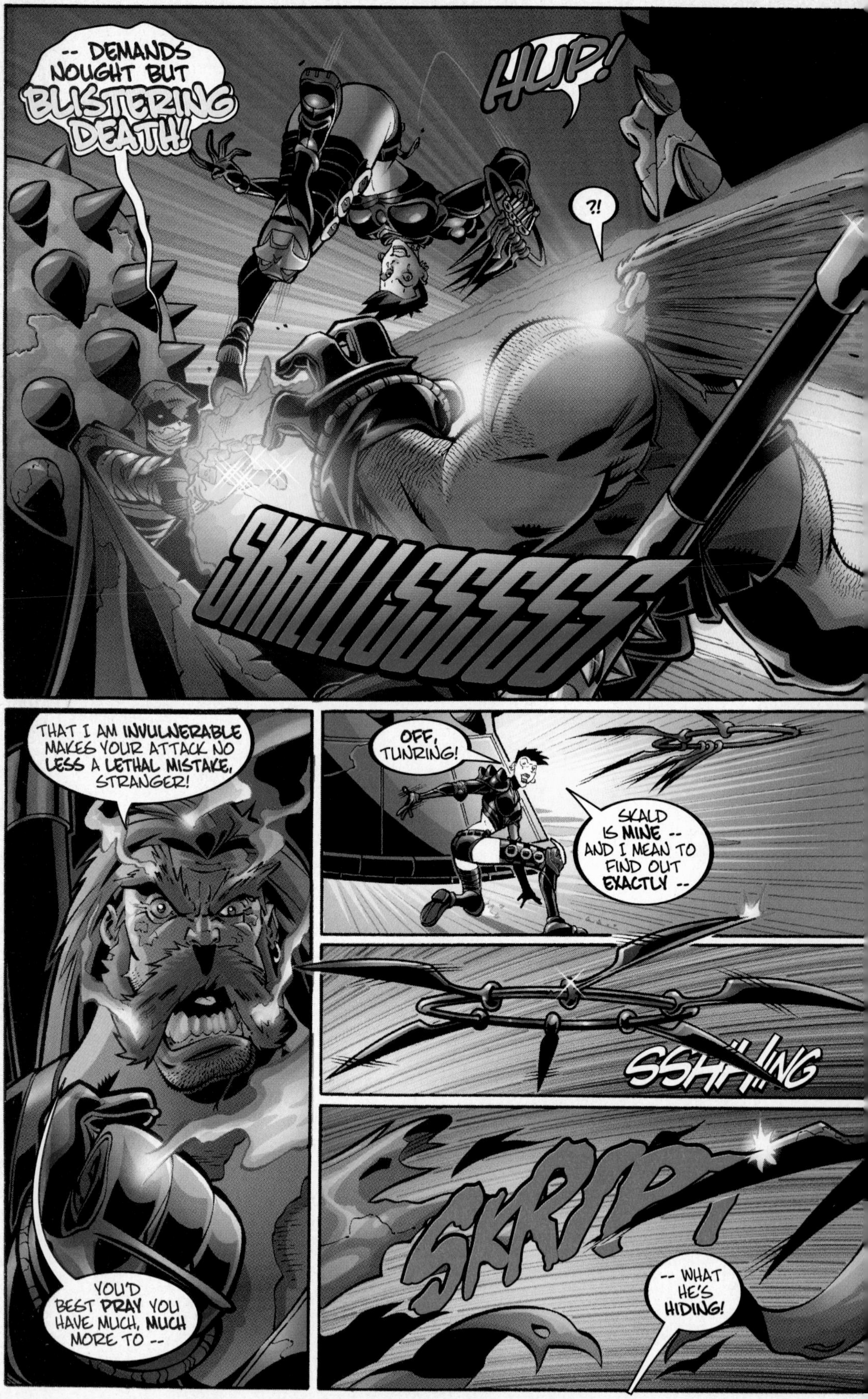
-- DEMANDS NOUGHT BUT BLISTERING DEATH!
HUP!
?!
SKALLSSSSS
THAT I AM INVULNERABLE MAKES YOUR ATTACK NO LESS A LETHAL MISTAKE, STRANGER!
YOU'D BEST PRAY YOU HAVE MUCH, MUCH MORE TO --
OFF, TUNRING!
SKALD IS MINE -- AND I MEAN TO FIND OUT EXACTLY --
SSHHING
SKRIP!
-- WHAT HE'S HIDING!

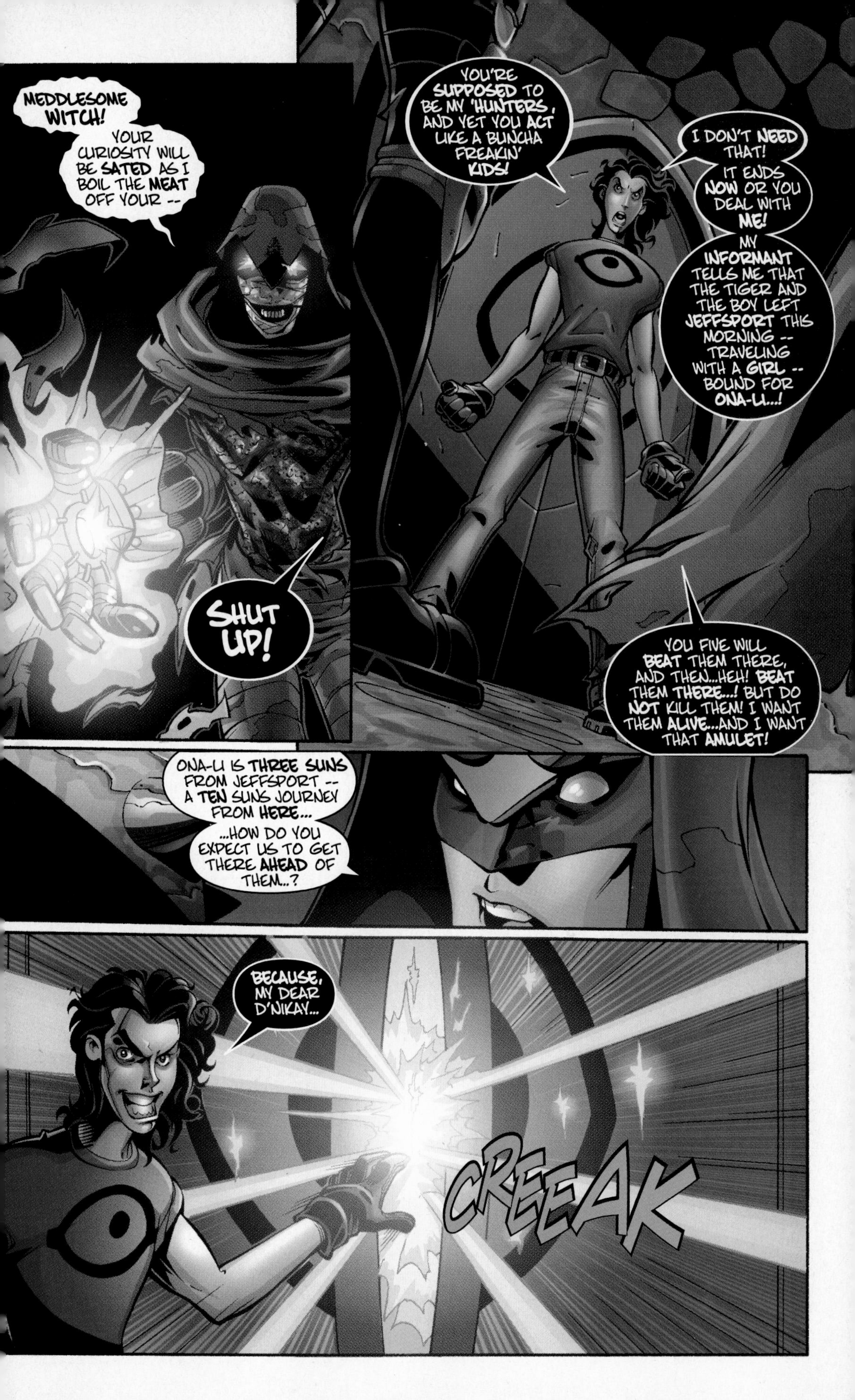
MEDDLESOME WITCH!
YOUR CURIOSITY WILL BE SATED AS I BOIL THE MEAT OFF YOUR --
YOU'RE SUPPOSED TO BE MY 'HUNTERS', AND YET YOU ACT LIKE A BUNCHA FREAKIN' KIDS!
I DON'T NEED THAT!
IT ENDS NOW OR YOU DEAL WITH ME!
MY INFORMANT TELLS ME THAT THE TIGER AND THE BOY LEFT JEFFSPORT THIS MORNING -- TRAVELING WITH A GIRL -- BOUND FOR ONA-LI...!
SHUT UP!
YOU FIVE WILL BEAT THEM THERE, AND THEN...HEH! BEAT THEM THERE...! BUT DO NOT KILL THEM! I WANT THEM ALIVE...AND I WANT THAT AMULET!
ONA-LI IS THREE SUNS FROM JEFFSPORT -- A TEN SUNS JOURNEY FROM HERE...
...HOW DO YOU EXPECT US TO GET THERE AHEAD OF THEM...?
BECAUSE, MY DEAR D'NIKAY...
CREEAK

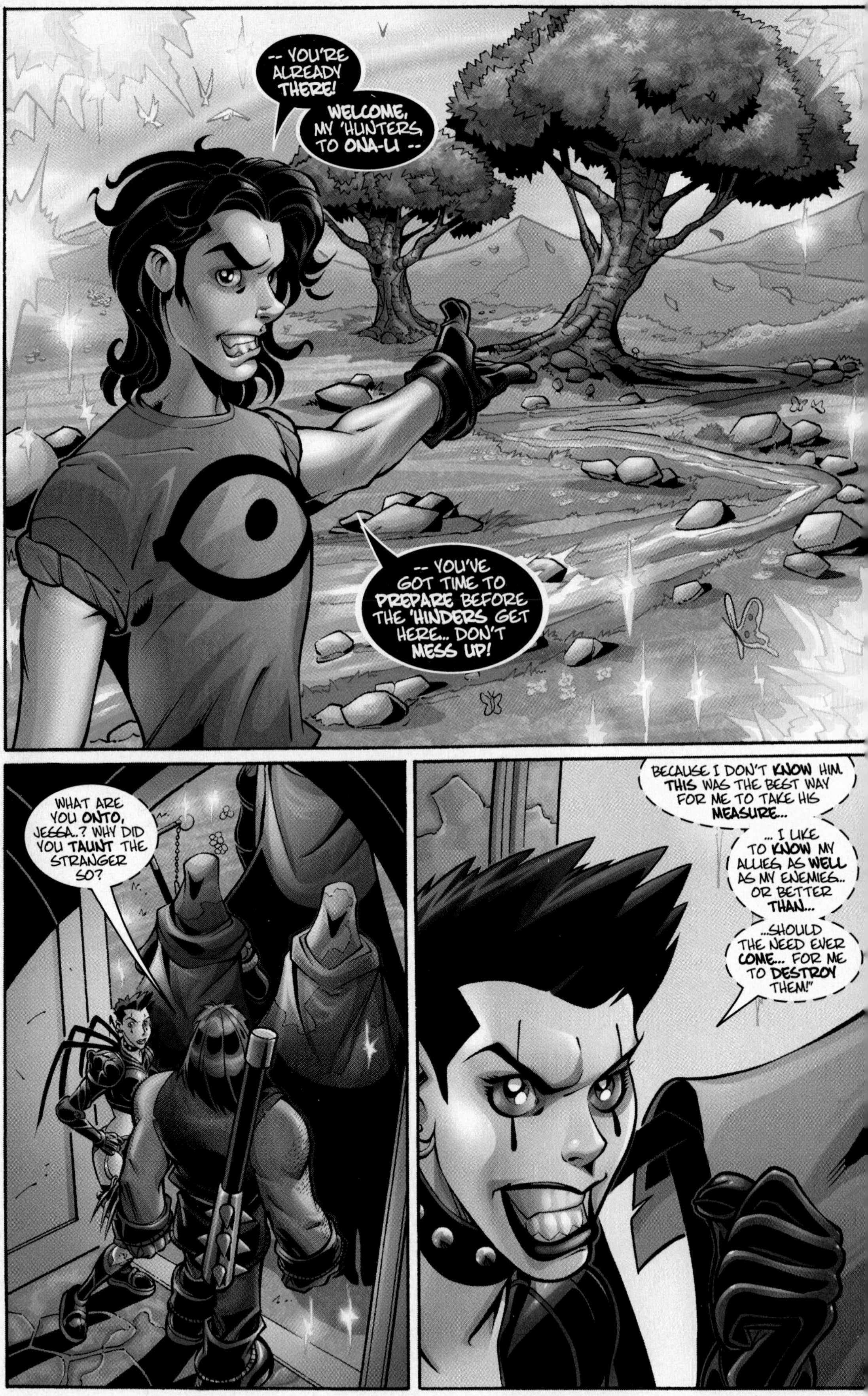

-- YOU'RE ALREADY THERE!
WELCOME, MY 'HUNTERS TO ONA-LI --
-- YOU'VE GOT TIME TO PREPARE BEFORE THE 'HINDERS GET HERE... DON'T MESS UP!
WHAT ARE YOU ONTO, JESSA..? WHY DID YOU TAUNT THE STRANGER SO?
BECAUSE I DON'T KNOW HIM THIS WAS THE BEST WAY FOR ME TO TAKE HIS MEASURE...
... I LIKE TO KNOW MY ALLIES AS WELL AS MY ENEMIES... OR BETTER THAN...
...SHOULD THE NEED EVER COME... FOR ME TO DESTROY THEM!"

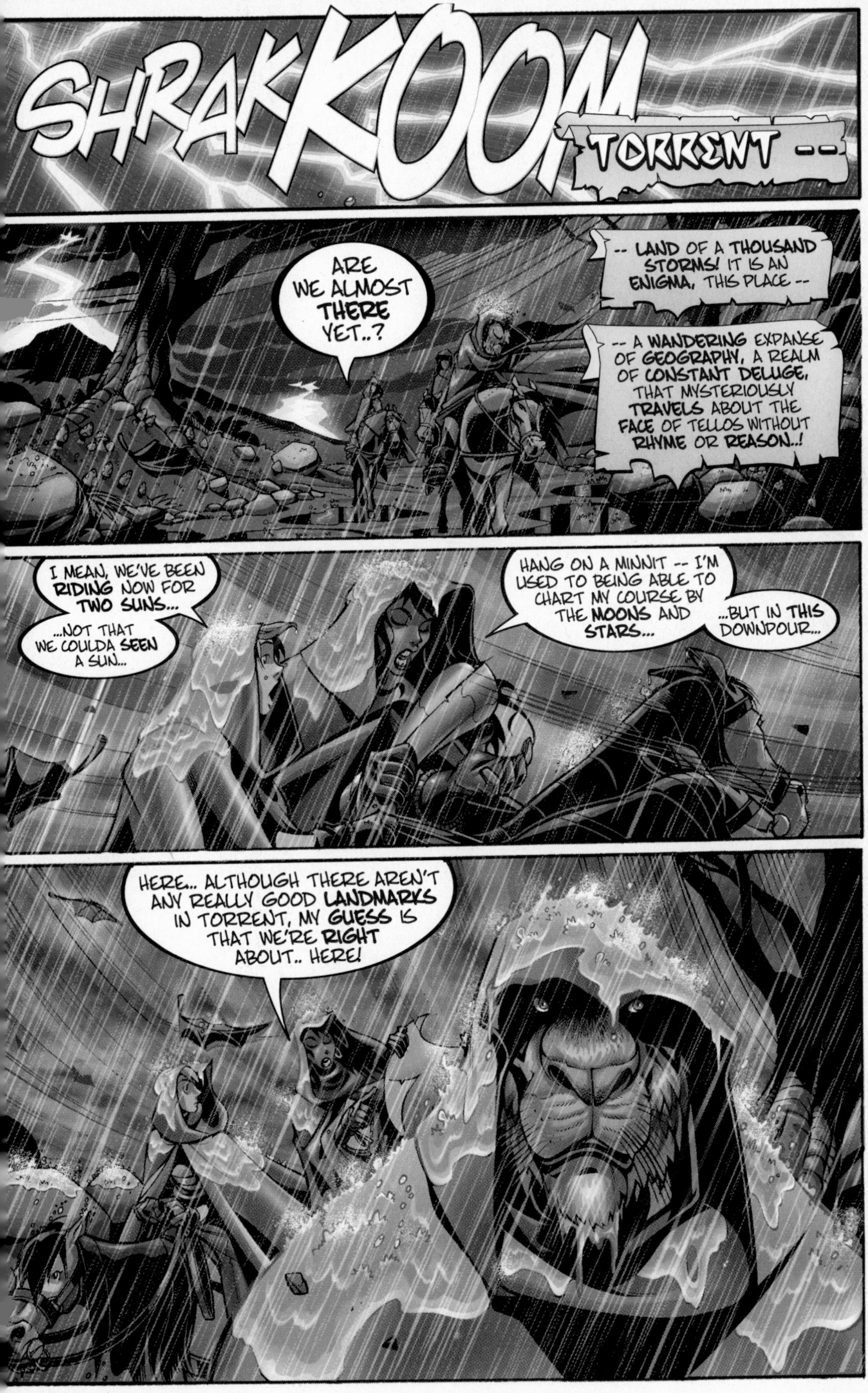

SHRAKKOOM
TORRENT --
-- LAND OF A THOUSAND STORMS! IT IS AN ENIGMA, THIS PLACE --
ARE WE ALMOST THERE YET..?
-- A WANDERING EXPANSE OF GEOGRAPHY, A REALM OF CONSTANT DELUGE, THAT MYSTERIOUSLY TRAVELS ABOUT THE FACE OF TELLOS WITHOUT RHYME OR REASON..!
I MEAN, WE'VE BEEN RIDING NOW FOR TWO SUNS...
...NOT THAT WE COULDA SEEN A SUN...
HANG ON A MINNIT -- I'M USED TO BEING ABLE TO CHART MY COURSE BY THE MOONS AND STARS...
...BUT IN THIS DOWNPOUR...
HERE... ALTHOUGH THERE AREN'T ANY REALLY GOOD LANDMARKS IN TORRENT, MY GUESS IS THAT WE'RE RIGHT ABOUT.. HERE!

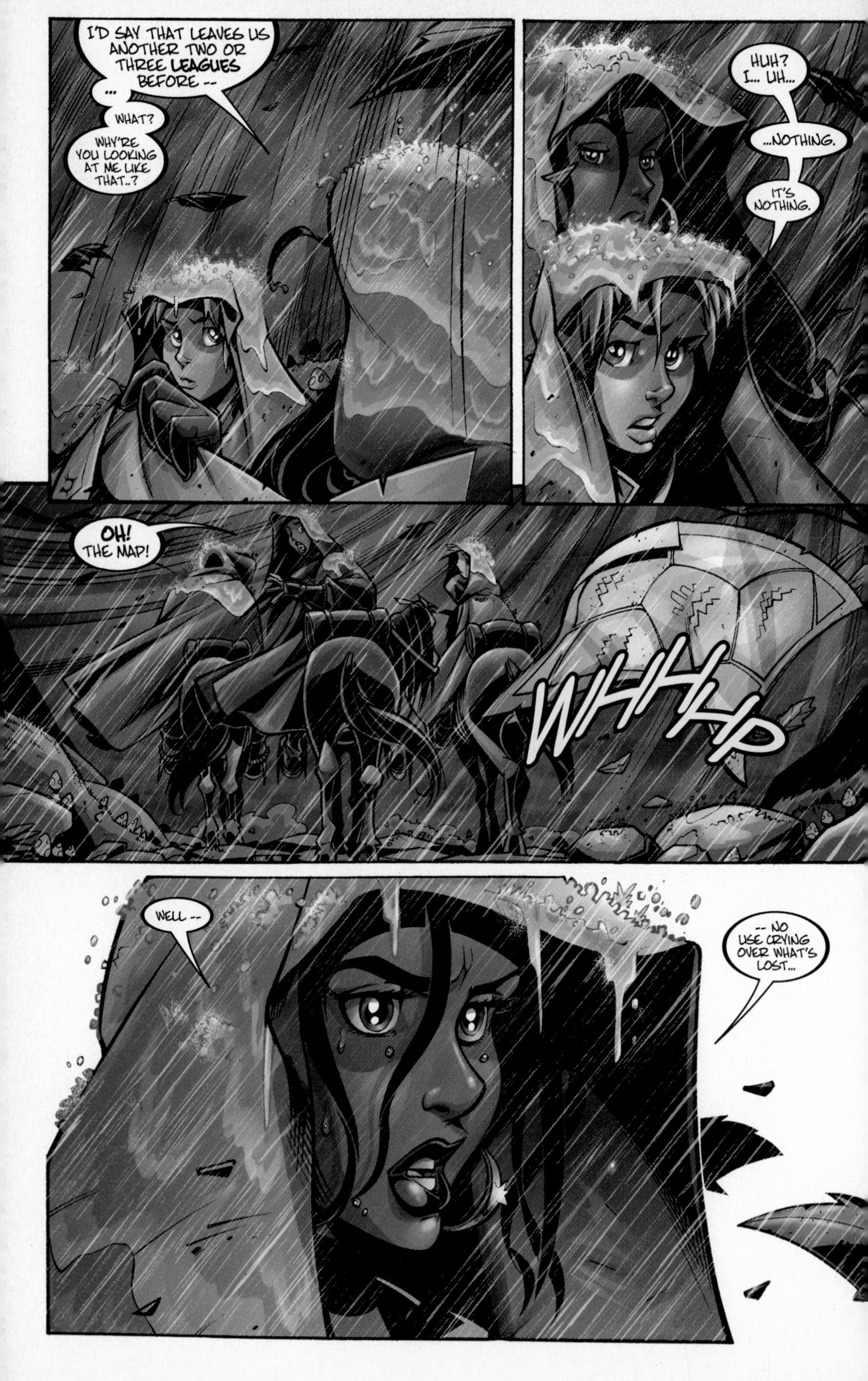
I'D SAY THAT LEAVES US ANOTHER TWO OR THREE LEAGUES BEFORE --
...
WHAT?
WHY'RE YOU LOOKING AT ME LIKE THAT..?
HUH? I... UH...
...NOTHING.
IT'S NOTHING.
OH! THE MAP!
WHHHP
WELL --
-- NO USE CRYING OVER WHAT'S LOST...

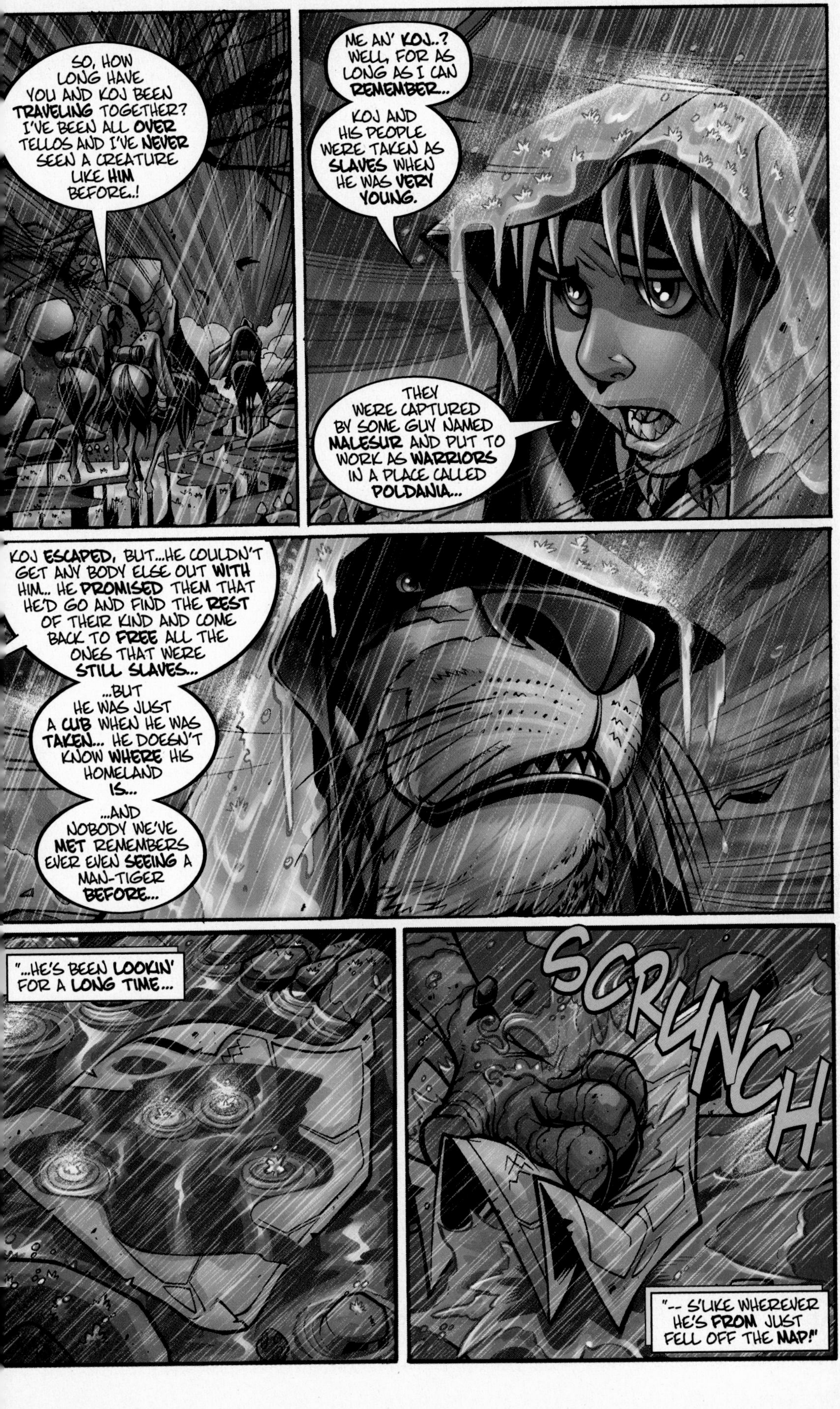
SO, HOW LONG HAVE YOU AND KOJ BEEN TRAVELING TOGETHER? I'VE BEEN ALL OVER TELLOS AND I'VE NEVER SEEN A CREATURE LIKE HIM BEFORE..!
ME AN' KOJ..? WELL, FOR AS LONG AS I CAN REMEMBER...
KOJ AND HIS PEOPLE WERE TAKEN AS SLAVES WHEN HE WAS VERY YOUNG.
THEY WERE CAPTURED BY SOME GUY NAMED MALESUR AND PUT TO WORK AS WARRIORS IN A PLACE CALLED POLDANIA...
KOJ ESCAPED, BUT...HE COULDN'T GET ANY BODY ELSE OUT WITH HIM... HE PROMISED THEM THAT HE'D GO AND FIND THE REST OF THEIR KIND AND COME BACK TO FREE ALL THE ONES THAT WERE STILL SLAVES...
...BUT HE WAS JUST A CUB WHEN HE WAS TAKEN... HE DOESN'T KNOW WHERE HIS HOMELAND IS...
...AND NOBODY WE'VE MET REMEMBERS EVER EVEN SEEING A MAN-TIGER BEFORE...
"...HE'S BEEN LOOKIN' FOR A LONG TIME...
SCRUNCH
"-- S'LIKE WHEREVER HE'S FROM JUST FELL OFF THE MAP!"

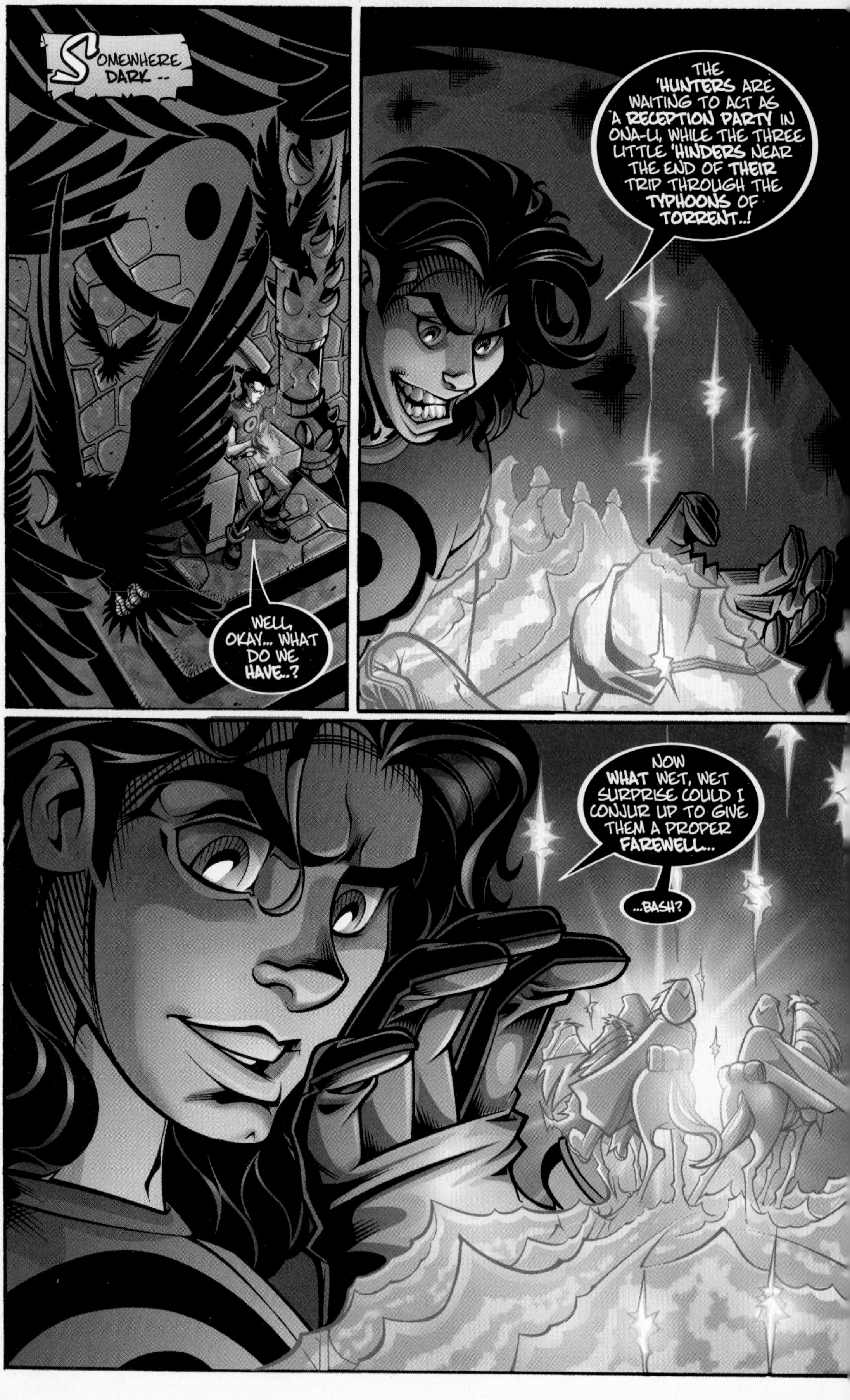
SOMEWHERE DARK --
WELL, OKAY... WHAT DO WE HAVE..?
THE 'HUNTERS ARE WAITING TO ACT AS A RECEPTION PARTY IN ONA-LI, WHILE THE THREE LITTLE 'HINDERS NEAR THE END OF THEIR TRIP THROUGH THE TYPHOONS OF TORRENT..!
NOW WHAT WET, WET SURPRISE COULD I CONJUR UP TO GIVE THEM A PROPER FAREWELL...
...BASH?

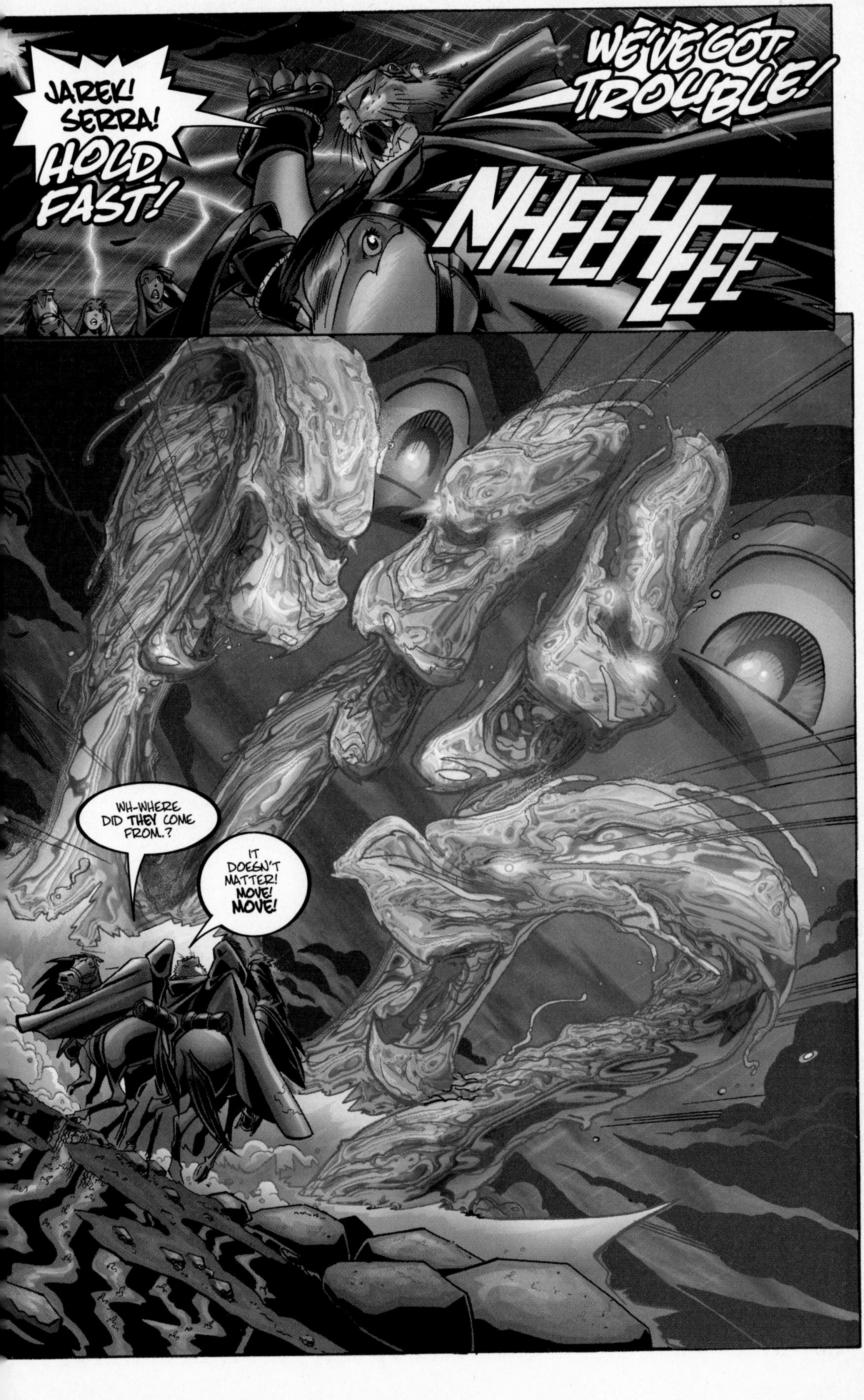
JAREK! SERRA! HOLD FAST!
WE'VE GOT TROUBLE!
NHEEHEEE
WH-WHERE DID THEY COME FROM..?
IT DOESN'T MATTER! MOVE! MOVE!

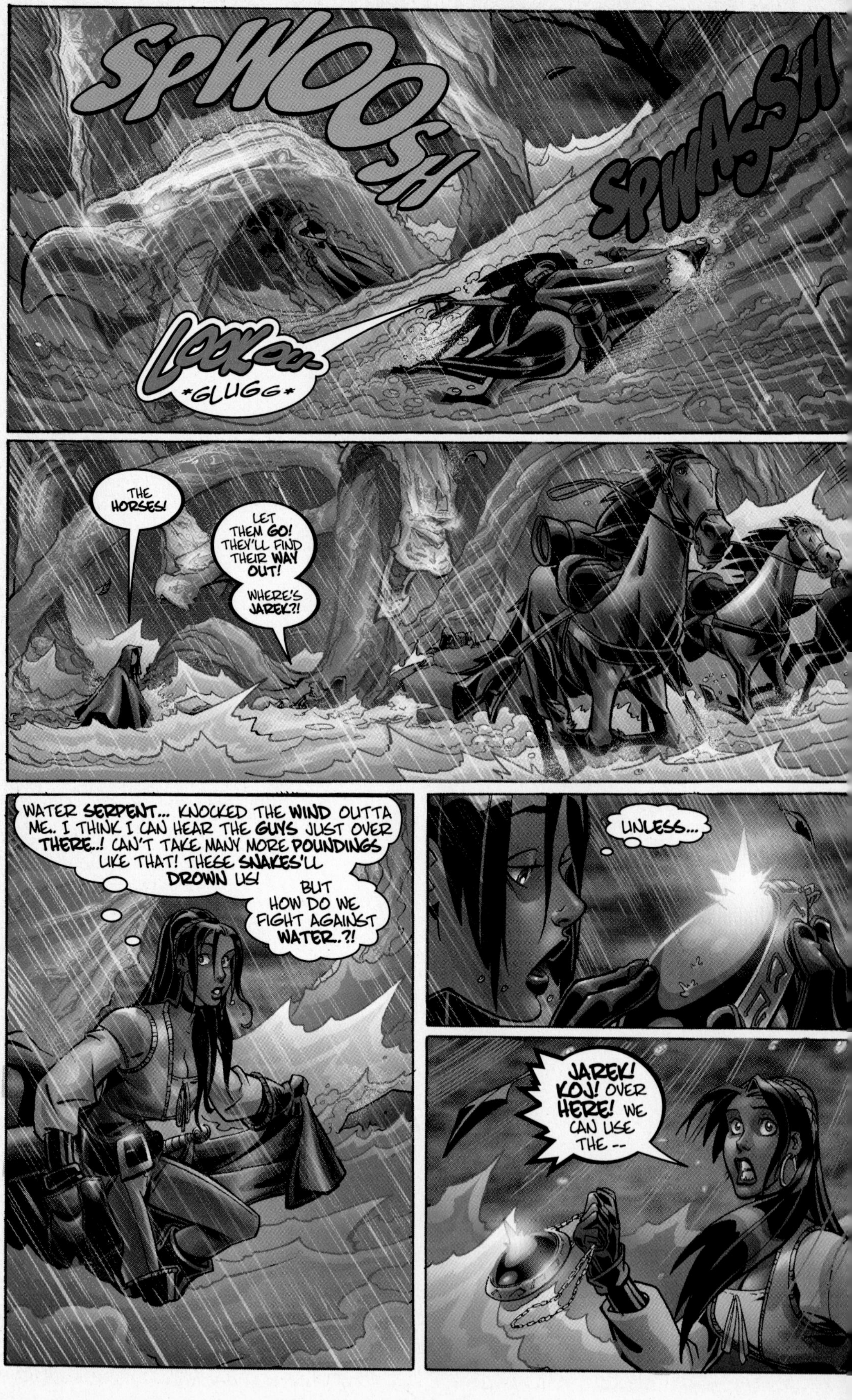
SPWOOSH
SPWASSH
LOOK OUT-
GLUGG
THE HORSES!
LET THEM GO! THEY'LL FIND THEIR WAY OUT!
WHERE'S JAREK?!
WATER SERPENT... KNOCKED THE WIND OUTTA ME.. I THINK I CAN HEAR THE GUYS JUST OVER THERE..! CAN'T TAKE MANY MORE POUNDINGS LIKE THAT! THESE SNAKES'LL DROWN US!
BUT HOW DO WE FIGHT AGAINST WATER..?!
UNLESS...
JAREK! KOJ! OVER HERE! WE CAN USE THE --

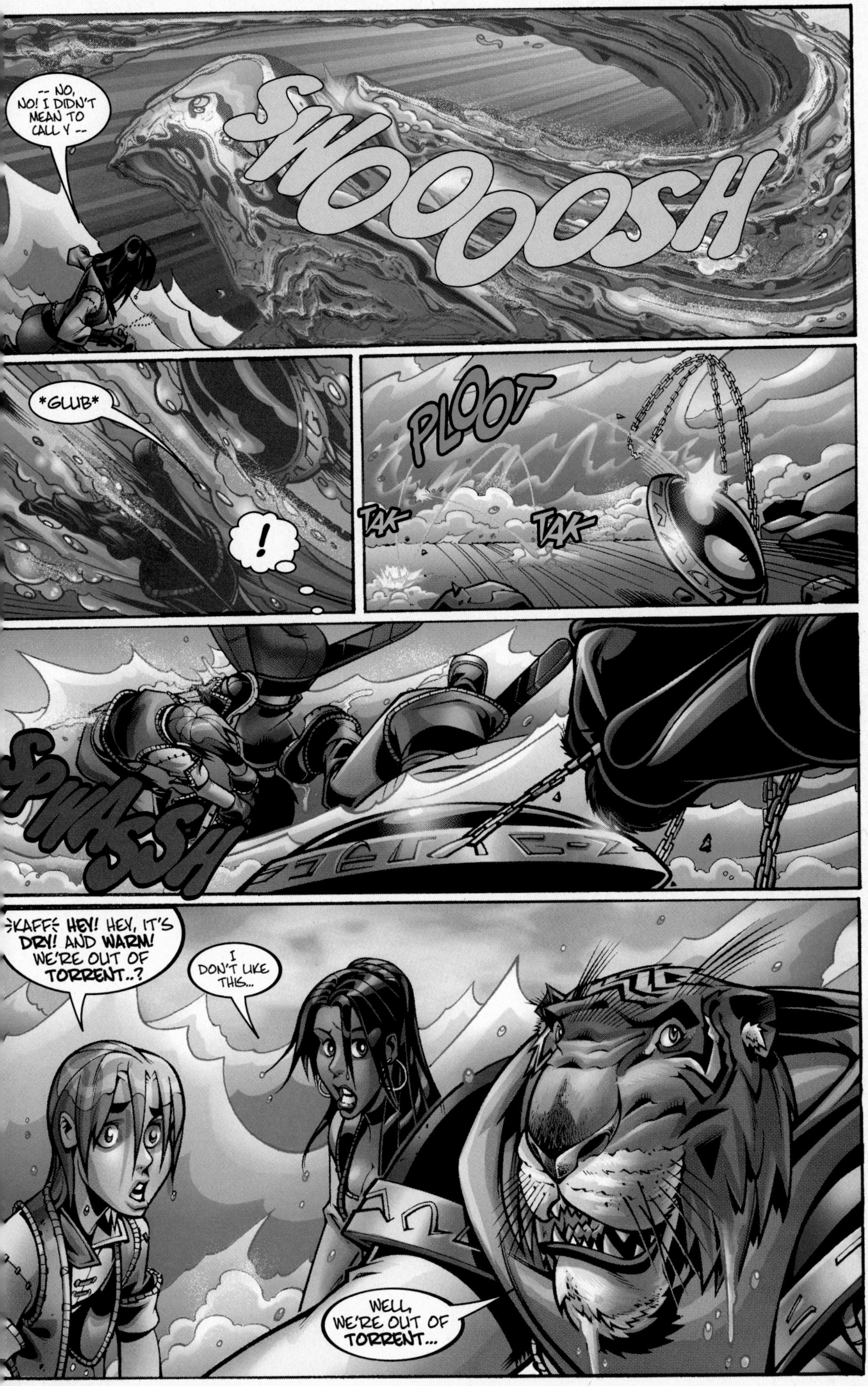
-- NO, NO! I DIDN'T MEAN TO CALL Y --
SWOOOOSH
GLUB
!
PLOOT
TAK
TAK
SPWASSH
KAFF HEY! HEY, IT'S DRY! AND WARM! WE'RE OUT OF TORRENT..?
I DON'T LIKE THIS...
WELL, WE'RE OUT OF TORRENT...

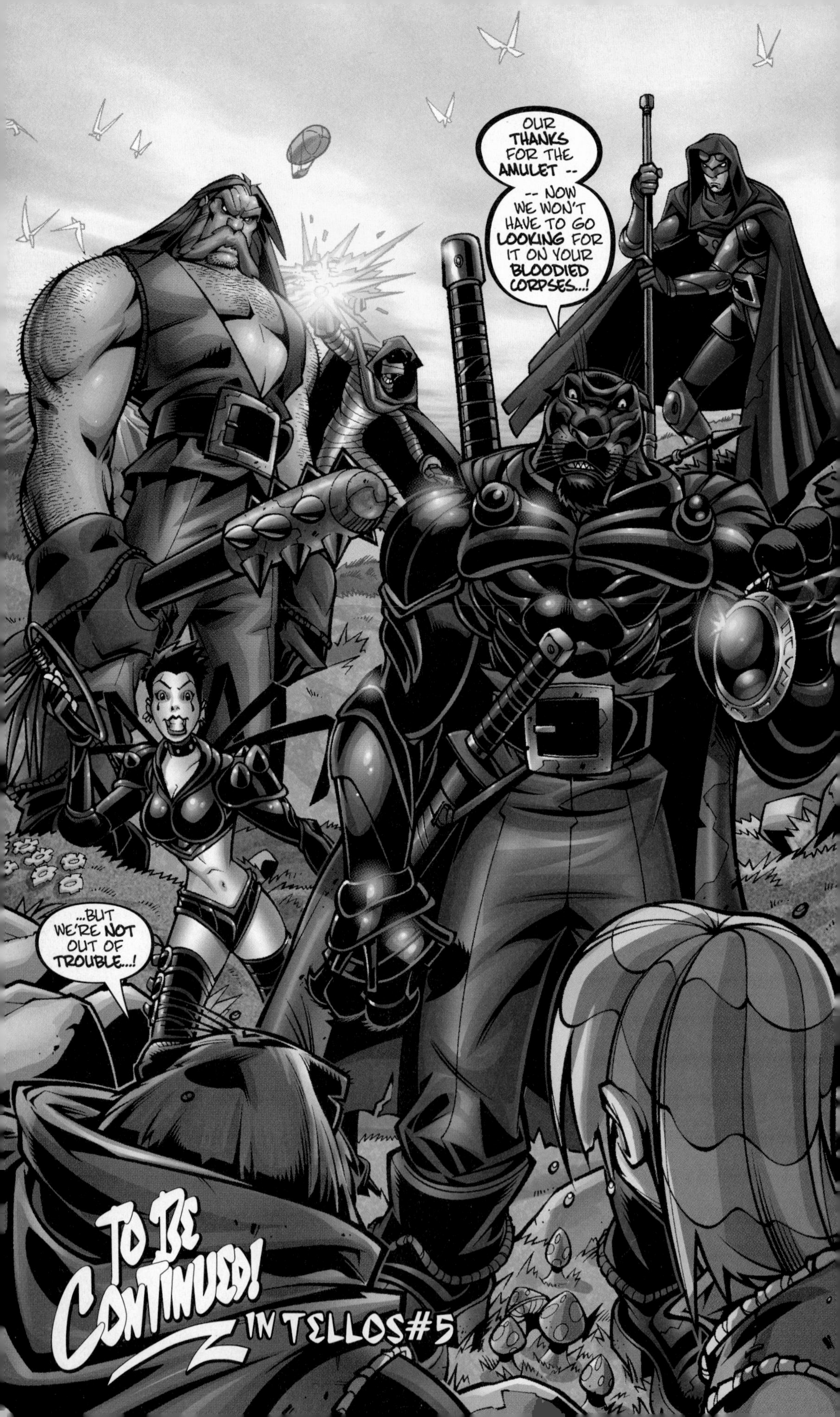
OUR THANKS FOR THE AMULET --
-- NOW WE WON'T HAVE TO GO LOOKING FOR IT ON YOUR BLOODIED CORPSES...!
...BUT WE'RE NOT OUT OF TROUBLE...!
TO BE CONTINUED! IN TELLOS #5

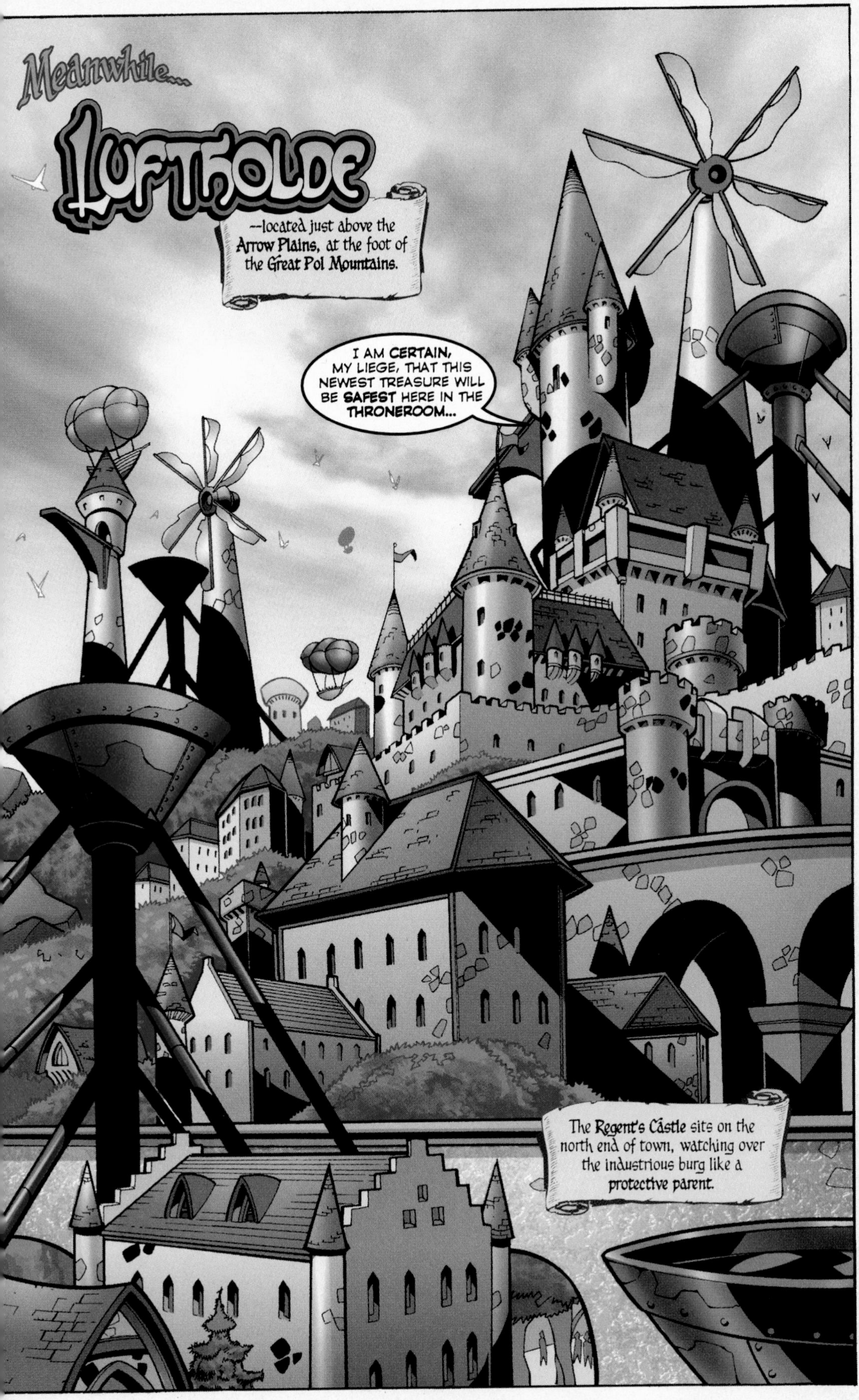
Meanwhile...
Lufth°lde
--located just above the Arrow Plains, at the foot of the Great Pol Mountains.
I AM CERTAIN, MY LIEGE, THAT THIS NEWEST TREASURE WILL BE SAFEST HERE IN THE THRONEROOM...
The Regent's Castle sits on the north end of town, watching over the industrious burg like a protective parent.

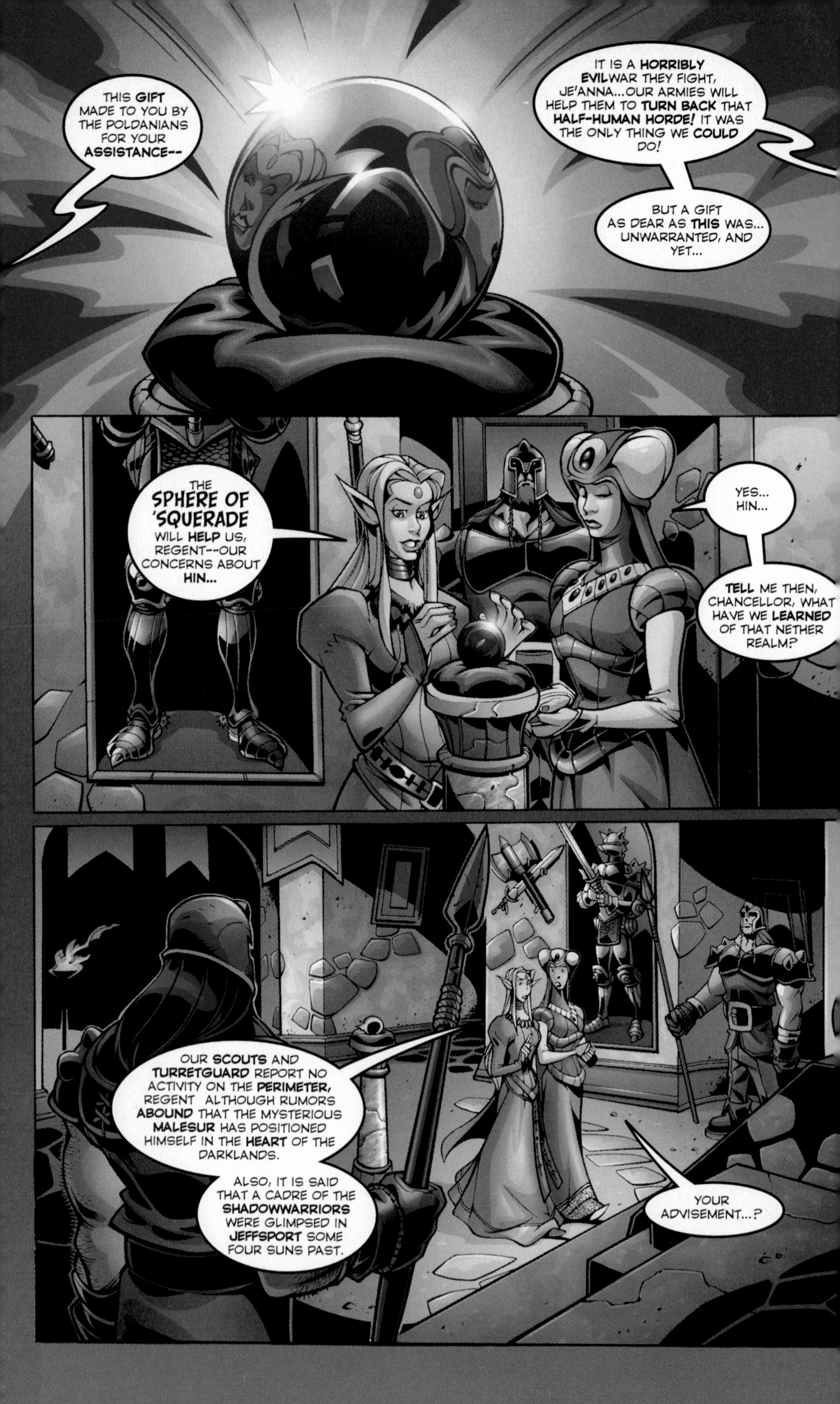
THIS GIFT MADE TO YOU BY THE POLDANIANS FOR YOUR ASSISTANCE--
IT IS A HORRIBLY EVIL WAR THEY FIGHT, JE'ANNA...OUR ARMIES WILL HELP THEM TO TURN BACK THAT HALF-HUMAN HORDE! IT WAS THE ONLY THING WE COULD DO!
BUT A GIFT AS DEAR AS THIS WAS... UNWARRANTED, AND YET...
THE SPHERE OF 'SQUERADE WILL HELP US, REGENT--OUR CONCERNS ABOUT HIN...
YES... HIN...
TELL ME THEN, CHANCELLOR, WHAT HAVE WE LEARNED OF THAT NETHER REALM?
OUR SCOUTS AND TURRETGUARD REPORT NO ACTIVITY ON THE PERIMETER, REGENT ALTHOUGH RUMORS ABOUND THAT THE MYSTERIOUS MALESUR HAS POSITIONED HIMSELF IN THE HEART OF THE DARKLANDS.
ALSO, IT IS SAID THAT A CADRE OF THE SHADOWWARRIORS WERE GLIMPSED IN JEFFSPORT SOME FOUR SUNS PAST.
YOUR ADVISEMENT...?

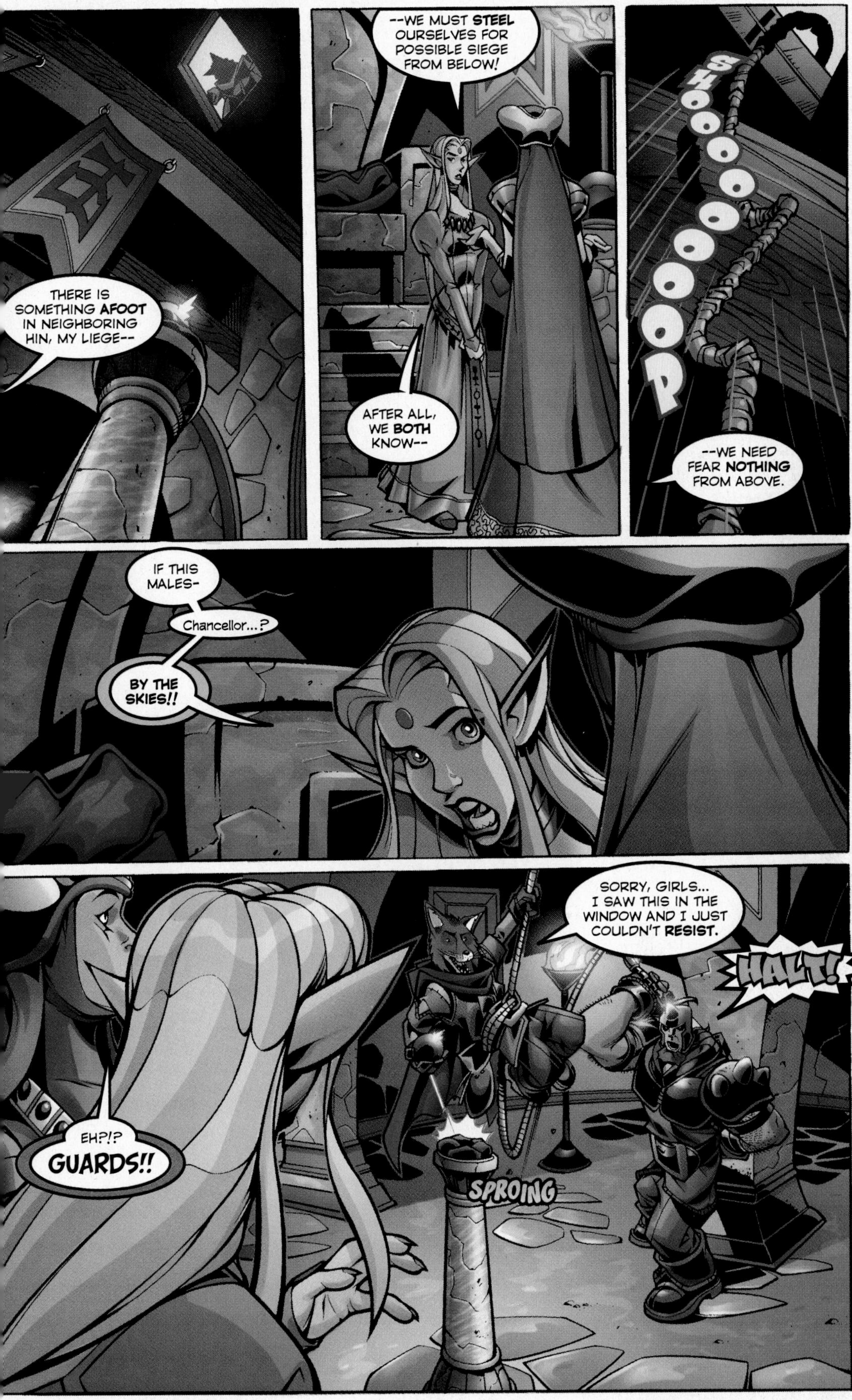
THERE IS SOMETHING AFOOT IN NEIGHBORING HIN, MY LIEGE--
--WE MUST STEEL OURSELVES FOR POSSIBLE SIEGE FROM BELOW!
AFTER ALL, WE BOTH KNOW--
SHOOOOOOOOP
--WE NEED FEAR NOTHING FROM ABOVE.
IF THIS MALES-
Chancellor...?
BY THE SKIES!!
EH?!? GUARDS!!
SORRY, GIRLS... I SAW THIS IN THE WINDOW AND I JUST COULDN'T RESIST.
HALT!
SPROING

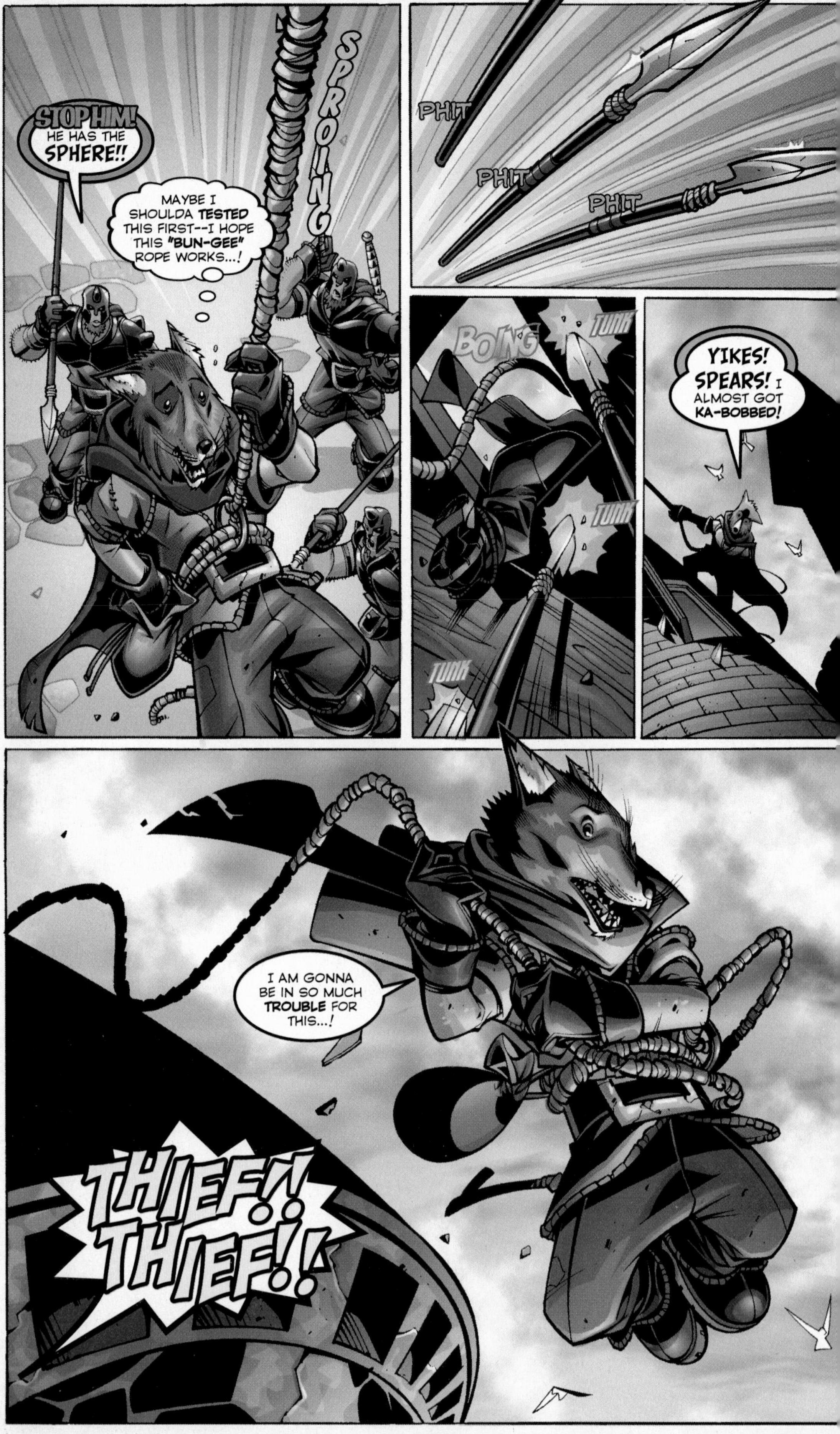
STOP HIM! HE HAS THE SPHERE!!
MAYBE I SHOULDA TESTED THIS FIRST--I HOPE THIS "BUN-GEE" ROPE WORKS...!
SPROING
PHIT
PHIT
PHIT
BOING
TUNK
TUNK
TUNK
YIKES! SPEARS! I ALMOST GOT KA-BOBBED!
I AM GONNA BE IN SO MUCH TROUBLE FOR THIS...!
THIEF!! THIEF!!

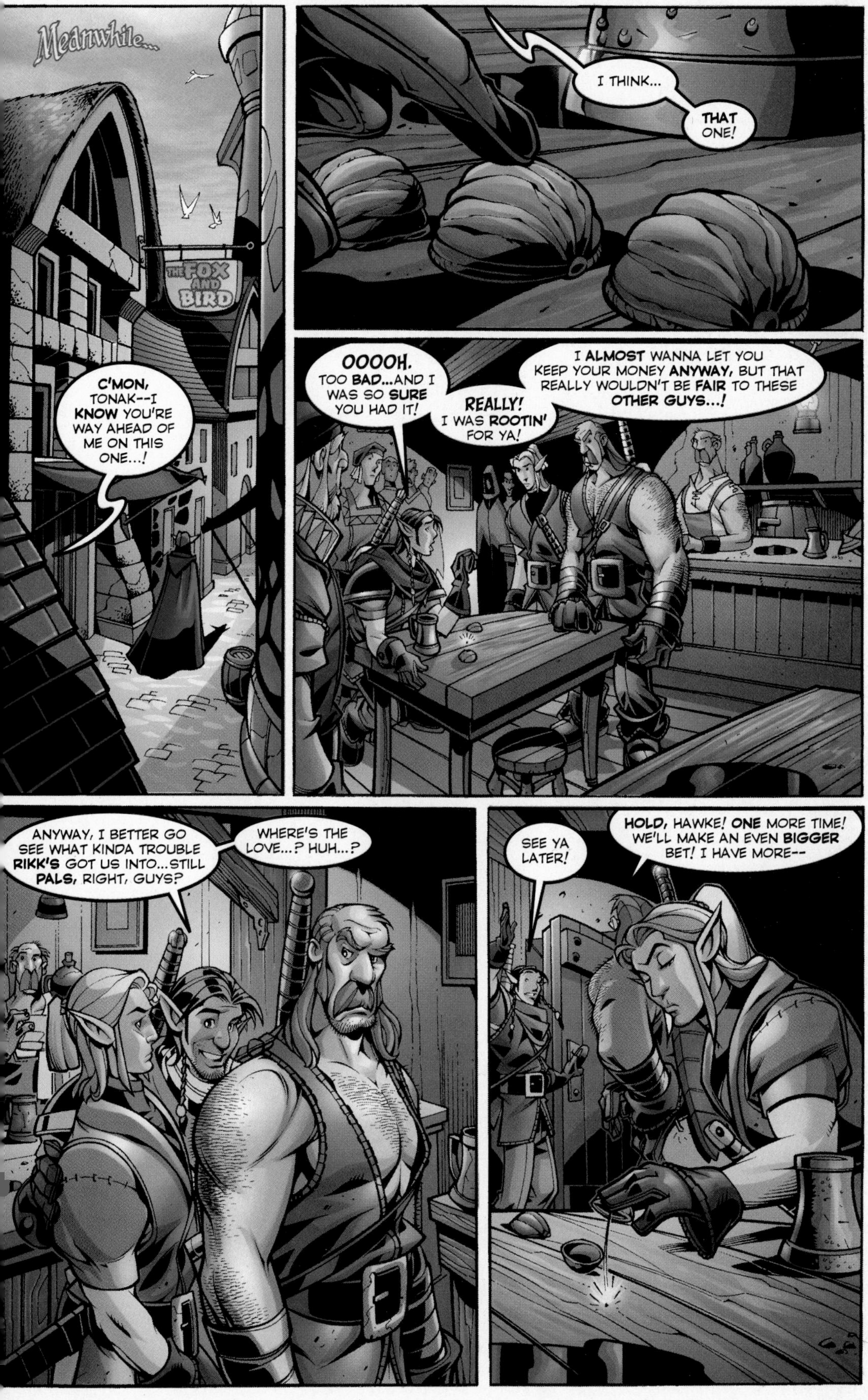
Meanwhile...
THE FOX AND BIRD
C'MON, TONAK--I KNOW YOU'RE WAY AHEAD OF ME ON THIS ONE...!
I THINK...
THAT ONE!
OOOOH. TOO BAD...AND I WAS SO SURE YOU HAD IT!
REALLY! I WAS ROOTIN' FOR YA!
I ALMOST WANNA LET YOU KEEP YOUR MONEY ANYWAY, BUT THAT REALLY WOULDN'T BE FAIR TO THESE OTHER GUYS...!
ANYWAY, I BETTER GO SEE WHAT KINDA TROUBLE RIKK'S GOT US INTO...STILL PALS, RIGHT, GUYS?
WHERE'S THE LOVE...? HUH...?
SEE YA LATER!
HOLD, HAWKE! ONE MORE TIME! WE'LL MAKE AN EVEN BIGGER BET! I HAVE MORE--

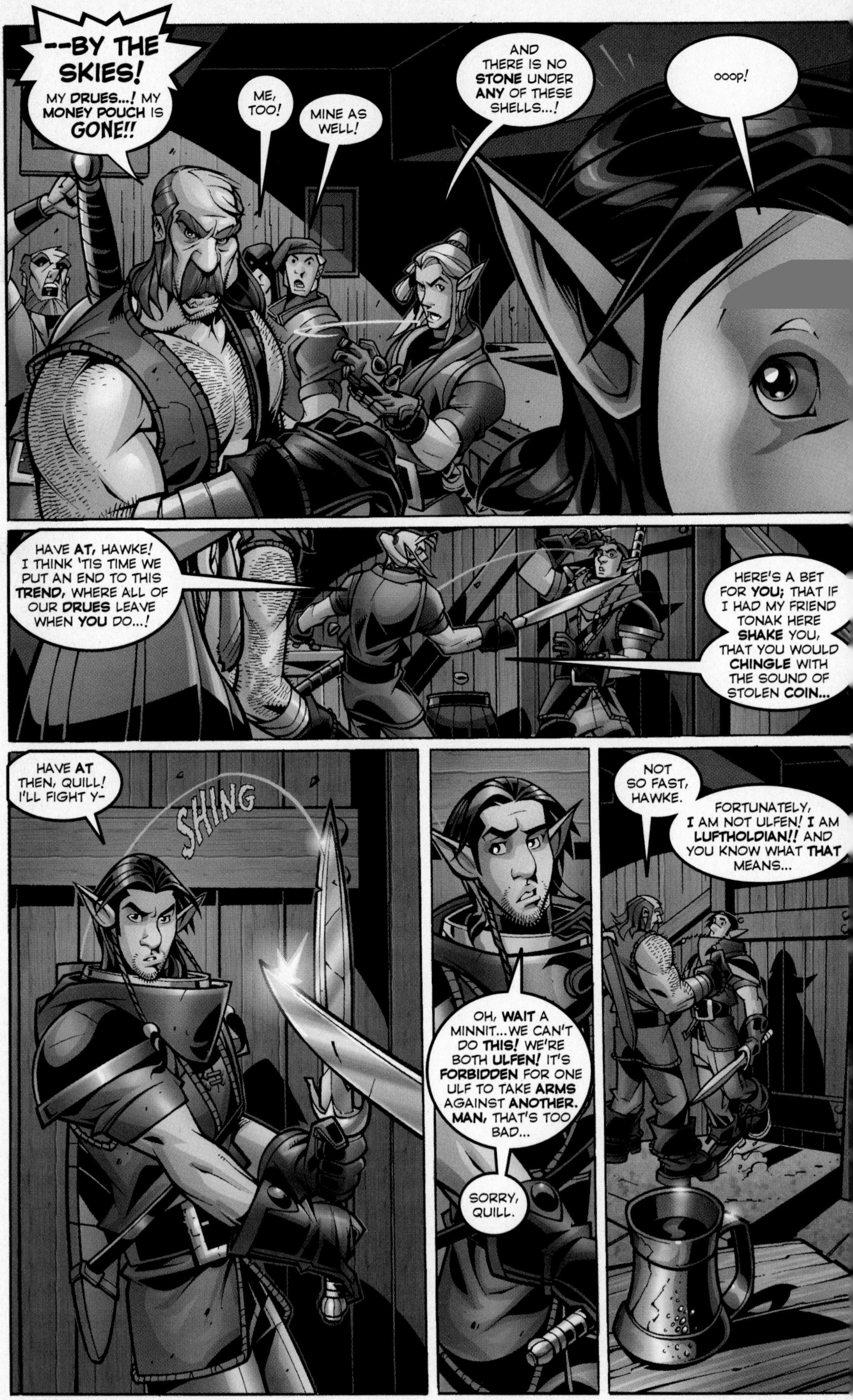
--BY THE SKIES!
MY DRUES...! MY MONEY POUCH IS GONE!!
ME, TOO!
MINE AS WELL!
AND THERE IS NO STONE UNDER ANY OF THESE SHELLS...!
ooop!
HAVE AT, HAWKE! I THINK 'TIS TIME WE PUT AN END TO THIS TREND, WHERE ALL OF OUR DRUES LEAVE WHEN YOU DO...!
HERE'S A BET FOR YOU; THAT IF I HAD MY FRIEND TONAK HERE SHAKE YOU, THAT YOU WOULD CHINGLE WITH THE SOUND OF STOLEN COIN...
HAVE AT THEN, QUILL! I'LL FIGHT Y-
SHING
OH, WAIT A MINNIT...WE CAN'T DO THIS! WE'RE BOTH ULFEN! IT'S FORBIDDEN FOR ONE ULF TO TAKE ARMS AGAINST ANOTHER. MAN, THAT'S TOO BAD...
SORRY, QUILL.
NOT SO FAST, HAWKE.
FORTUNATELY, I AM NOT ULFEN! I AM LUFTHOLDIAN!! AND YOU KNOW WHAT THAT MEANS...

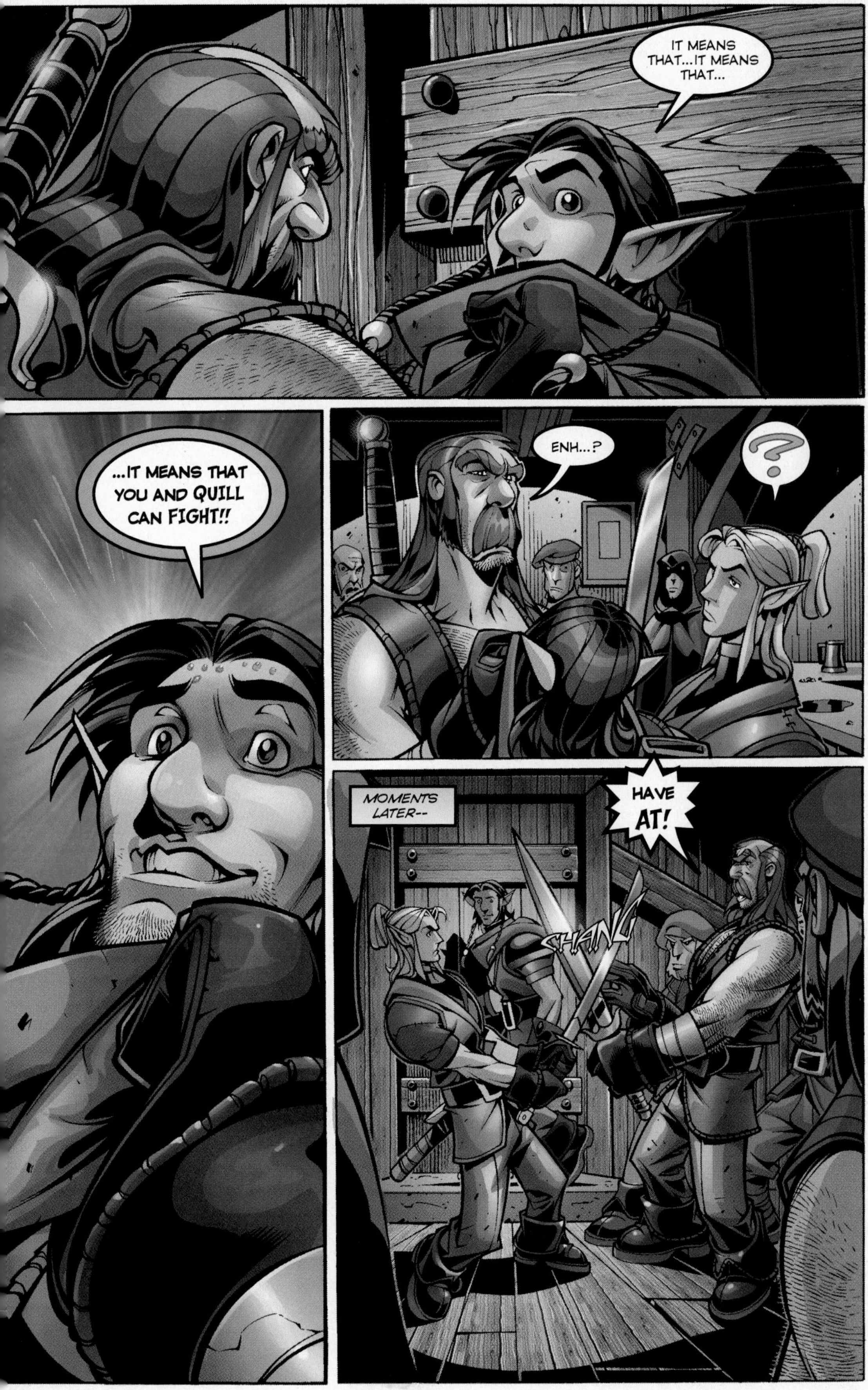
IT MEANS THAT...IT MEANS THAT...
...IT MEANS THAT YOU AND QUILL CAN FIGHT!!
ENH...?
?
MOMENTS LATER--
HAVE AT!
SHANG

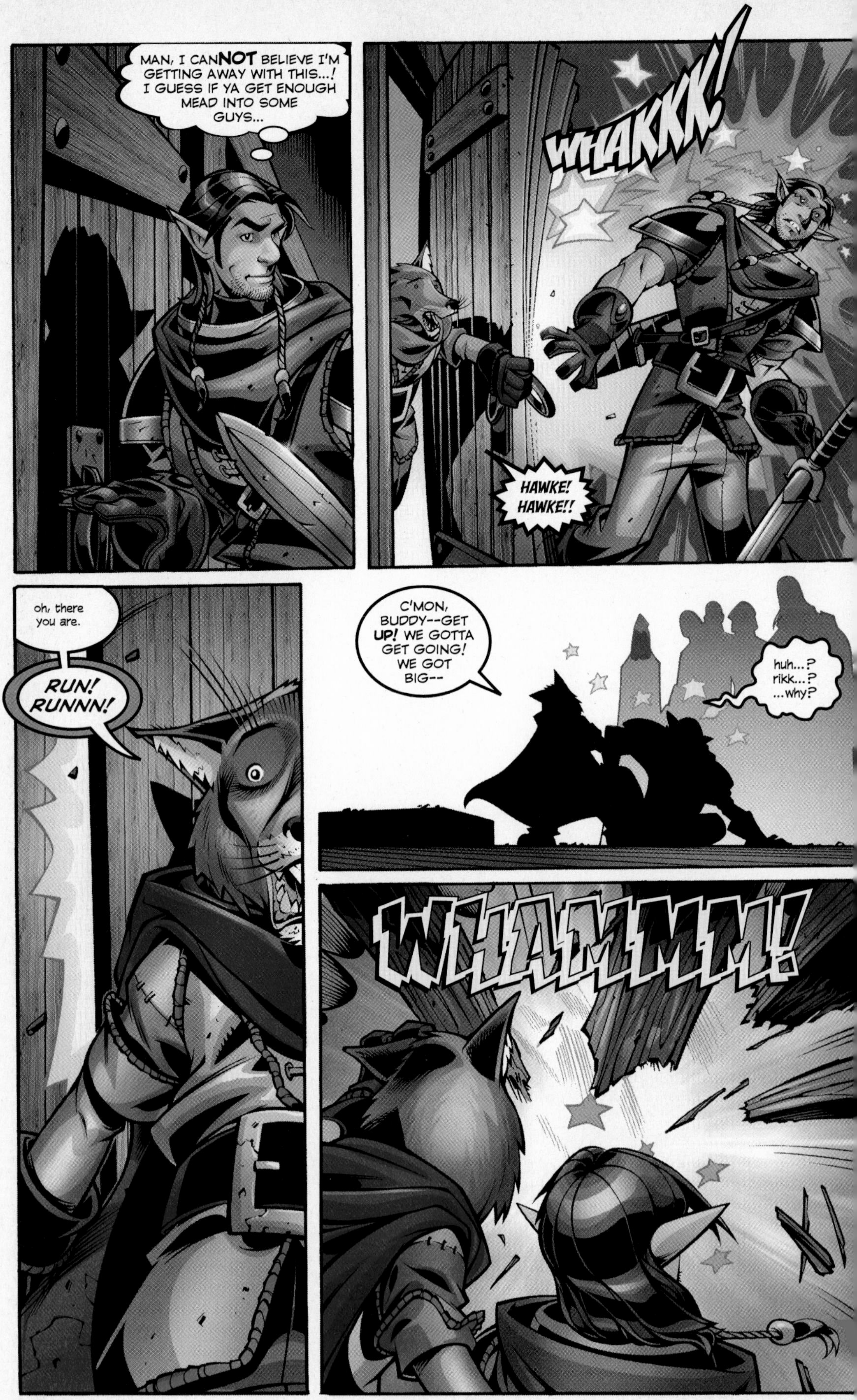
MAN, I CANNOT BELIEVE I'M GETTING AWAY WITH THIS...! I GUESS IF YA GET ENOUGH MEAD INTO SOME GUYS...
WHAKKK!
HAWKE! HAWKE!!
oh, there you are.
RUN! RUNNN!
C'MON, BUDDY--GET UP! WE GOTTA GET GOING! WE GOT BIG--
huh...? rikk...? ...why?
WHAMMM!

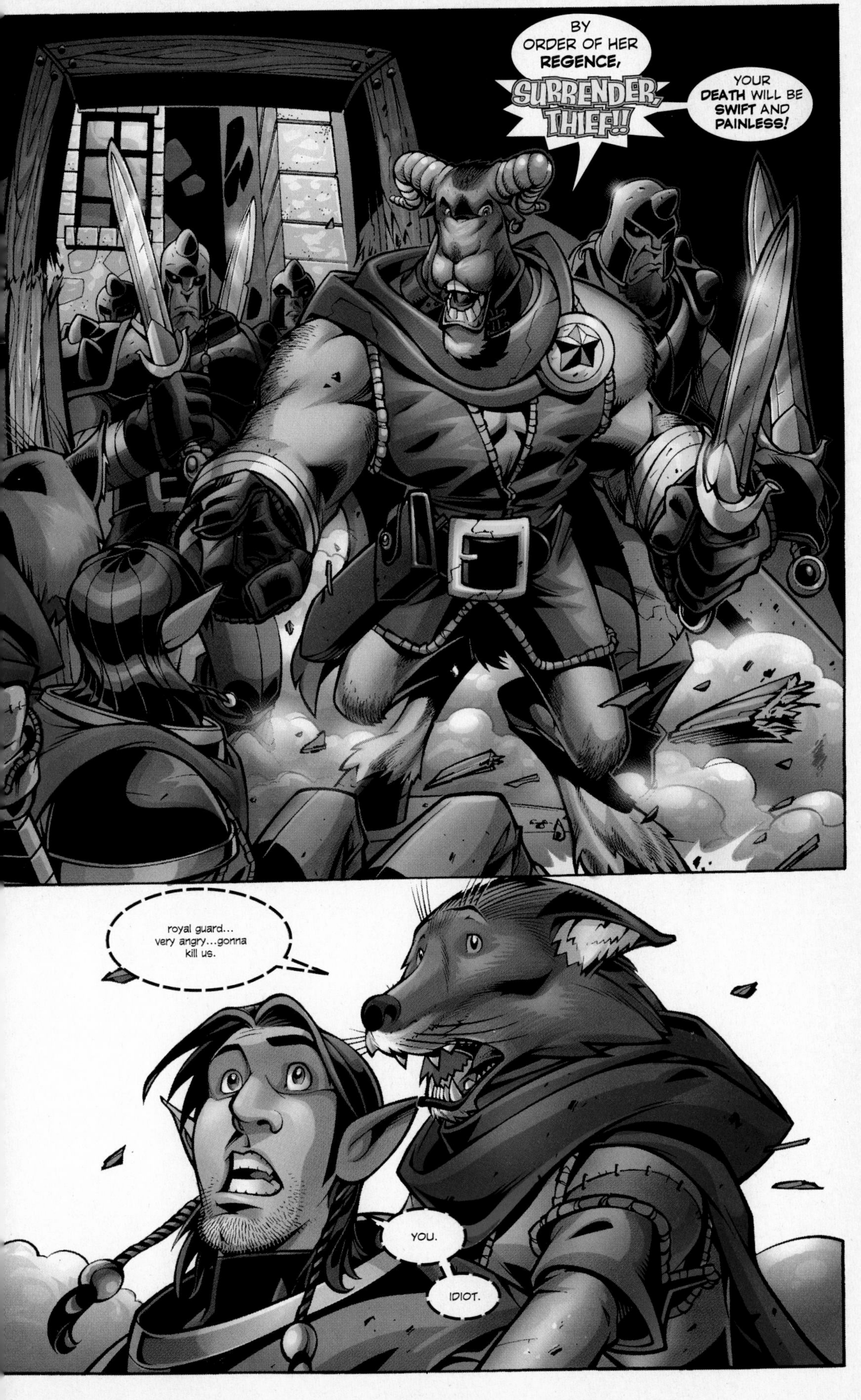
BY ORDER OF HER REGENCE,
SURRENDER, THIEF!!
YOUR DEATH WILL BE SWIFT AND PAINLESS!
royal guard... very angry...gonna kill us.
YOU.
IDIOT.

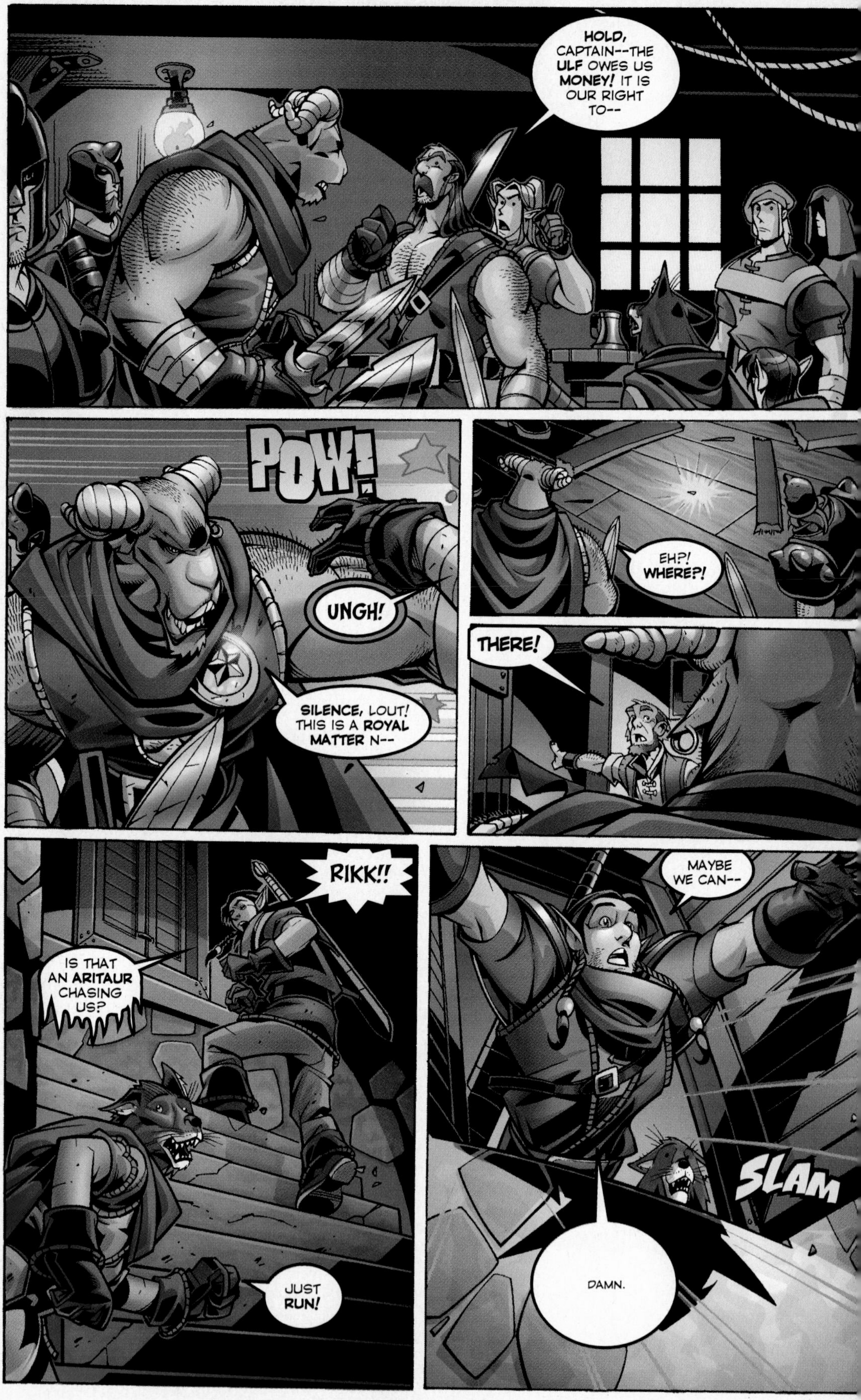
HOLD, CAPTAIN--THE ULF OWES US MONEY! IT IS OUR RIGHT TO--
POW!
UNGH!
SILENCE, LOUT! THIS IS A ROYAL MATTER N--
EH?! WHERE?!
THERE!
RIKK!!
IS THAT AN ARITAUR CHASING US?
JUST RUN!
MAYBE WE CAN--
SLAM
DAMN.

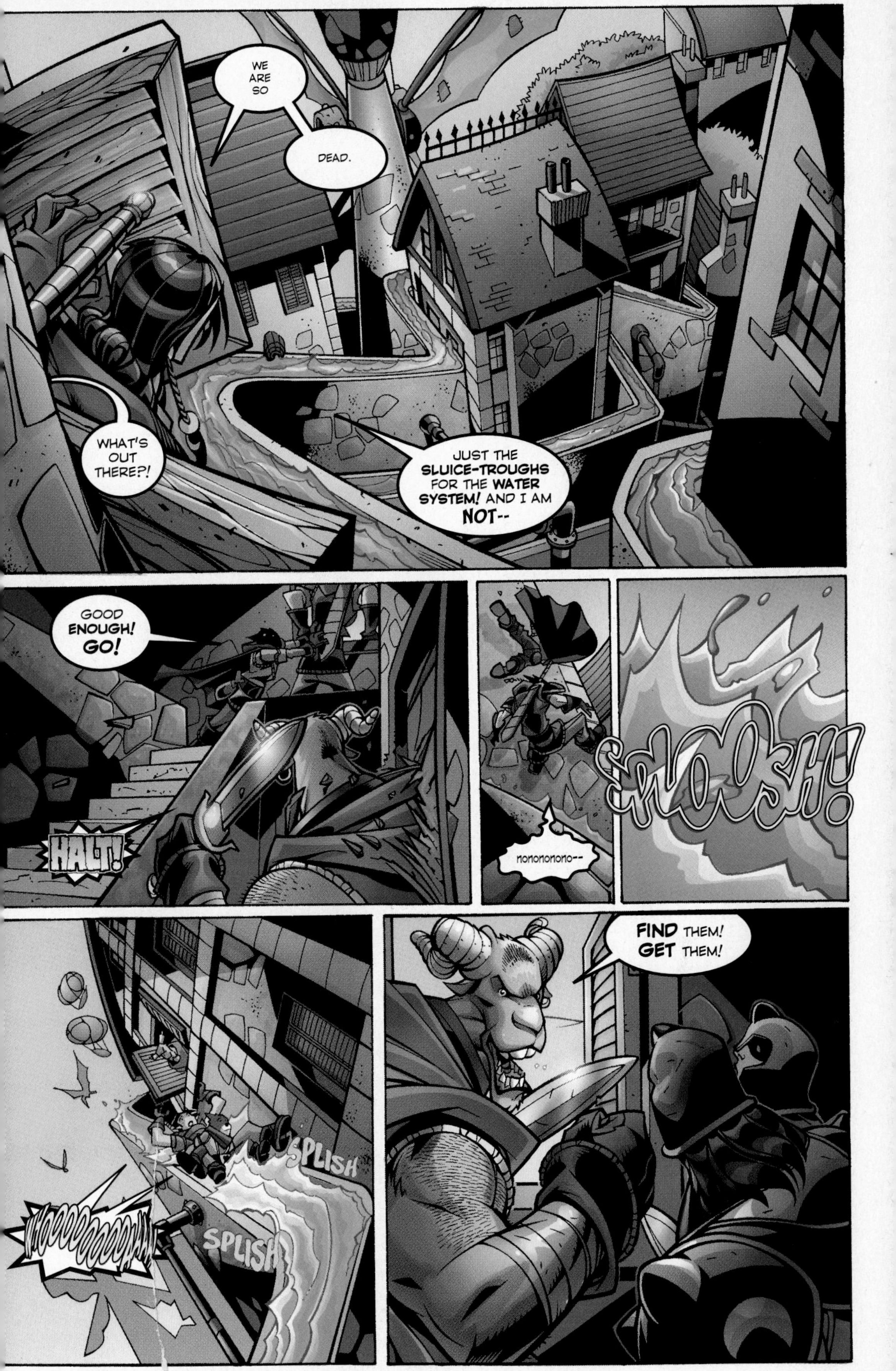
WE ARE SO
DEAD.
WHAT'S OUT THERE?!
JUST THE SLUICE-TROUGHS FOR THE WATER SYSTEM! AND I AM NOT--
GOOD ENOUGH! GO!
HALT!
nononononono--
SHOOSH!
SPLISH
SPLISH
FIND THEM! GET THEM!

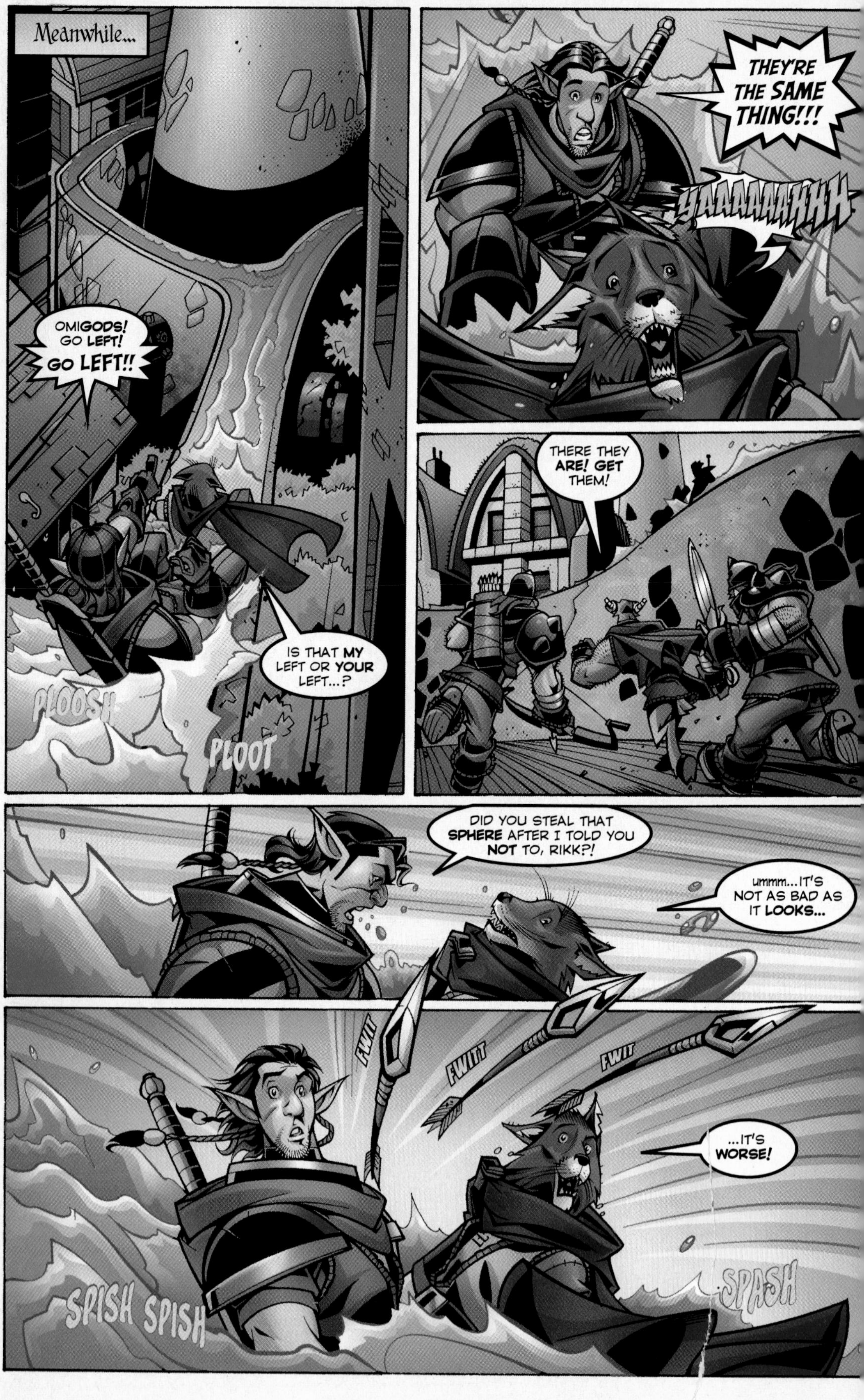
Meanwhile...
OMIGODS! GO LEFT! GO LEFT!!
IS THAT MY LEFT OR YOUR LEFT...?
PLOOSH
PLOOT
THEY'RE THE SAME THING!!!
YAAAAAAHHH
THERE THEY ARE! GET THEM!
DID YOU STEAL THAT SPHERE AFTER I TOLD YOU NOT TO, RIKK?!
ummm...IT'S NOT AS BAD AS IT LOOKS...
FWIT
FWITT
FWIT
...IT'S WORSE!
SPISH SPISH
SPASH

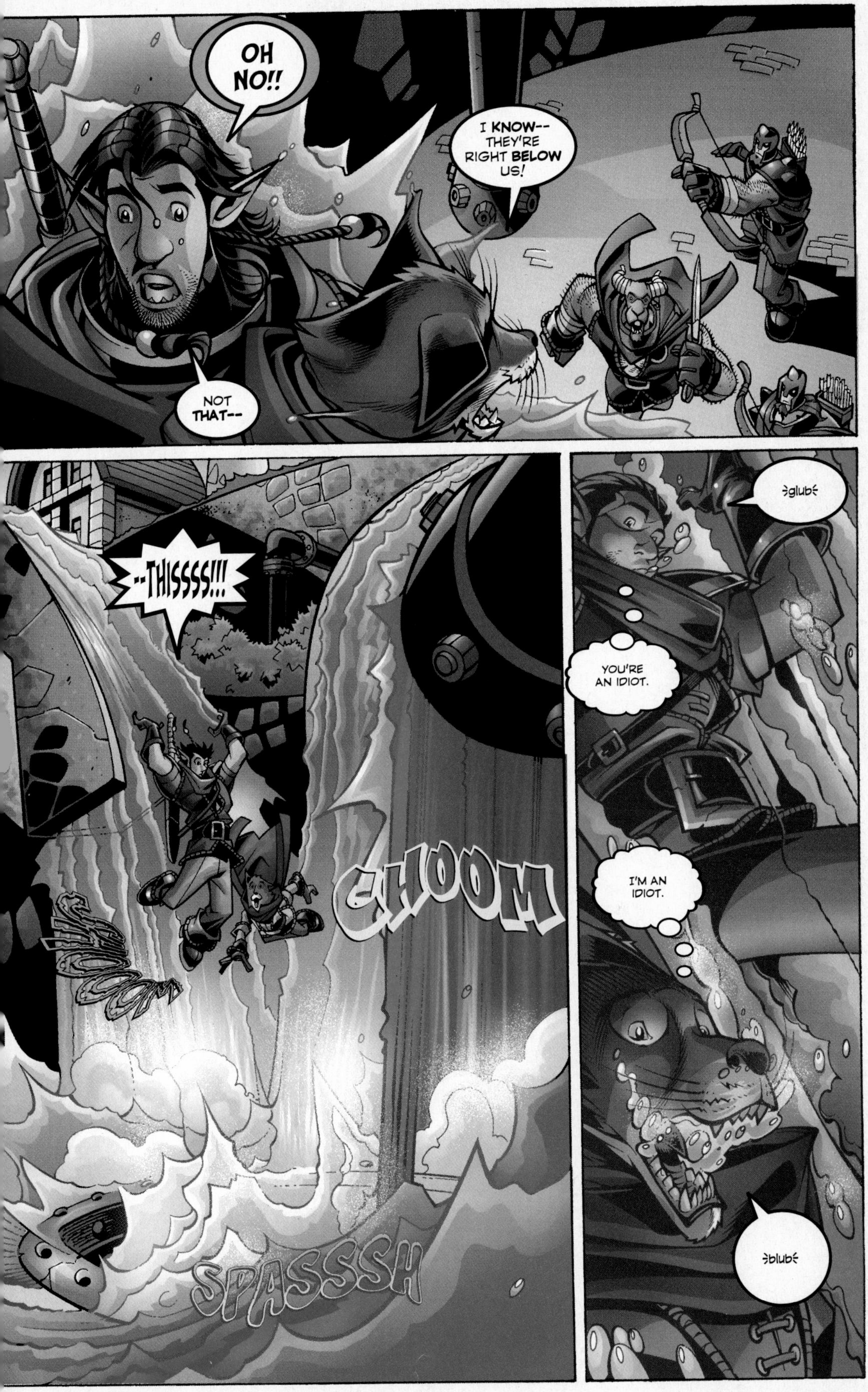
OH NO!!
I KNOW-- THEY'RE RIGHT BELOW US!
NOT THAT--
--THISSSS!!!
CHOOM
SPASSSH
glub
YOU'RE AN IDIOT.
I'M AN IDIOT.
blub

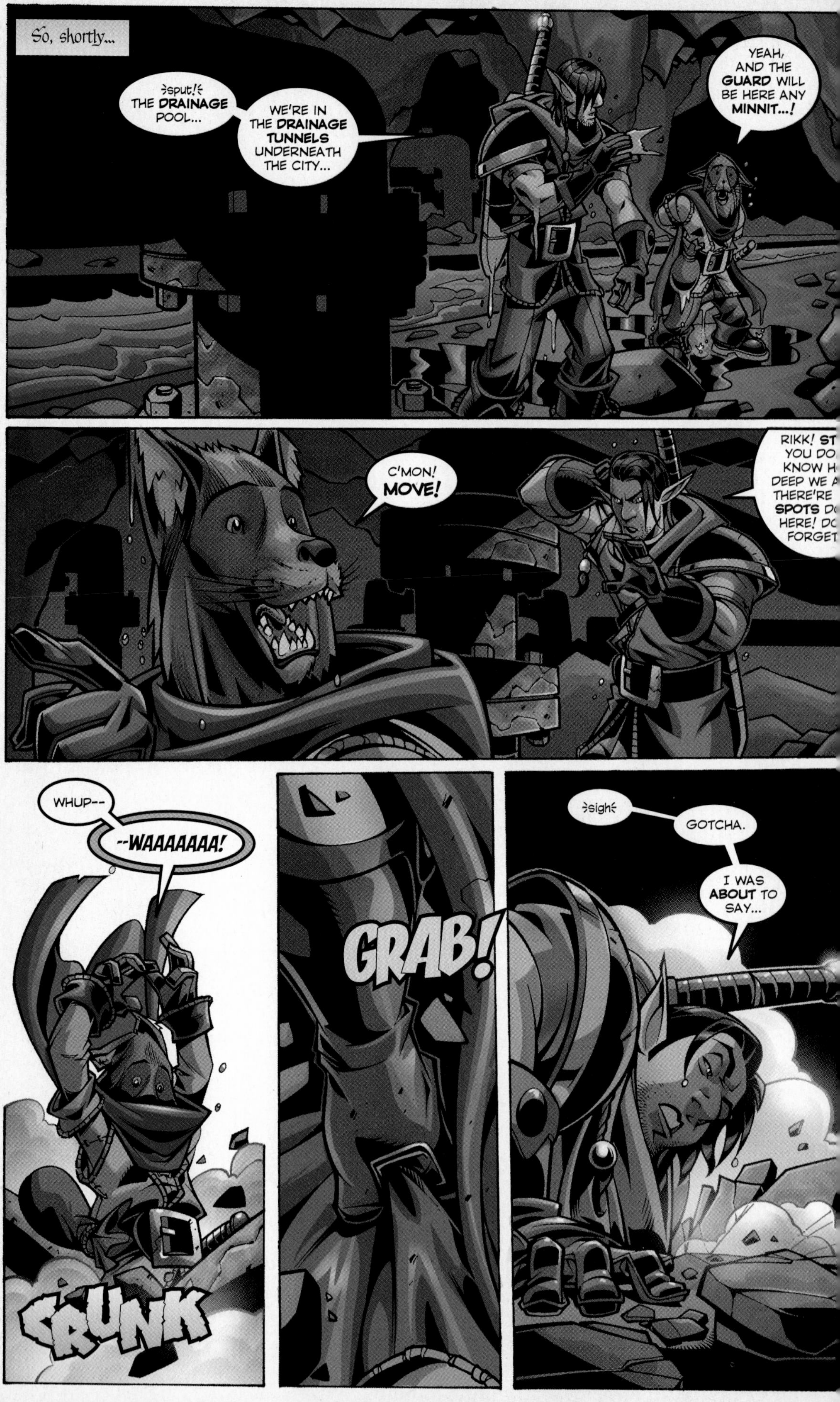
So, shortly...
⊰sput!⊱ THE DRAINAGE POOL...
WE'RE IN THE DRAINAGE TUNNELS UNDERNEATH THE CITY...
YEAH, AND THE GUARD WILL BE HERE ANY MINNIT...!
C'MON! MOVE!
RIKK! ST YOU DO KNOW H DEEP WE A THERE'RE SPOTS D HERE! DO FORGET
WHUP--
--WAAAAAAA!
CRUNK
GRAB!
⊰sigh⊱
GOTCHA.
I WAS ABOUT TO SAY...

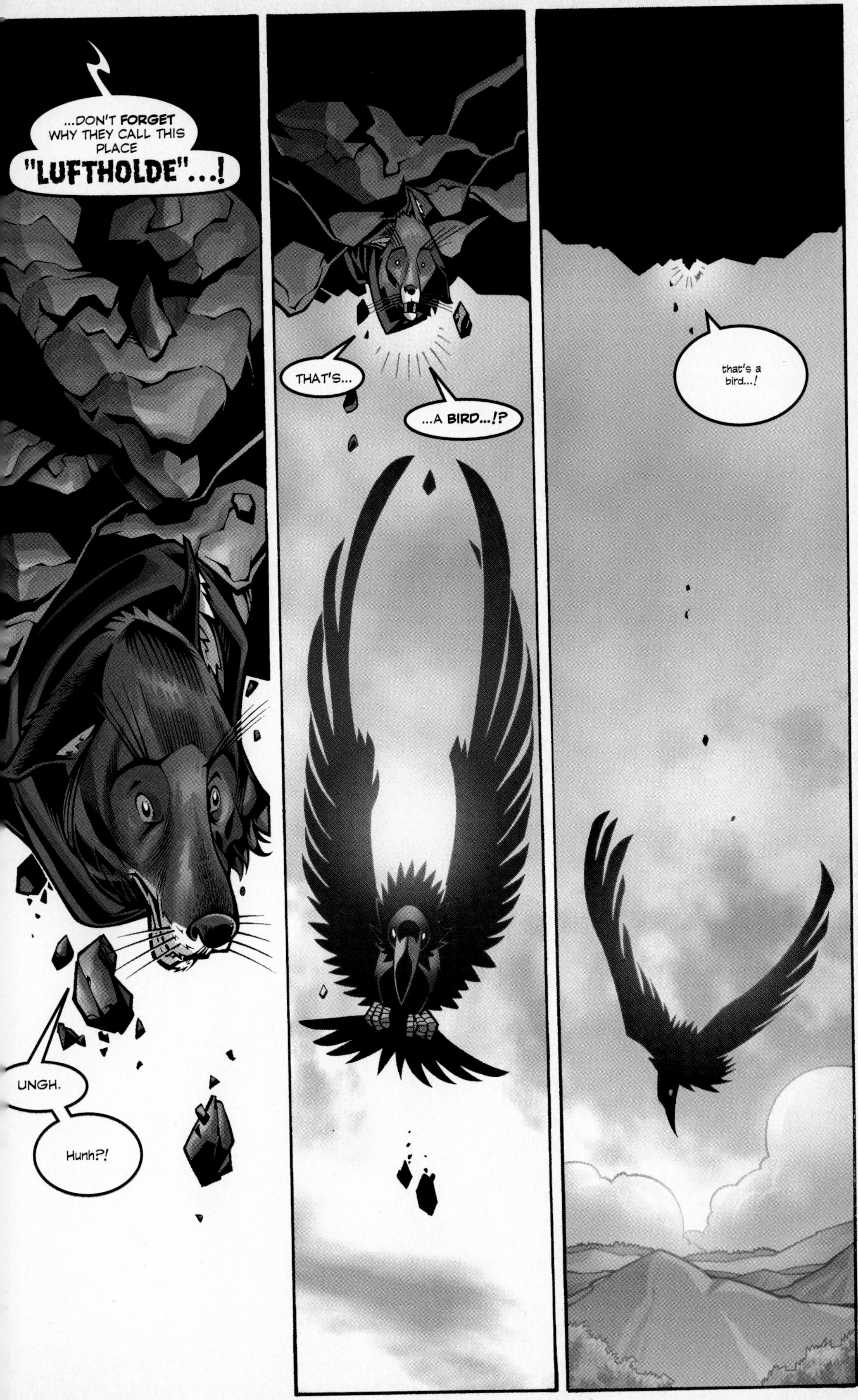
...DON'T FORGET WHY THEY CALL THIS PLACE "LUFTHOLDE"...!
UNGH.
Hunh?!
THAT'S...
...A BIRD...!?
that's a bird...!

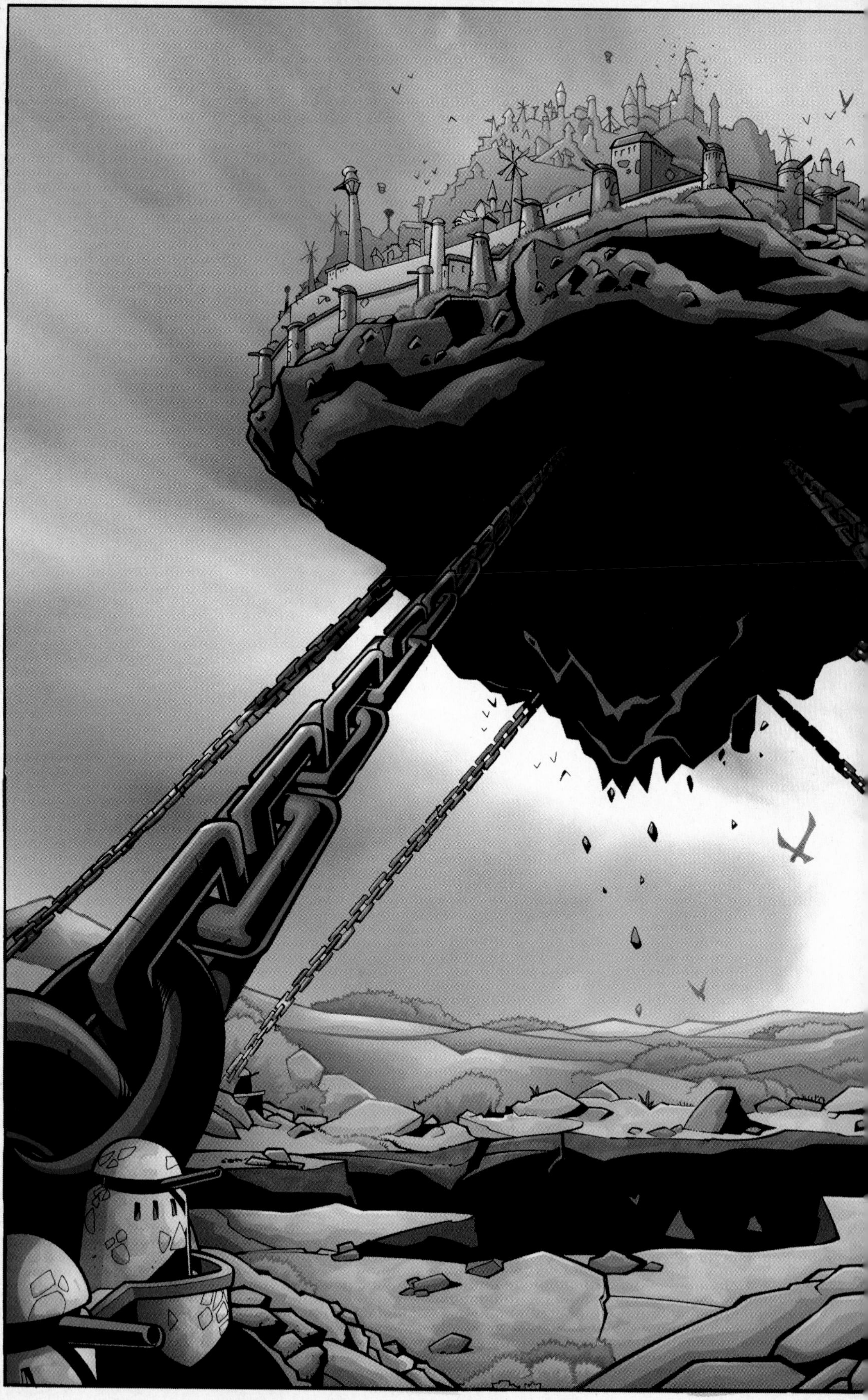

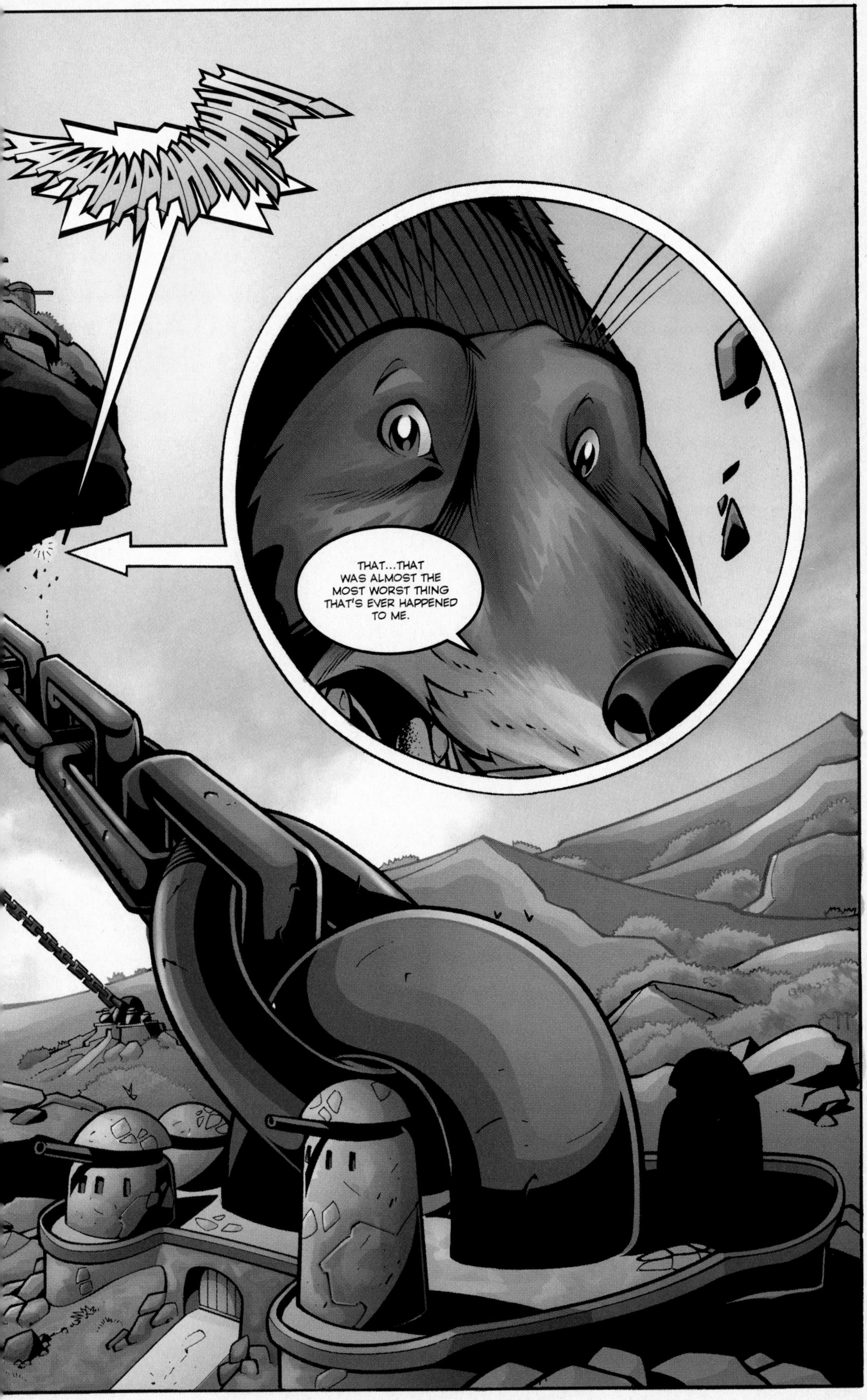
AAAAAAAAHHHH!!!
THAT...THAT WAS ALMOST THE MOST WORST THING THAT'S EVER HAPPENED TO ME.

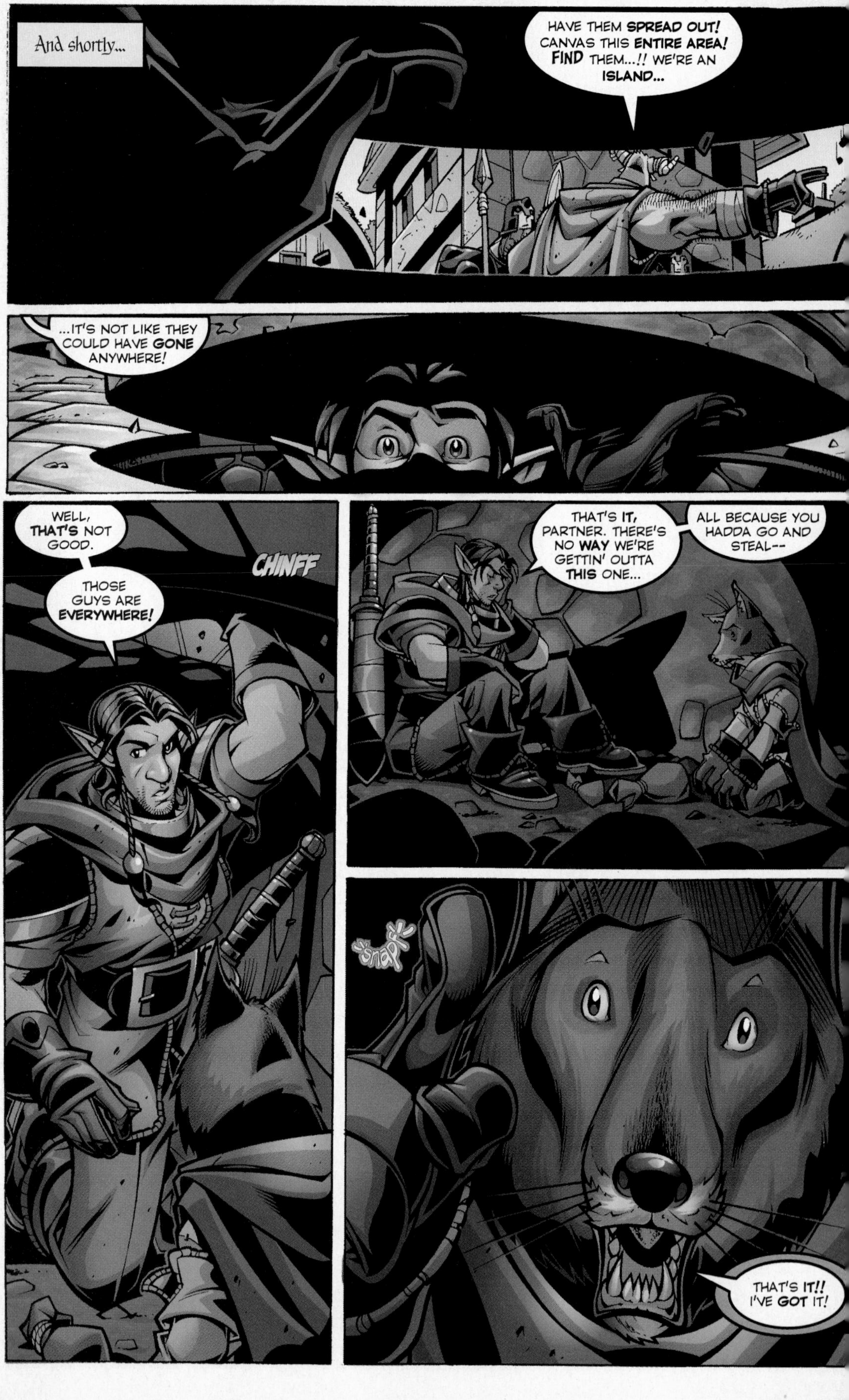
And shortly...
HAVE THEM SPREAD OUT! CANVAS THIS ENTIRE AREA! FIND THEM...!! WE'RE AN ISLAND...
...IT'S NOT LIKE THEY COULD HAVE GONE ANYWHERE!
WELL, THAT'S NOT GOOD.
THOSE GUYS ARE EVERYWHERE!
CHINFF
THAT'S IT, PARTNER. THERE'S NO WAY WE'RE GETTIN' OUTTA THIS ONE...
ALL BECAUSE YOU HADDA GO AND STEAL--
snap
THAT'S IT!! I'VE GOT IT!

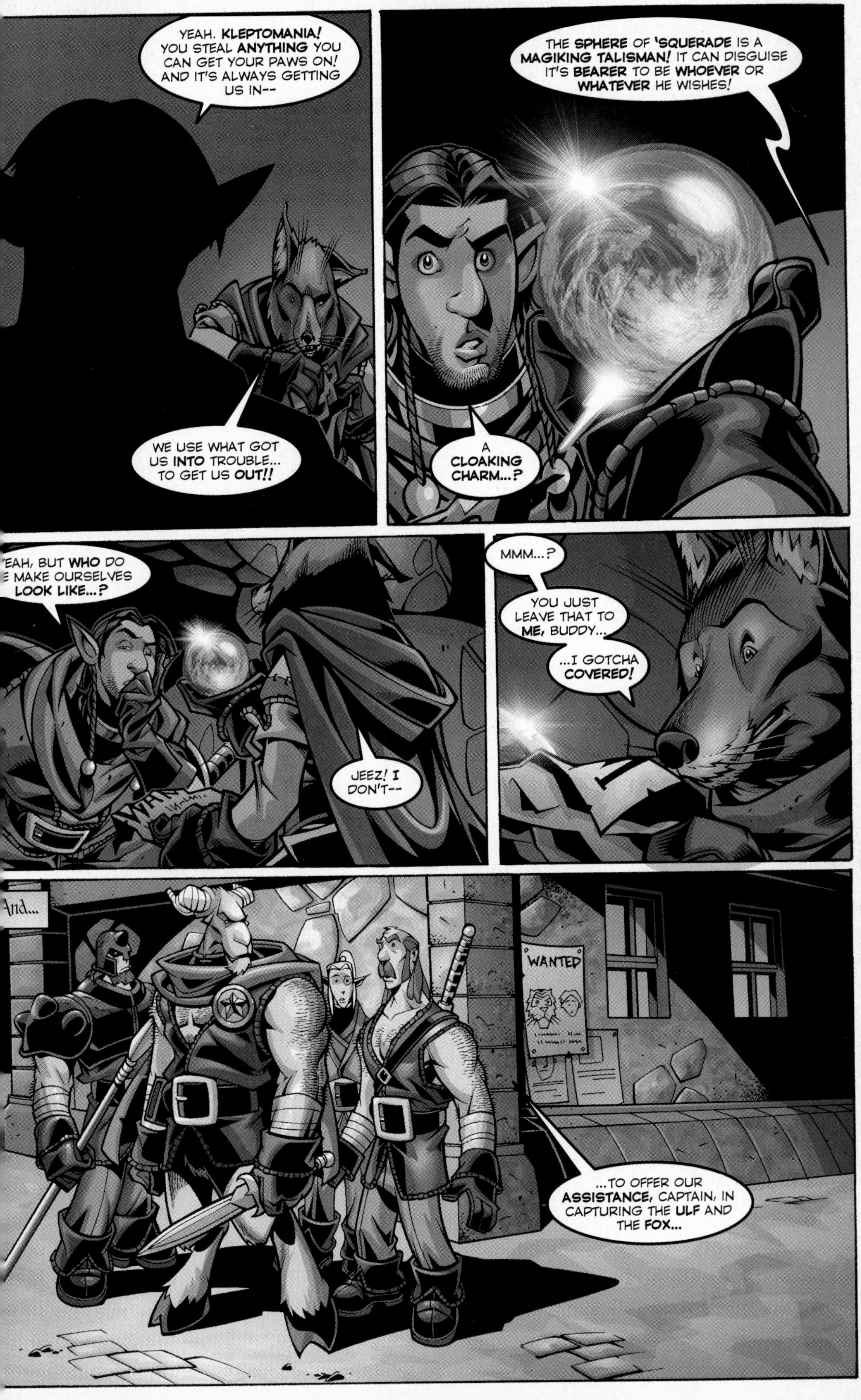

YEAH. KLEPTOMANIA! YOU STEAL ANYTHING YOU CAN GET YOUR PAWS ON! AND IT'S ALWAYS GETTING US IN--
WE USE WHAT GOT US INTO TROUBLE... TO GET US OUT!!
THE SPHERE OF 'SQUERADE IS A MAGIKING TALISMAN! IT CAN DISGUISE IT'S BEARER TO BE WHOEVER OR WHATEVER HE WISHES!
A CLOAKING CHARM...?
EAH, BUT WHO DO E MAKE OURSELVES LOOK LIKE...?
JEEZ! I DON'T--
MMM...?
YOU JUST LEAVE THAT TO ME, BUDDY...
...I GOTCHA COVERED!
And...
WANTED
...TO OFFER OUR ASSISTANCE, CAPTAIN, IN CAPTURING THE ULF AND THE FOX...

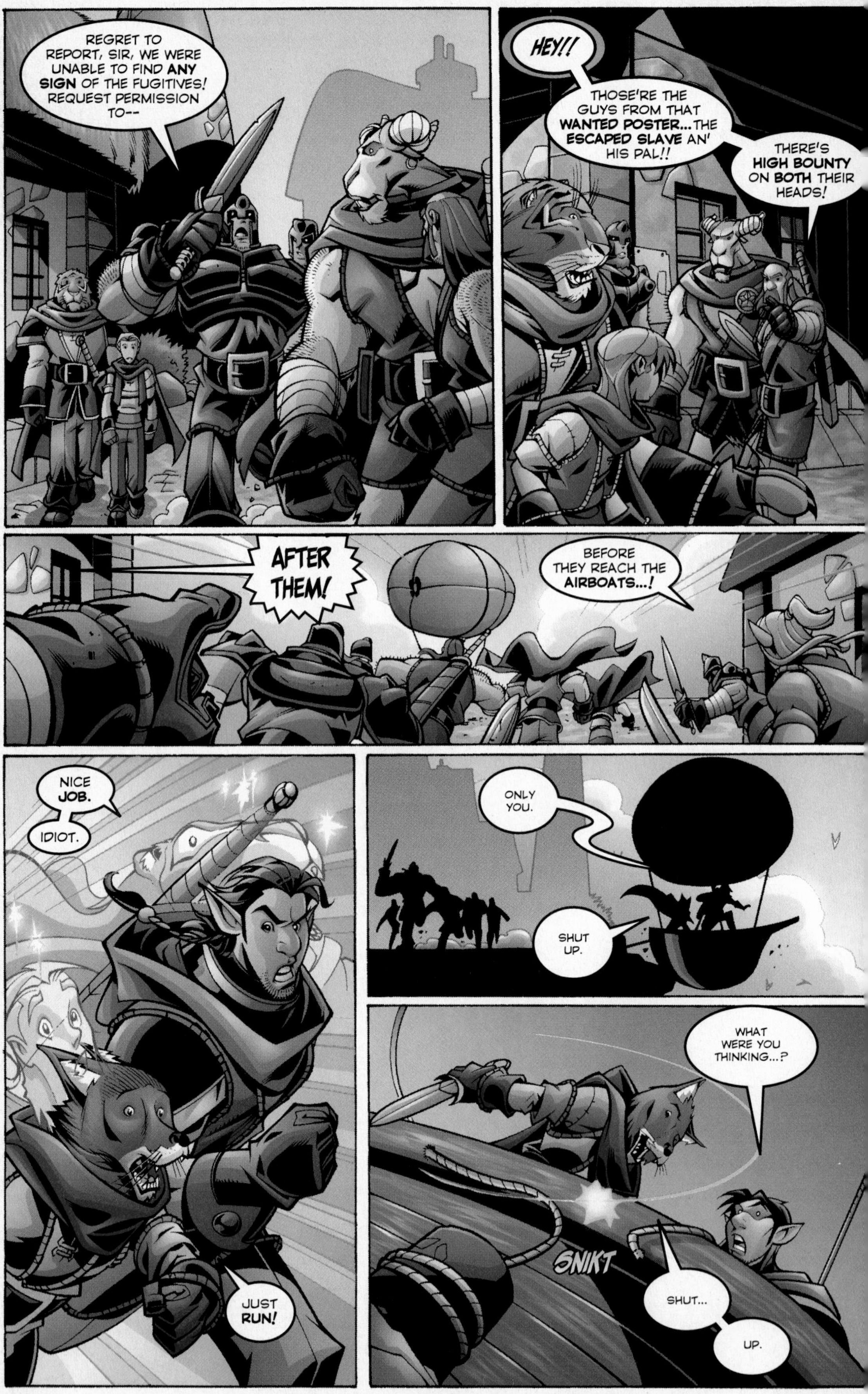
REGRET TO REPORT, SIR, WE WERE UNABLE TO FIND ANY SIGN OF THE FUGITIVES! REQUEST PERMISSION TO--
HEY!!
THOSE'RE THE GUYS FROM THAT WANTED POSTER... THE ESCAPED SLAVE AN' HIS PAL!!
THERE'S HIGH BOUNTY ON BOTH THEIR HEADS!
AFTER THEM!
BEFORE THEY REACH THE AIRBOATS...!
NICE JOB.
IDIOT.
JUST RUN!
ONLY YOU.
SHUT UP.
WHAT WERE YOU THINKING...?
SNIKT
SHUT...
UP.

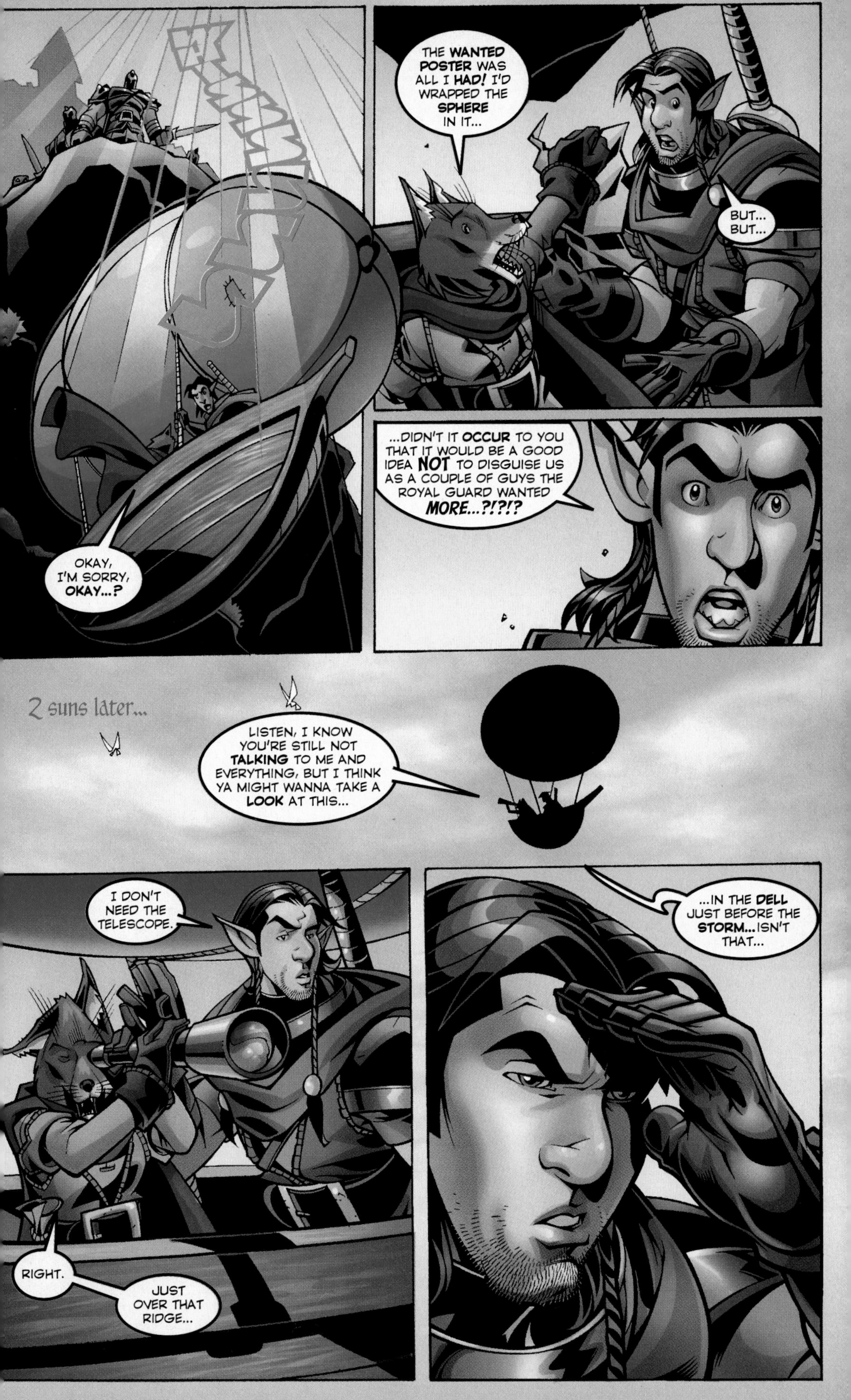
THE WANTED POSTER WAS ALL I HAD! I'D WRAPPED THE SPHERE IN IT...
BUT... BUT...
...DIDN'T IT OCCUR TO YOU THAT IT WOULD BE A GOOD IDEA NOT TO DISGUISE US AS A COUPLE OF GUYS THE ROYAL GUARD WANTED MORE...?!?!?
OKAY, I'M SORRY, OKAY...?
2 suns later...
LISTEN, I KNOW YOU'RE STILL NOT TALKING TO ME AND EVERYTHING, BUT I THINK YA MIGHT WANNA TAKE A LOOK AT THIS...
I DON'T NEED THE TELESCOPE.
RIGHT.
JUST OVER THAT RIDGE...
...IN THE DELL JUST BEFORE THE STORM...ISN'T THAT...

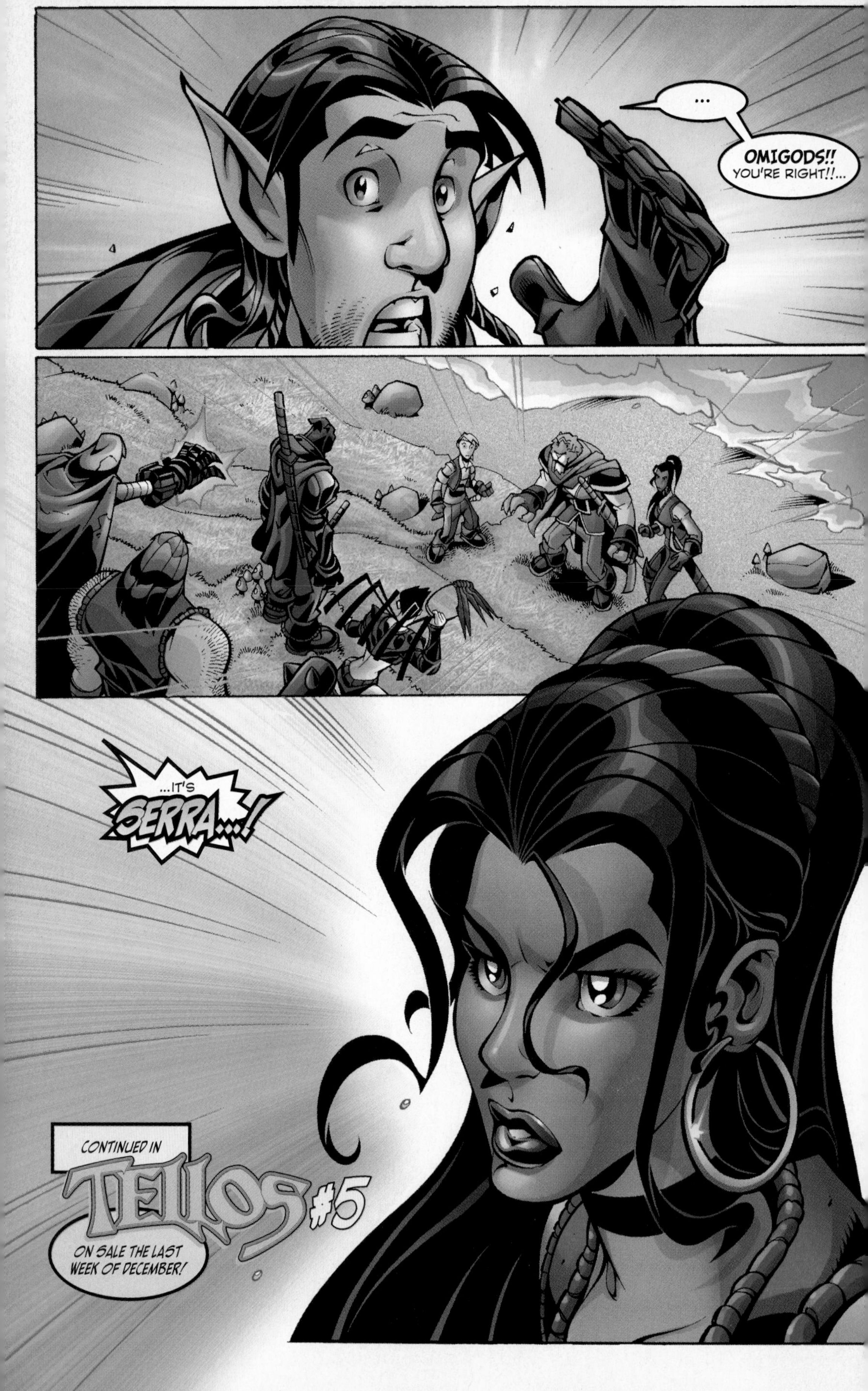

...
OMIGODS!! YOU'RE RIGHT!!...
...IT'S SERRA...!
CONTINUED IN
TELLOS #5
ON SALE THE LAST WEEK OF DECEMBER!

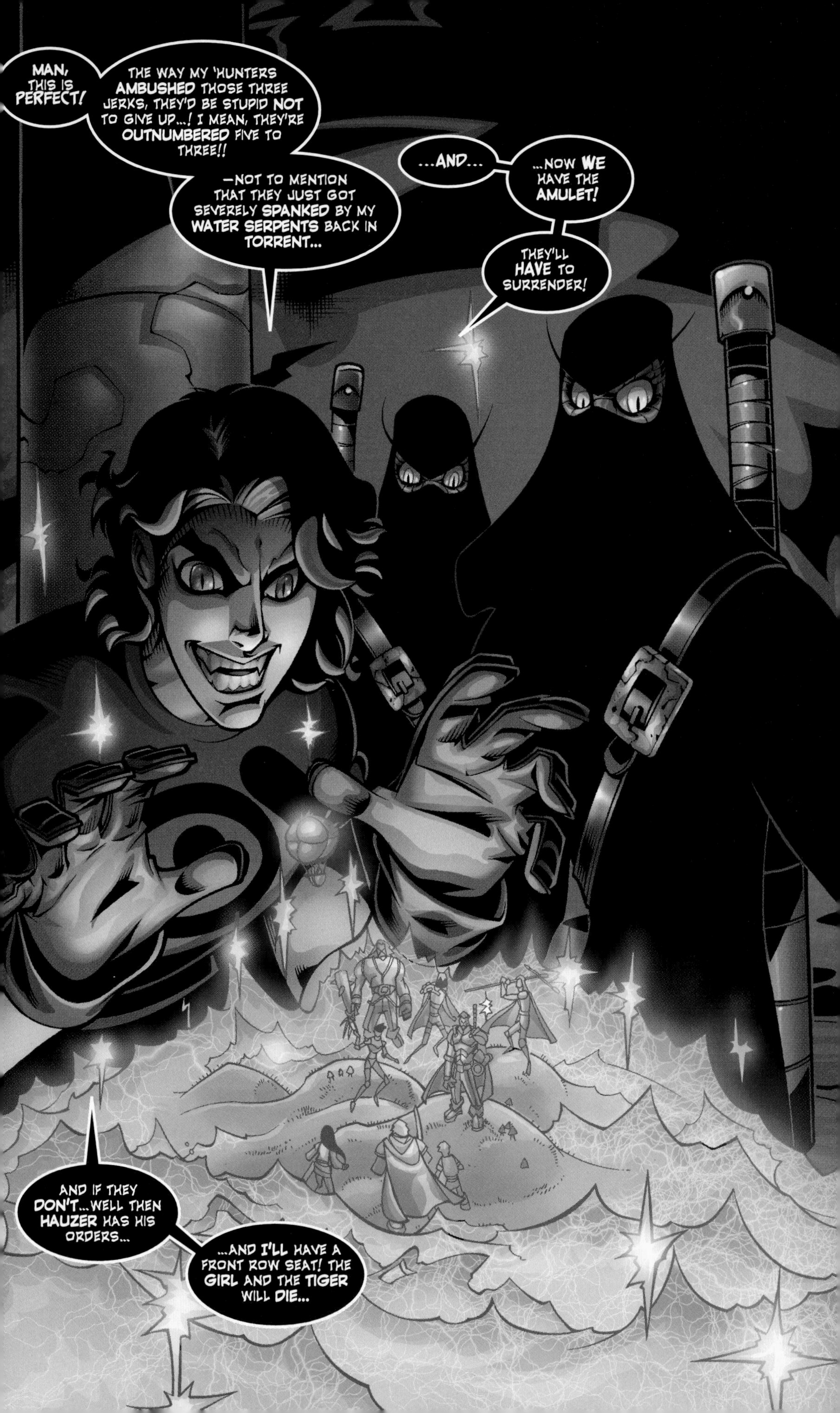
MAN, THIS IS PERFECT!
THE WAY MY 'HUNTERS AMBUSHED THOSE THREE JERKS, THEY'D BE STUPID NOT TO GIVE UP...! I MEAN, THEY'RE OUTNUMBERED FIVE TO THREE!!
—NOT TO MENTION THAT THEY JUST GOT SEVERELY SPANKED BY MY WATER SERPENTS BACK IN TORRENT...
...AND...
...NOW WE HAVE THE AMULET!
THEY'LL HAVE TO SURRENDER!
AND IF THEY DON'T...WELL THEN HAUZER HAS HIS ORDERS...
...AND I'LL HAVE A FRONT ROW SEAT! THE GIRL AND THE TIGER WILL DIE...

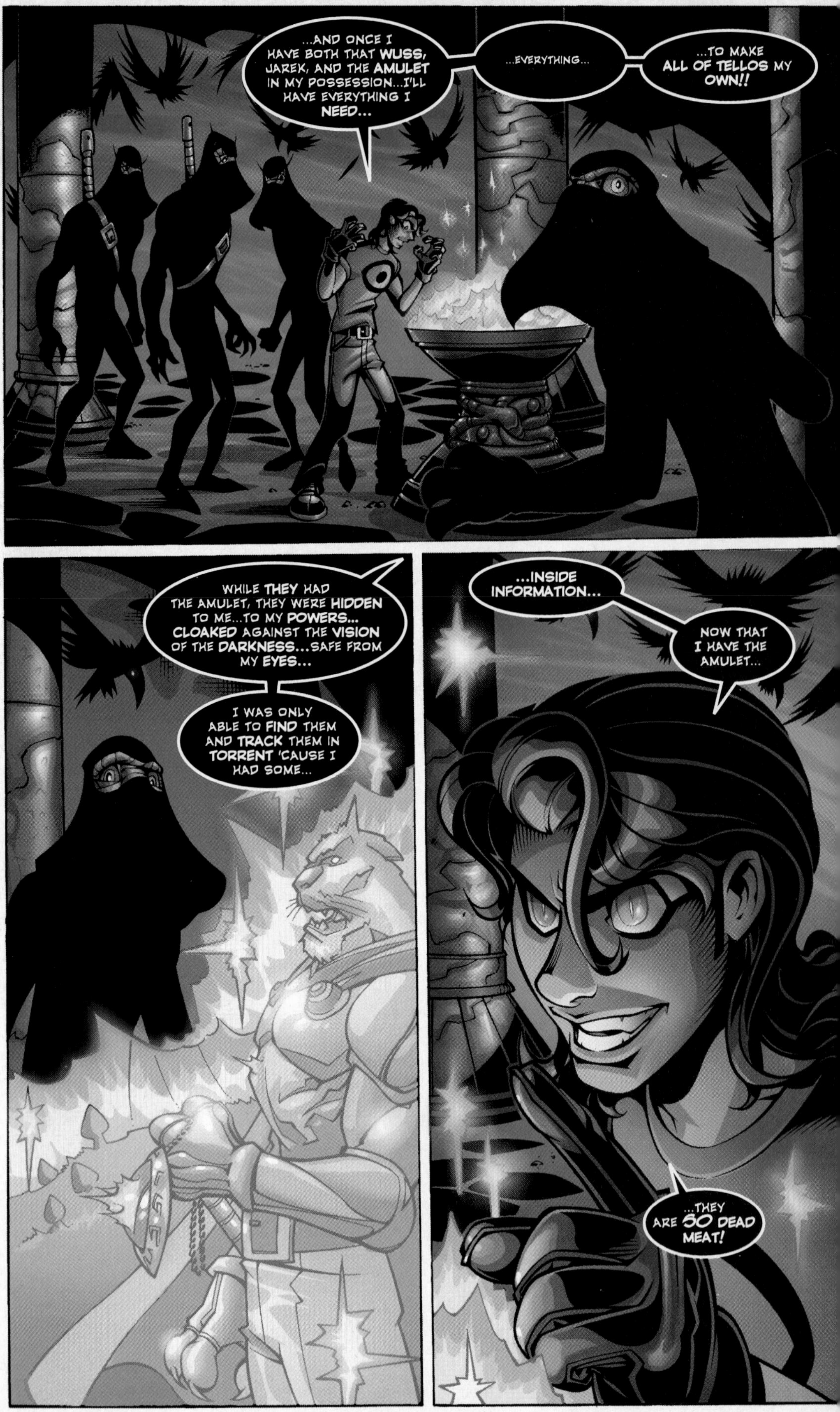
...AND ONCE I HAVE BOTH THAT WUSS, JAREK, AND THE AMULET IN MY POSSESSION...I'LL HAVE EVERYTHING I NEED...
...EVERYTHING...
...TO MAKE ALL OF TELLOS MY OWN!!
WHILE THEY HAD THE AMULET, THEY WERE HIDDEN TO ME...TO MY POWERS... CLOAKED AGAINST THE VISION OF THE DARKNESS...SAFE FROM MY EYES...
I WAS ONLY ABLE TO FIND THEM AND TRACK THEM IN TORRENT 'CAUSE I HAD SOME...
...INSIDE INFORMATION...
NOW THAT I HAVE THE AMULET...
...THEY ARE SO DEAD MEAT!

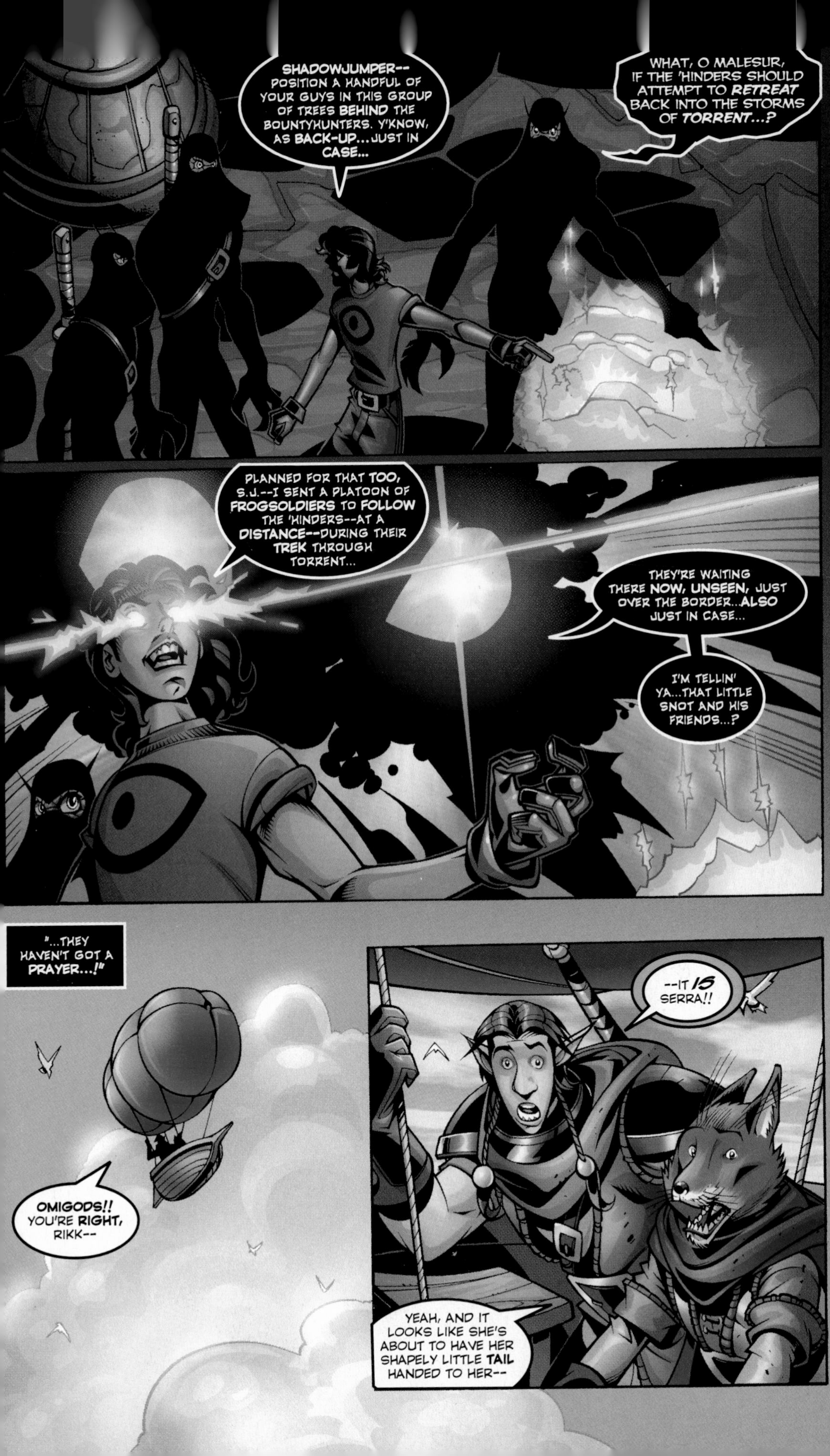
SHADOWJUMPER--POSITION A HANDFUL OF YOUR GUYS IN THIS GROUP OF TREES BEHIND THE BOUNTYHUNTERS. Y'KNOW, AS BACK-UP...JUST IN CASE...
WHAT, O MALESUR, IF THE 'HINDERS SHOULD ATTEMPT TO RETREAT BACK INTO THE STORMS OF TORRENT...?
PLANNED FOR THAT TOO, S.J.--I SENT A PLATOON OF FROGSOLDIERS TO FOLLOW THE 'HINDERS--AT A DISTANCE--DURING THEIR TREK THROUGH TORRENT...
THEY'RE WAITING THERE NOW, UNSEEN, JUST OVER THE BORDER...ALSO JUST IN CASE...
I'M TELLIN' YA...THAT LITTLE SNOT AND HIS FRIENDS...?
"...THEY HAVEN'T GOT A PRAYER...!"
OMIGODS!! YOU'RE RIGHT, RIKK--
--IT IS SERRA!!
YEAH, AND IT LOOKS LIKE SHE'S ABOUT TO HAVE HER SHAPELY LITTLE TAIL HANDED TO HER--

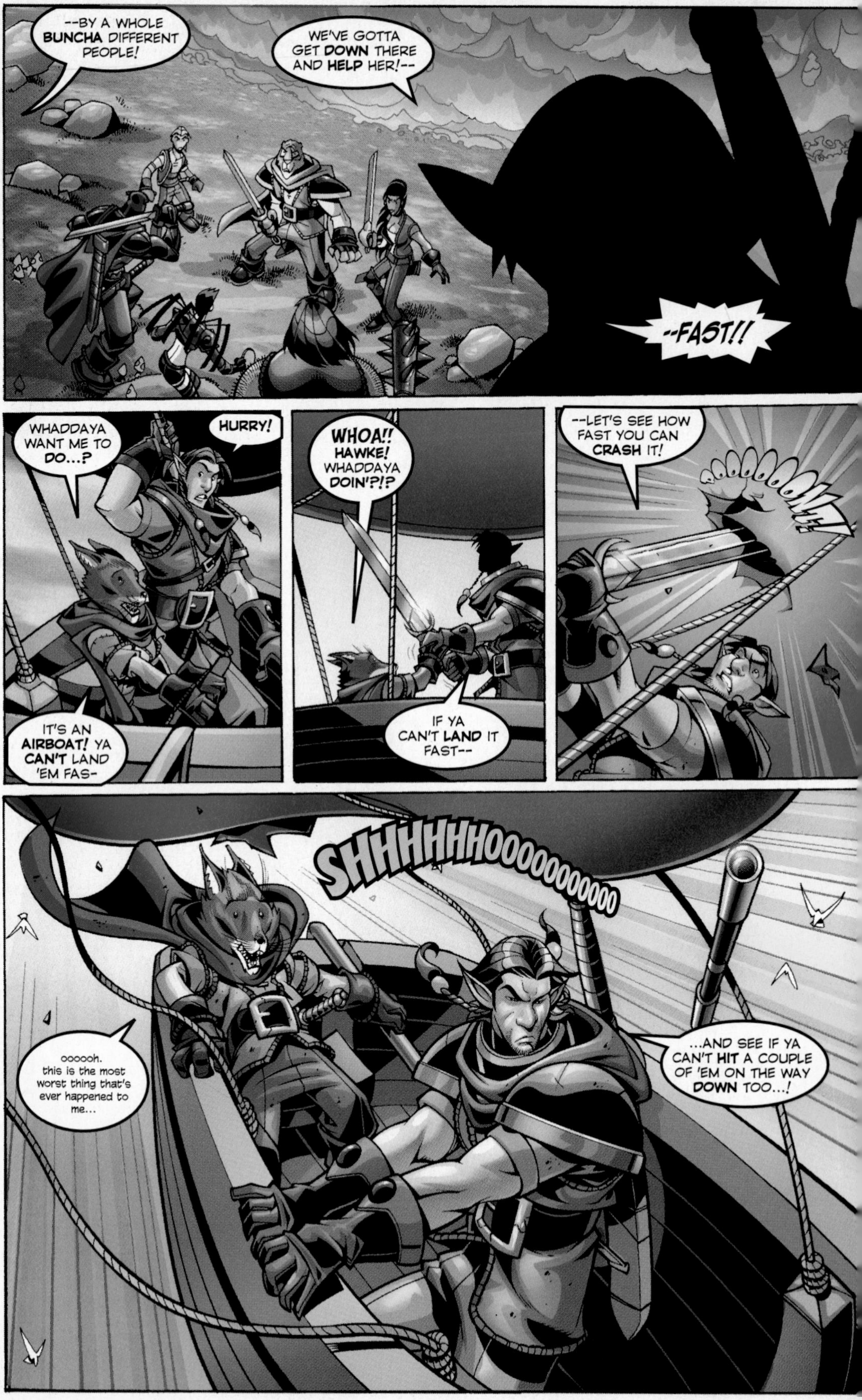

--BY A WHOLE BUNCHA DIFFERENT PEOPLE!
WE'VE GOTTA GET DOWN THERE AND HELP HER!--
--FAST!!
WHADDAYA WANT ME TO DO...?
HURRY!
IT'S AN AIRBOAT! YA CAN'T LAND 'EM FAS-
WHOA!! HAWKE! WHADDAYA DOIN'?!?
IF YA CAN'T LAND IT FAST--
--LET'S SEE HOW FAST YOU CAN CRASH IT!
SHHHHHHOOOOOOOOOOOO
oooooh. this is the most worst thing that's ever happened to me...
...AND SEE IF YA CAN'T HIT A COUPLE OF 'EM ON THE WAY DOWN TOO...!

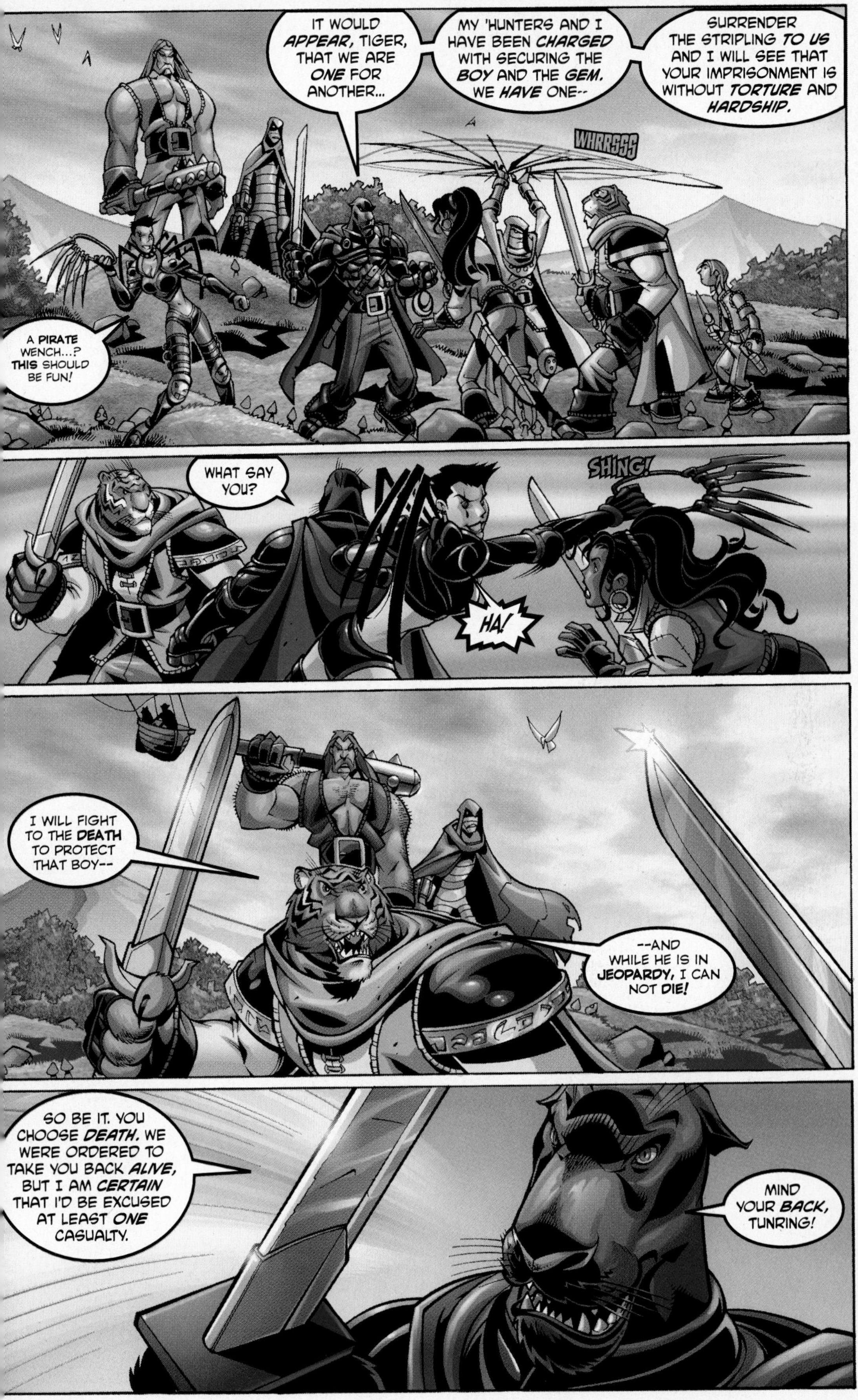
IT WOULD APPEAR, TIGER, THAT WE ARE ONE FOR ANOTHER...
MY 'HUNTERS AND I HAVE BEEN CHARGED WITH SECURING THE BOY AND THE GEM. WE HAVE ONE--
SURRENDER THE STRIPLING TO US AND I WILL SEE THAT YOUR IMPRISONMENT IS WITHOUT TORTURE AND HARDSHIP.
WHRRSSS
A PIRATE WENCH...? THIS SHOULD BE FUN!
WHAT SAY YOU?
SHING!
HA!
I WILL FIGHT TO THE DEATH TO PROTECT THAT BOY--
--AND WHILE HE IS IN JEOPARDY, I CAN NOT DIE!
SO BE IT. YOU CHOOSE DEATH. WE WERE ORDERED TO TAKE YOU BACK ALIVE, BUT I AM CERTAIN THAT I'D BE EXCUSED AT LEAST ONE CASUALTY.
MIND YOUR BACK, TUNRING!

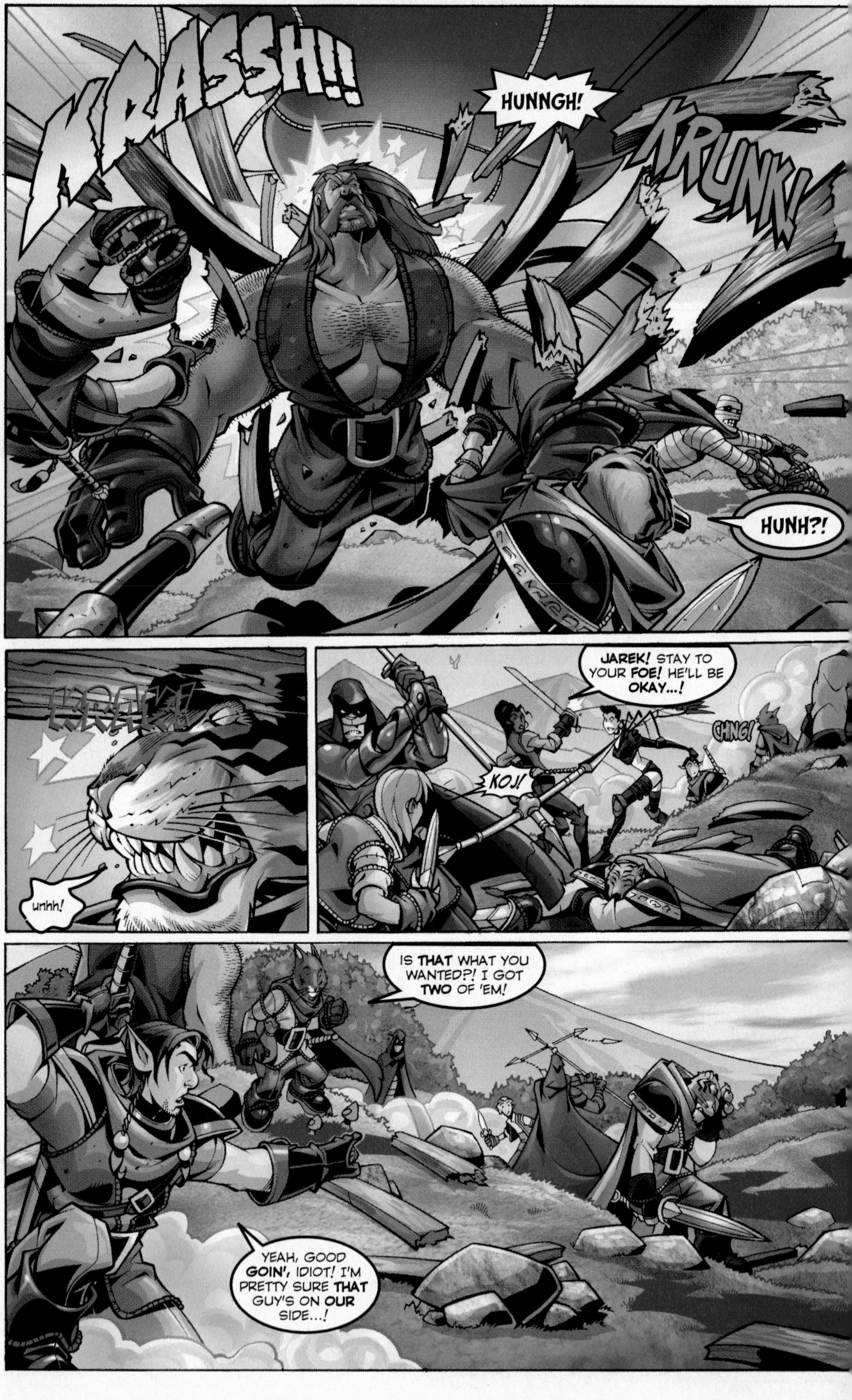

KRASSH!!
HUNNGH!
KRUNK!
HUNH?!
unhh!
JAREK! STAY TO YOUR FOE! HE'LL BE OKAY...!
KOJ!
CHNG!
IS THAT WHAT YOU WANTED?! I GOT TWO OF 'EM!
YEAH, GOOD GOIN', IDIOT! I'M PRETTY SURE THAT GUY'S ON OUR SIDE...!

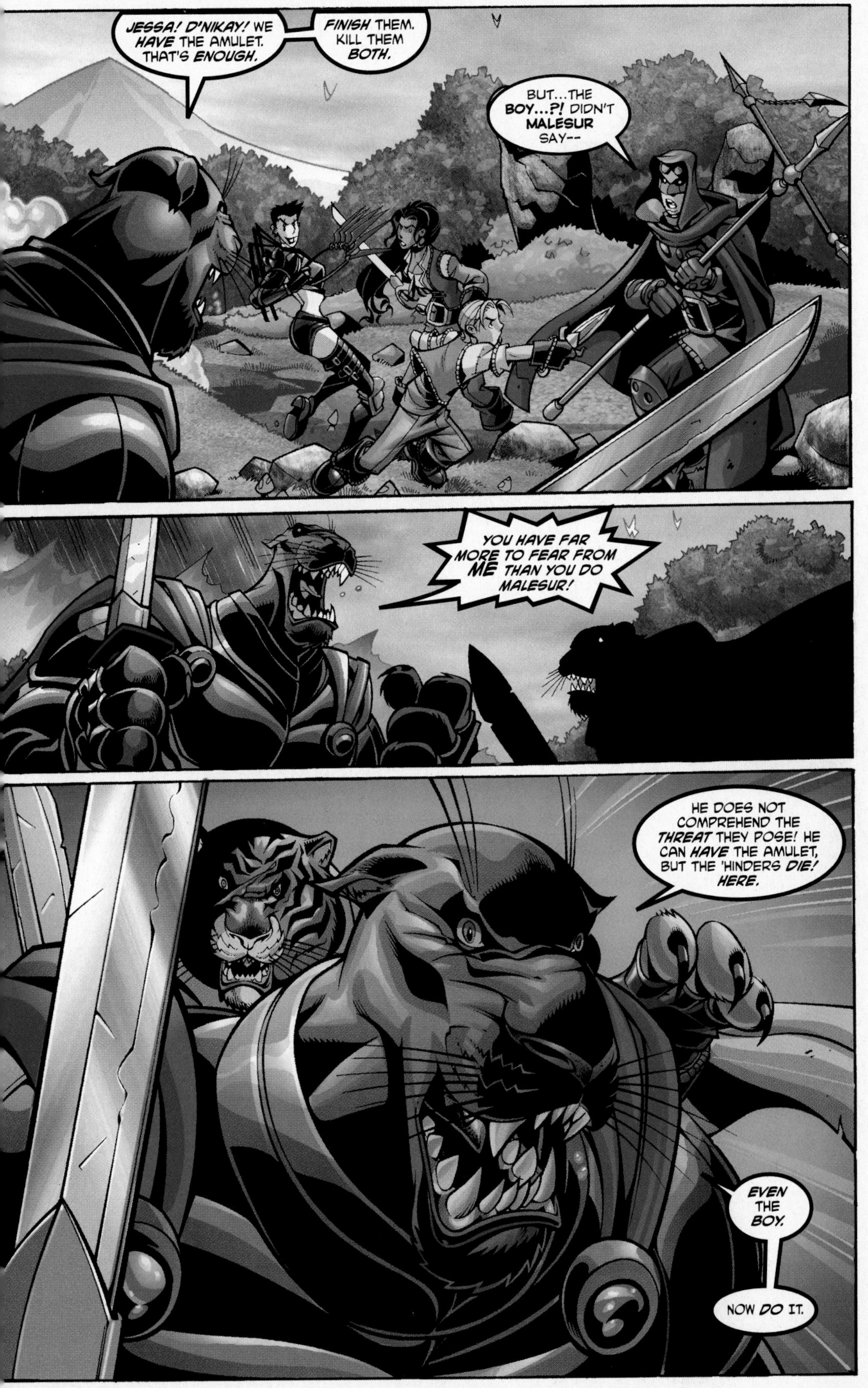
JESSA! D'NIKAY! WE HAVE THE AMULET. THAT'S ENOUGH.
FINISH THEM. KILL THEM BOTH.
BUT...THE BOY...?! DIDN'T MALESUR SAY--
YOU HAVE FAR MORE TO FEAR FROM ME THAN YOU DO MALESUR!
HE DOES NOT COMPREHEND THE THREAT THEY POSE! HE CAN HAVE THE AMULET, BUT THE 'HINDERS DIE! HERE.
EVEN THE BOY.
NOW DO IT.

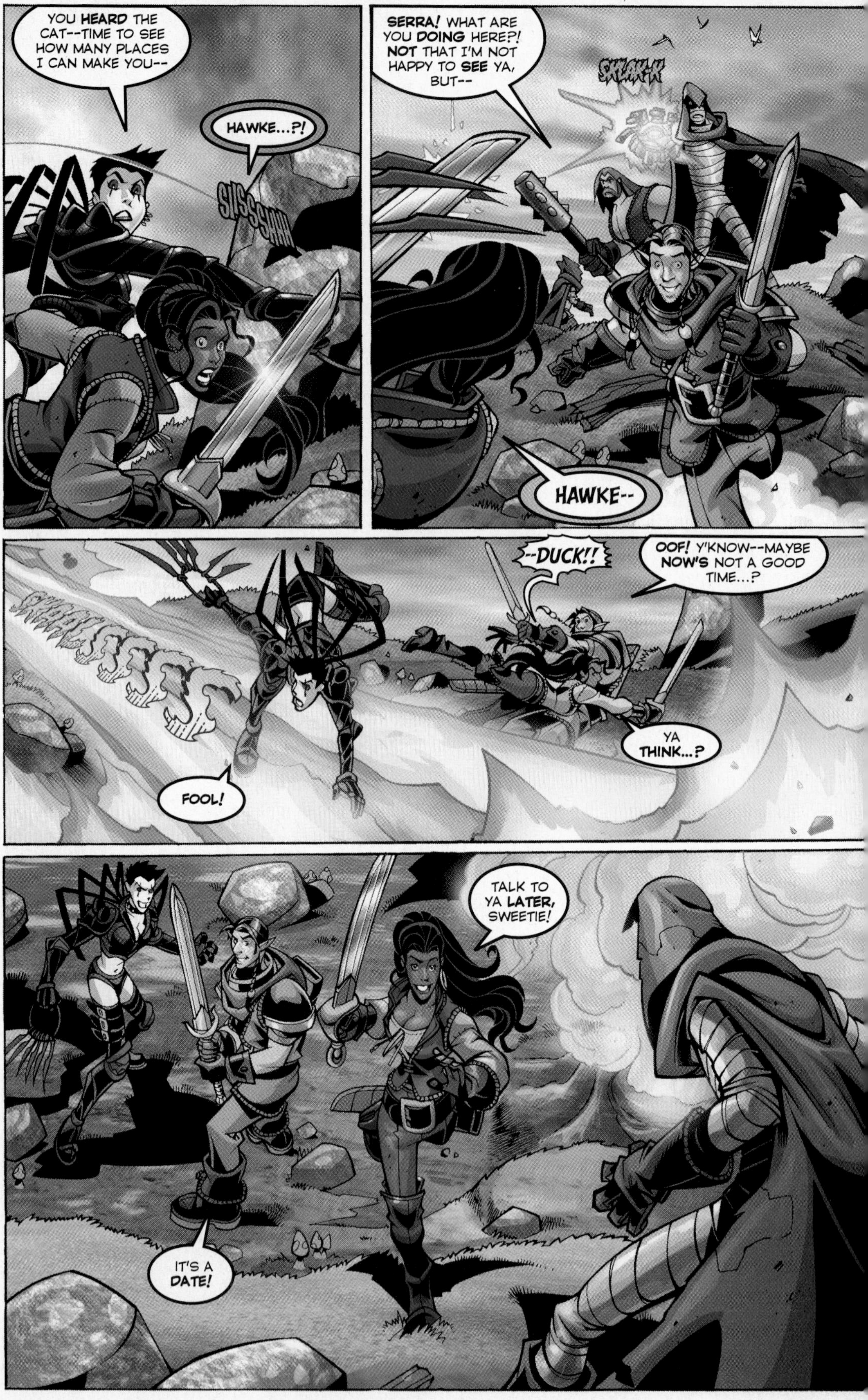
YOU HEARD THE CAT--TIME TO SEE HOW MANY PLACES I CAN MAKE YOU--
HAWKE...?!
SLISSSHHH
SERRA! WHAT ARE YOU DOING HERE?! NOT THAT I'M NOT HAPPY TO SEE YA, BUT--
SKLAK-K
HAWKE--
--DUCK!!
OOF! Y'KNOW--MAYBE NOW'S NOT A GOOD TIME...?
YA THINK...?
FOOL!
TALK TO YA LATER, SWEETIE!
IT'S A DATE!

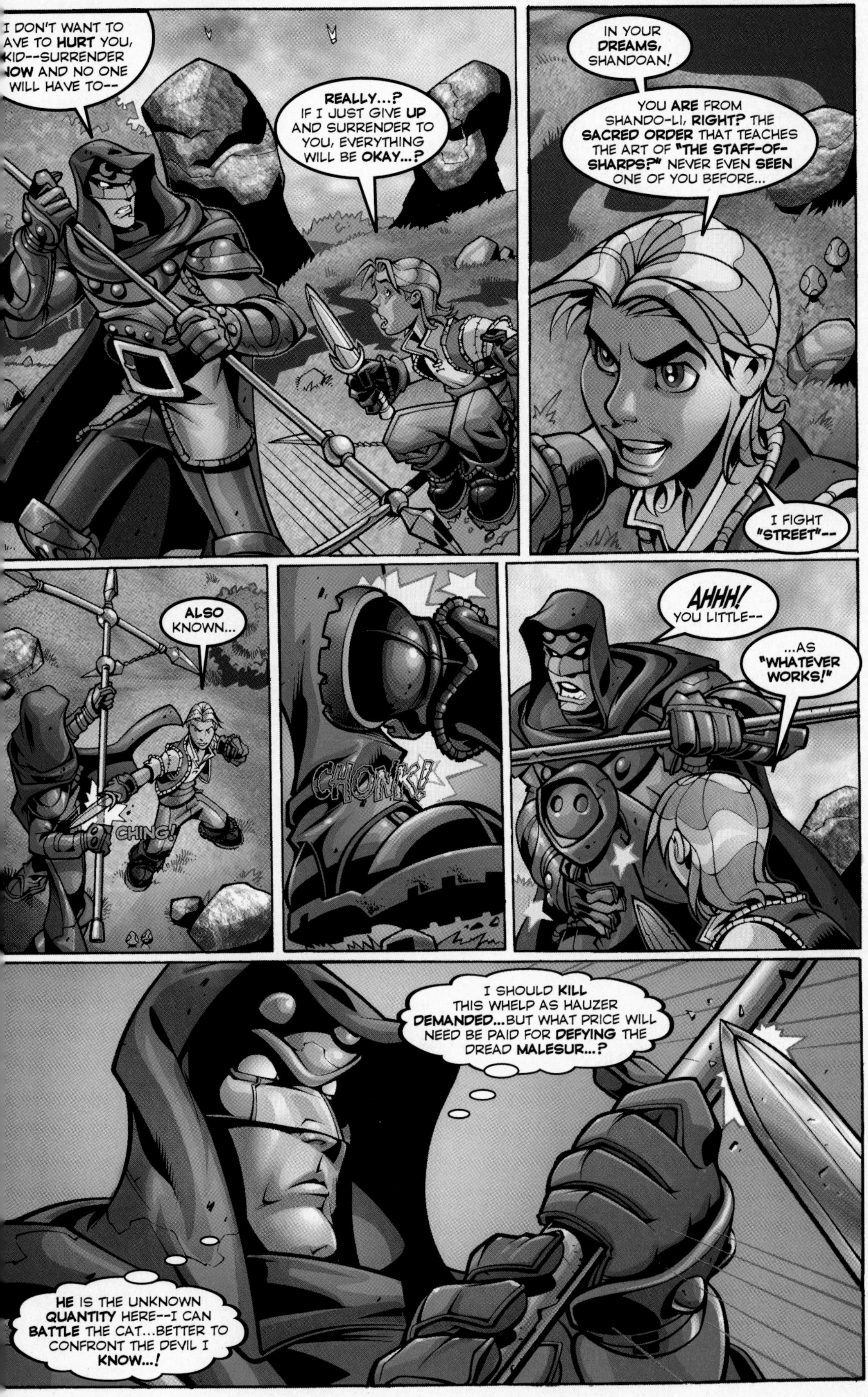
I DON'T WANT TO AVE TO HURT YOU, KID--SURRENDER NOW AND NO ONE WILL HAVE TO--
REALLY...? IF I JUST GIVE UP AND SURRENDER TO YOU, EVERYTHING WILL BE OKAY...?
IN YOUR DREAMS, SHANDOAN!
YOU ARE FROM SHANDO-LI, RIGHT? THE SACRED ORDER THAT TEACHES THE ART OF "THE STAFF-OF-SHARPS?" NEVER EVEN SEEN ONE OF YOU BEFORE...
I FIGHT "STREET"--
ALSO KNOWN...
CHING!
CHONK!
AHHH! YOU LITTLE--
...AS "WHATEVER WORKS!"
I SHOULD KILL THIS WHELP AS HAUZER DEMANDED...BUT WHAT PRICE WILL NEED BE PAID FOR DEFYING THE DREAD MALESUR...?
HE IS THE UNKNOWN QUANTITY HERE--I CAN BATTLE THE CAT...BETTER TO CONFRONT THE DEVIL I KNOW...!

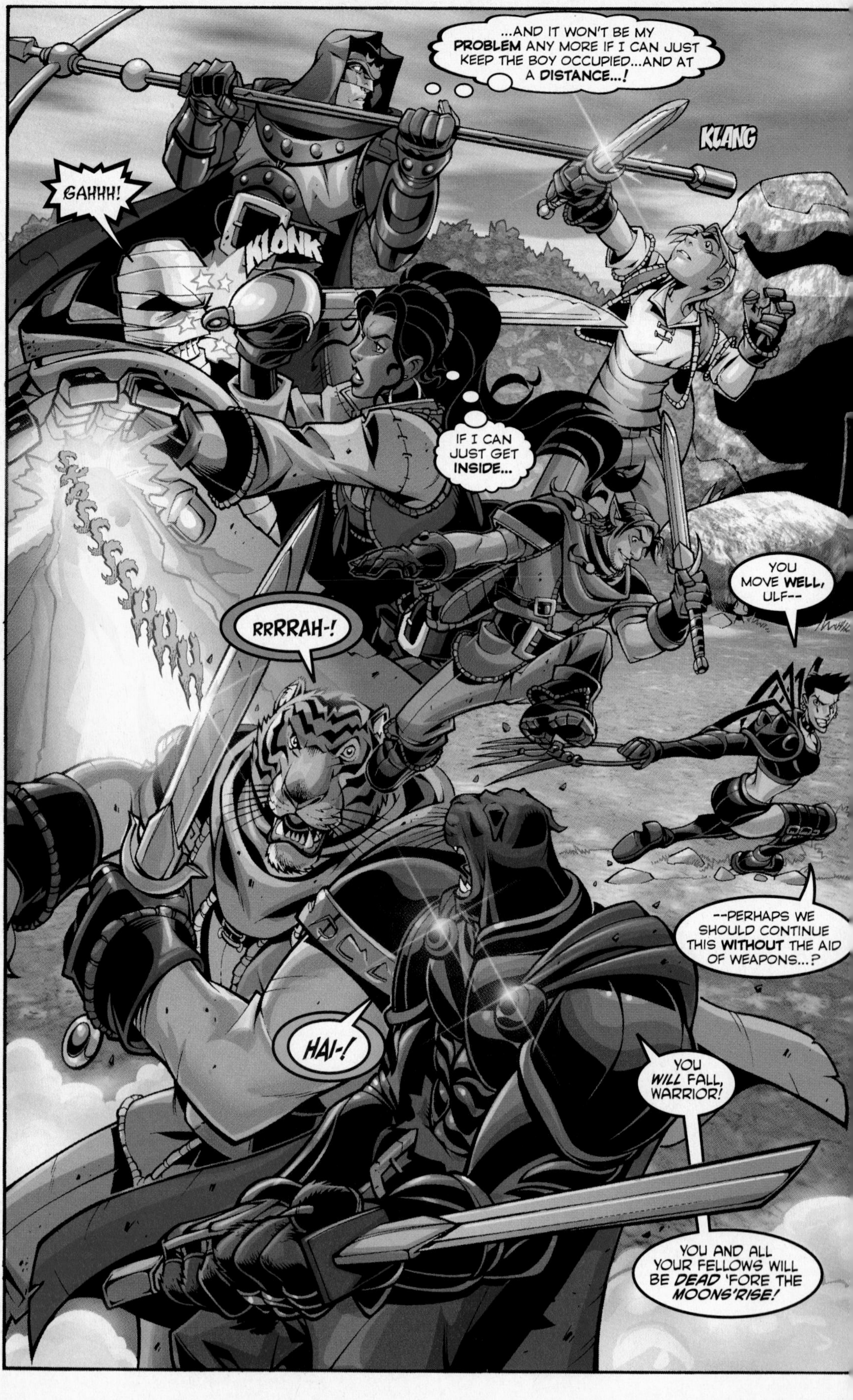
...AND IT WON'T BE MY PROBLEM ANY MORE IF I CAN JUST KEEP THE BOY OCCUPIED...AND AT A DISTANCE...!
KLANG
GAHHH!
KLONK
IF I CAN JUST GET INSIDE...
SKSSSSHHH
YOU MOVE WELL, ULF--
RRRRAH-!
--PERHAPS WE SHOULD CONTINUE THIS WITHOUT THE AID OF WEAPONS...?
HAI-!
YOU WILL FALL, WARRIOR!
YOU AND ALL YOUR FELLOWS WILL BE DEAD 'FORE THE MOONS'RISE!

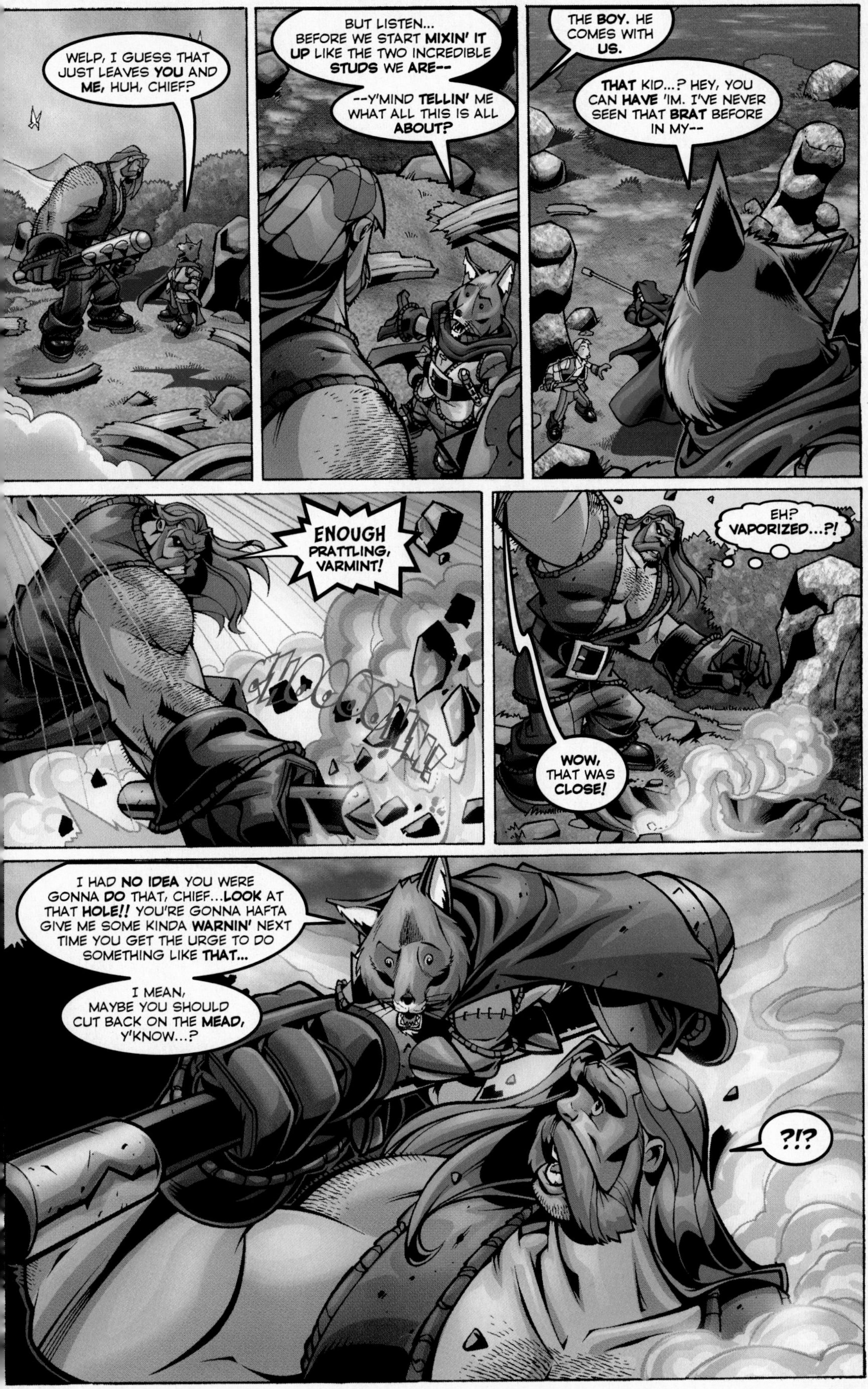
WELP, I GUESS THAT JUST LEAVES YOU AND ME, HUH, CHIEF?
BUT LISTEN... BEFORE WE START MIXIN' IT UP LIKE THE TWO INCREDIBLE STUDS WE ARE--
--Y'MIND TELLIN' ME WHAT ALL THIS IS ALL ABOUT?
THE BOY. HE COMES WITH US.
THAT KID...? HEY, YOU CAN HAVE 'IM. I'VE NEVER SEEN THAT BRAT BEFORE IN MY--
ENOUGH PRATTLING, VARMINT!
EH? VAPORIZED...?!
WOW, THAT WAS CLOSE!
I HAD NO IDEA YOU WERE GONNA DO THAT, CHIEF...LOOK AT THAT HOLE!! YOU'RE GONNA HAFTA GIVE ME SOME KINDA WARNIN' NEXT TIME YOU GET THE URGE TO DO SOMETHING LIKE THAT...
I MEAN, MAYBE YOU SHOULD CUT BACK ON THE MEAD, Y'KNOW...?
?!?

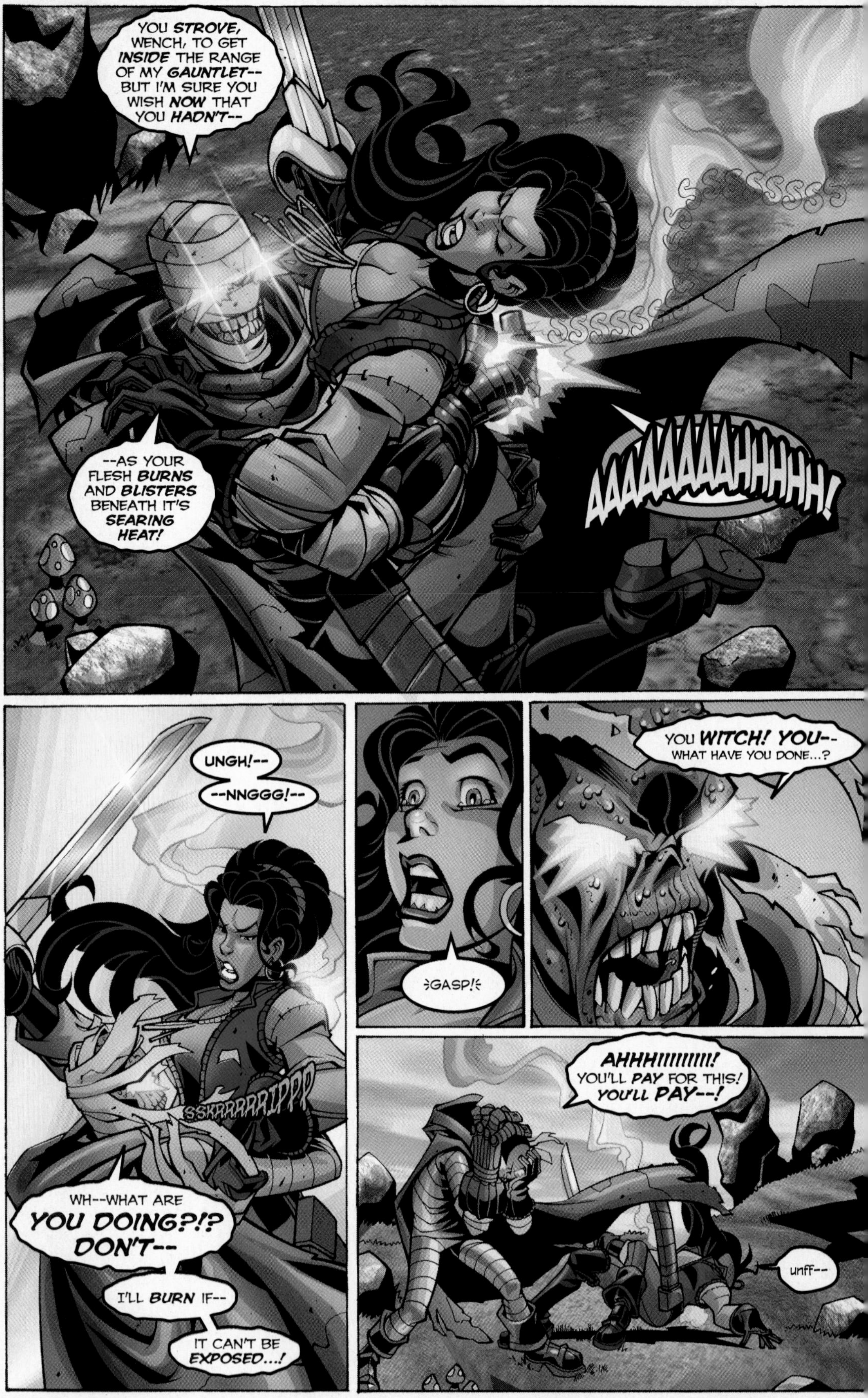
YOU STROVE, WENCH, TO GET INSIDE THE RANGE OF MY GAUNTLET-- BUT I'M SURE YOU WISH NOW THAT YOU HADN'T--
--AS YOUR FLESH BURNS AND BLISTERS BENEATH IT'S SEARING HEAT!
SSSSSSSSSSSSSS
AAAAAAAAHHHHH!
UNGH!--
--NNGGG!--
SSKRRRRRRIPPP
WH--WHAT ARE YOU DOING?!? DON'T--
I'LL BURN IF--
IT CAN'T BE EXPOSED...!
GASP!
YOU WITCH! YOU-- WHAT HAVE YOU DONE...?
AHHH!!!!!!!!!!! YOU'LL PAY FOR THIS! YOU'LL PAY--!
unff--

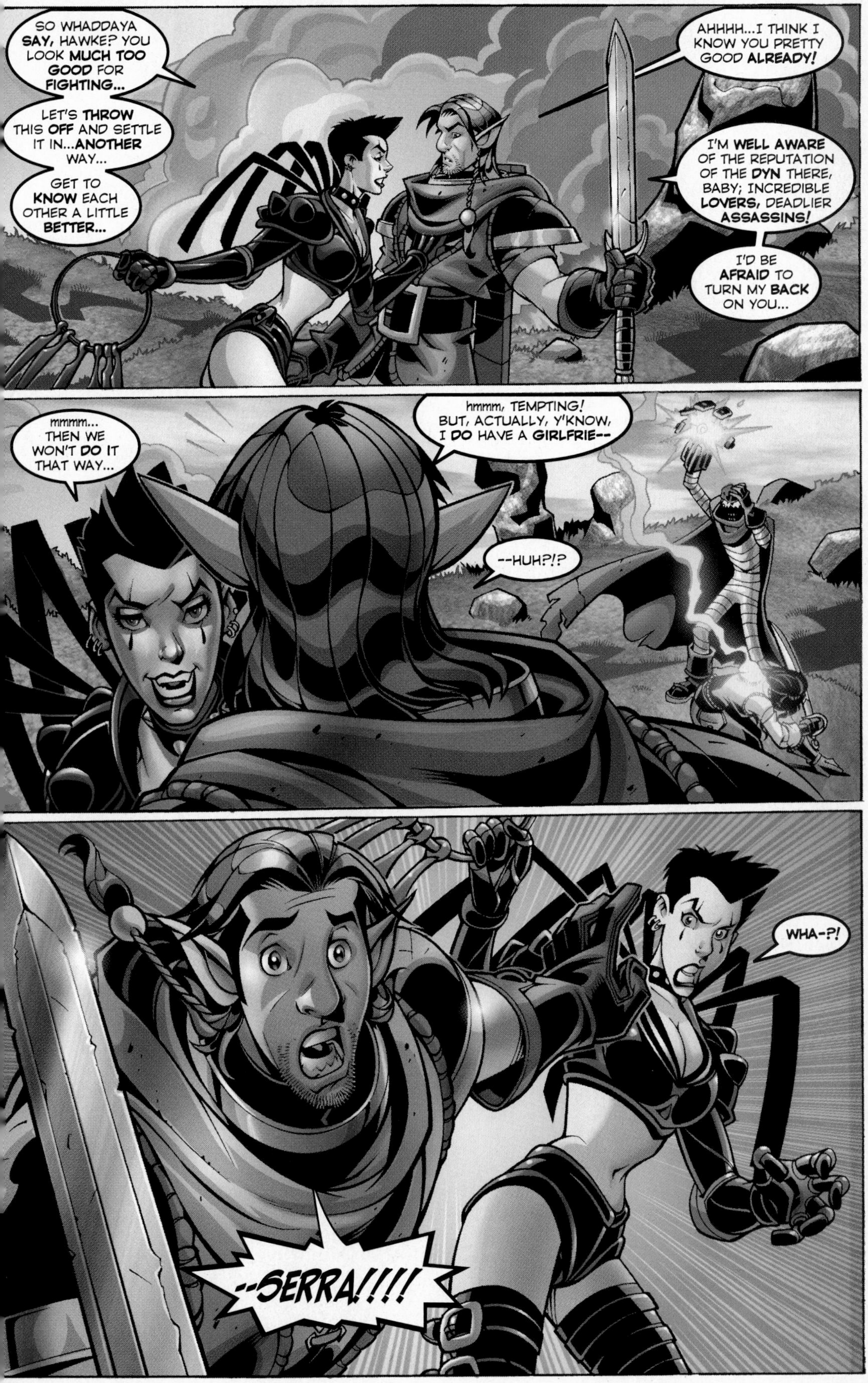
SO WHADDAYA SAY, HAWKE? YOU LOOK MUCH TOO GOOD FOR FIGHTING...
LET'S THROW THIS OFF AND SETTLE IT IN...ANOTHER WAY...
GET TO KNOW EACH OTHER A LITTLE BETTER...
AHHHH...I THINK I KNOW YOU PRETTY GOOD ALREADY!
I'M WELL AWARE OF THE REPUTATION OF THE DYN THERE, BABY; INCREDIBLE LOVERS, DEADLIER ASSASSINS!
I'D BE AFRAID TO TURN MY BACK ON YOU...
mmmm... THEN WE WON'T DO IT THAT WAY...
hmmm, TEMPTING! BUT, ACTUALLY, Y'KNOW, I DO HAVE A GIRLFRIE--
--HUH?!?
WHA-?!
--SERRA!!!!

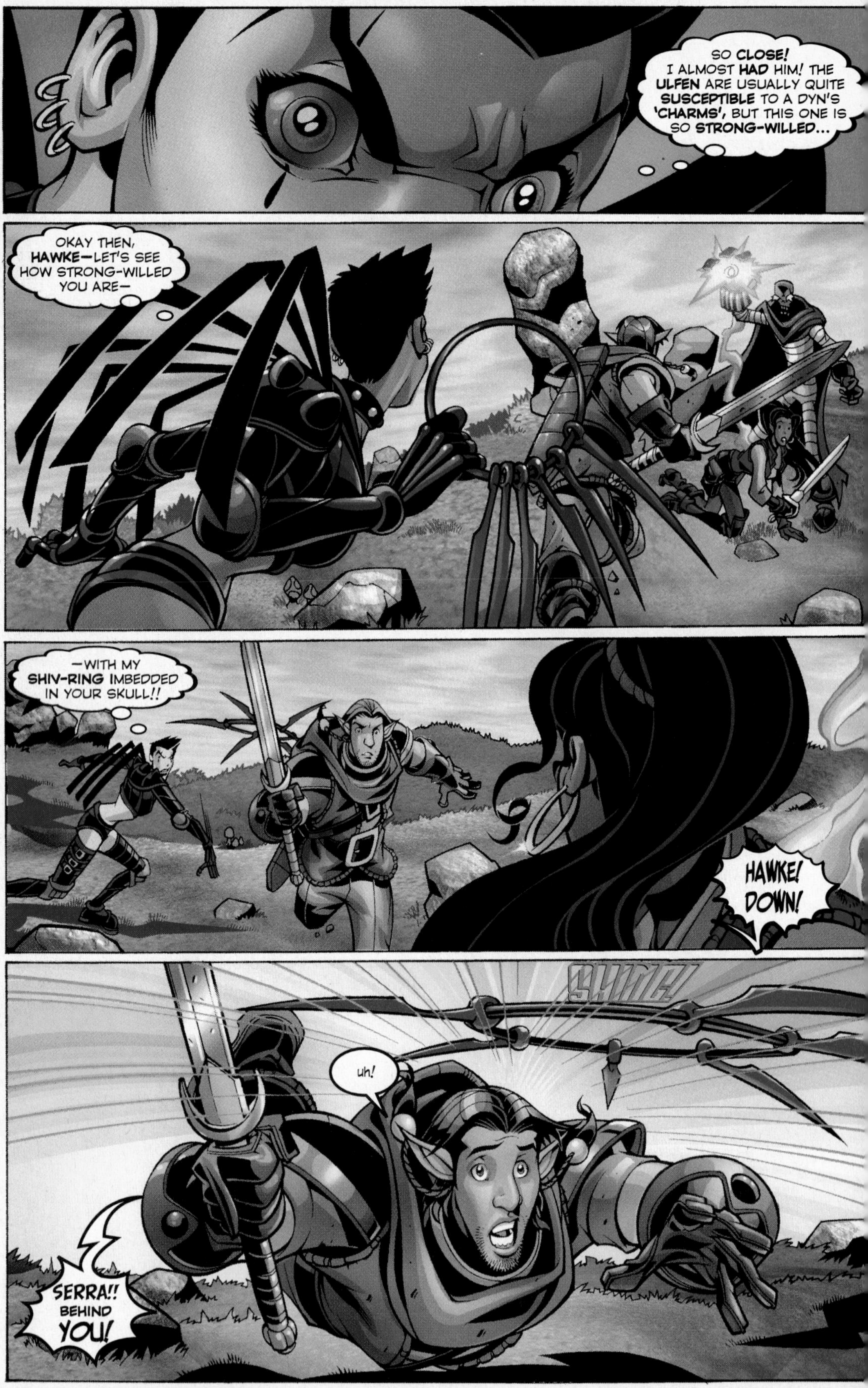

SO CLOSE! I ALMOST HAD HIM! THE ULFEN ARE USUALLY QUITE SUSCEPTIBLE TO A DYN'S 'CHARMS', BUT THIS ONE IS SO STRONG-WILLED...
OKAY THEN, HAWKE—LET'S SEE HOW STRONG-WILLED YOU ARE—
—WITH MY SHIV-RING IMBEDDED IN YOUR SKULL!!
HAWKE! DOWN!
SHING!
uh!
SERRA!! BEHIND YOU!

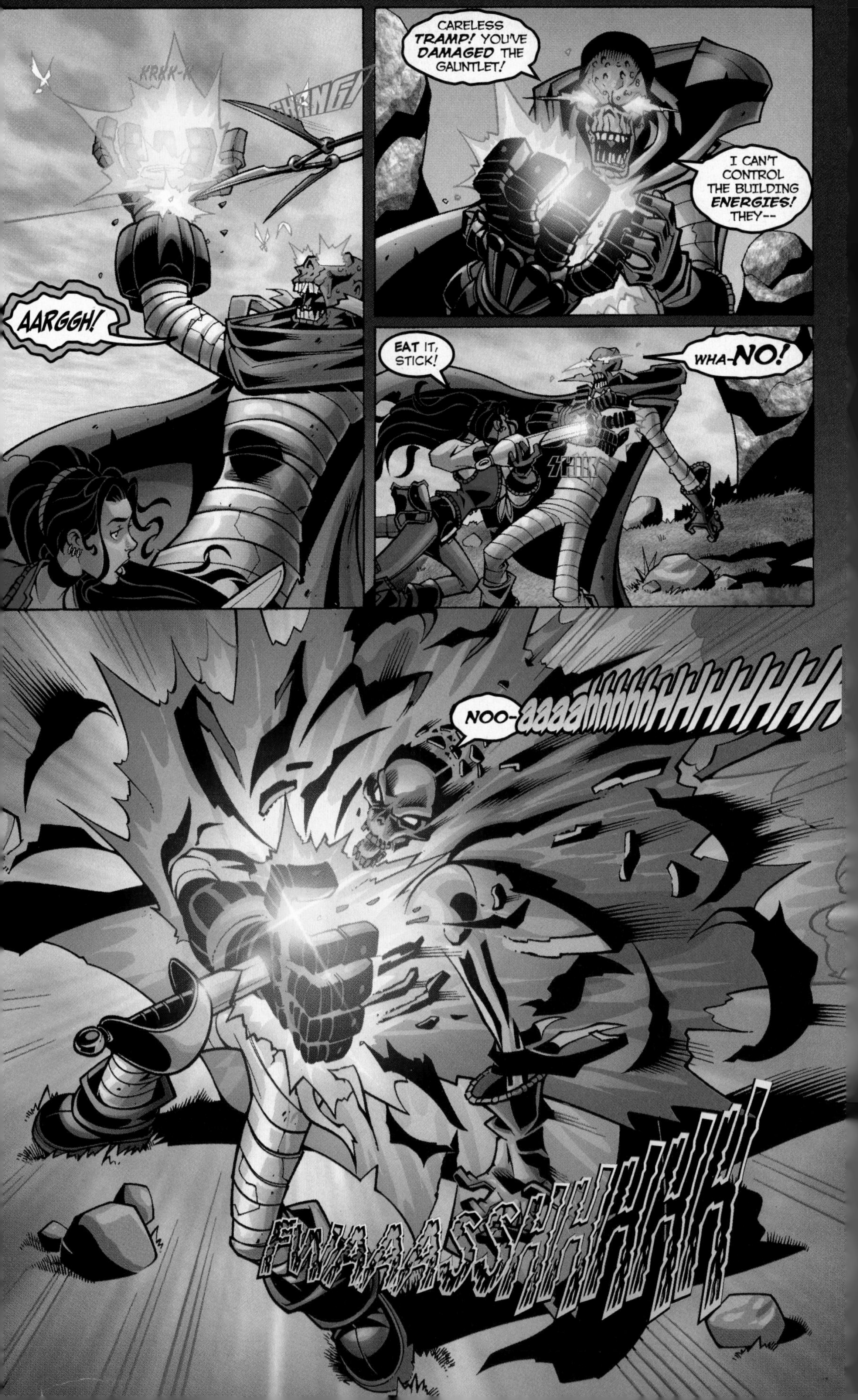
KRKK-K
SHING!
AARGGH!
CARELESS TRAMP! YOU'VE DAMAGED THE GAUNTLET!
I CAN'T CONTROL THE BUILDING ENERGIES! THEY--
EAT IT, STICK!
WHA-NO!
NOO-aaaahhhhhHHHHHH!
FWHAAASSHHHRRK!

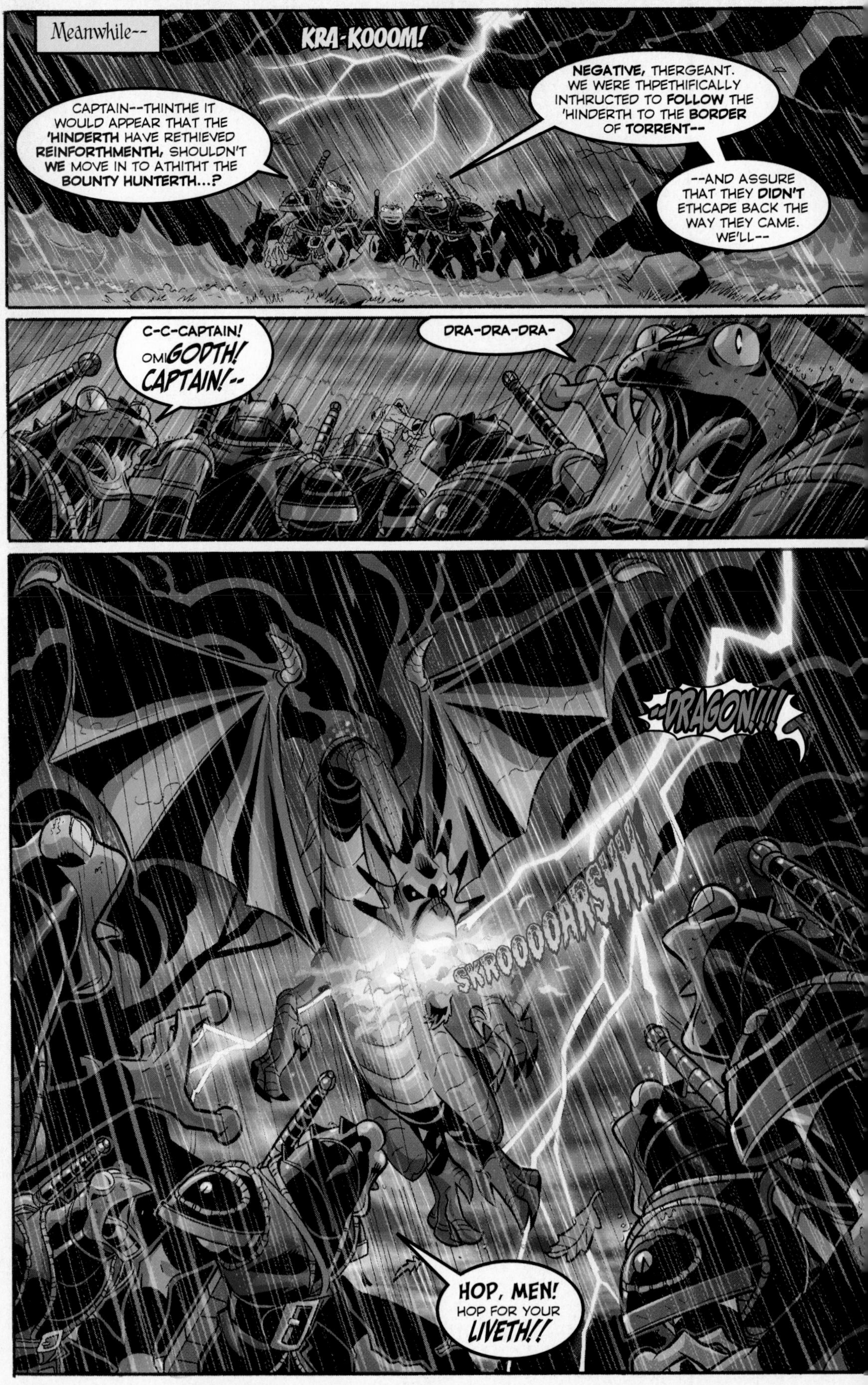
Meanwhile--
KRA-KOOOM!
CAPTAIN--THINTHE IT WOULD APPEAR THAT THE 'HINDERTH HAVE RETHIEVED REINFORTHMENTH, SHOULDN'T WE MOVE IN TO ATHITHT THE BOUNTY HUNTERTH...?
NEGATIVE, THERGEANT. WE WERE THPETHIFICALLY INTHRUCTED TO FOLLOW THE 'HINDERTH TO THE BORDER OF TORRENT--
--AND ASSURE THAT THEY DIDN'T ETHCAPE BACK THE WAY THEY CAME. WE'LL--
C-C-CAPTAIN! OMIGODTH! CAPTAIN!--
DRA-DRA-DRA-
--DRAGON!!!!
SKROOOOOARSHH
HOP, MEN! HOP FOR YOUR LIVETH!!

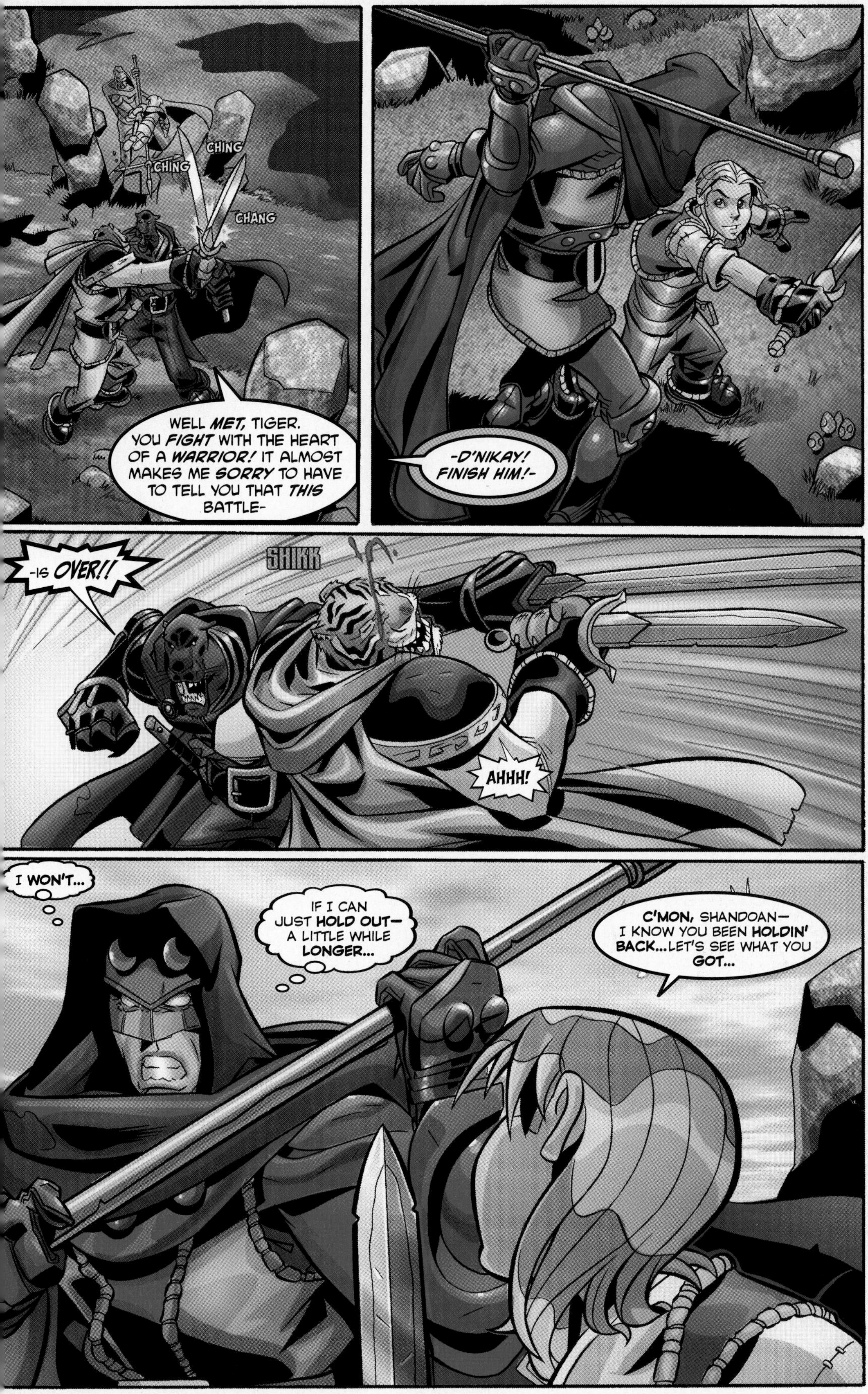

CHING
CHING
CHANG
WELL MET, TIGER. YOU FIGHT WITH THE HEART OF A WARRIOR! IT ALMOST MAKES ME SORRY TO HAVE TO TELL YOU THAT THIS BATTLE-
-D'NIKAY! FINISH HIM!-
-IS OVER!!
SHIKK
AHHH!
I WON'T...
IF I CAN JUST HOLD OUT— A LITTLE WHILE LONGER...
C'MON, SHANDOAN— I KNOW YOU BEEN HOLDIN' BACK...LET'S SEE WHAT YOU GOT...

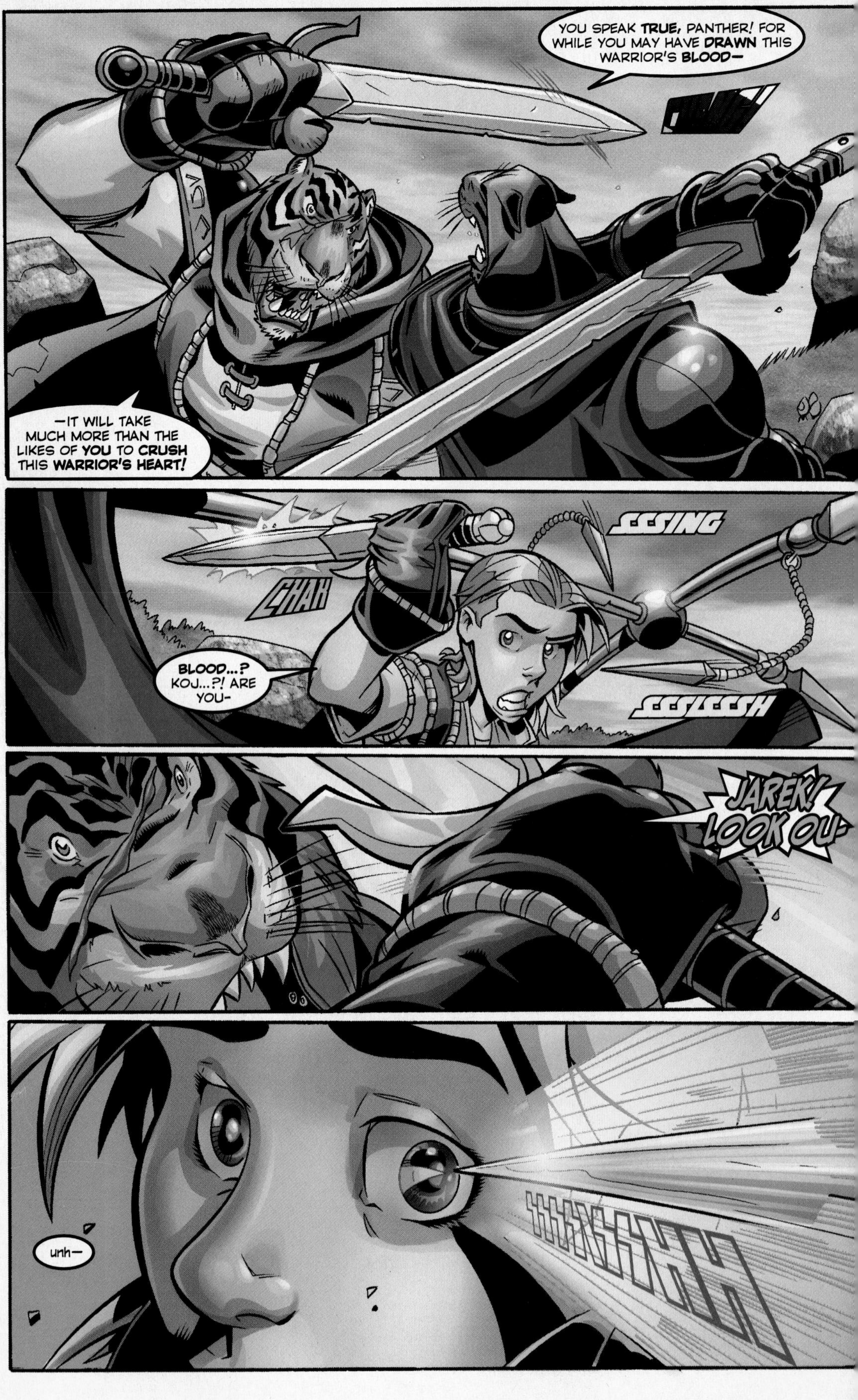
YOU SPEAK TRUE, PANTHER! FOR WHILE YOU MAY HAVE DRAWN THIS WARRIOR'S BLOOD—
—IT WILL TAKE MUCH MORE THAN THE LIKES OF YOU TO CRUSH THIS WARRIOR'S HEART!
SSSING
CHAK
BLOOD...? KOJ...?! ARE YOU-
JAREK! LOOK OU-
unh—

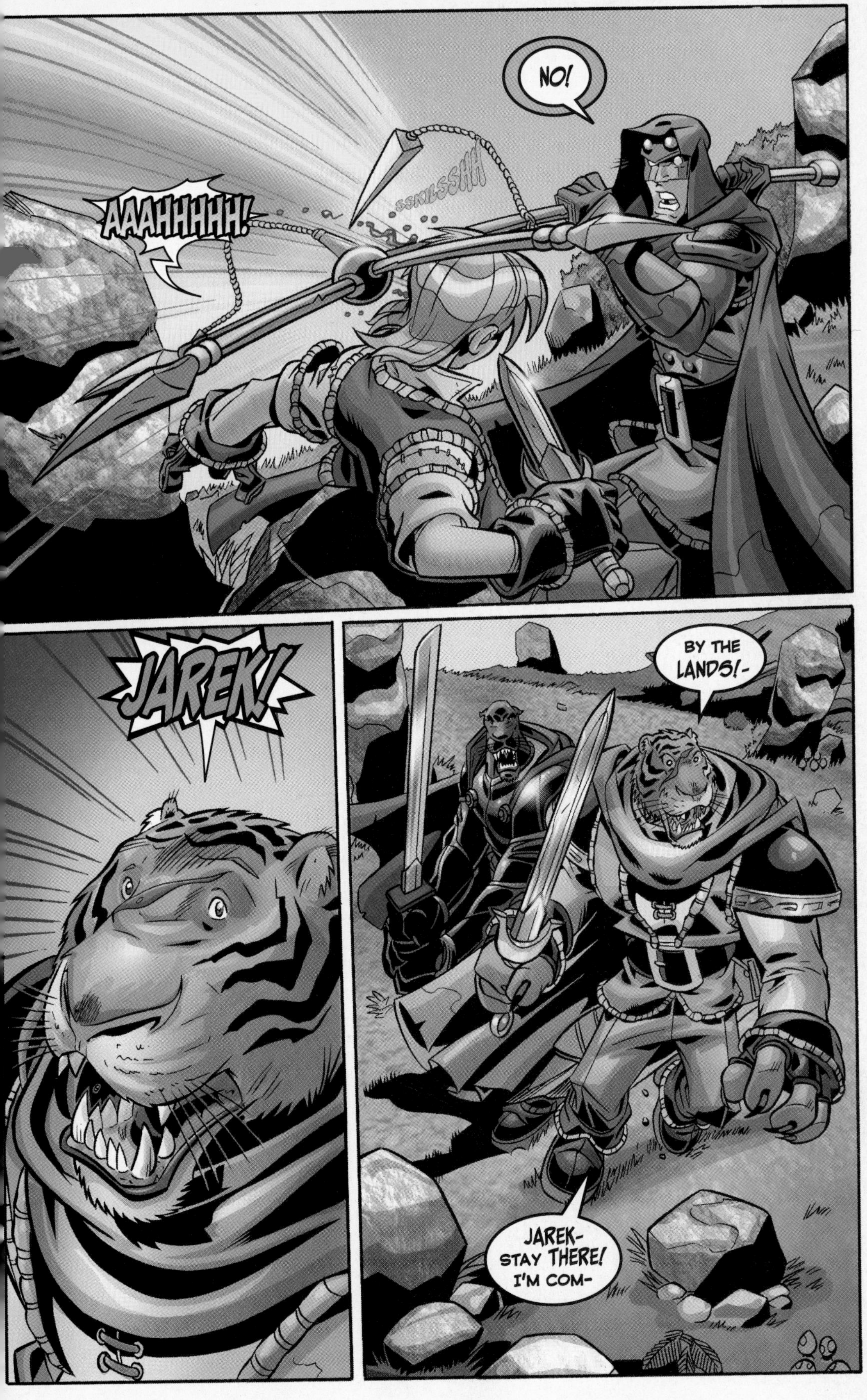
AAAHHHHH!
SSKILSSHH
NO!
JAREK!
BY THE LANDS!-
JAREK- STAY THERE! I'M COM-

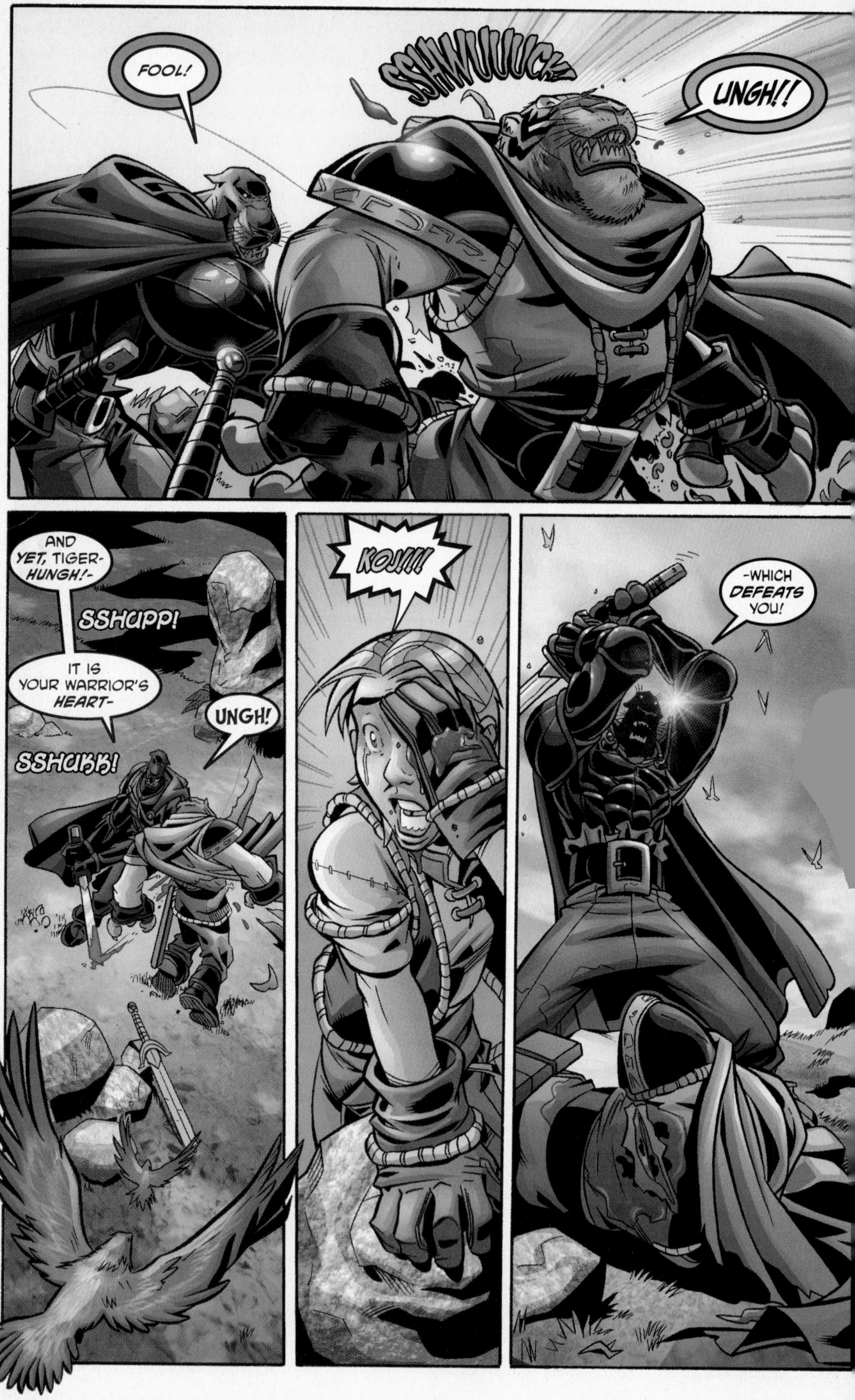
FOOL!
SSHWUUUCK!
UNGH!!
AND YET, TIGER-HUNGH!-
SSHUPP!
IT IS YOUR WARRIOR'S HEART-
UNGH!
SSHUKK!
KOJ!!!
-WHICH DEFEATS YOU!

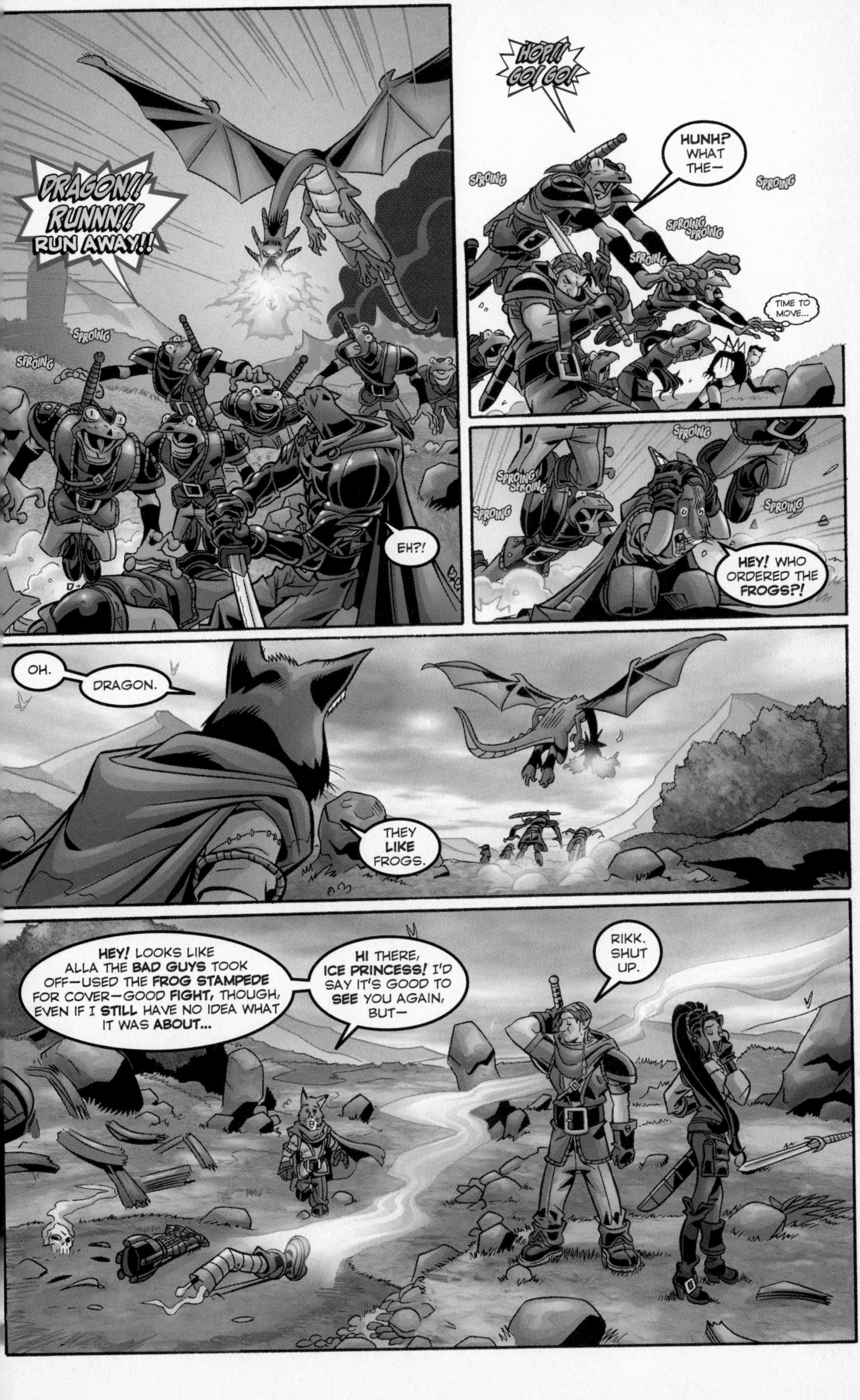

DRAGON!! RUNNN!! RUN AWAY!!
SPROING
SPROING
EH?!
HOP!! GO! GO!
HUNH? WHAT THE—
SPROING
SPROING
SPROING SPROING
SPROING
TIME TO MOVE...
SPROING
SPROING SPROING
SPROING
SPROING
HEY! WHO ORDERED THE FROGS?!
OH.
DRAGON.
THEY LIKE FROGS.
HEY! LOOKS LIKE ALLA THE BAD GUYS TOOK OFF—USED THE FROG STAMPEDE FOR COVER—GOOD FIGHT, THOUGH, EVEN IF I STILL HAVE NO IDEA WHAT IT WAS ABOUT...
HI THERE, ICE PRINCESS! I'D SAY IT'S GOOD TO SEE YOU AGAIN, BUT—
RIKK. SHUT UP.

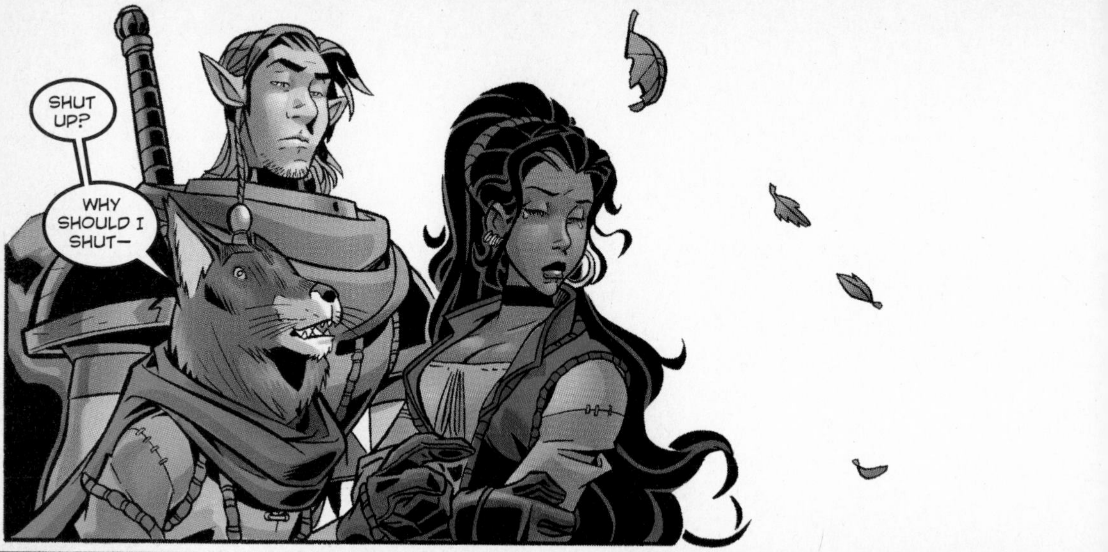
SHUT UP?
WHY SHOULD I SHUT—

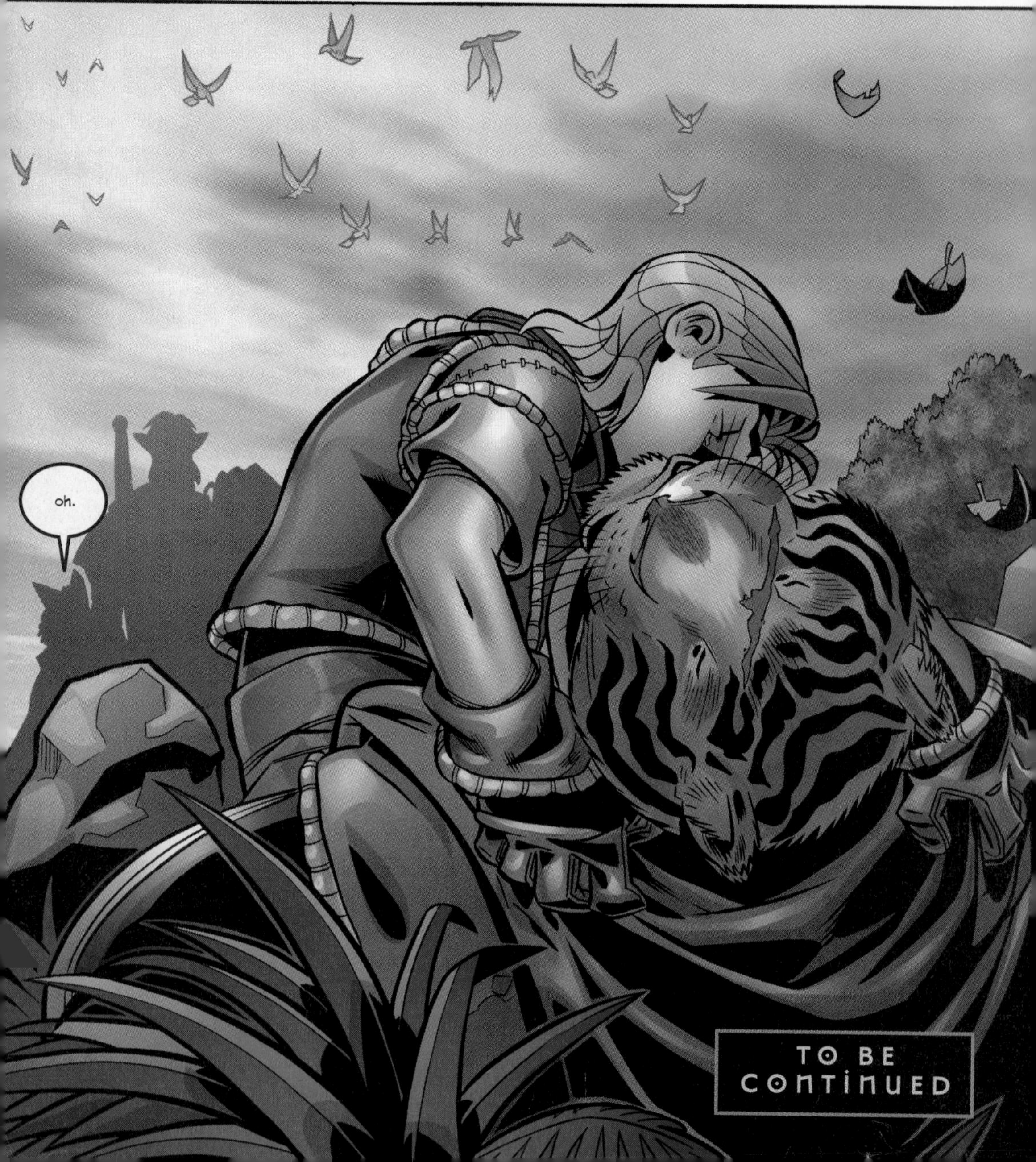
oh.
TO BE CONTINUED

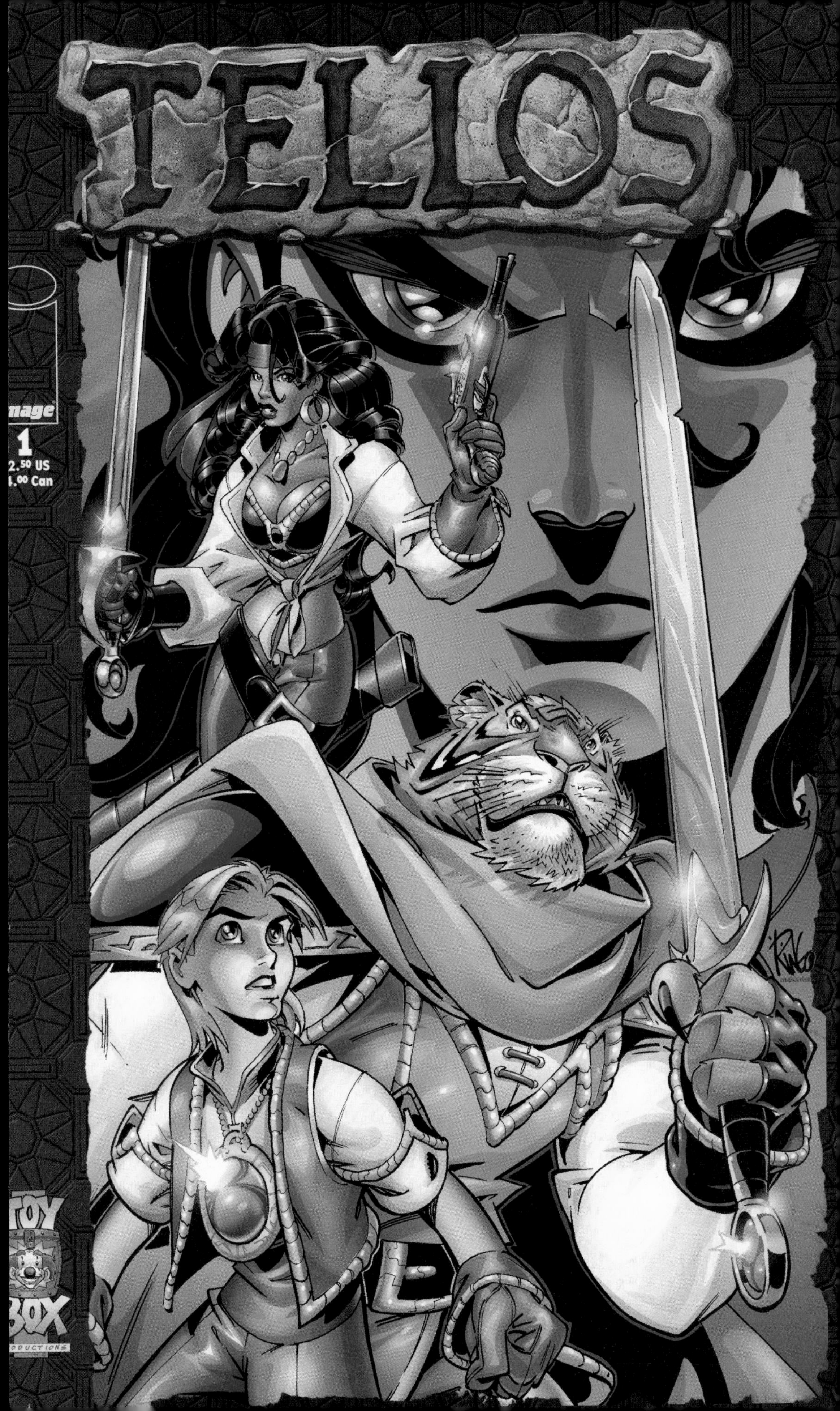
TELLOS
mage
1
2.50 US
4.00 Can
TOY BOX
ODUCTIONS

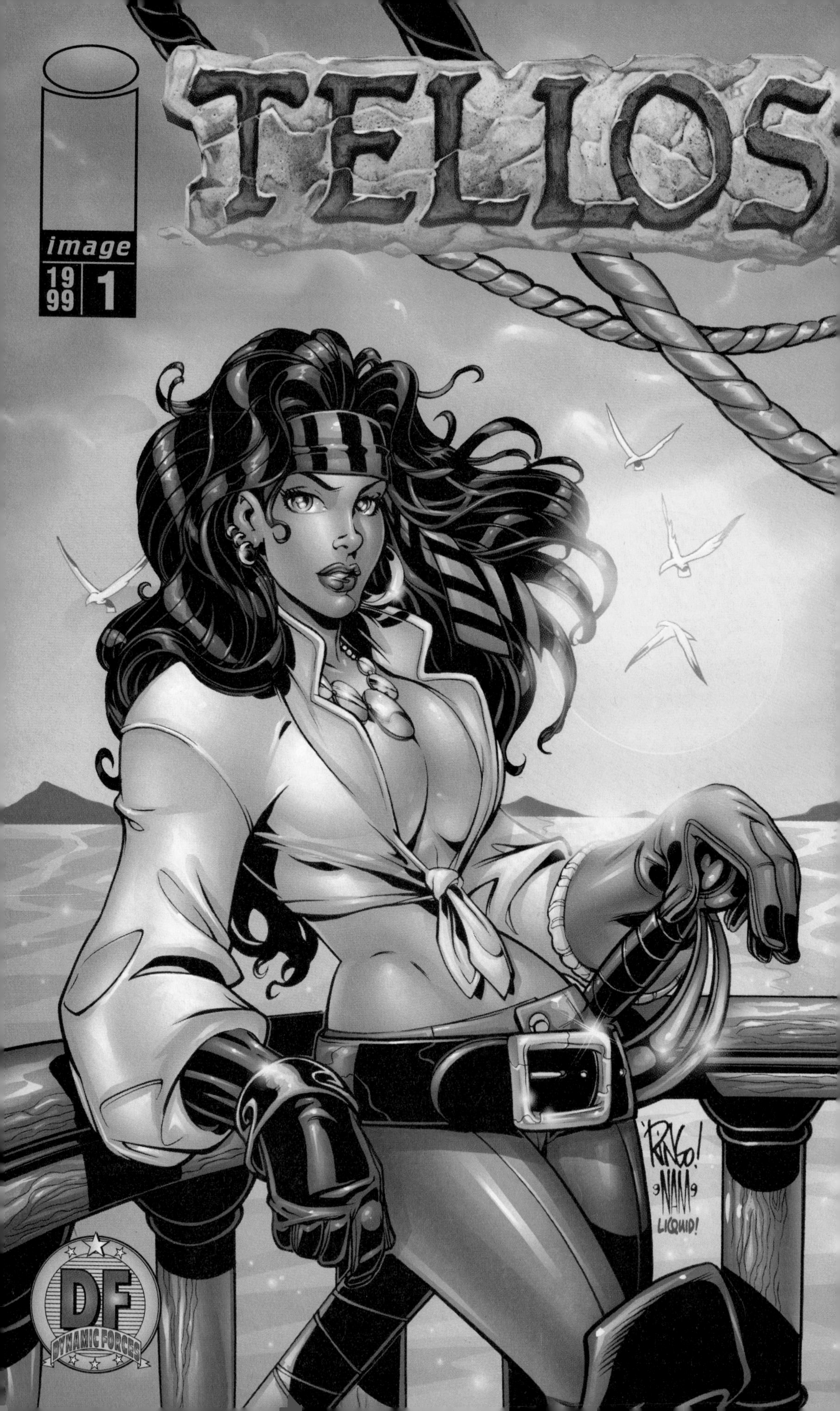
TELLOS
image
1999 1
'RINGO!
NAM
LICQUID!
DF
DYNAMIC FORCES

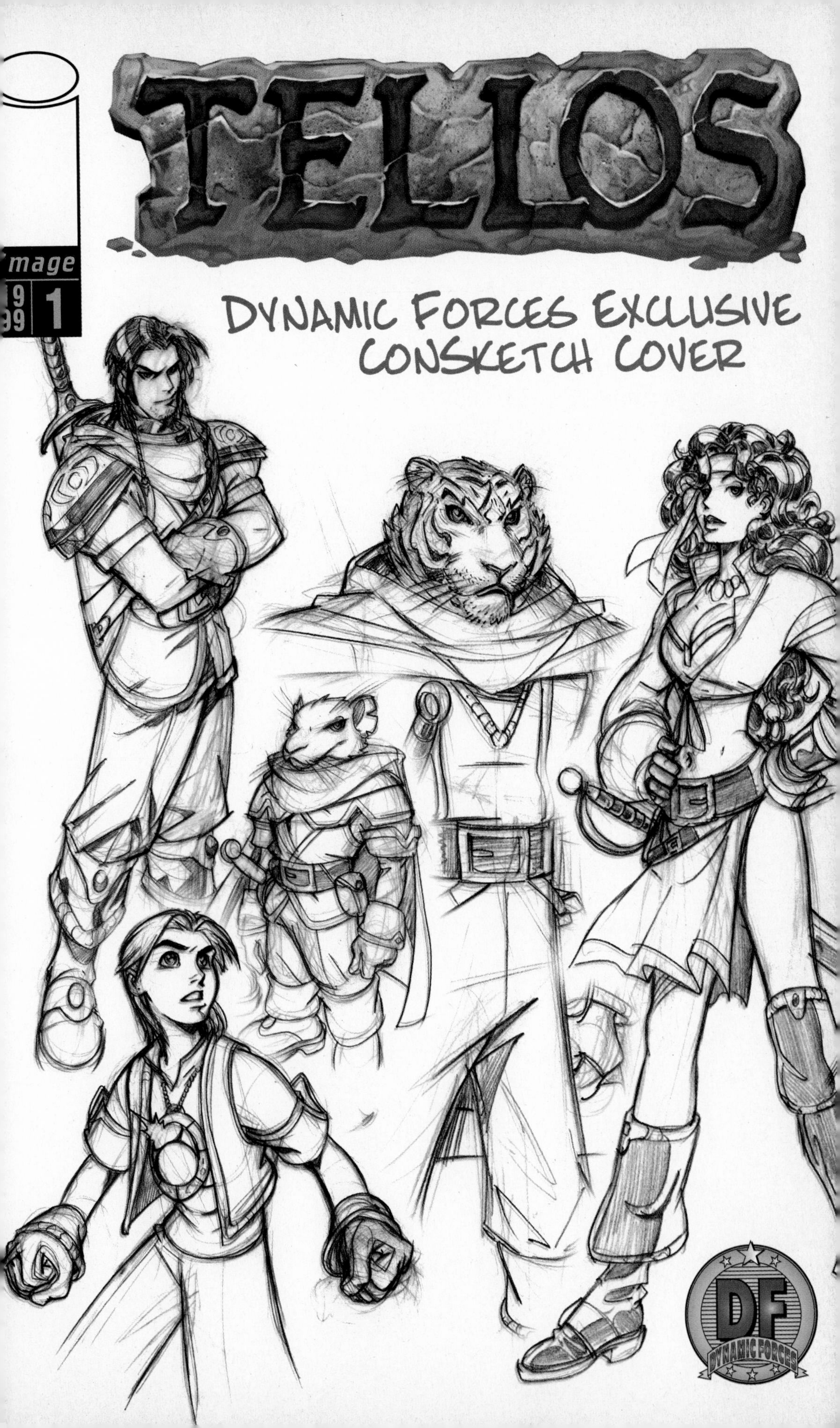
TELLOS
DYNAMIC FORCES EXCLUSIVE
CONSKETCH COVER
DF
DYNAMIC FORCES

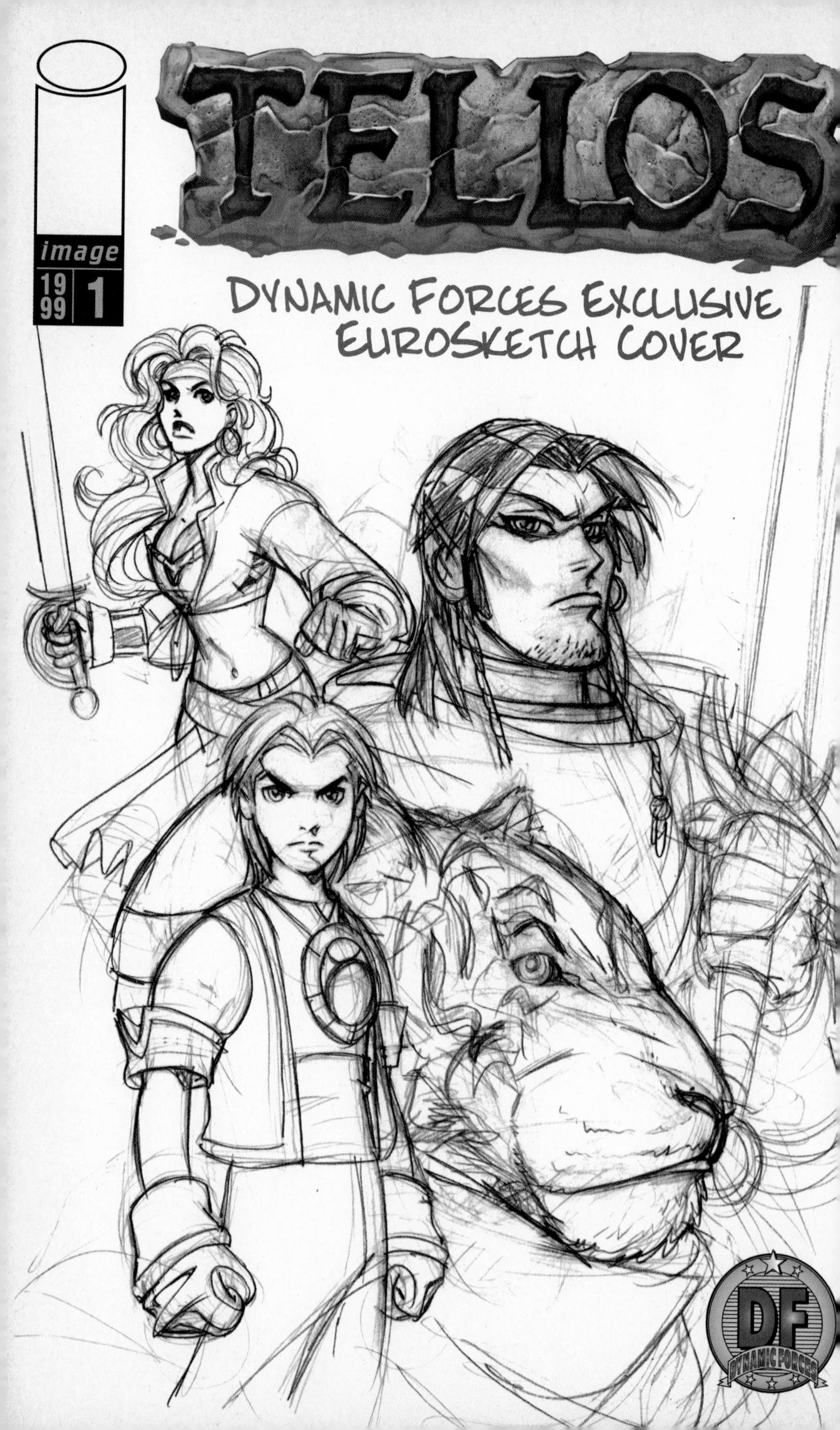
TELLOS
image
1999 1
DYNAMIC FORCES EXCLUSIVE
EUROSKETCH COVER
DF
DYNAMIC FORCES

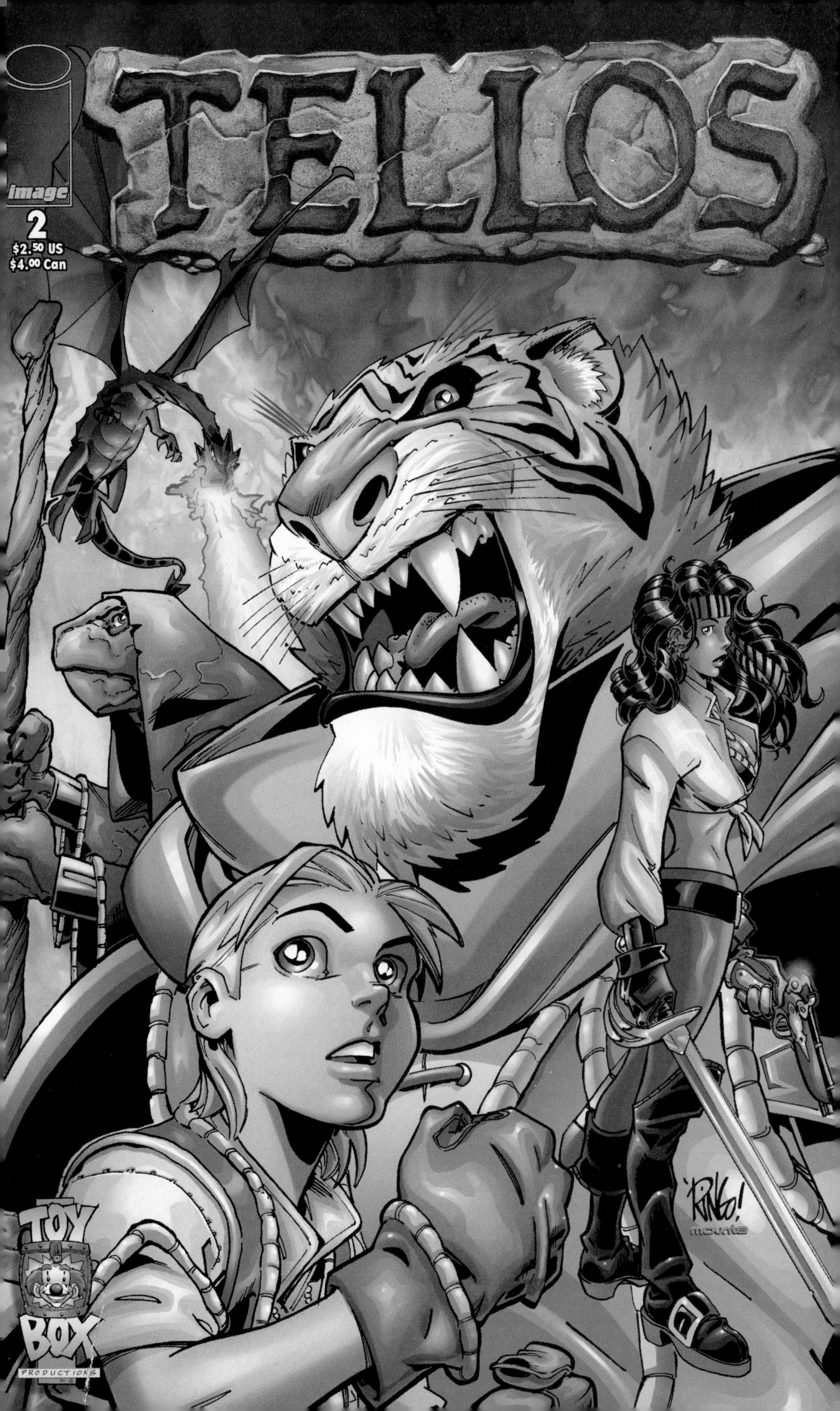
image
2
$2.50 US
$4.00 Can
TELOS
RINGO!
mounts
TOY BOX PRODUCTIONS

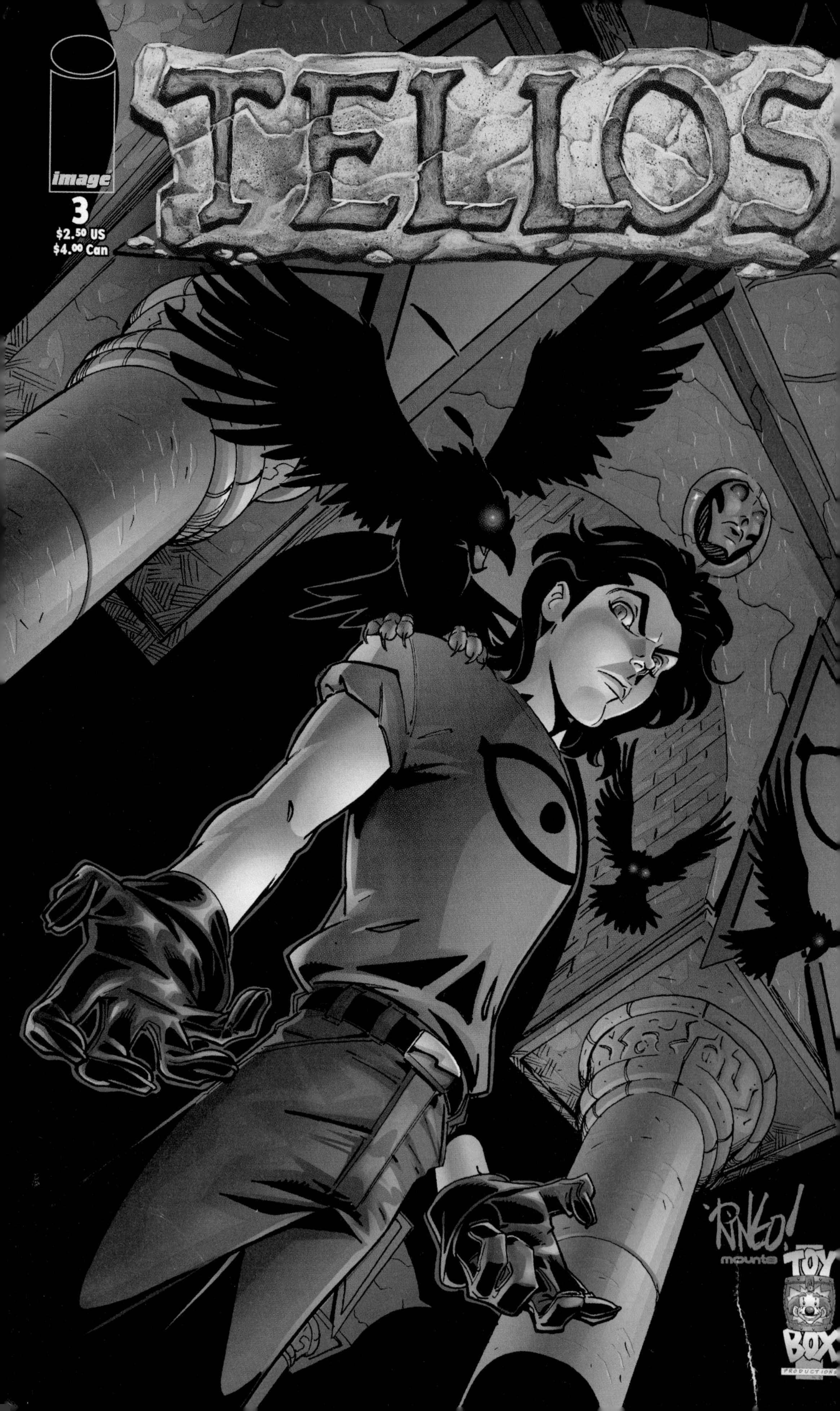

image
3
$2.50 US
$4.00 Can
TELLOS
RINGO!
mounts
TOY BOX
PRODUCTIONS

image COMICS

ILLUSTRATION QUALITY PAPER FULL BLEED COMIC PAGES

MAY 99-E.L. VERSION

xerox	stats	code

BOOK ISSUE PG#

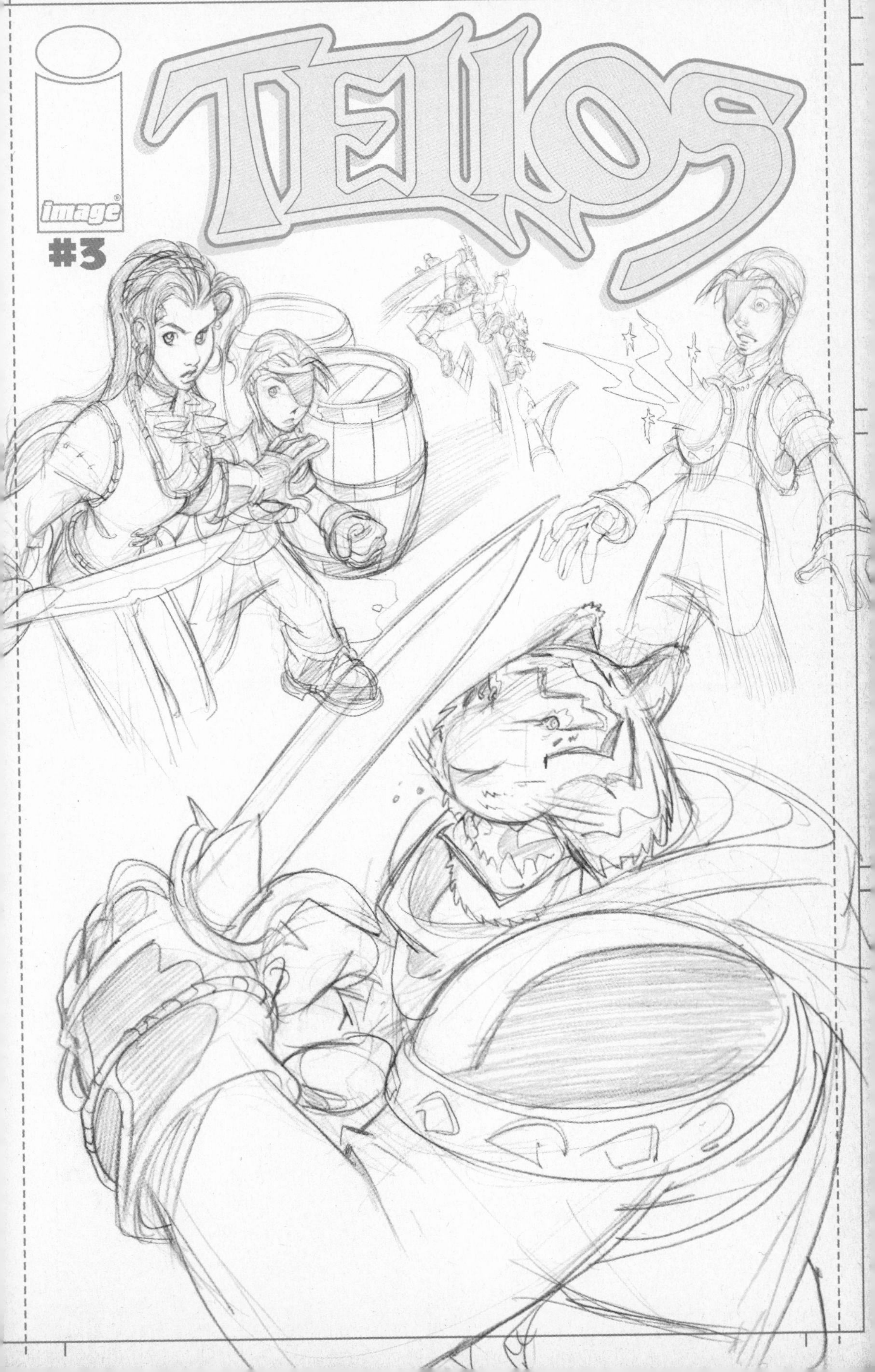
TELLOS
image
#3

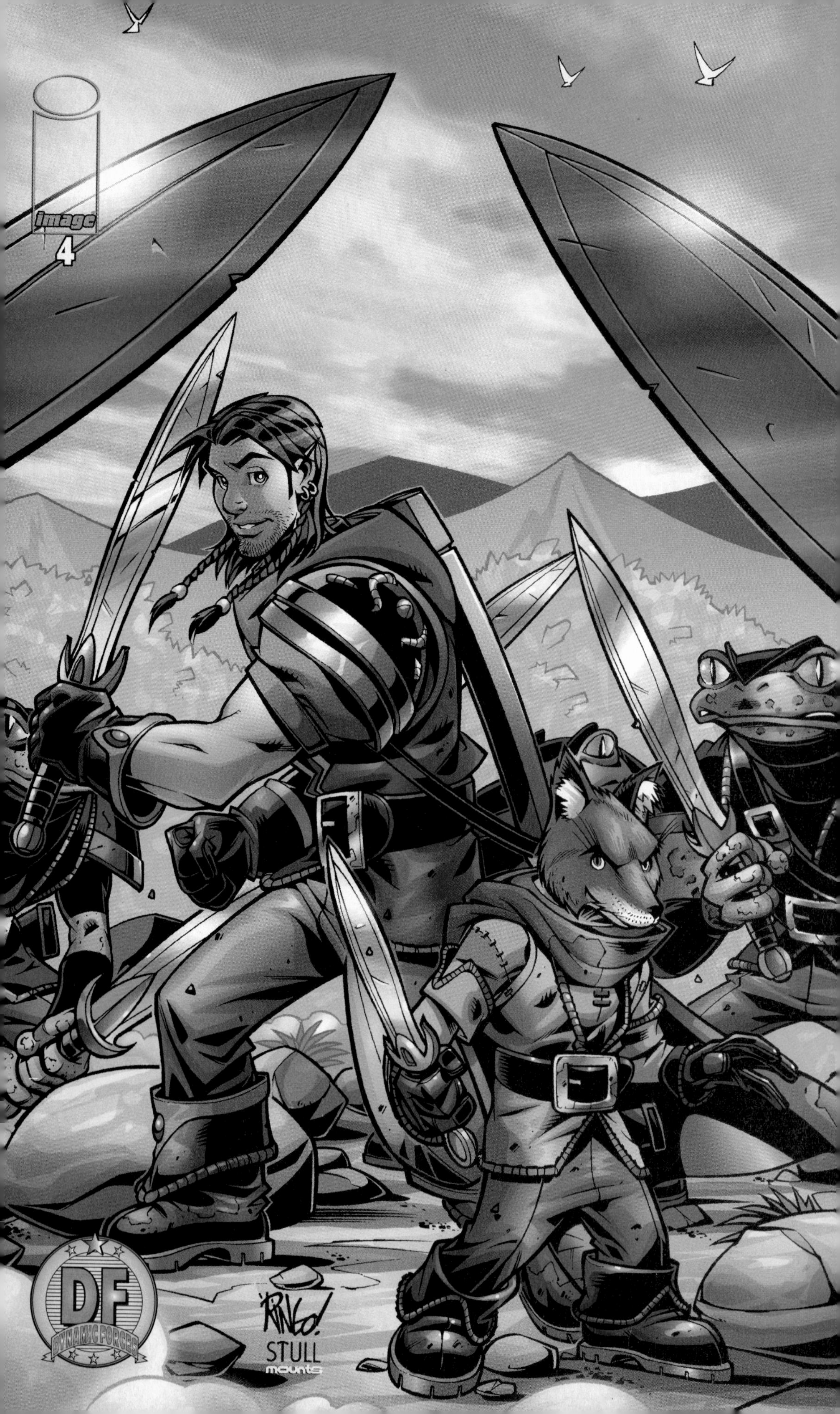
image
4
RINGO!
STULL
mounts
DF
DYNAMIC FORCES

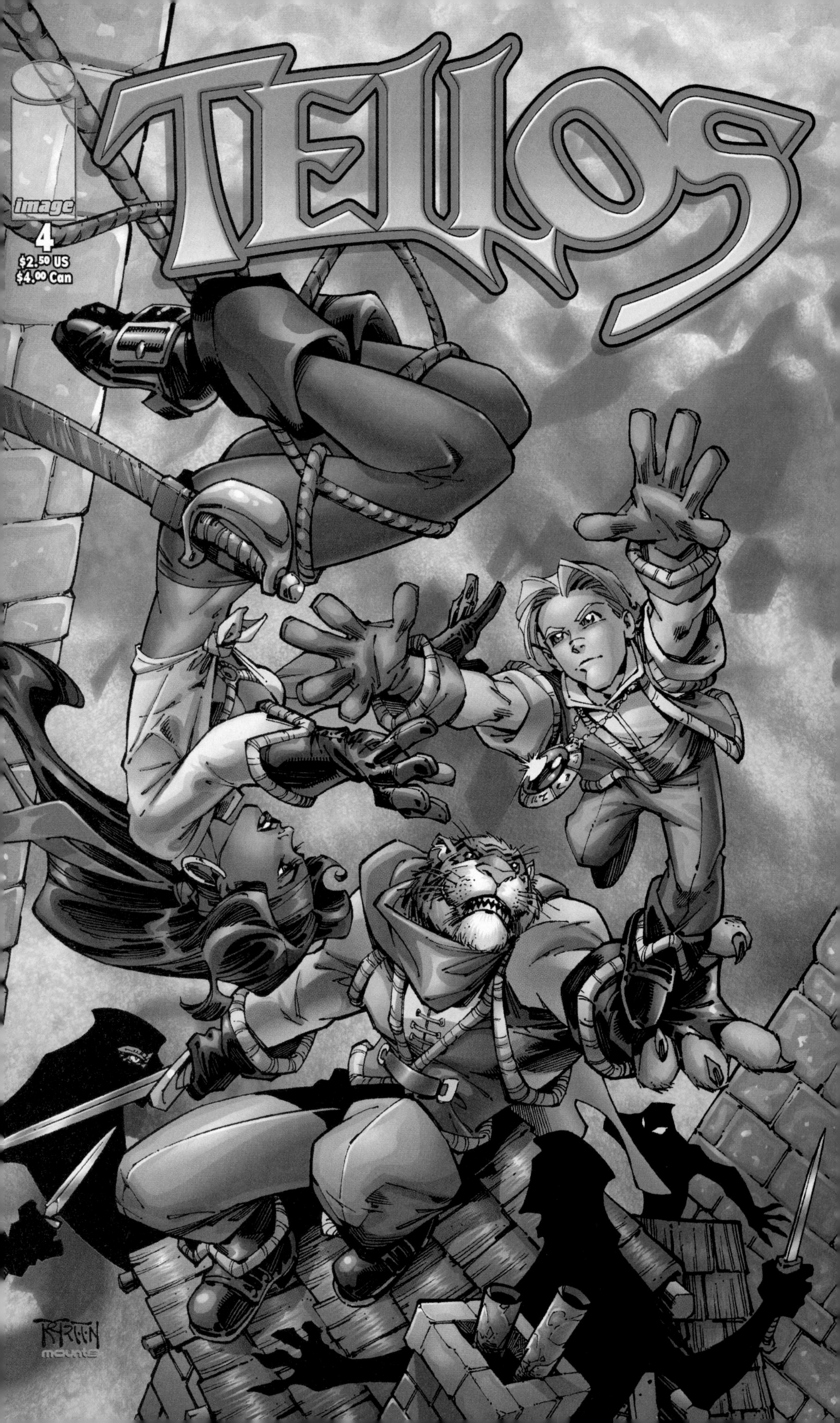

TELLOS
image
4
$2.50 US
$4.00 Can

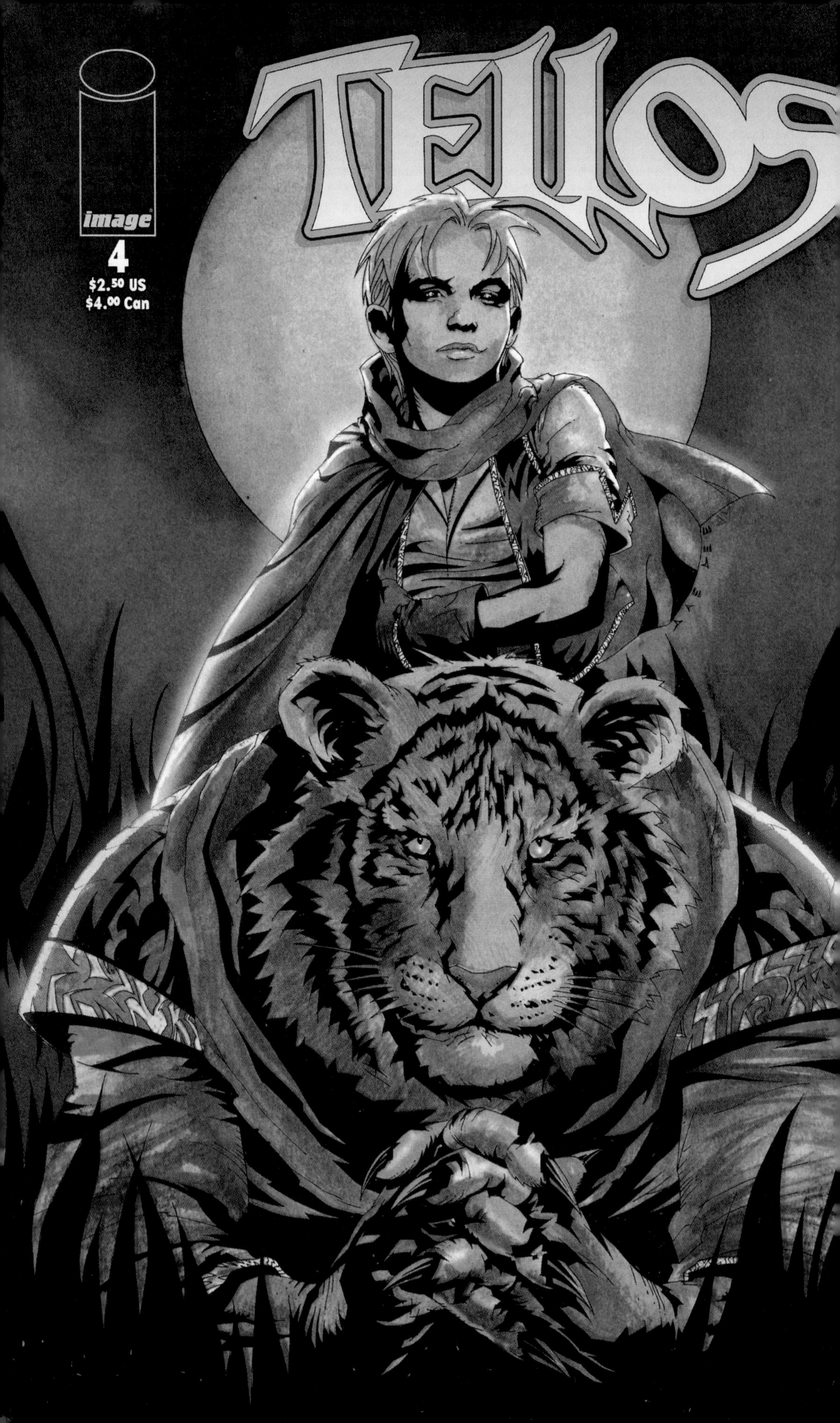
TELLOS
image
4
$2.50 US
$4.00 Can

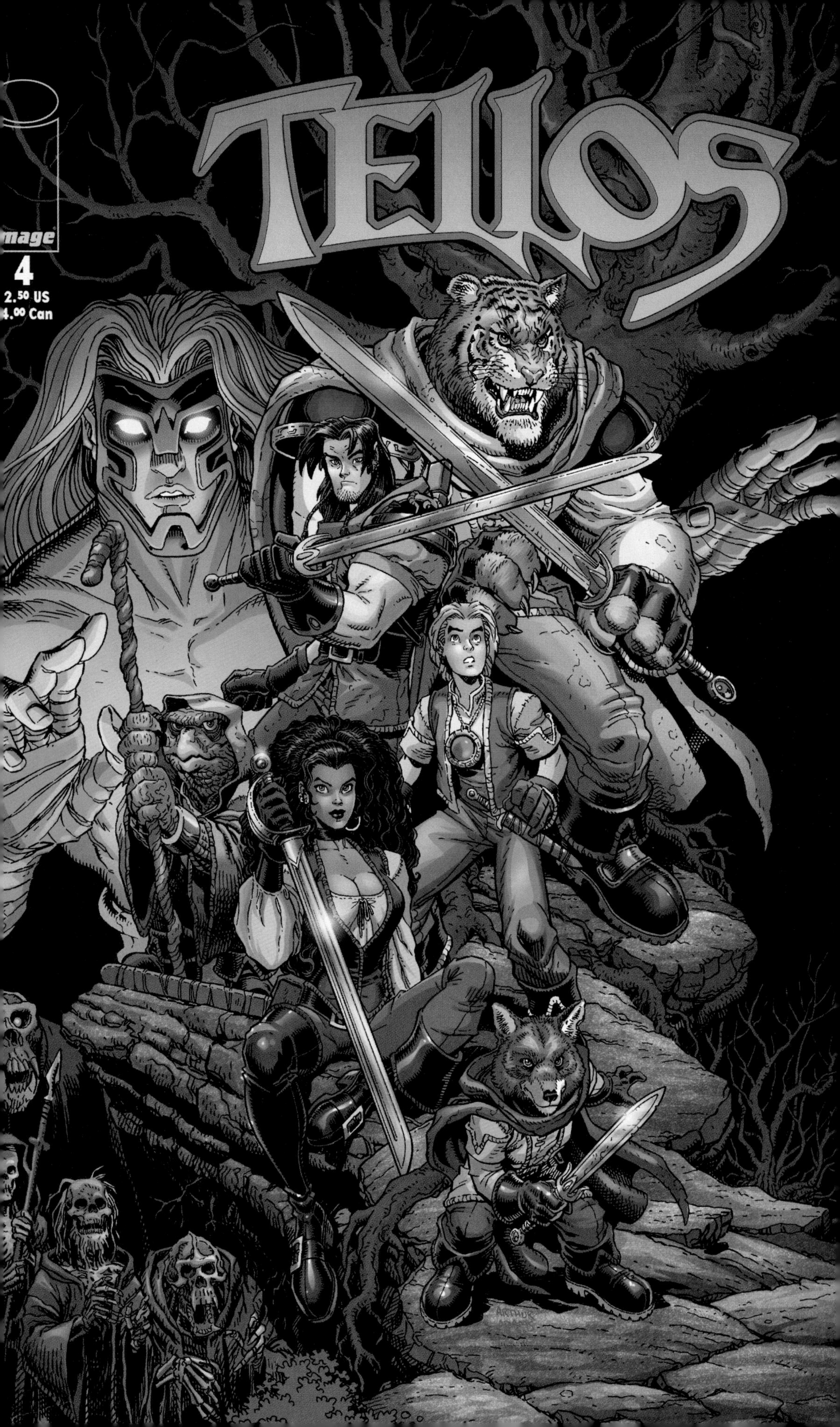
mage
4
2.50 US
4.00 Can
TELLOS

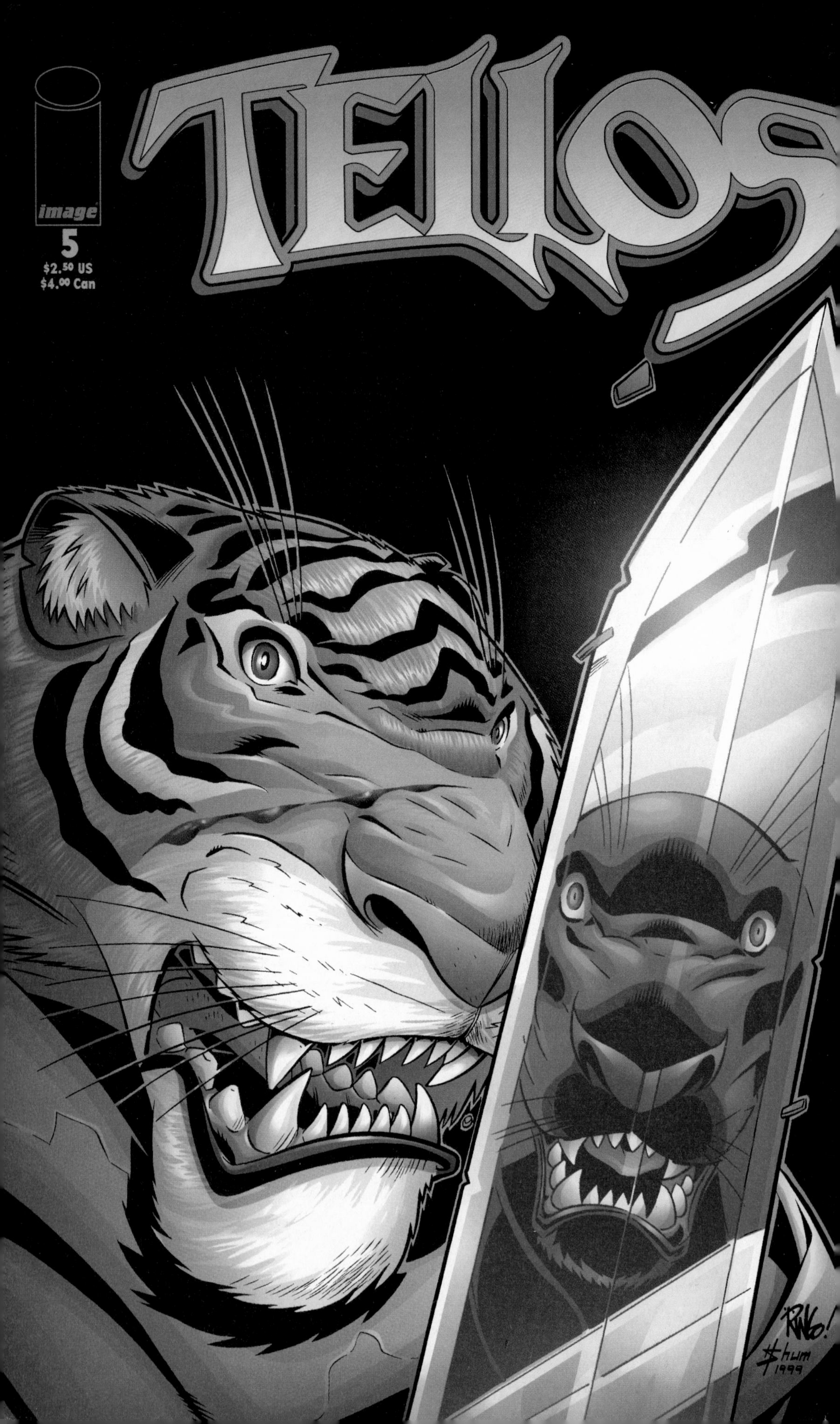

image
5
$2.50 US
$4.00 Can
TELLOS
RINGO!
$hum
1999

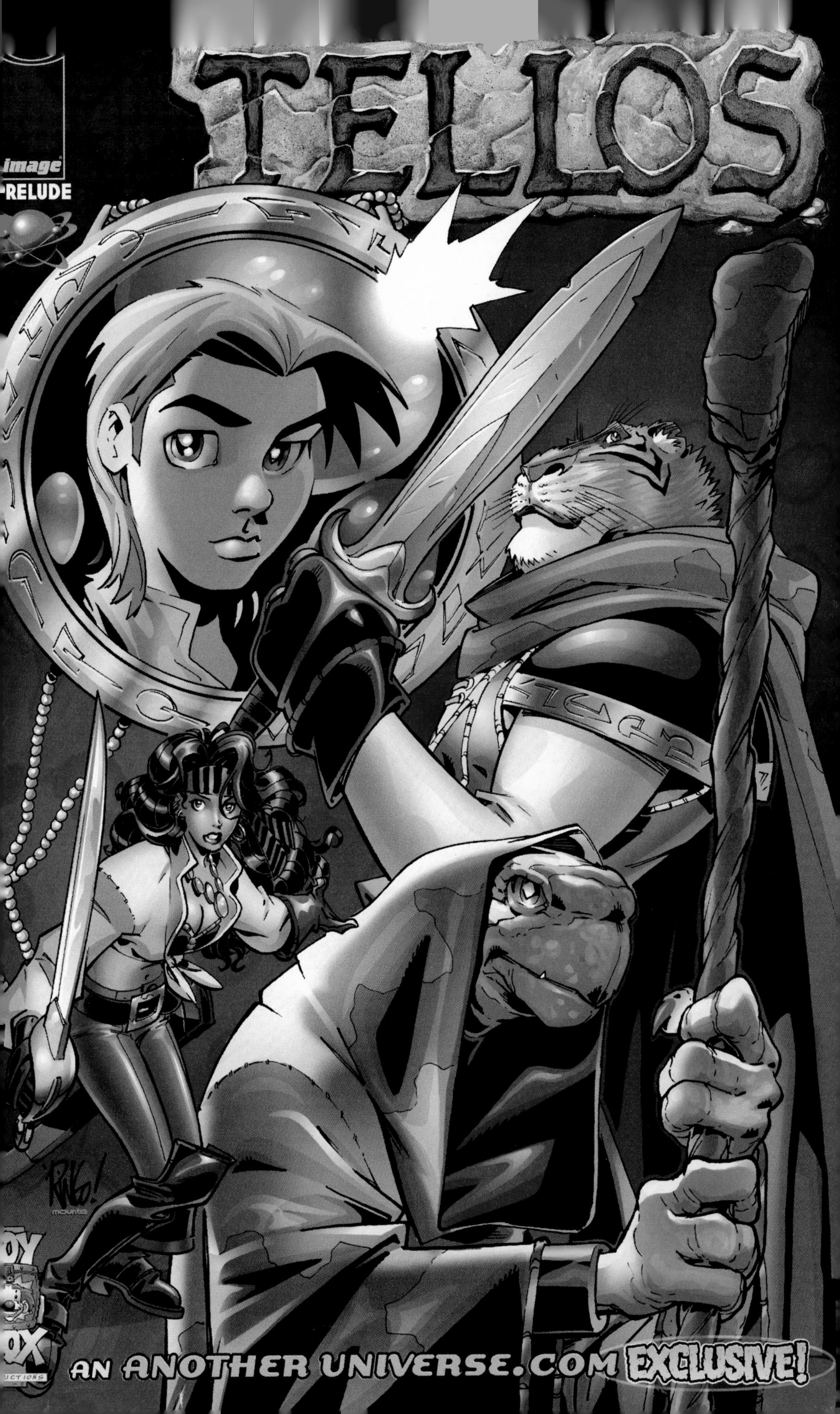

image
PRELUDE
TELLOS
AN ANOTHER UNIVERSE.COM EXCLUSIVE!

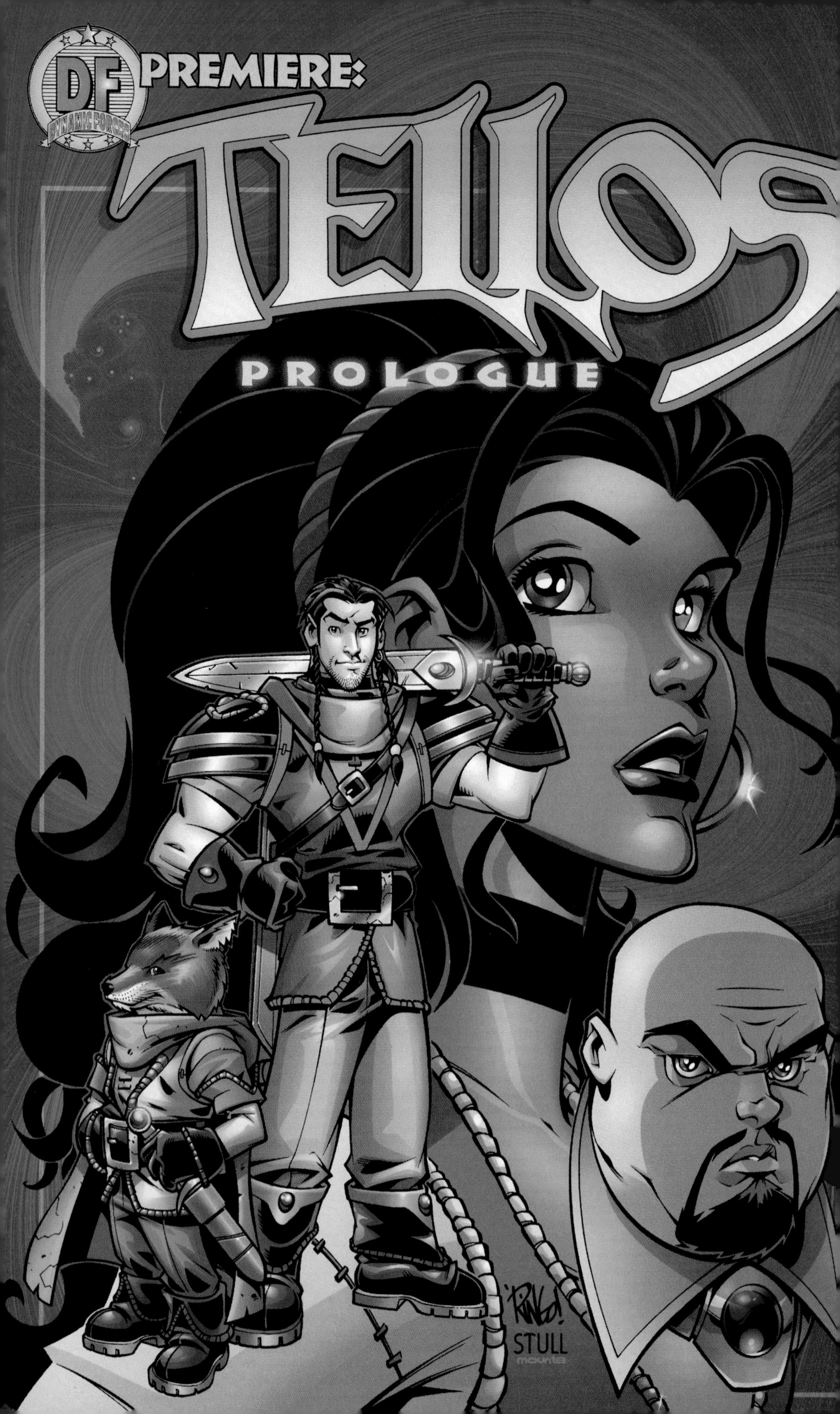

DF
DYNAMIC FORCES
PREMIERE:
TELLOS
PROLOGUE
RINGO!
STULL

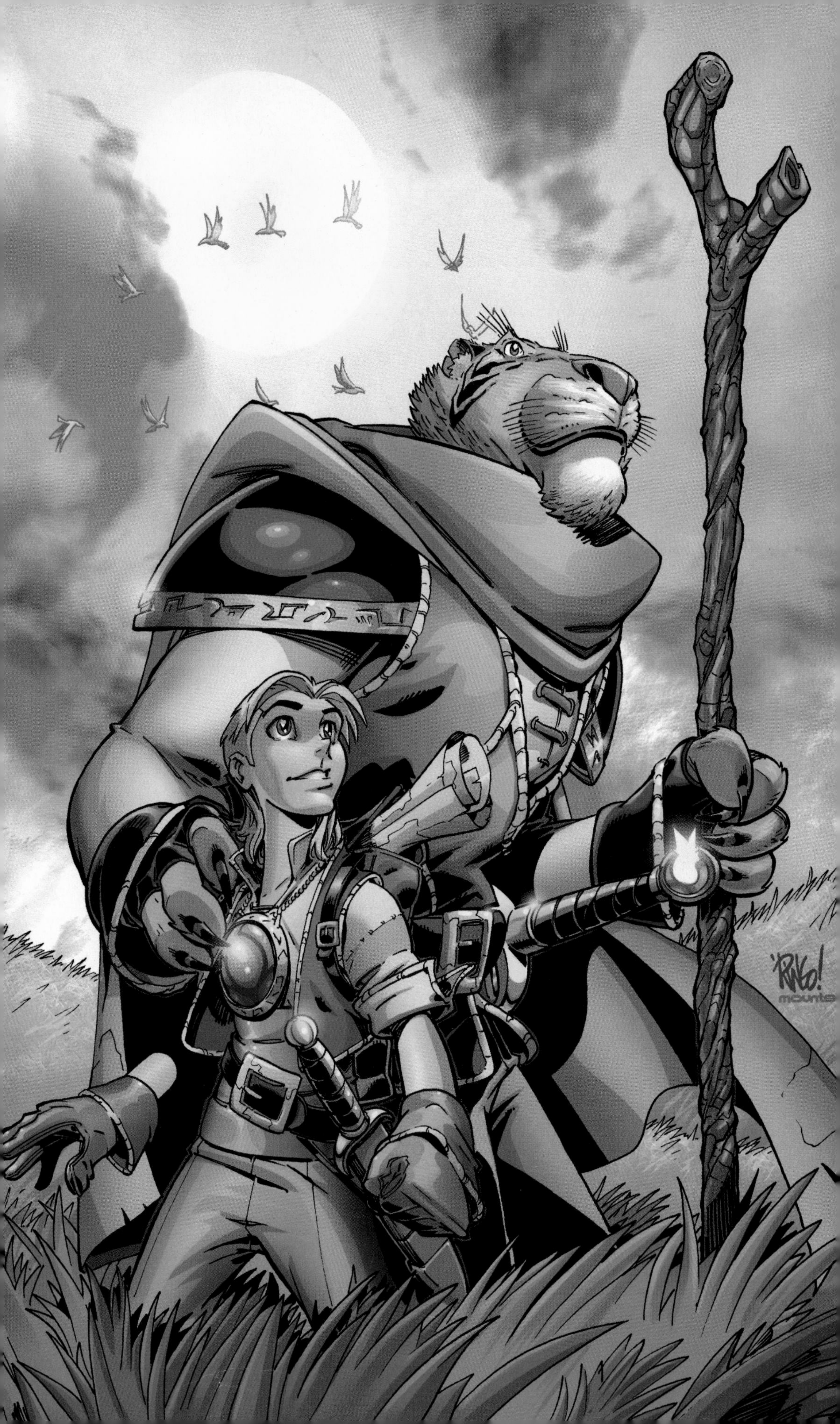
'RINGO!
mounts

TELLOS
PRELUDE

As we leapt headfirst into the realm of creator-owned comics, we soon found that variant covers and co-produced exclusives were the bartering chip of the day. While both Mike and I were a bit reluctant to create products that would be difficult for our Readers to get, we soon discovered that the hunting down and 'capturing' of these hidden treasures was, to many, half the fun!

The TELLOS PRELUDE was intended to be an 'eyes-in' for any new Readers, revealing to them the wonders of this fantastic new world and hoping that they might opt to visit again sometime...it features a short little verse, three pages shot from Mike's pencils (without the benefit of inks), and the early designs of Hawke and Rikk, before the latter was upgraded to fox.

Originally published to coincide with the release of TELLOS #3, the TELLOS PRELUDE was produced under the auspices of AnotherUniverse.com.

TELLOS
PROLOGUE

Intended to be a true prologue to the events of TELLOS #1, the TELLOS PROLOGUE introduced the larcenous team of HAWKE and RIKK to our faithful Tellos Readers. Presenting some elements and situations that dove-tail directly into our first issue, this story was also designed to establish our intent to taunt the Reader with secrets and mysteries. We hope it worked.

Published in cooperation with Nick Barrucci and the gang at Dynamic Forces, the TELLOS PROLOGUE was released between TELLOS 4 and 5.

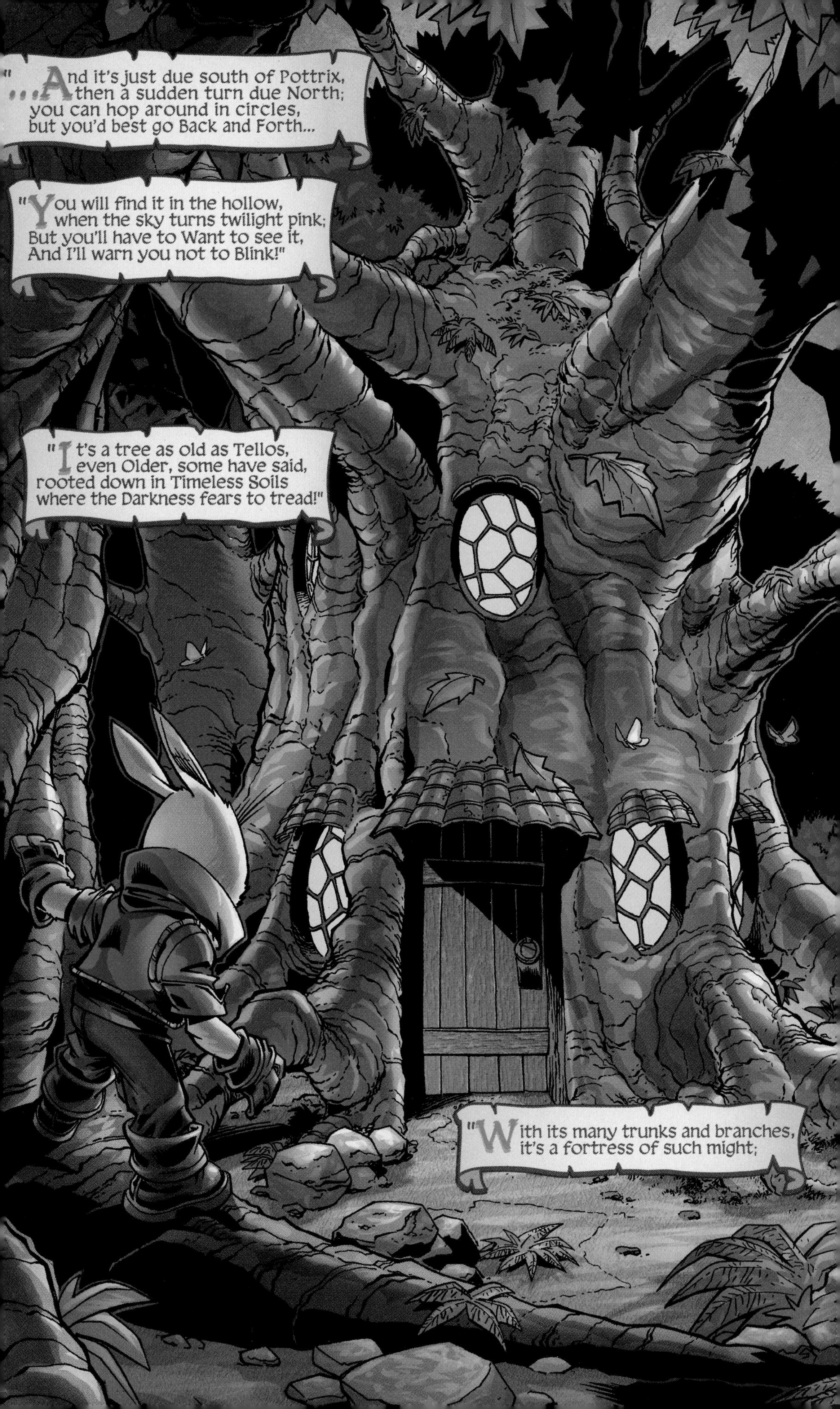
"...And it's just due south of Pottrix, then a sudden turn due North; you can hop around in circles, but you'd best go Back and Forth...
"You will find it in the hollow, when the sky turns twilight pink; But you'll have to Want to see it, And I'll warn you not to Blink!"
"It's a tree as old as Tellos, even Older, some have said, rooted down in Timeless Soils where the Darkness fears to tread!"
"With its many trunks and branches, it's a fortress of such might;

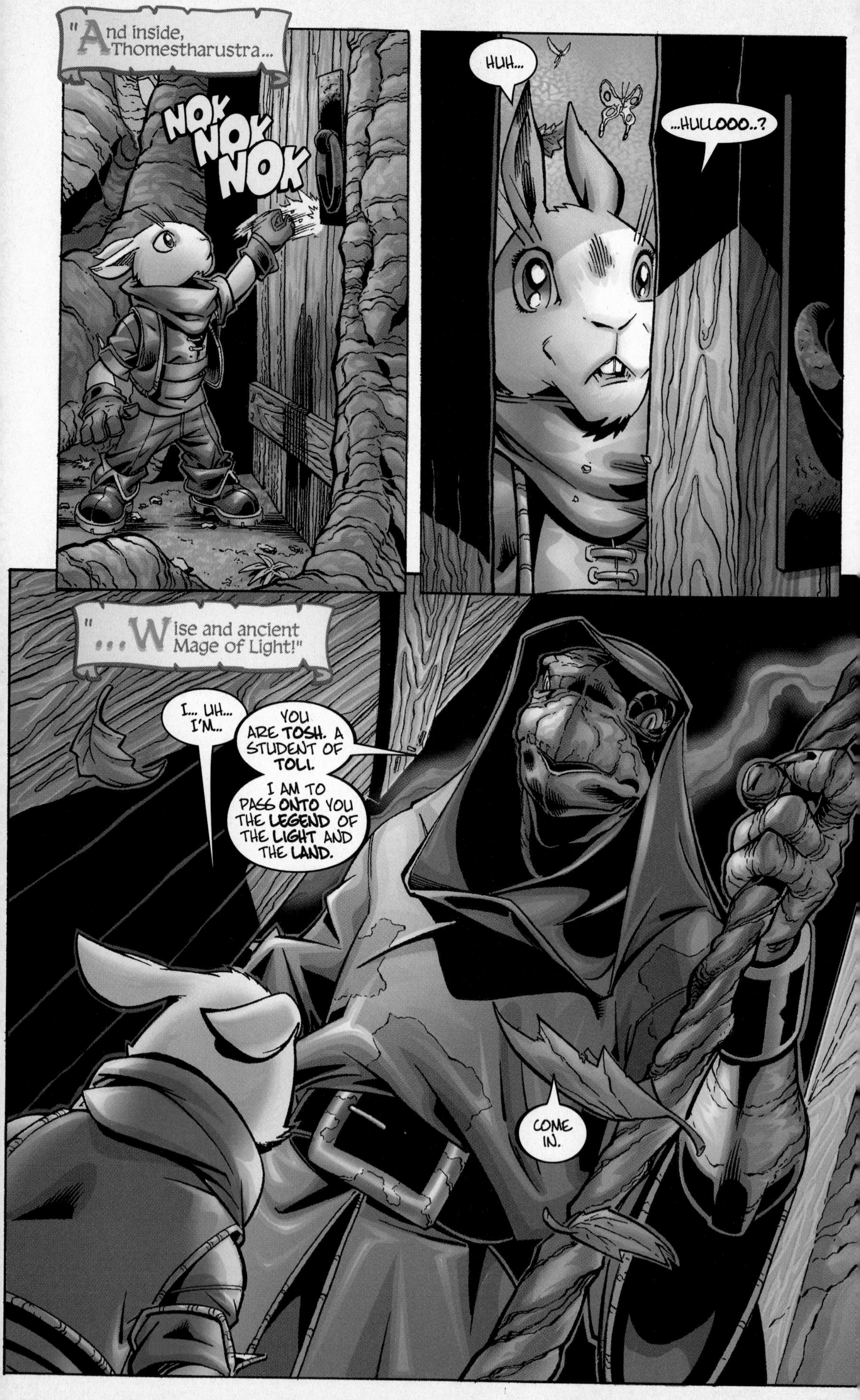
"And inside, Thomestharustra...
NOK NOK NOK
HUH...
...HULLOOO..?
"...Wise and ancient Mage of Light!"
I... UH... I'M...
YOU ARE TOSH. A STUDENT OF TOLI.
I AM TO PASS ONTO YOU THE LEGEND OF THE LIGHT AND THE LAND.
COME IN.

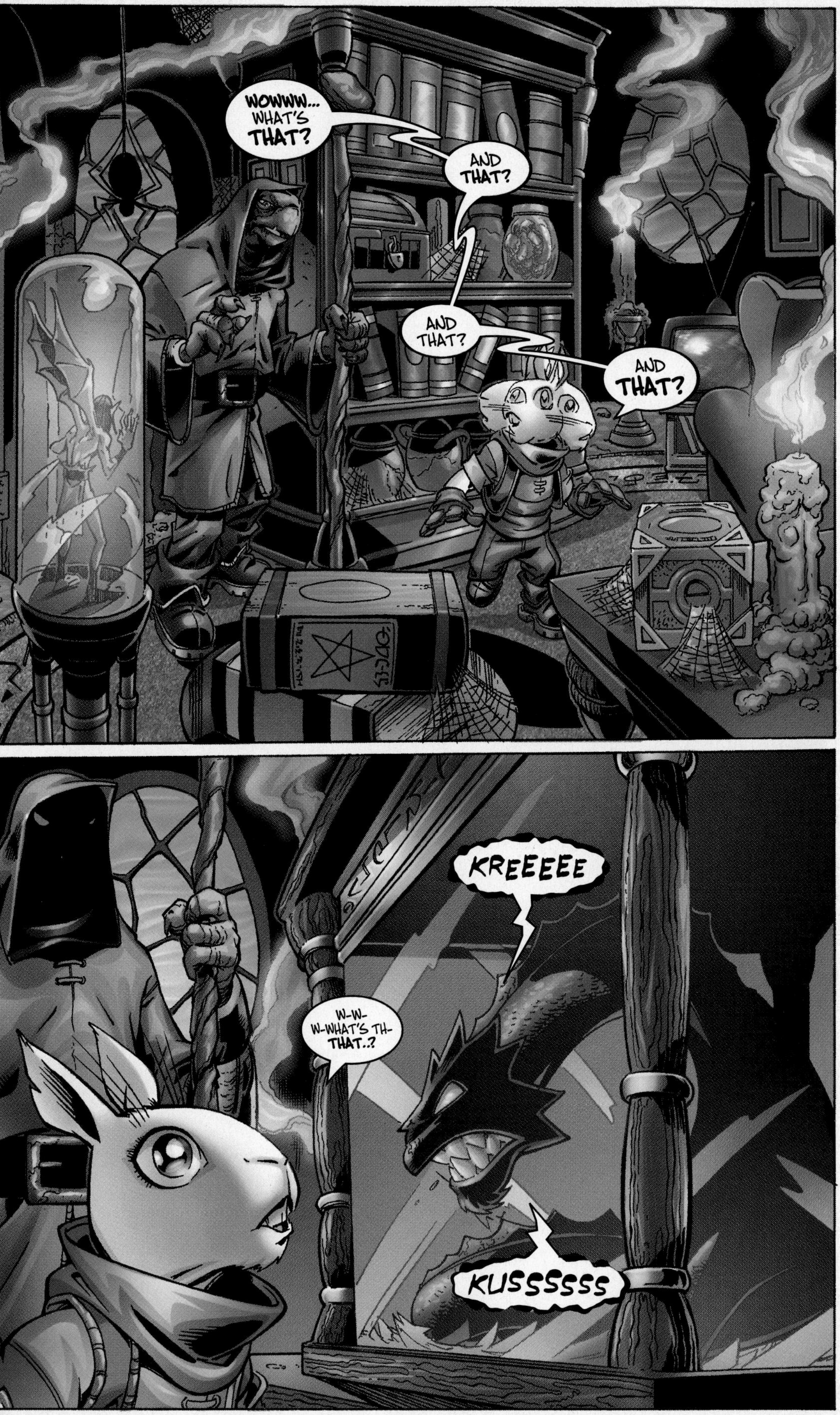
WOWWW... WHAT'S THAT?
AND THAT?
AND THAT?
AND THAT?
KREEEEE
W-W- W-WHAT'S TH- THAT..?
KUSSSSSS

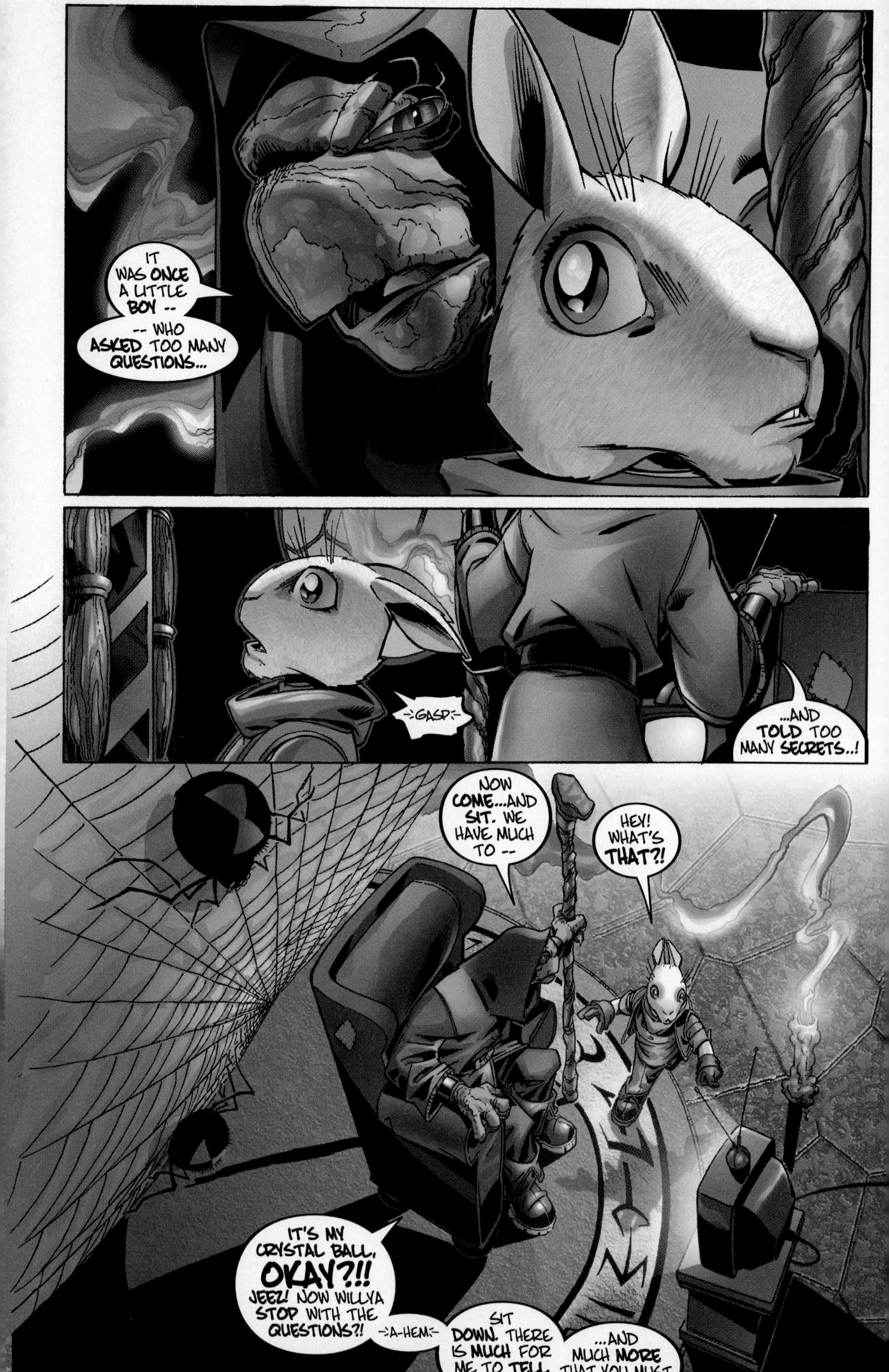
IT WAS ONCE A LITTLE BOY --
-- WHO ASKED TOO MANY QUESTIONS...
-:GASP:-
...AND TOLD TOO MANY SECRETS...!
NOW COME...AND SIT. WE HAVE MUCH TO --
HEY! WHAT'S THAT?!
IT'S MY CRYSTAL BALL, OKAY?!! JEEZ! NOW WILLYA STOP WITH THE QUESTIONS?!
-:A-HEM:-
SIT DOWN. THERE IS MUCH FOR ME TO TELL YOU...
...AND MUCH MORE THAT YOU MUST LEARN...

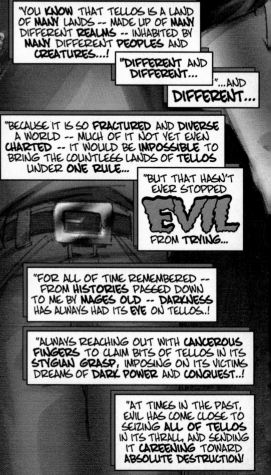

"YOU **KNOW** THAT TELLOS IS A LAND OF **MANY** LANDS -- MADE UP OF MANY DIFFERENT **REALMS** -- INHABITED BY **MANY** DIFFERENT **PEOPLES** AND CREATURES...!

"DIFFERENT AND DIFFERENT...

"...AND DIFFERENT...

"BECAUSE IT IS SO FRACTURED AND DIVERSE A WORLD -- MUCH OF IT NOT YET EVEN **CHARTED** -- IT WOULD BE **IMPOSSIBLE** TO BRING THE COUNTLESS LANDS OF TELLOS UNDER **ONE** RULE...

"BUT THAT HASN'T EVER STOPPED **EVIL** FROM TRYING...

"FOR ALL OF TIME REMEMBERED -- FROM **HISTORIES** PASSED DOWN TO ME BY **MAGES** OLD -- DARKNESS HAS ALWAYS HAD ITS **EYE** ON TELLOS..!

"ALWAYS REACHING OUT WITH **CANCEROUS** FINGERS TO CLAIM BITS OF TELLOS IN ITS **STYGIAN** GRASP, IMPOSING ON ITS VICTIMS DREAMS OF **DARK** POWER AND CONQUEST..!

"AT TIMES IN THE PAST, EVIL HAS COME CLOSE TO SEIZING ALL OF TELLOS IN ITS THRALL, AND SENDING IT **CAREENING** TOWARD ABSOLUTE DESTRUCTION!

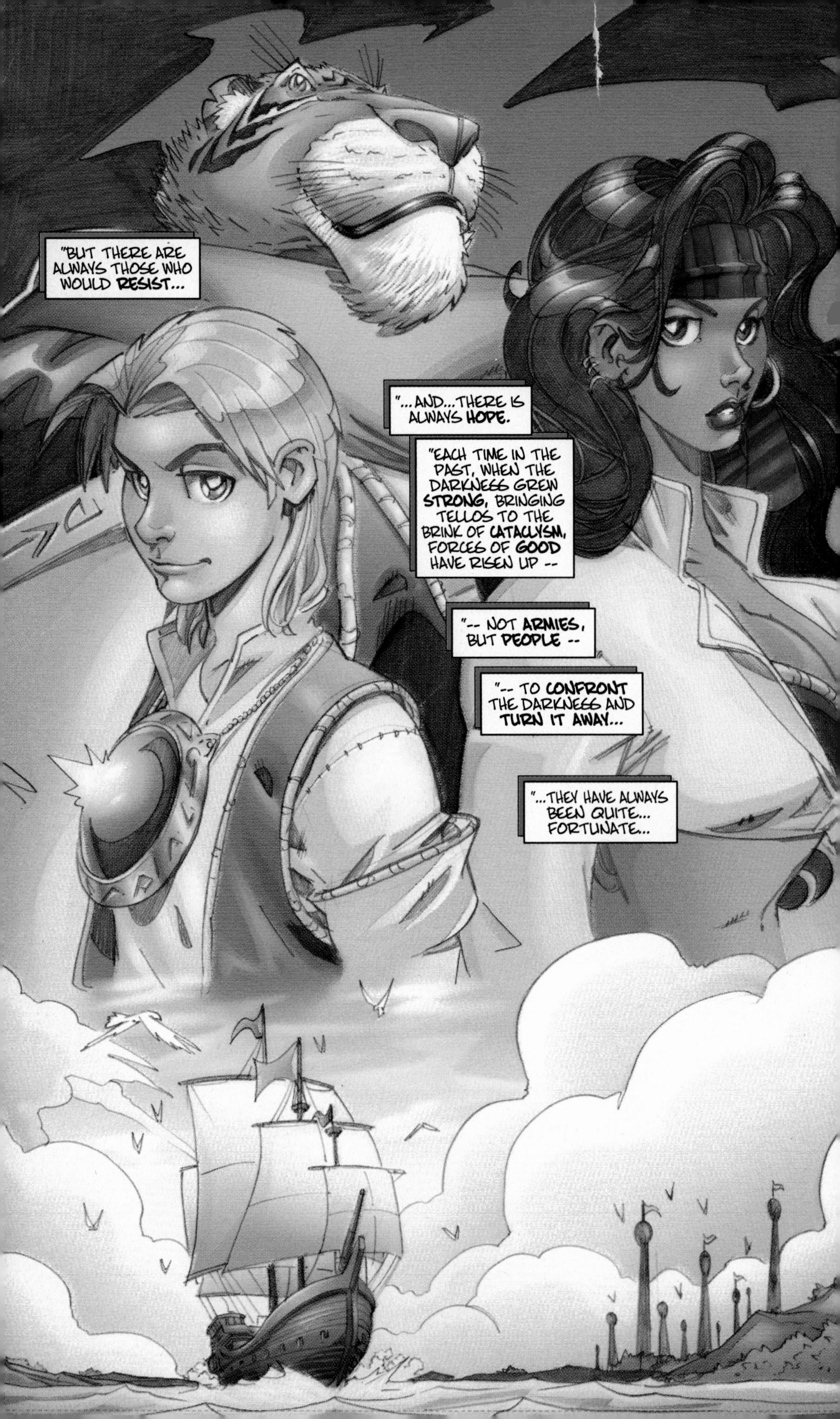
"BUT THERE ARE ALWAYS THOSE WHO WOULD **RESIST**...
"...AND...THERE IS ALWAYS **HOPE**.
"EACH TIME IN THE PAST, WHEN THE DARKNESS GREW **STRONG**, BRINGING TELLOS TO THE BRINK OF **CATACLYSM**, FORCES OF **GOOD** HAVE RISEN UP --
"-- NOT **ARMIES**, BUT **PEOPLE** --
"-- TO **CONFRONT** THE DARKNESS AND **TURN IT AWAY**...
"...THEY HAVE ALWAYS BEEN QUITE... FORTUNATE...

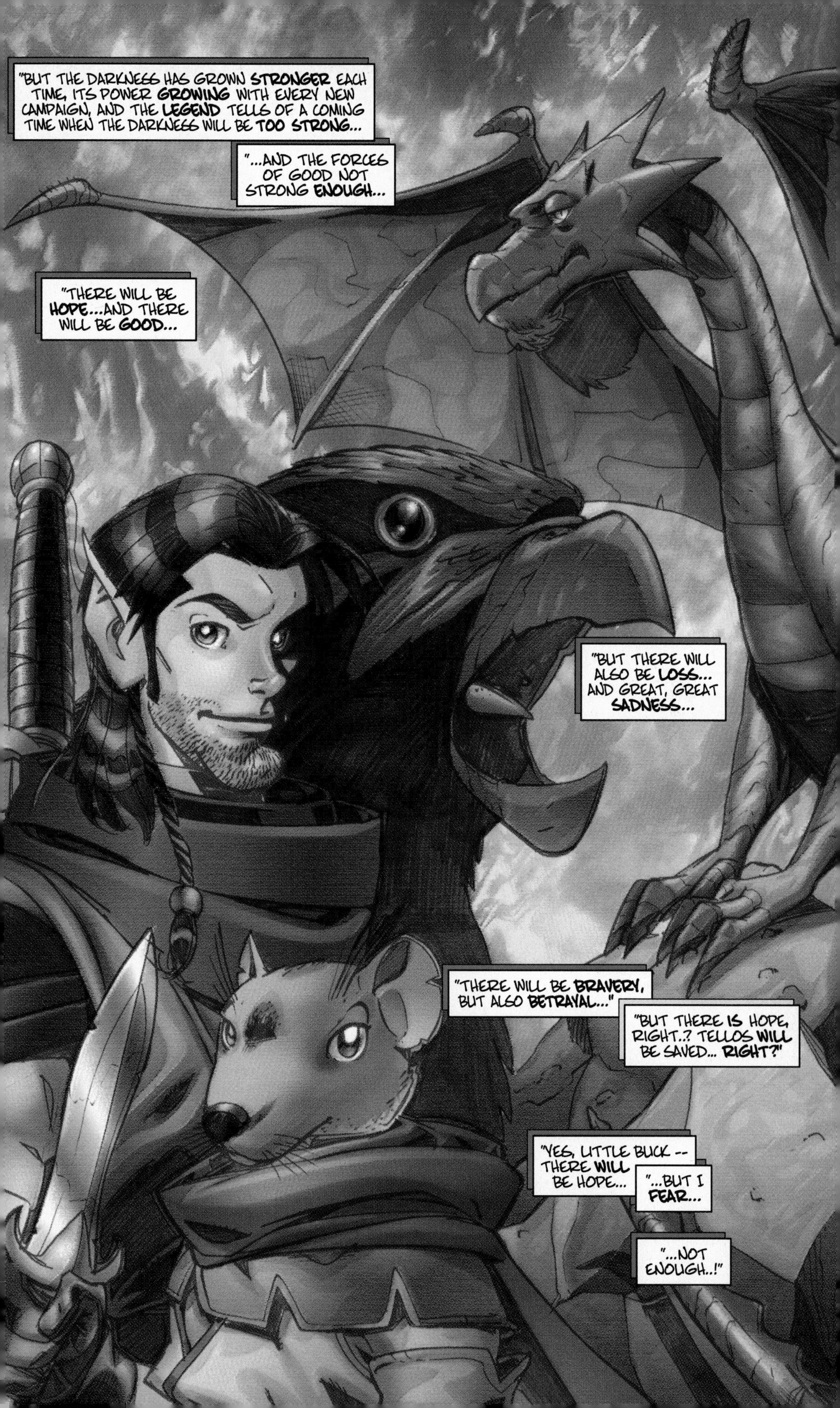
"BUT THE DARKNESS HAS GROWN STRONGER EACH TIME, ITS POWER GROWING WITH EVERY NEW CAMPAIGN, AND THE LEGEND TELLS OF A COMING TIME WHEN THE DARKNESS WILL BE TOO STRONG...
"...AND THE FORCES OF GOOD NOT STRONG ENOUGH...
"THERE WILL BE HOPE...AND THERE WILL BE GOOD...
"BUT THERE WILL ALSO BE LOSS... AND GREAT, GREAT SADNESS...
"THERE WILL BE BRAVERY, BUT ALSO BETRAYAL..."
"BUT THERE IS HOPE, RIGHT..? TELLOS WILL BE SAVED... RIGHT?"
"YES, LITTLE BUCK -- THERE WILL BE HOPE...
"...BUT I FEAR...
"...NOT ENOUGH..!"

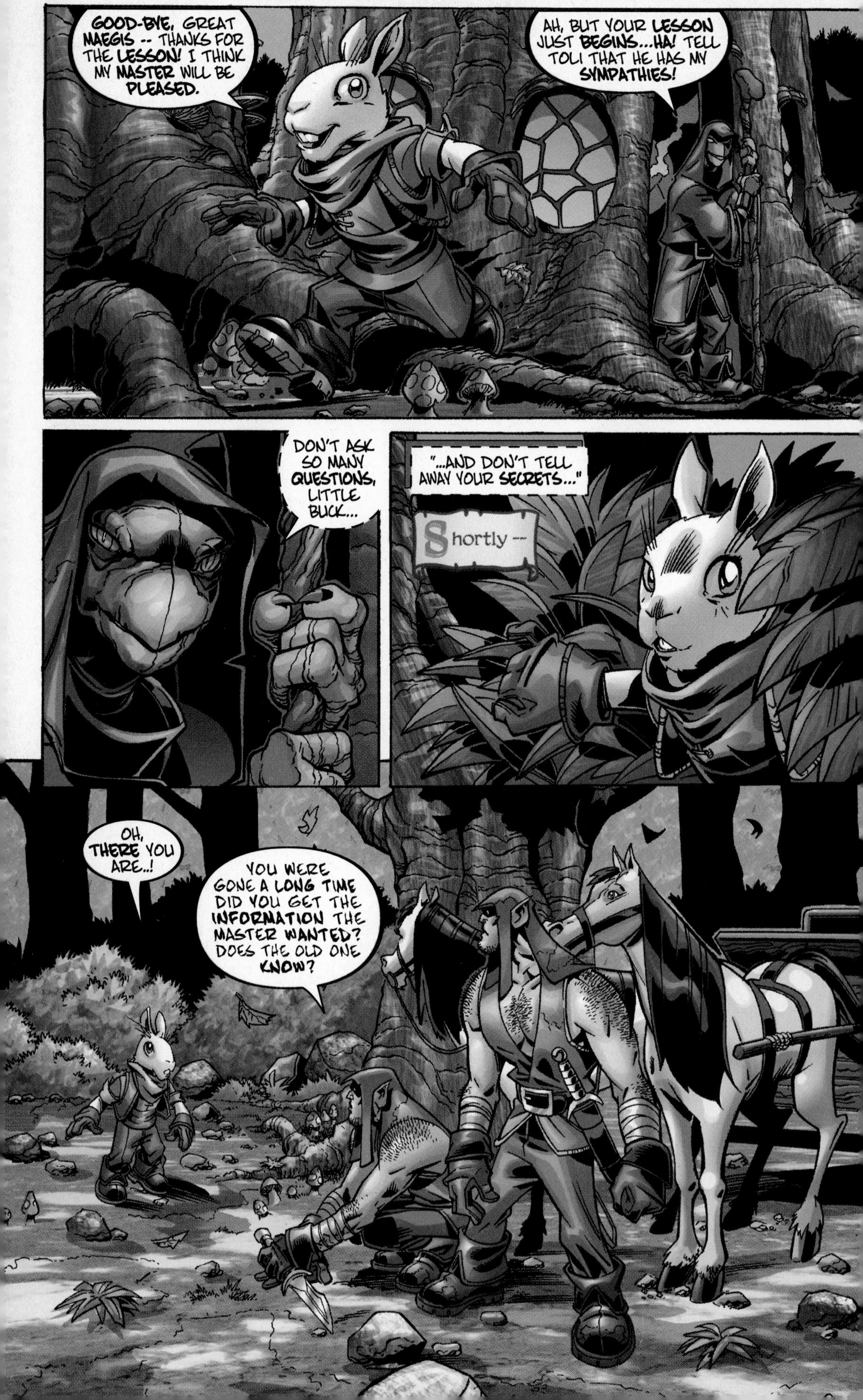
GOOD-BYE, GREAT MAEGIS -- THANKS FOR THE LESSON! I THINK MY MASTER WILL BE PLEASED.
AH, BUT YOUR LESSON JUST BEGINS...HA! TELL TOLI THAT HE HAS MY SYMPATHIES!
DON'T ASK SO MANY QUESTIONS, LITTLE BUCK...
"...AND DON'T TELL AWAY YOUR SECRETS..."
Shortly --
OH, THERE YOU ARE..!
YOU WERE GONE A LONG TIME DID YOU GET THE INFORMATION THE MASTER WANTED? DOES THE OLD ONE KNOW?

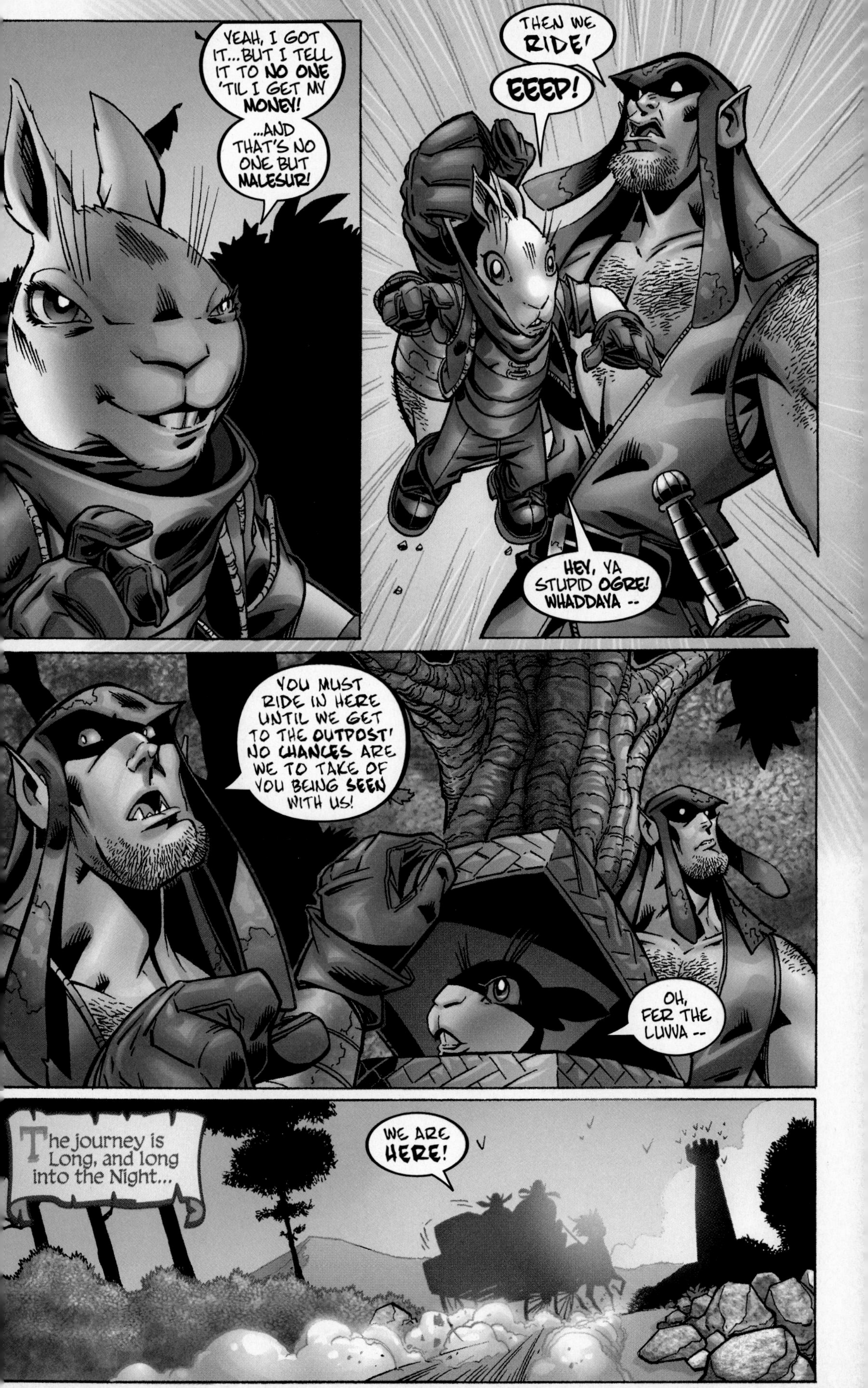
YEAH, I GOT IT...BUT I TELL IT TO NO ONE 'TIL I GET MY MONEY!
...AND THAT'S NO ONE BUT MALESUR!
THEN WE RIDE!
EEEP!
HEY, YA STUPID OGRE! WHADDAYA --
YOU MUST RIDE IN HERE UNTIL WE GET TO THE OUTPOST! NO CHANCES ARE WE TO TAKE OF YOU BEING SEEN WITH US!
OH, FER THE LUVVA --
The journey is Long, and long into the Night...
WE ARE HERE!

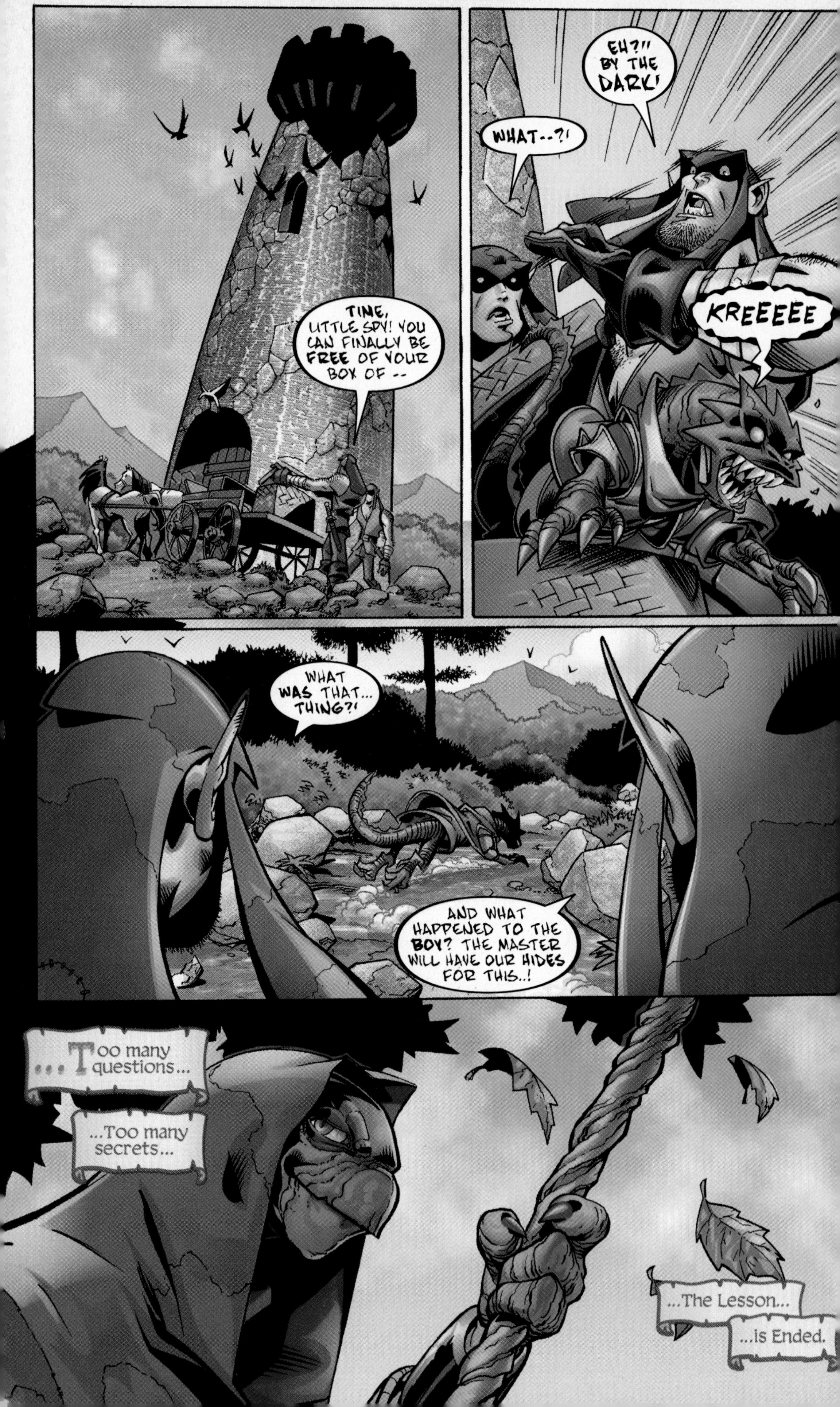
TIME, LITTLE SPY! YOU CAN FINALLY BE FREE OF YOUR BOX OF --
WHAT--?!
EH?!! BY THE DARK!
KREEEEE
WHAT WAS THAT... THING?!
AND WHAT HAPPENED TO THE BOY? THE MASTER WILL HAVE OUR HIDES FOR THIS..!
...Too many questions...
...Too many secrets...
...The Lesson...
...is Ended.

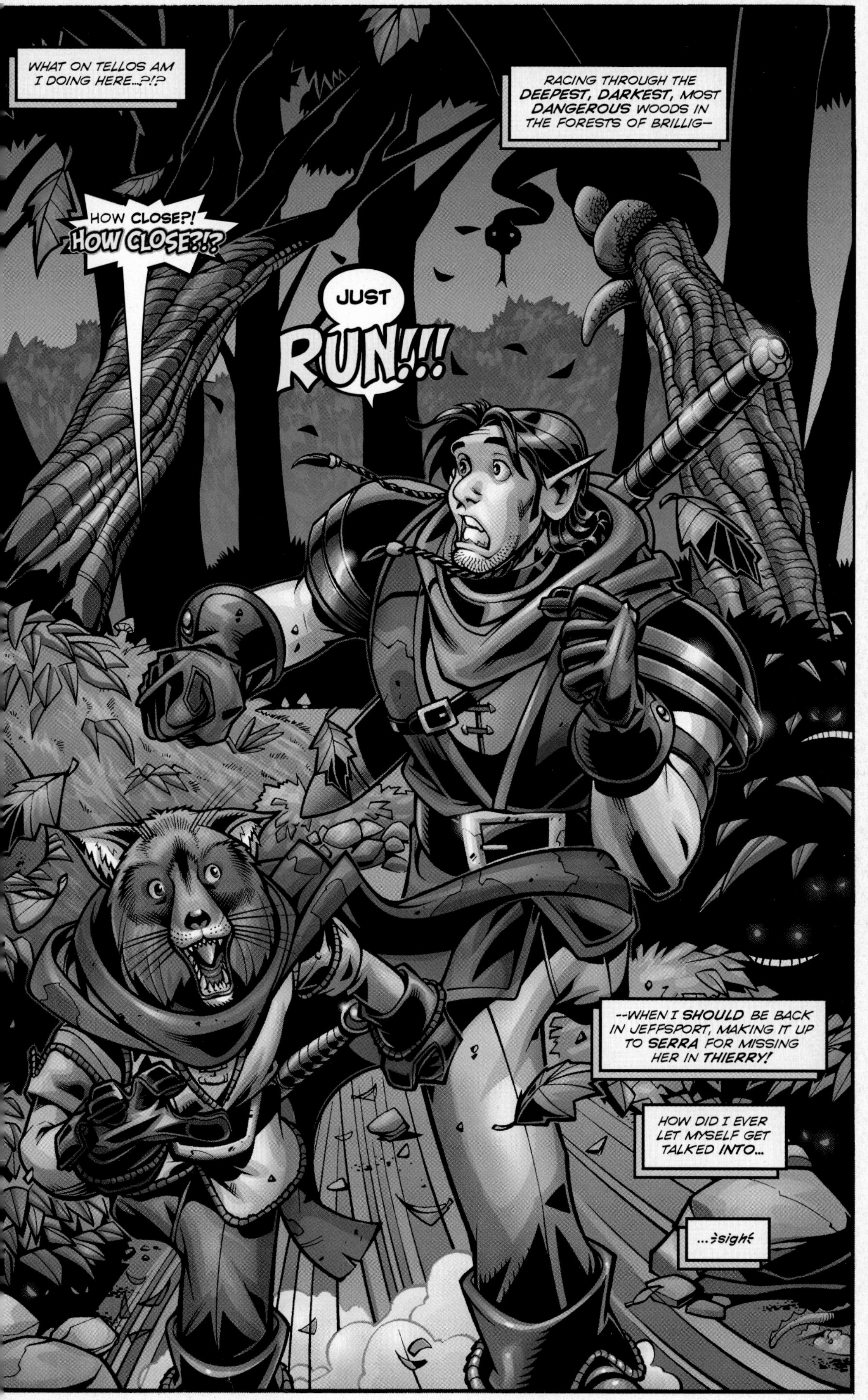
WHAT ON TELLOS AM I DOING HERE...?!?
RACING THROUGH THE DEEPEST, DARKEST, MOST DANGEROUS WOODS IN THE FORESTS OF BRILLIG--
HOW CLOSE?! HOW CLOSE?!?
JUST RUN!!!
--WHEN I SHOULD BE BACK IN JEFFSPORT, MAKING IT UP TO SERRA FOR MISSING HER IN THIERRY!
HOW DID I EVER LET MYSELF GET TALKED INTO...
...sigh

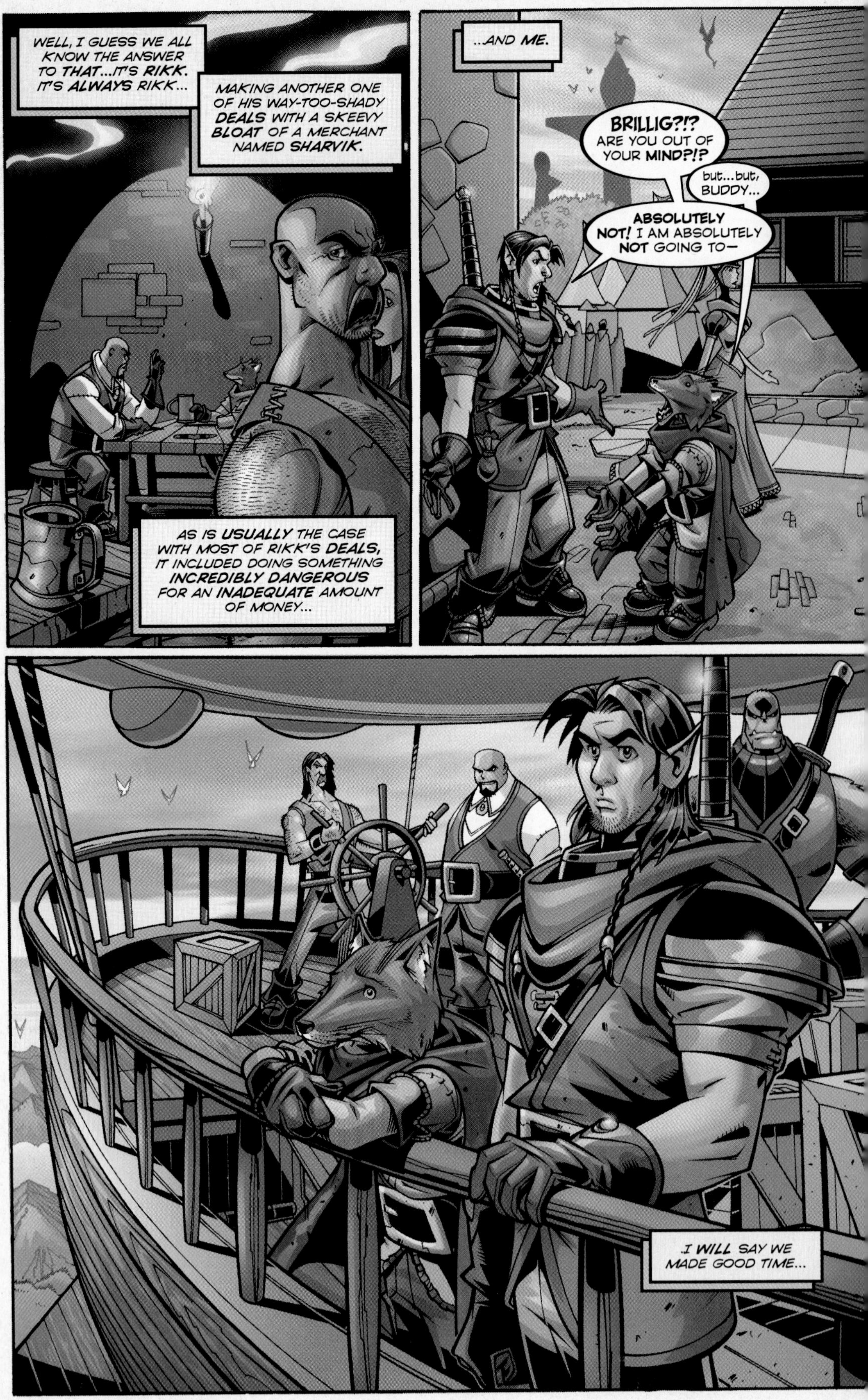
WELL, I GUESS WE ALL KNOW THE ANSWER TO THAT...IT'S RIKK. IT'S ALWAYS RIKK...
MAKING ANOTHER ONE OF HIS WAY-TOO-SHADY DEALS WITH A SKEEVY BLOAT OF A MERCHANT NAMED SHARVIK.
AS IS USUALLY THE CASE WITH MOST OF RIKK'S DEALS, IT INCLUDED DOING SOMETHING INCREDIBLY DANGEROUS FOR AN INADEQUATE AMOUNT OF MONEY...
...AND ME.
BRILLIG?!? ARE YOU OUT OF YOUR MIND?!?
but...but, BUDDY...
ABSOLUTELY NOT! I AM ABSOLUTELY NOT GOING TO—
..I WILL SAY WE MADE GOOD TIME...

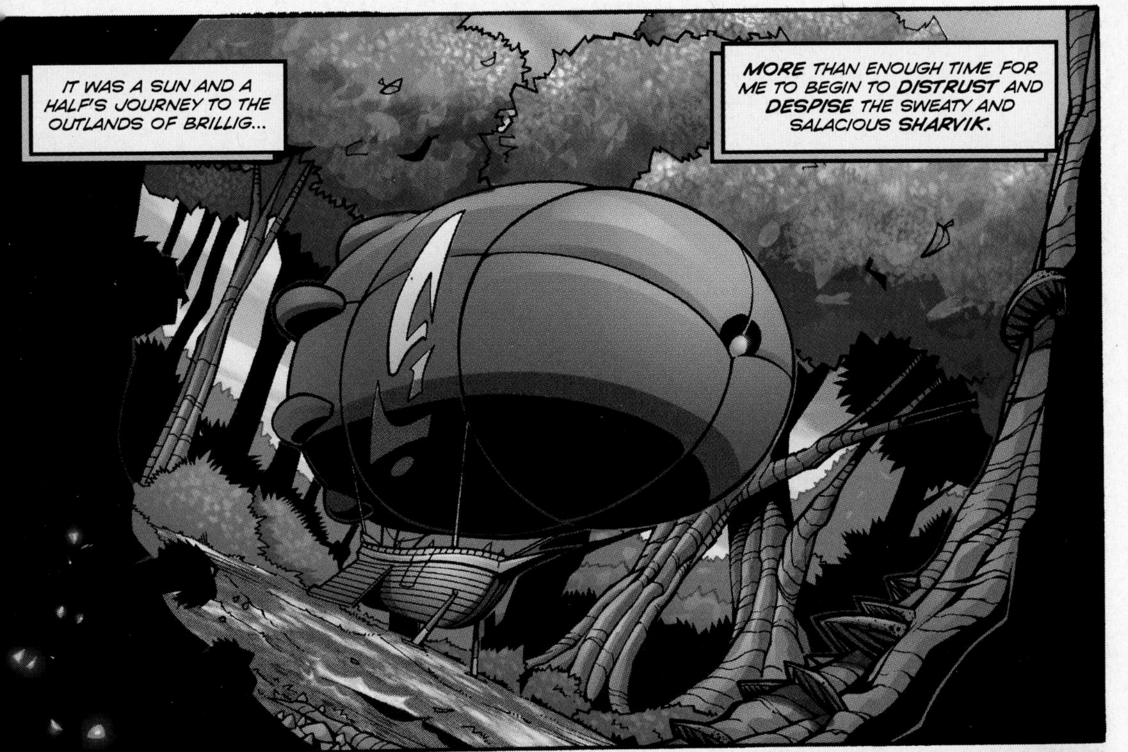
IT WAS A SUN AND A HALF'S JOURNEY TO THE OUTLANDS OF BRILLIG...
MORE THAN ENOUGH TIME FOR ME TO BEGIN TO DISTRUST AND DESPISE THE SWEATY AND SALACIOUS SHARVIK.

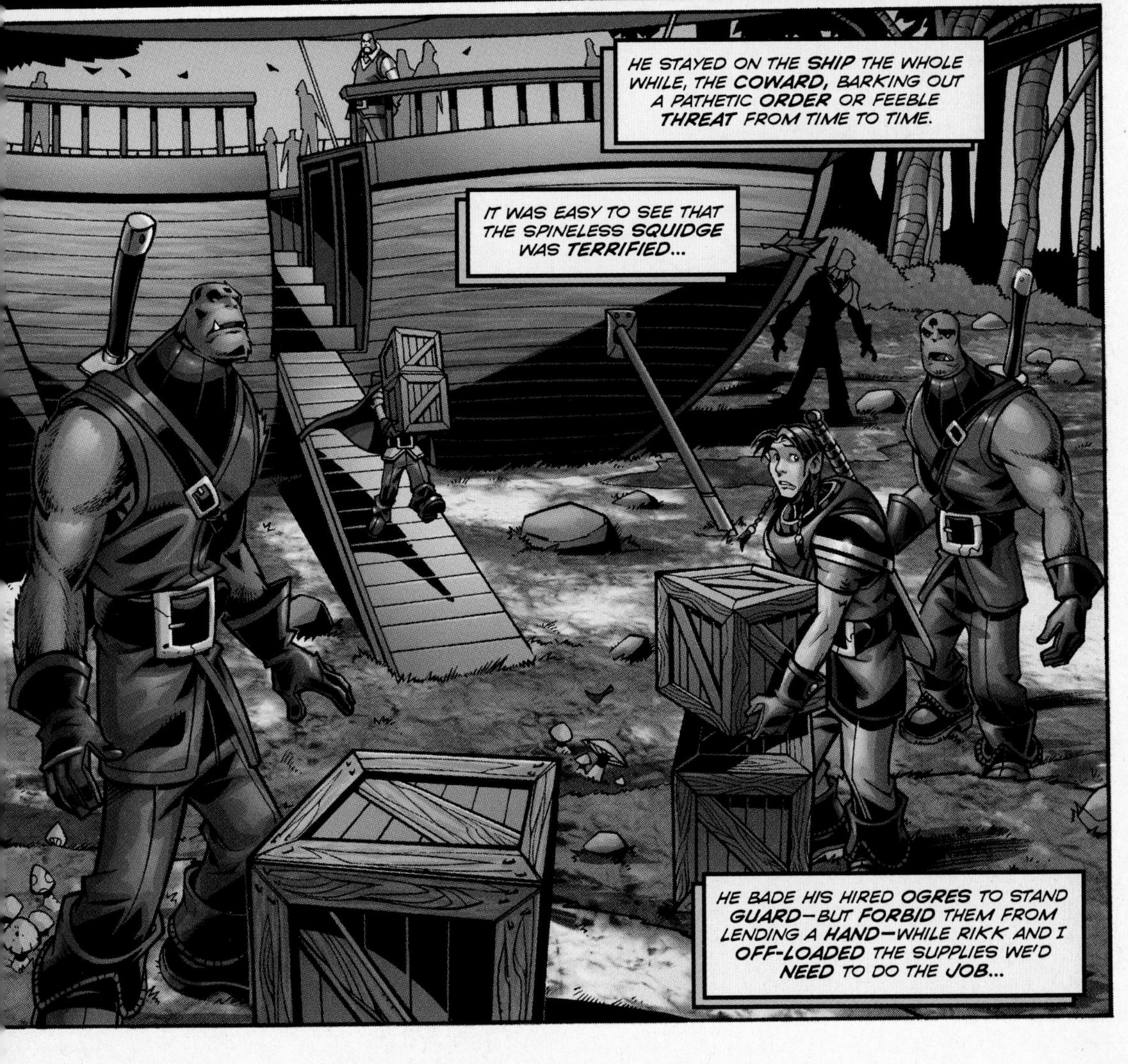
HE STAYED ON THE SHIP THE WHOLE WHILE, THE COWARD, BARKING OUT A PATHETIC ORDER OR FEEBLE THREAT FROM TIME TO TIME.
IT WAS EASY TO SEE THAT THE SPINELESS SQUIDGE WAS TERRIFIED...
HE BADE HIS HIRED OGRES TO STAND GUARD—BUT FORBID THEM FROM LENDING A HAND—WHILE RIKK AND I OFF-LOADED THE SUPPLIES WE'D NEED TO DO THE JOB...

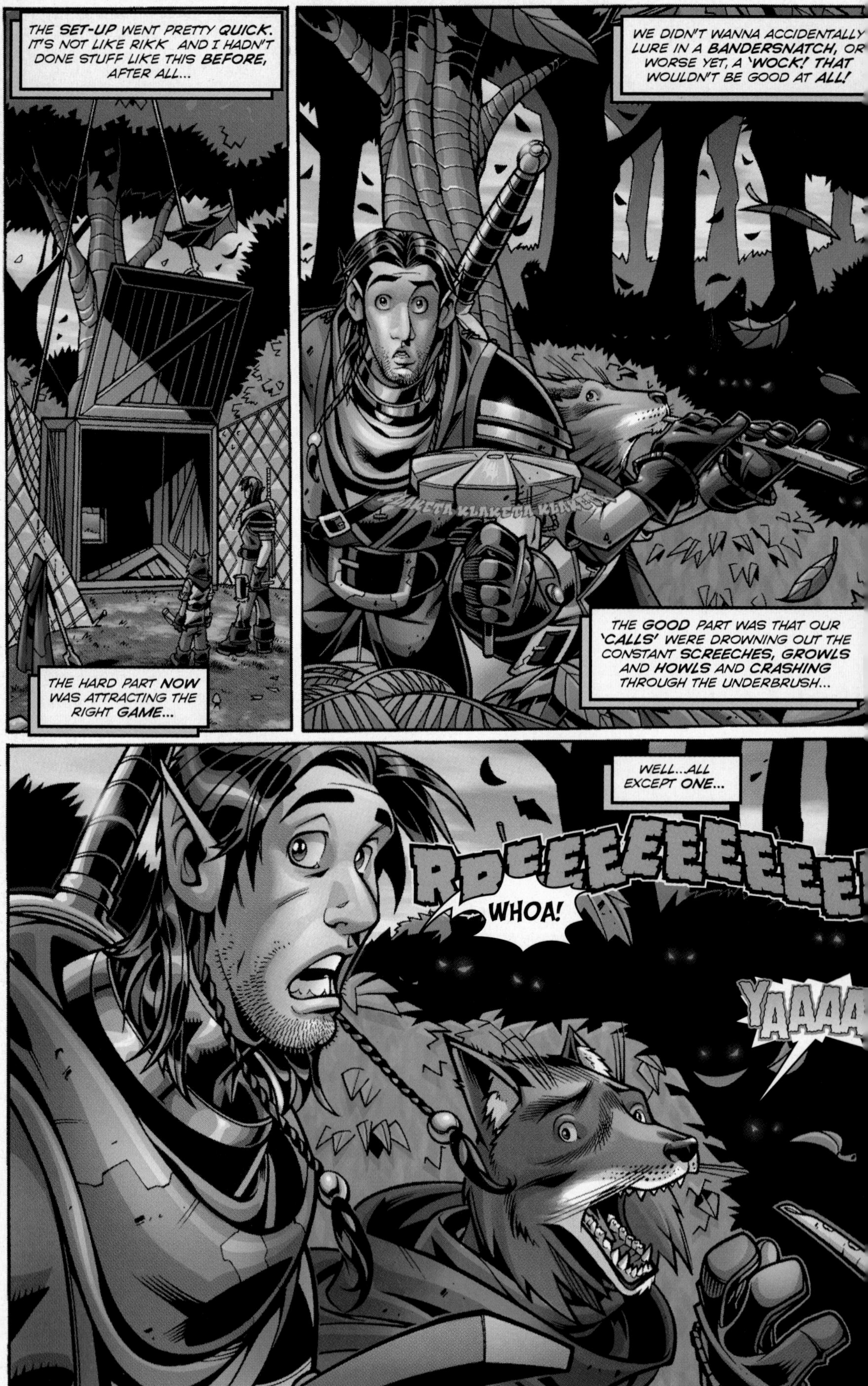
THE SET-UP WENT PRETTY QUICK. IT'S NOT LIKE RIKK AND I HADN'T DONE STUFF LIKE THIS BEFORE, AFTER ALL...
THE HARD PART NOW WAS ATTRACTING THE RIGHT GAME...
WE DIDN'T WANNA ACCIDENTALLY LURE IN A BANDERSNATCH, OR WORSE YET, A 'WOCK! THAT WOULDN'T BE GOOD AT ALL!
THE GOOD PART WAS THAT OUR 'CALLS' WERE DROWNING OUT THE CONSTANT SCREECHES, GROWLS AND HOWLS AND CRASHING THROUGH THE UNDERBRUSH...
WELL...ALL EXCEPT ONE...
WHOA!
YAAAA

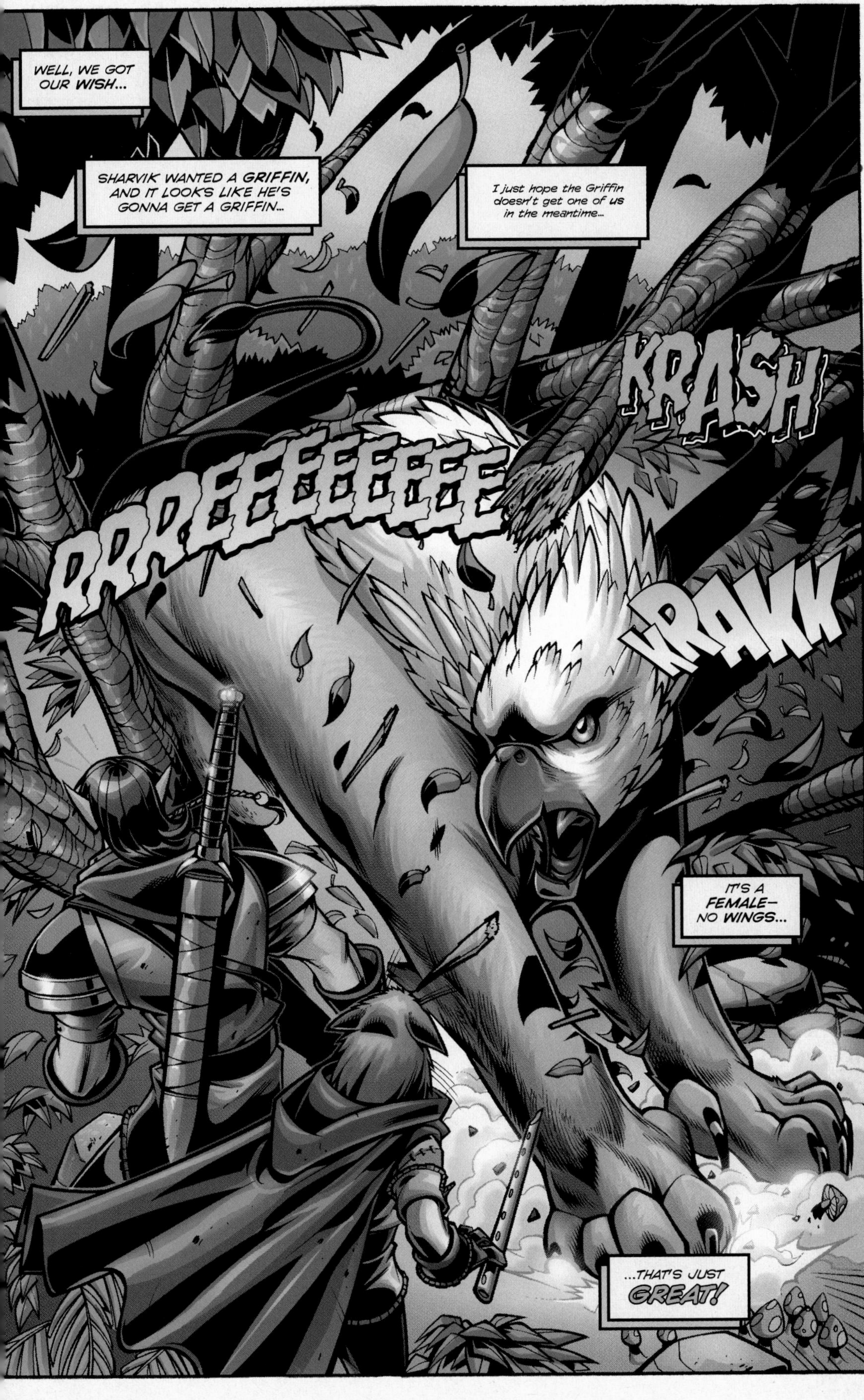
WELL, WE GOT OUR WISH...
SHARVIK WANTED A GRIFFIN, AND IT LOOKS LIKE HE'S GONNA GET A GRIFFIN...
I just hope the Griffin doesn't get one of us in the meantime...
KRASH
RRREEEEEEEEEEE
KRAKK
IT'S A FEMALE— NO WINGS...
...THAT'S JUST GREAT!

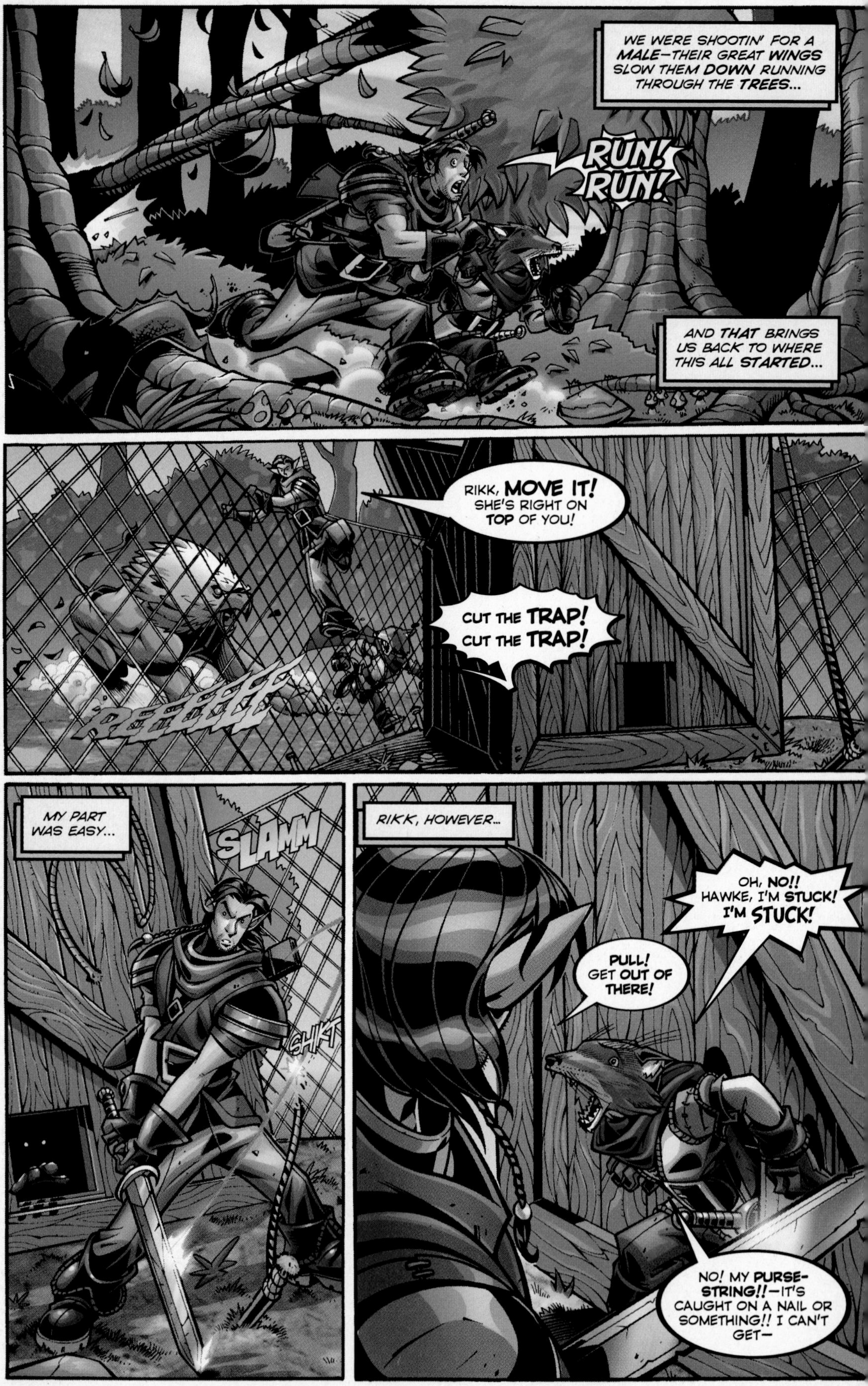
WE WERE SHOOTIN' FOR A MALE—THEIR GREAT WINGS SLOW THEM DOWN RUNNING THROUGH THE TREES...
RUN! RUN!
AND THAT BRINGS US BACK TO WHERE THIS ALL STARTED...
RIKK, MOVE IT! SHE'S RIGHT ON TOP OF YOU!
CUT THE TRAP! CUT THE TRAP!
MY PART WAS EASY...
SLAMM
SHIKT
RIKK, HOWEVER...
OH, NO!! HAWKE, I'M STUCK! I'M STUCK!
PULL! GET OUT OF THERE!
NO! MY PURSE-STRING!!—IT'S CAUGHT ON A NAIL OR SOMETHING!! I CAN'T GET—

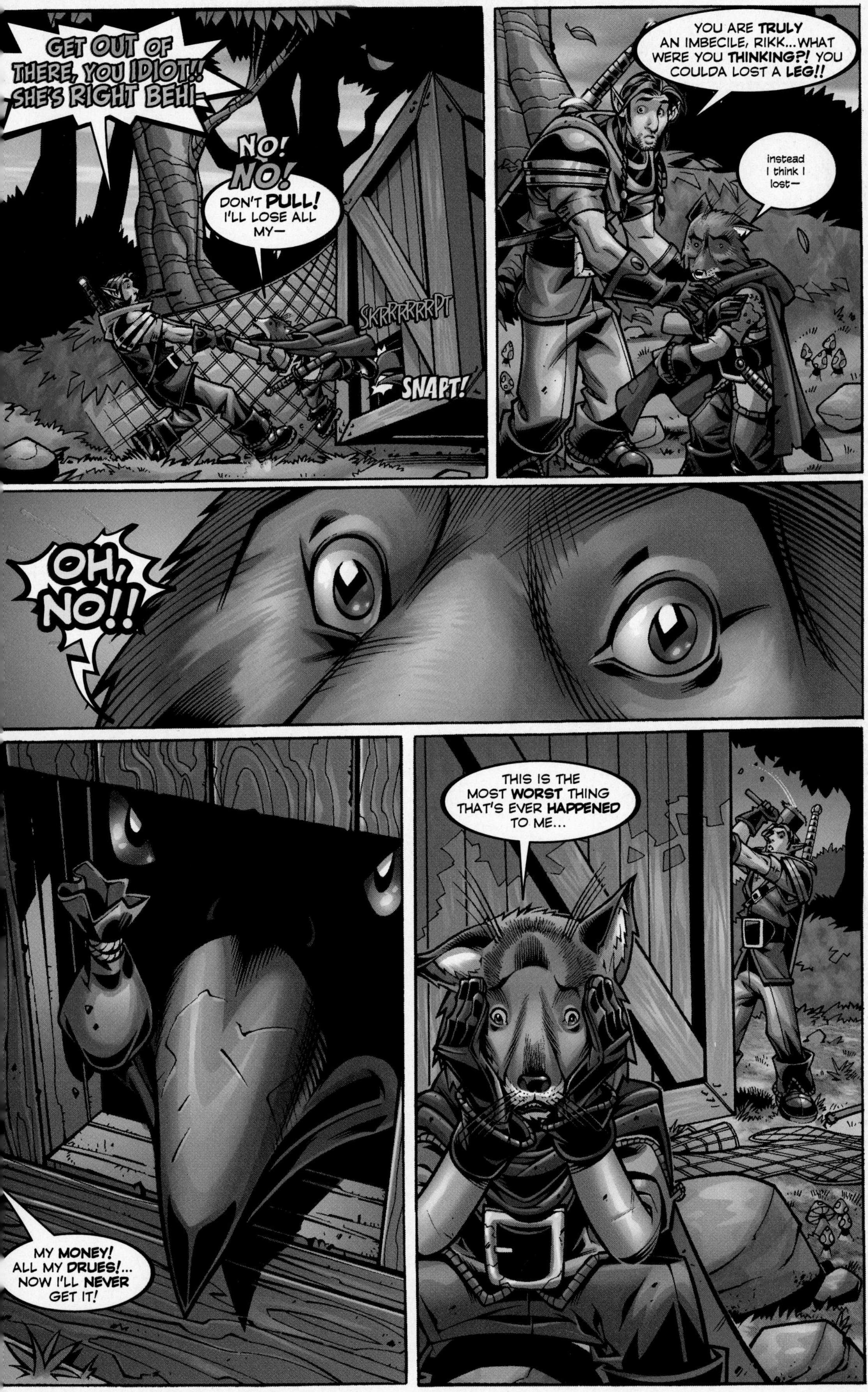
GET OUT OF THERE, YOU IDIOT!! SHE'S RIGHT BEHI–
NO! NO! DON'T PULL! I'LL LOSE ALL MY—
SKRRRRRRPT
SNAPT!
YOU ARE TRULY AN IMBECILE, RIKK...WHAT WERE YOU THINKING?! YOU COULDA LOST A LEG!!
instead I think I lost—
OH, NO!!
MY MONEY! ALL MY DRUES!... NOW I'LL NEVER GET IT!
THIS IS THE MOST WORST THING THAT'S EVER HAPPENED TO ME...

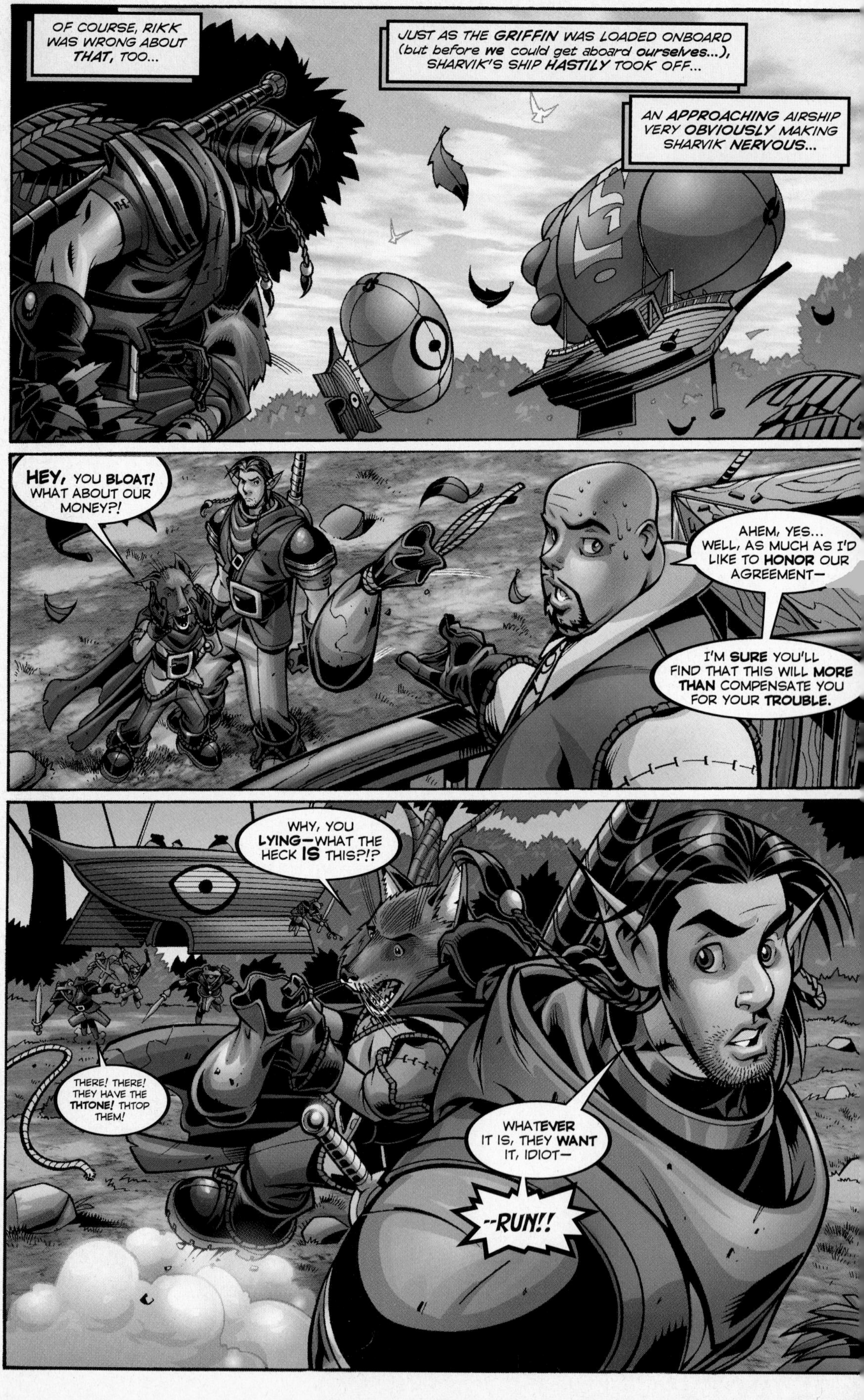
OF COURSE, RIKK WAS WRONG ABOUT THAT, TOO...
JUST AS THE GRIFFIN WAS LOADED ONBOARD (but before we could get aboard ourselves...), SHARVIK'S SHIP HASTILY TOOK OFF...
AN APPROACHING AIRSHIP VERY OBVIOUSLY MAKING SHARVIK NERVOUS...
HEY, YOU BLOAT! WHAT ABOUT OUR MONEY?!
AHEM, YES... WELL, AS MUCH AS I'D LIKE TO HONOR OUR AGREEMENT—
I'M SURE YOU'LL FIND THAT THIS WILL MORE THAN COMPENSATE YOU FOR YOUR TROUBLE.
WHY, YOU LYING—WHAT THE HECK IS THIS?!?
THERE! THERE! THEY HAVE THE THTONE! THTOP THEM!
WHATEVER IT IS, THEY WANT IT, IDIOT—
--RUN!!

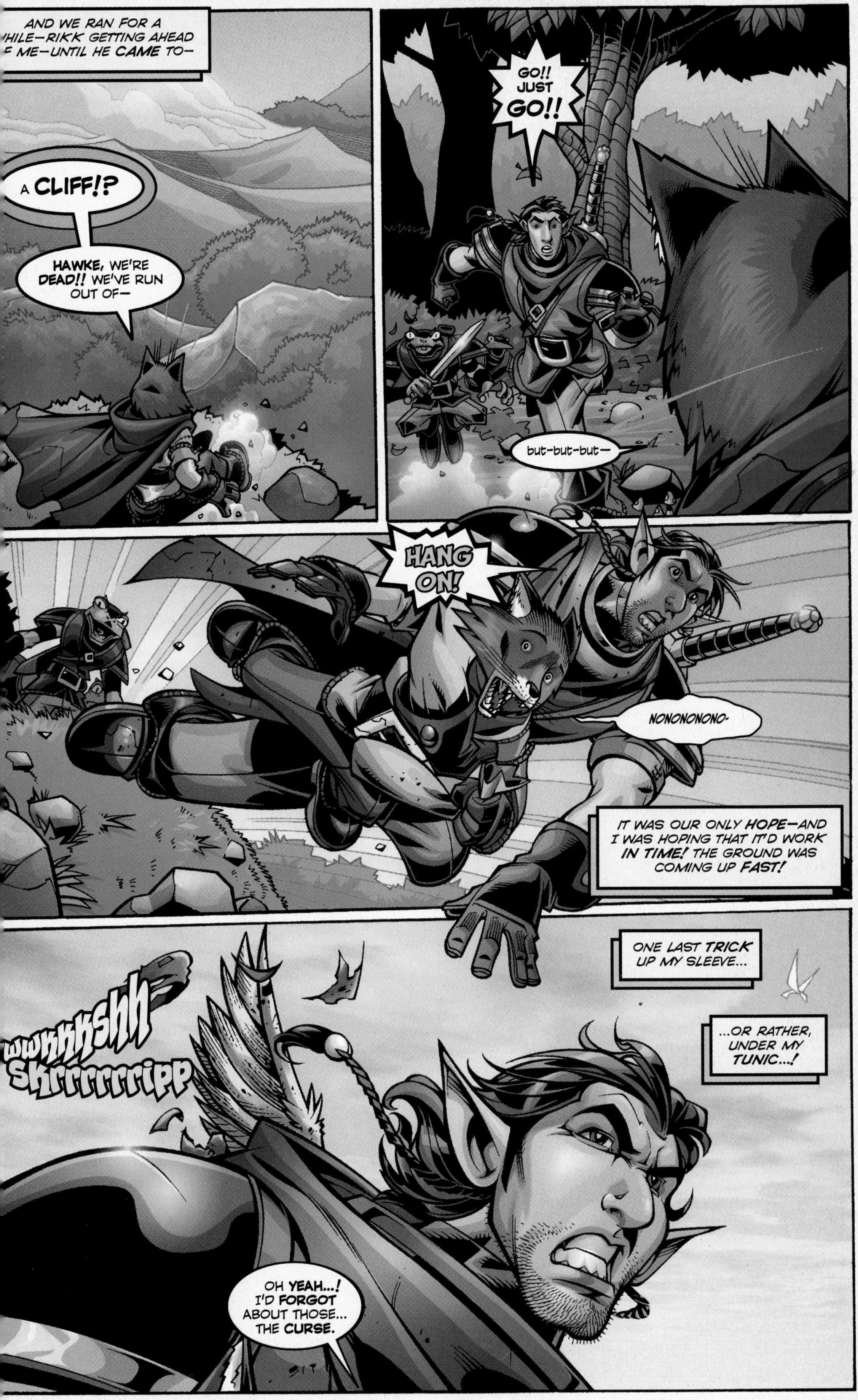
AND WE RAN FOR A WHILE—RIKK GETTING AHEAD OF ME—UNTIL HE CAME TO—
A CLIFF!?
HAWKE, WE'RE DEAD!! WE'VE RUN OUT OF—
GO!! JUST GO!!
but-but-but—
HANG ON!
NONONONONO-
IT WAS OUR ONLY HOPE—AND I WAS HOPING THAT IT'D WORK IN TIME! THE GROUND WAS COMING UP FAST!
ONE LAST TRICK UP MY SLEEVE...
...OR RATHER, UNDER MY TUNIC...!
wwhhkshh
skrrrrrripp
OH YEAH...! I'D FORGOT ABOUT THOSE... THE CURSE.

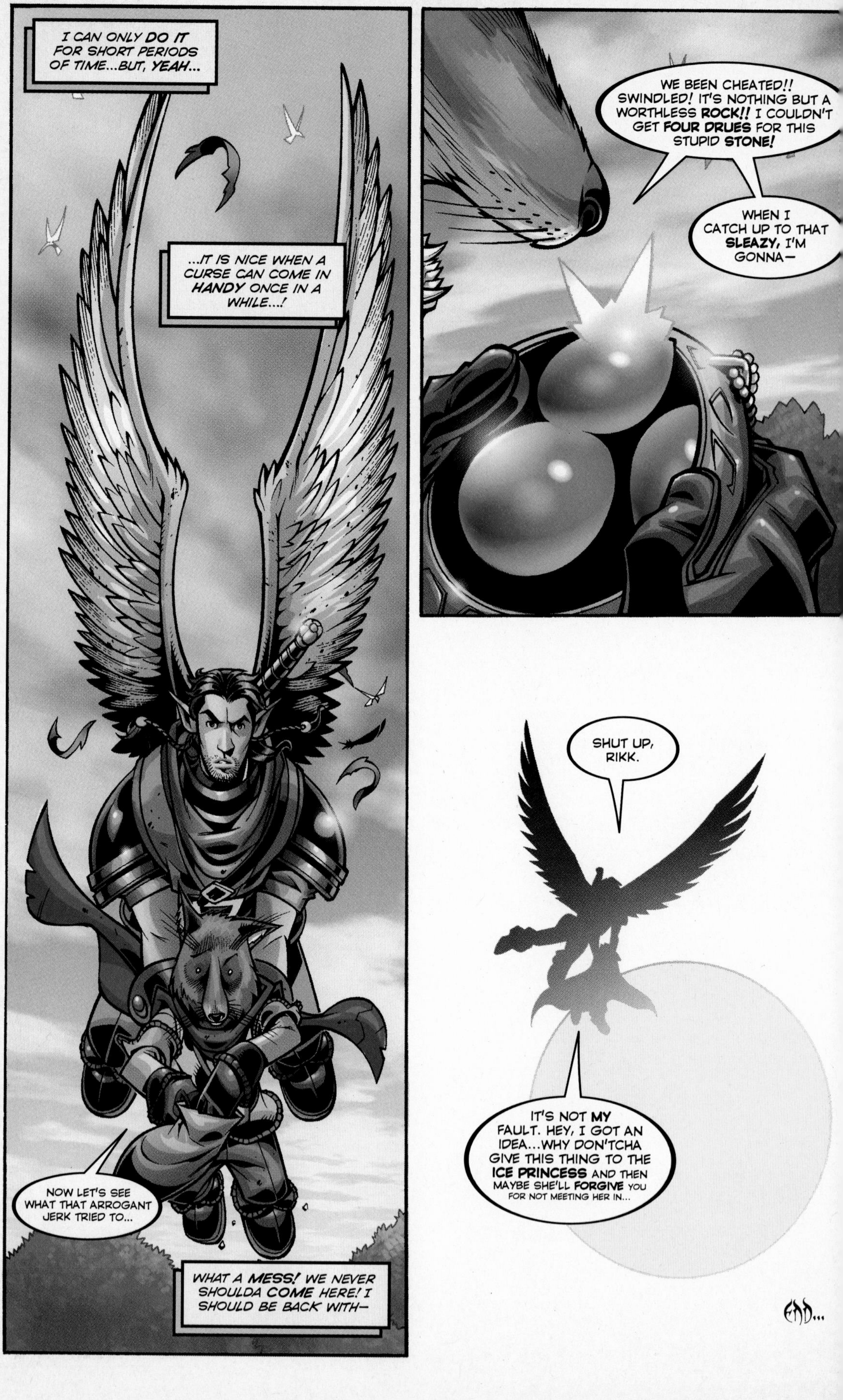
I CAN ONLY DO IT FOR SHORT PERIODS OF TIME...BUT, YEAH...
...IT IS NICE WHEN A CURSE CAN COME IN HANDY ONCE IN A WHILE...!
NOW LET'S SEE WHAT THAT ARROGANT JERK TRIED TO...
WHAT A MESS! WE NEVER SHOULDA COME HERE! I SHOULD BE BACK WITH—
WE BEEN CHEATED!! SWINDLED! IT'S NOTHING BUT A WORTHLESS ROCK!! I COULDN'T GET FOUR DRUES FOR THIS STUPID STONE!
WHEN I CATCH UP TO THAT SLEAZY, I'M GONNA—
SHUT UP, RIKK.
IT'S NOT MY FAULT. HEY, I GOT AN IDEA...WHY DON'TCHA GIVE THIS THING TO THE ICE PRINCESS AND THEN MAYBE SHE'LL FORGIVE YOU FOR NOT MEETING HER IN...
END...

JAREK

"NO WAY! NOT ME! . . .
really! I just touched that
thing and the light went
on. I'm not this 'ONE' guy!
Your Prophecy's gotta
mean somebody else!"

*JAREK, the reluctant hero,
after being presented
with his Destiny.*

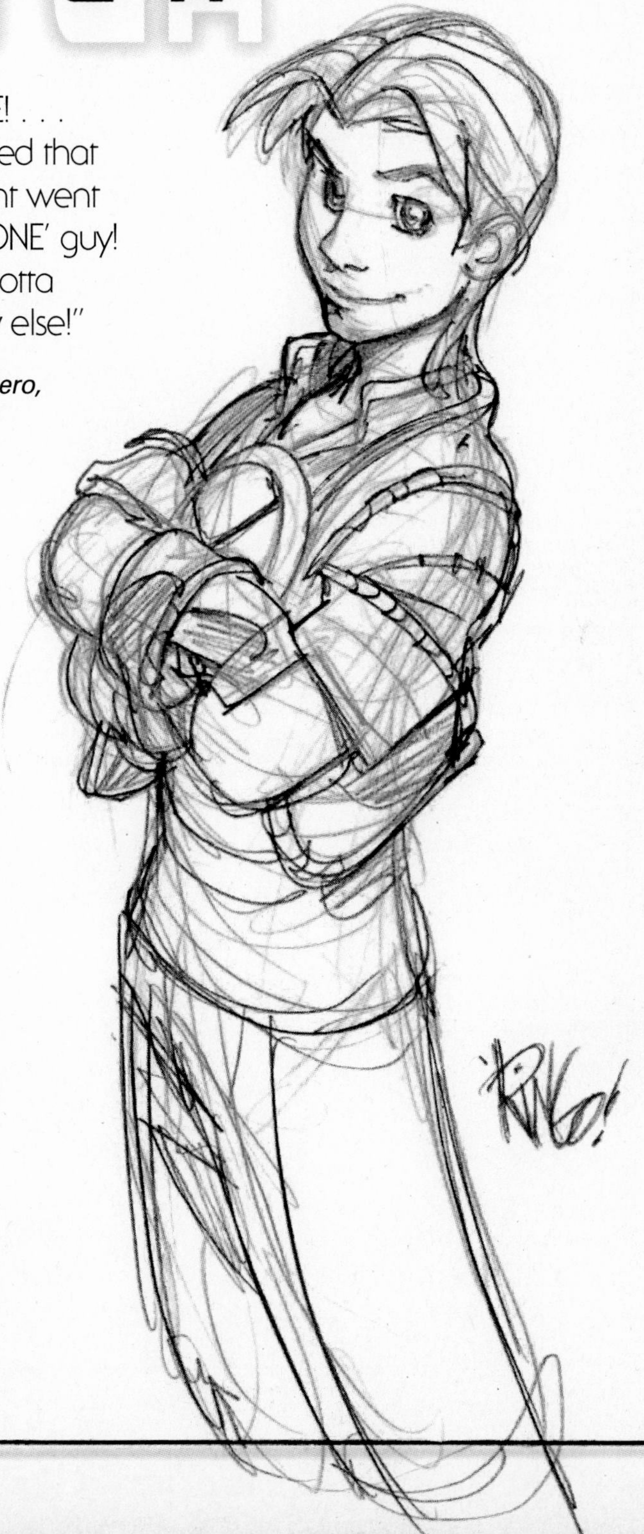

KOJ

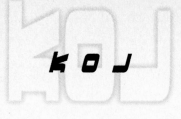

"KOJ and his People were taken as slaves when he was very young. They were captured by some guy named MALESUR and put to work as warriors in a place called Poldania...KOJ escaped, . . . but he couldn't get anybody else out with him. He promised them that he'd go out to find the rest of their kind and come back to free all the ones that were still slaves—but he was just a cub when he was taken—he doesn't know where his homeland is . . ."

JAREK, on the tragedy that haunts his best friend and partner.

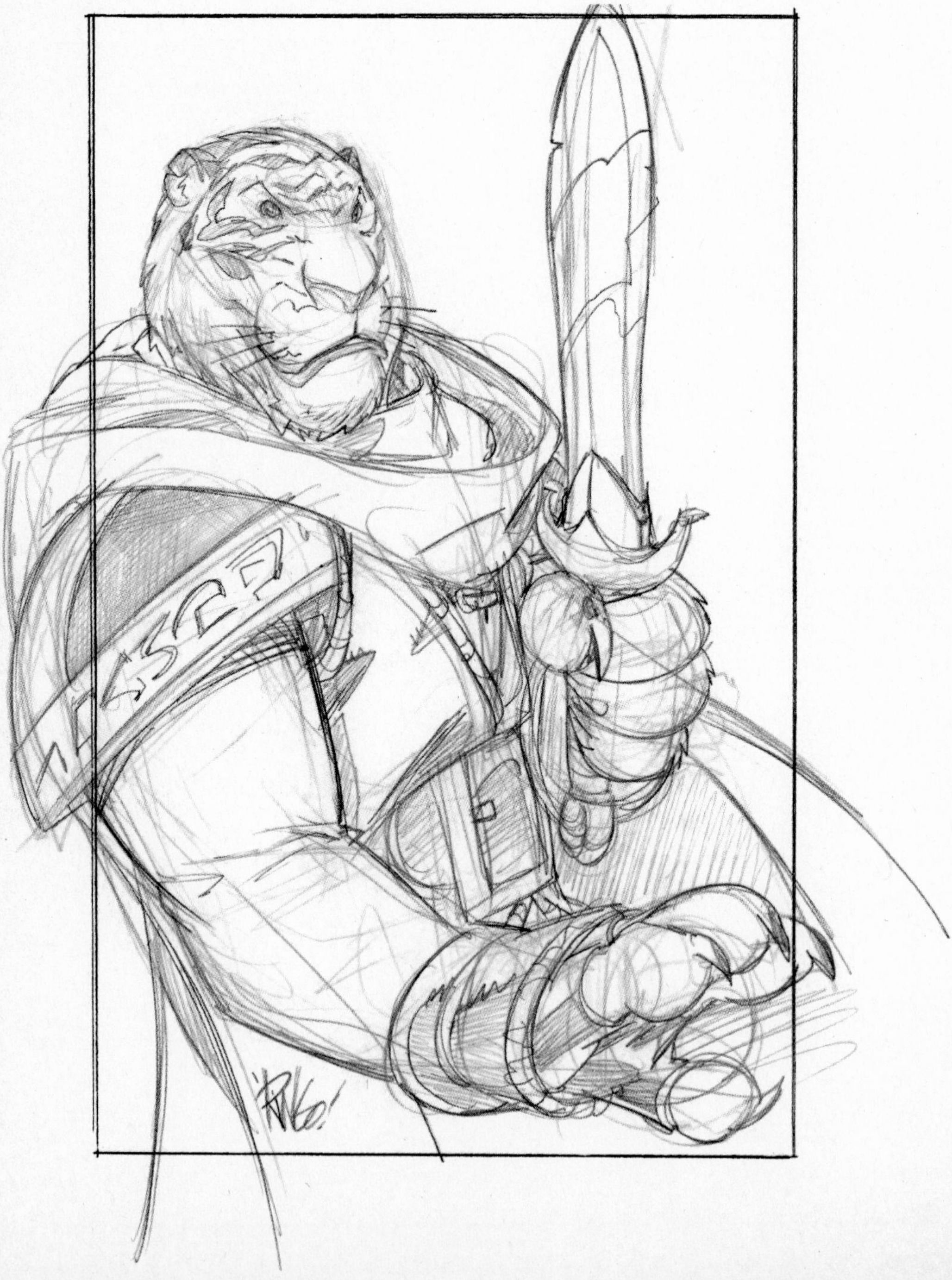

SERRA

"The SHEVA-NOVA is my ship . . . I'm the Captain . . .
and I'll decide what does or doesn't go on my boat!"
SERRA, to the Sleazy Merchant, SHARVIK . . . keepin' it real!

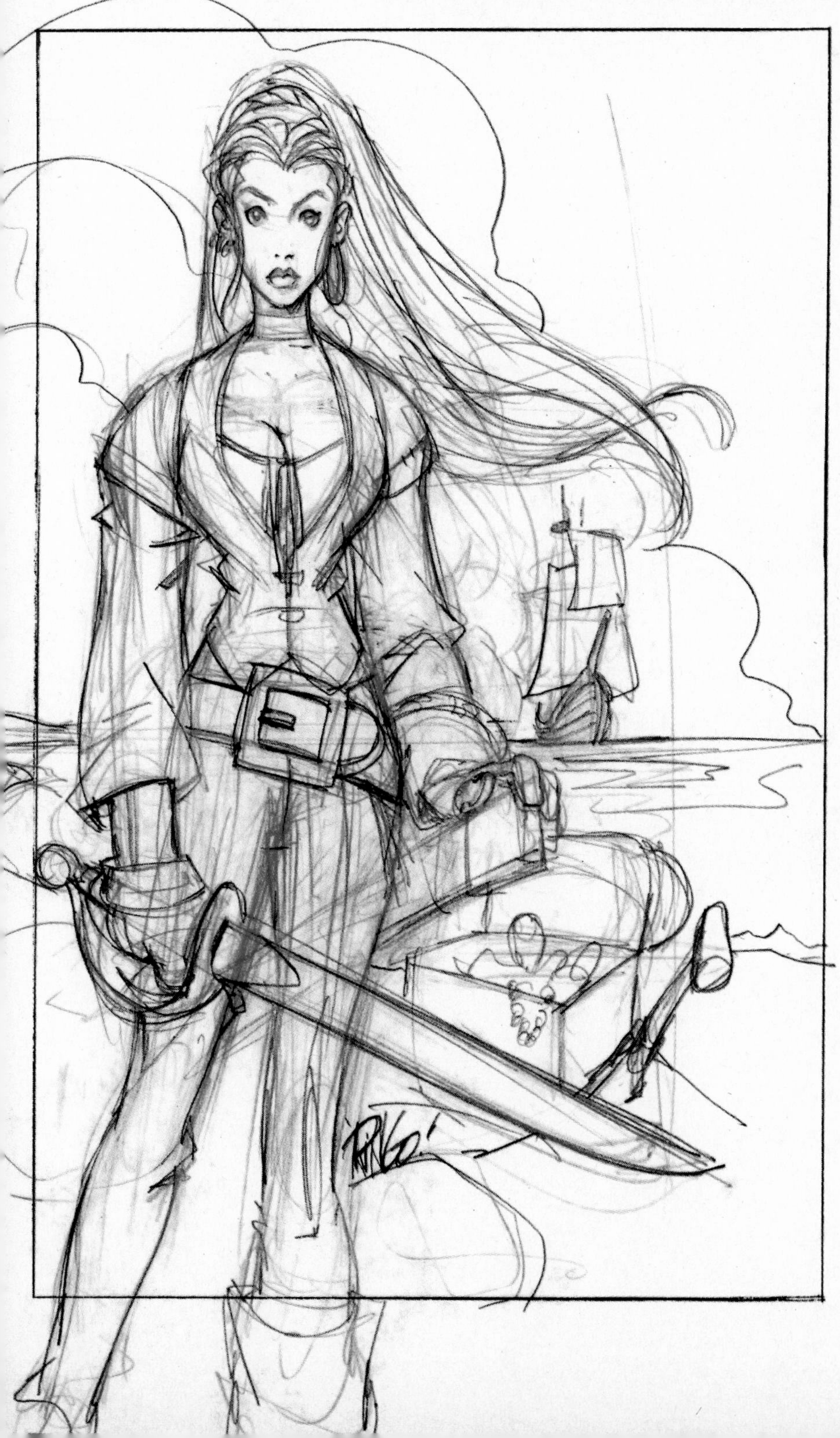
RINGO!

HAWKE

"Damn you HAWKE . . . you couldn'a just sent flowers . . . ya just hadda send me something that everyone in the Lands is after?"

SERRA, as she realizes that the Amulet (and maybe her boyfriend!) is more trouble than they're worth.

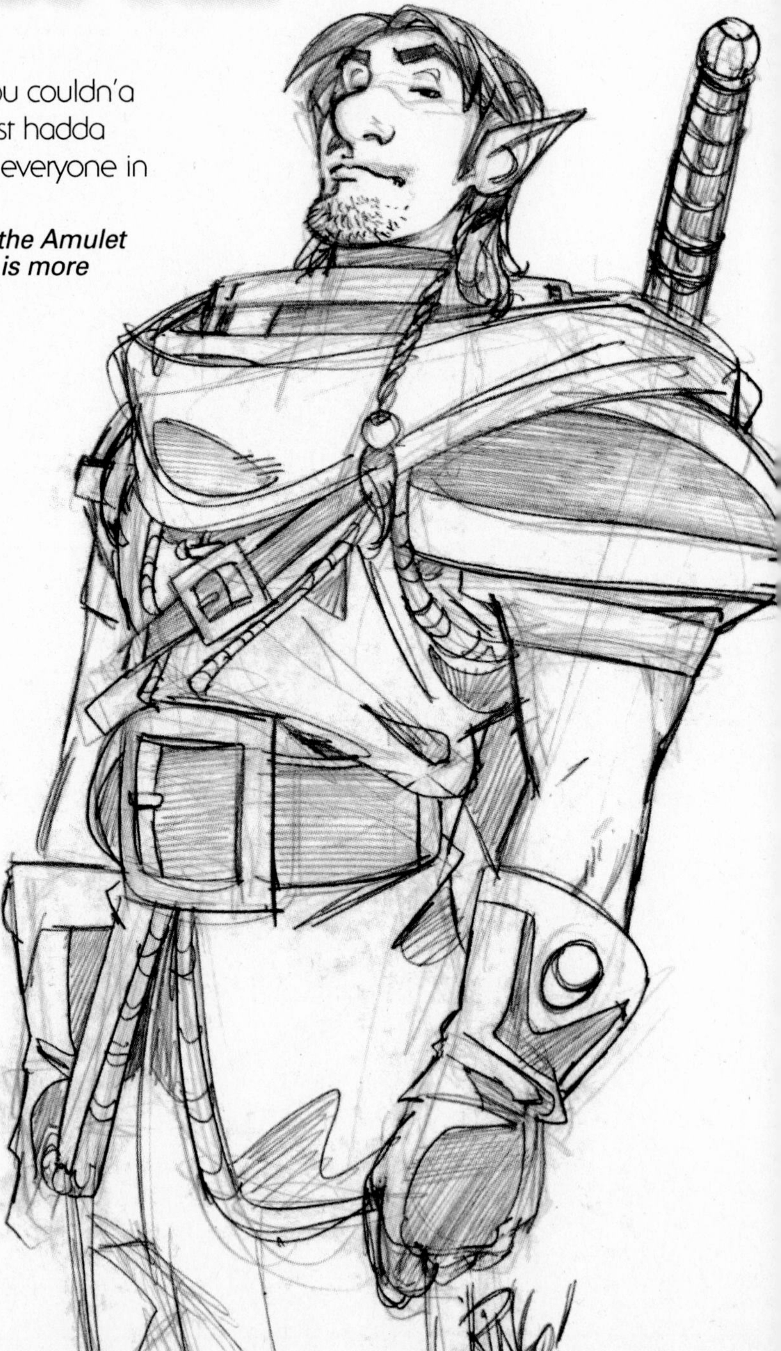

. MINOTAUR, RIKK!?!? Are we being chased by
MINOTAUR?!?"
'mon, HAWKE . . . it's not how it looks!"
)h, we're NOT being chased by the ROYAL
UARD because you went ahead and stole the
querade Sphere after I told you not to?!?"
)h . . . I guess it IS how it looks then . . ."
AWKE and RIKK, just about every day . . .

RIKK

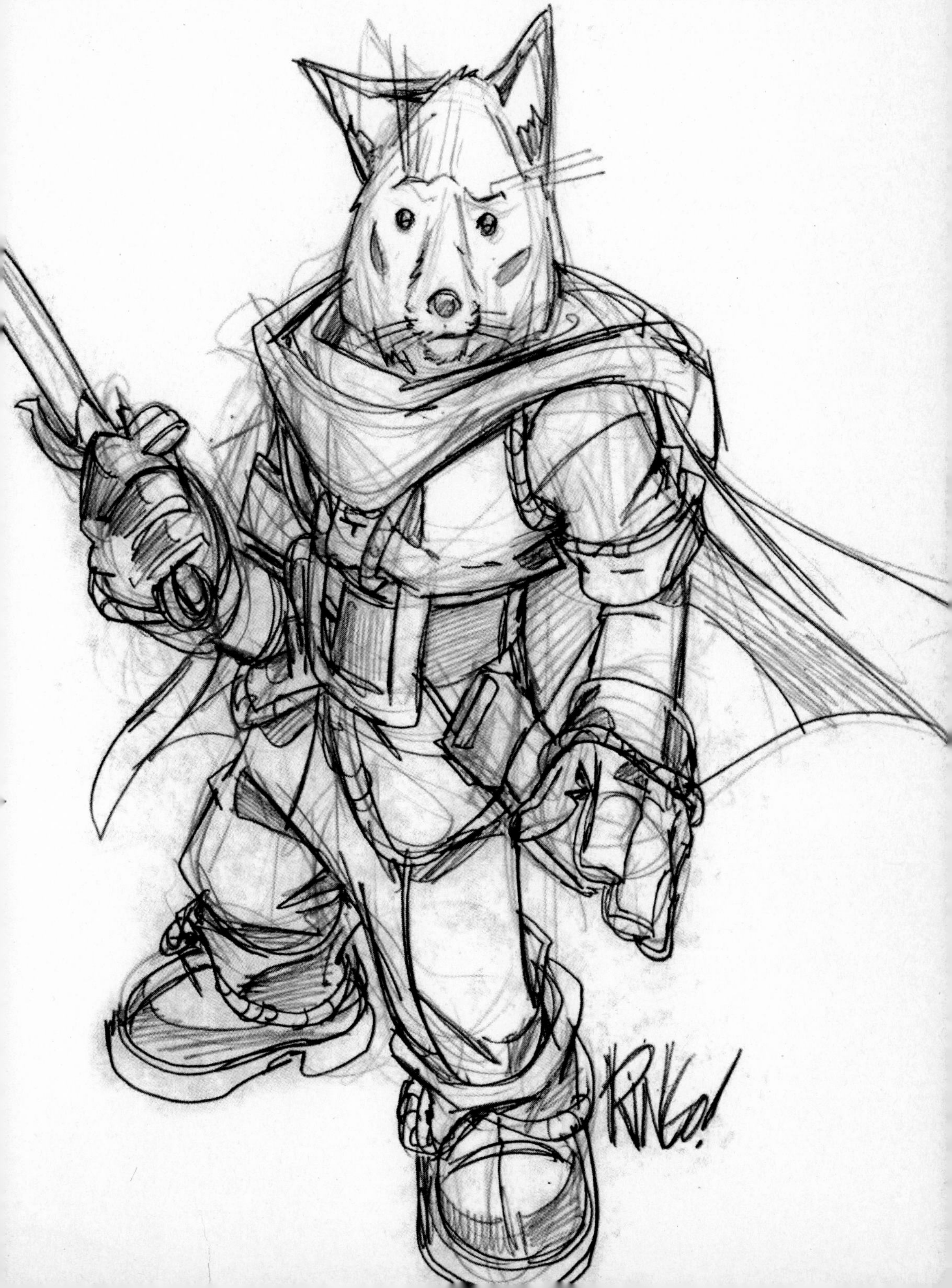

Ringo!

MALESUR

"So he's already got the Amulet? S'okay. He still doesn't know what it is, and he's not gonna figure it out alone...! And I'M about to make sure that I have IT, and him, long before he ever has a chance to learn about it!..."

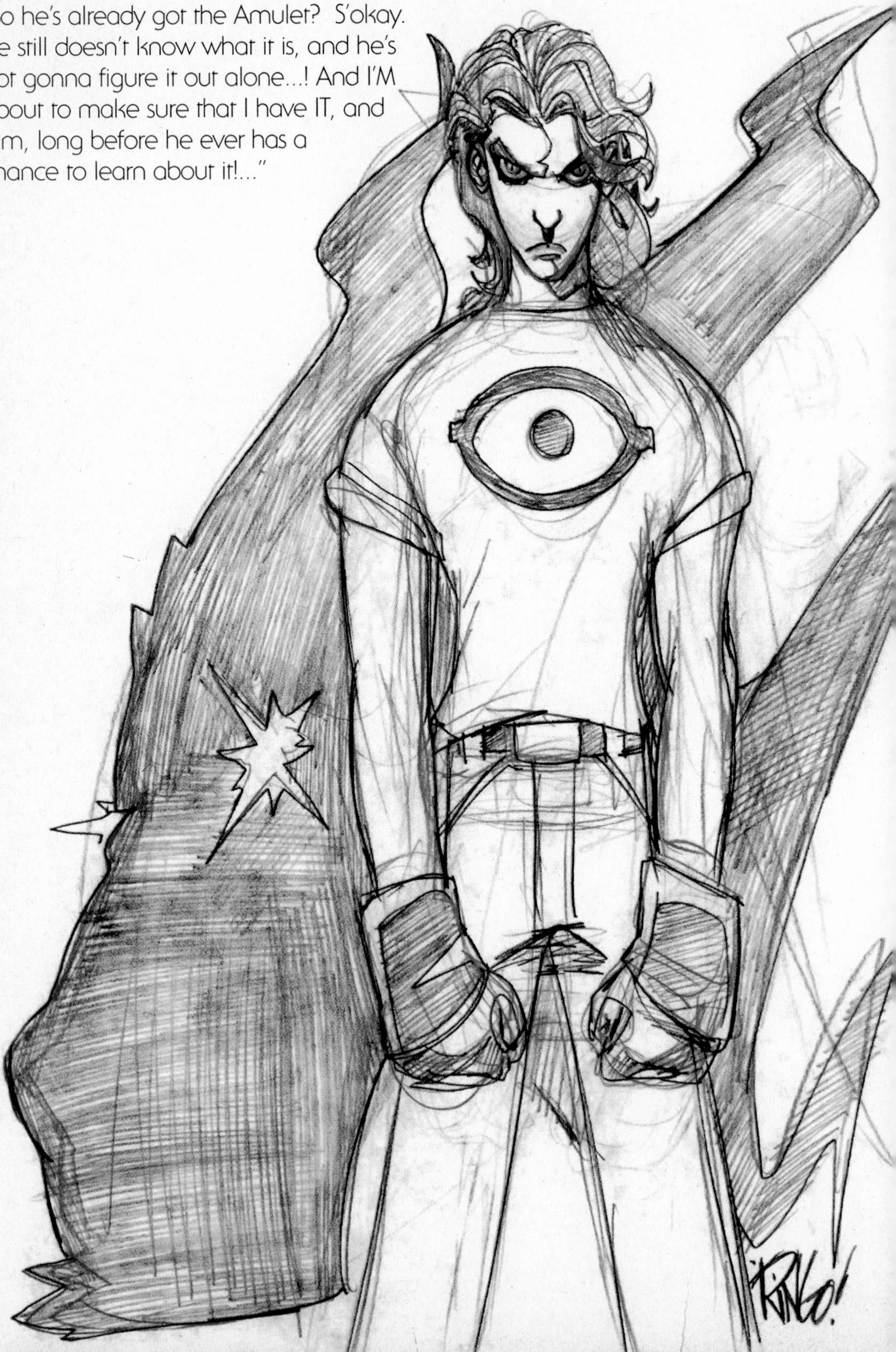

RINGO!

MIKE WIERINGO

has worked on most of the major characters for practically every major publisher in the comic book business. Mike has penciled FLASH, ROBIN and ADVENTURES OF SUPERMAN for DC Comics and for Marvel Comics he has worked on SENSATIONAL SPIDER-MAN (with TELLOS co-creator Todd Dezago) the ROGUE mini-series and HEROES REBORN: FANTASTIC FOUR. TELLOS is by far his proudest moment in this business.

Mike lives in Durham, North Carolina with his cat Butch—who is at once his best friend and personal therapist.

TODD DEZAGO

studied Acting and worked in a myriad of different jobs before coming to Comics in 1994. At Marvel, he began by working on the X-Men offshoot, X-FACTOR, and was soon tapped to pen several of the Spider-man books, such as The SPECTACULAR SPIDER-MAN and SENSATIONAL SPIDER-MAN. It was on the latter of these two that he was teamed with future Partner and Pal, Mike Wieringo. At DC Comics, Todd has worked on IMPULSE and JLA: WORLD WITHOUT GROWN-UPS, the story that introduced the super-teen team of Young Justice. For Todd as well, TELLOS is his most proudest achievement.

Todd lives in upstate New York with his girlfriend, Dani, and his two dogs, Gretchen and Jake. Gretchen is good. Jake is the devil.

Mike and Todd at HeroesCon 2000.
Photo courtesy Stuart Immonen